CONSTRUCTION LAW FOR OWNERS AND BUILDERS

CONSTRUCTION LAW FOR OWNERS AND BUILDERS

McNEILL STOKES
Stokes, Shapiro, Fussell & Genberg

JUDITH L. FINUF
Medical University of South Carolina

AN *Engineering News-Record* BOOK

McGRAW-HILL BOOK COMPANY
New York   St. Louis   San Francisco   Auckland
Bogotá   Hamburg   Johannesburg   London
Madrid   Mexico   Montreal   New Delhi
Panama   Paris   São Paulo   Singapore
Sydney   Tokyo   Toronto

Library of Congress Cataloging in Publication Data

Stokes, McNeill.
  Construction law for owners and builders.

  Includes index.
  1. Building — Contracts and specifications — United
States. 2. Construction industry — Law and legislation —
United States. I. Finuf, Judith L. II. Title.
KF902.S77 1986   343.73'07869   84-27868
ISBN 0-07-061647-7   347.3037869

1234567890 KGP/KGP 8932109876

The editor for this book was Joan Zseleczky.
The designer was Naomi Auerbach and the production supervisor was Teresa F. Leaden .
It was set in Century Schoolbook, by Osborne/McGraw-Hill.

Printed and bound by The Kingsport Press.

CONTENTS

PREFACE

Most public and private owners are in the part-time business of building or construction. When an owner starts to develop a project or build a building, as a practical matter it has to invent the wheel all over again. This book is an attempt to blend the practical and legal knowledge that public and private owners need in order to participate successfully in the building process.

At the outset, owners must know the various choices and methods available for the design of the project, beginning with the selection of a design professional. Public statutes mandate that the selection of design professionals for public works conform to certain requirements. Private selection processes are very similar if the owner puts maximum effort into selecting a design professional. This is well advised, for the design professional is, in fact, going to be the owner's quarterback for building construction. Therefore, the owner will need to evaluate the design professional's track record, intrinsic understanding of the project, problem-solving ability, and administrative capability so that the owner has confidence in the design professional it chooses.

Owners must also control the basic design whether it is contracted to outside professionals or controlled in-house. Owners must understand the various methods of contracting with design professionals and the necessity of defining the scope of work, responsibility, liability, and fees, as well as the legal and practical implications of contracts for architectural or engineering services. There are standard forms that owners must be aware of, and owners must be aware of the practical pitfalls of some of these forms.

Owners must also understand the various methods of contracting for construction and selecting general contractors. Public owners must understand public bidding, bid securities, and performance. In the past, contracts were let to a single contractor that in fact built the building substantially with its own labor and materials. This is changing now with the emergence of subcontracting, so that much of the construction work on a project is performed by specialty contractors. Many owners now work directly with multiple contractors and must either coordinate the contracts or provide construction managers to do so. Owners must be aware that they also have counter-responsibilities and that there are potential liabilities in coordinating the work of multiple specialty contractors. If construction managers are used, the owner must delineate their functions and responsibilities. The construction management function is vital to the smooth operation of final construction.

Some of the industry is beginning to use design-build contracts in which the owner contracts with one entity for design and construction. Owners must understand that although design-build has its advantages, it also has disadvantages. However, design-build contracts are an excellent opportunity for value engineering by the parties that actually perform the construction.

This is a buyer-financed industry and the owner must finance the construction process. Owners must therefore control cash flow from bidding through performance and final payment in order to pay an adequate amount of money to finance the work of the general contractor and each of its subcontractors. This is accomplished through the payment clauses in the construction contract that describe progress payments, the schedule of values, how to deal with front-end loading, payment for stored materials, retention, and final payment at substantial completion. But how do owners undertake to control cash flow and minimize the cost of construction? The owner must balance the need to finance the construction against front-end loading and other techniques so that cash flow is reasonable.

Owners often fail to recognize that the contract they sign is not graven in stone. Various practical driving forces dictate that the construction contract is going to be changed. Owners also fail to recognize the legal implications or extra costs of the problems that arise during performance of the contract. Work beyond the contract requirements may entitle the contractor to an increase in the contract price and may arise from many causes: defective plans and specifications, changes in methods of performance, misinterpretation of specifications, over-inspection, rejection of conforming work or equal substitutions, defective owner-furnished materials, or impossibility of performance. Owners must therefore understand their responsibility for constructive changes and the necessity of including a changes clause in the contract. The changes clause should clarify authority, notice requirements, changes within the scope of the contract, documentation, claims, and change procedures. The changes clause must also be practical in providing for the pricing of changes and their effect on the time of performance. The economic realities of changed conditions, differing site conditions, and other conditions beyond the contractor's control must be thoroughly understood by anyone undertaking the building process.

Of vital importance to an owner is the assurance of timely completion and performance of the work, the requirements of which are specified in scheduling clauses, excusable delay clauses, no-damages-for-delay clauses, liquidated damages clauses, and acceleration clauses. More fundamentally, the need for project coordination and scheduling is of vital interest both to the contractor and to the owner. It is the owner that is to provide maximum cooperation and efficient scheduling.

Owners obviously have an interest in ensuring that the work is performed in accordance with the plans and specifications. There are practical means of obtaining compliance with the contract, but inspection should not disrupt the contractor's procedures.

Another area of concern is claims management. Claims management is not just dealing with claims after they arise; it means avoiding claims by controlling the cost of the contract and minimizing the driving forces that may increase the scope of work. Preventive claims management is the most effective way to avoid legal entanglements and ensure that the project will be built on time and within the budget.

The key to claims management is knowledge. Owners must understand the realities of the change clause so they can manage it efficiently. Owners need to know what claims may be filed against them, what to do when a claim is filed, and what claims they may have against contractors or design professionals if something goes wrong. There are adequate remedies to protect the parties and they must be understood.

Insurance as a means of offsetting the uncertainty of construction cannot be overemphasized. Owners must know the special risk of financial loss that comes with construction. Owners must be aware that the additional hazards of construction require special endorsements, and they must be aware of the special protections made available by builder's risk insurance and other risk management techniques. As additional protection, private owners are well advised to use performance bonds and payment bonds, which are always required by public owners. But then, there is a whole different approach to dealing effectively with sureties if something goes wrong.

Settling disputes that arise during a construction project is a must, and it should be done at their inception. Negotiating disputes is a way of life in construction. Owners must be aware of ultimate remedies that they could bring to bear against contractors, design professionals, and their sureties, and must also understand that these same remedies may be brought to bear against them.

We have attempted to bring together in one volume a practical guide of things that owners and builders need to know in order to deal with the construction process. While not exhaustive, the illustrative examples of clauses, cases, and forms included in this book can be used as a general guide. The chapters are designed to point out some of the materials and are necessarily general; the legal doctrines and exceptions discussed may vary according to applicable contract clauses and the law. (Please note that architects and engineers will be referred to as design professionals or designers throughout this book except where either is specifically mentioned in a contract or illustrative case.) The statements that have been made are not intended to be a substitute for legal advice from an experienced attorney in a specific fact situation.

MCNEILL STOKES AND JUDITH L. FINUF

ACKNOWLEDGMENTS

The authors would like to acknowledge the invaluable contribution of the many associations and individual clients that have helped them gain insight into the specialized field of construction law.

They are also grateful to the American Institute of Architects (AIA) for its permission to reprint portions of its documents. These may be obtained by writing the AIA, 1735 New York Avenue, N.W., Washington, D.C. 20006.

In addition, they would like to express their gratitude for the individual assistance of

Bernard B. Rothchild, member and former chairman of the American Institute of Architects Documents Board;

John McPherson, Engineer for the State of South Carolina, who provided practical suggestions and information;

Victor S. Evans, former Deputy Attorney General of the State of South Carolina, for his encouragement and legal insights;

Judge Walter J. Bristow, 5th Judicial Circuit, State of South Carolina, who made all things possible; and

Elizabeth Collins Belden, of Stokes, Shapiro, Fussell & Genberg.

CONSTRUCTION LAW FOR OWNERS AND BUILDERS

1 SELECTING THE DESIGN PROFESSIONAL

Many owners begin the search for a designer without giving a great deal of thought or consideration to the needs and requirements of the project or to the actual services and responsibilities expected of the design professional. This has many times proved to be a serious error.

Selecting the "right" design firm should never be approached as a simple task. Just as in other industries today, the design professional is marketing a "product," and the designer's product is the capability of serving a certain market. Hospitals, public schools, local community colleges, technical and vocational schools, colleges and universities, prisons, hotels, and churches, to name a few, are all examples of individual markets with differing client needs and project design requirements. Therefore, a client's needs and requirements are the factors that should determine the type of design firm to be considered, the scope of services to be required, and the compensation to be paid to the design professional.

One of the primary sales tools of the designer is the ability to convince the client that the designer's capabilities are uniquely attuned to the specific needs and requirements of the project. However, the majority of design firms do not have a sophisticated marketing program and do not target specific markets. Many firms will seek any project that they think they have a chance of obtaining. A very few design firms will review specific market conditions within a specified territory and attempt to sell to that market.

The *Architect's Handbook of Professional Practice*,[1] published by the

---

[1]*Architect's Handbook of Professional Practice* (Washington D.C.: American Institute of Architects, Oct. 1975), Chapter 20.

American Institute of Architects (AIA), sets forth a specific marketing process that includes

(1) Prospecting for clients, referred to as "bird dogging";

(2) Strategy research, which identifies program requirements, construction money available, site location, and the method of selecting the design professional;

(3) Paperwork, that is, the preparation of a written brochure or prospect submittal tailored to the needs of the prospective clients;

(4) Interview presentations, which are interviews used by the design professional to demonstrate to the prospective client that their working relationship will be a good one. Quite often, this is accomplished by the design professional through the initiation of a dialogue with the owner that not only demonstrates the value of the owner's views, but also uses up the time allotted for the interview;

(5) The last step, the closing of the sale.

The design professional will often invite the prospective client to visit his office as well as buildings and projects he has already designed. It is at this stage that social and professional contacts most often come into play. In the private sector, the unsophisticated owner will usually request a proposal from the design professional at the conclusion of this interview.

EVALUATION TECHNIQUES

In selecting a design professional, the owner, whether public or private, should always require comprehensive information on the design firm, particularly on the management of the firm, the financial history of the firm, the type of work done in the past, the construction cost of past design work, and other related information. Selection questionnaires used by the State of New Jersey are included in Appendix A. These questionnaires can be easily adapted for either public or private use.

As a general rule, firms should have at least one principal who has been engaged in active design practice for a period of at least two years. The owner should develop files on design firms and should encourage firms to submit pamphlets, brochures, photographs, and other literature for inclusion in their files for review during the selection process. The federal government and Model Procurement Code methods of selecting design professionals outlined in "Public Selection Procedures" can easily be adapted for general use by any owner. Requests for design proposals may be advertised in such construction industry publications as the McGraw-Hill *F. W. Dodge Reports* and other design and construction industry publications. The notice requesting proposals should always include instructions that any design firm interested in the project must submit a letter of interest no later than a certain time and date. Upon receiving the letters of interest, the owner can mail out project questionnaires to the responding design firms.

The owner, relying on the files containing information about the firms and completed questionnaires, should carefully evaluate and rate each design firm. A minimum of three to five firms should be interviewed by the owner in order to obtain a broad view of the design for the proposed project. A pre-interview conference with the design firms is always a good idea. The purpose of the pre-interview conference is to allow all design firms an opportunity to review the scope of the work and to submit questions to the owner on particular features and requirements of the proposed project.

Prior to the interview with the design firm, the owner should furnish basic data about the proposed construction program:

(1) The project budget;

(2) Construction site information (the owner should have available the deed to the property and a plat, if possible, showing rights-of-way, easements, and topography);

(3) The owner's requirements for the proposed project, including:
   (a) the activities and functions that the construction must meet and serve; and
   (b) special requirements, such as service and storage needs, parking requirements, tentative space and volume requirements based on the number of persons to be incorporated into or served by the proposed project, the nature of the activity the project is to serve, and any special equipment needed.

Following the pre-interview conference, a schedule of interviews should be arranged with the selected design firms. The object of the individual interview is to establish a rapport between the design professional and the owner and to discuss that design professional's particular ideas and creative impressions for the proposed project.

Many sophisticated owners establish a predetermined standard list of criteria and, following deliberations at the completion of the interviews, score each design firm on a scale from 1 to 100. The design firms receiving the highest number of points are then requested to submit competitive cost proposals. The proposals may be submitted on a fixed-amount basis or on the basis of a percentage fee to be applied to the final construction cost estimate submitted by the design professional. The proposals are then approved by the owner.

PUBLIC SELECTION PROCEDURES

In the public sector, governmental agencies will frequently establish selection committees made up of individuals determined to be qualified to select the most competent and qualified design professional for the proposed project. A selection committee is generally responsible for (1) developing a description of the proposed project; (2) enumerating all required professional services for that project; and (3) preparing a formal invitation to design-professional firms for the submission of information concerning the firms' design capabilities. This invitation usually includes the project title, the general scope of the work involved, a

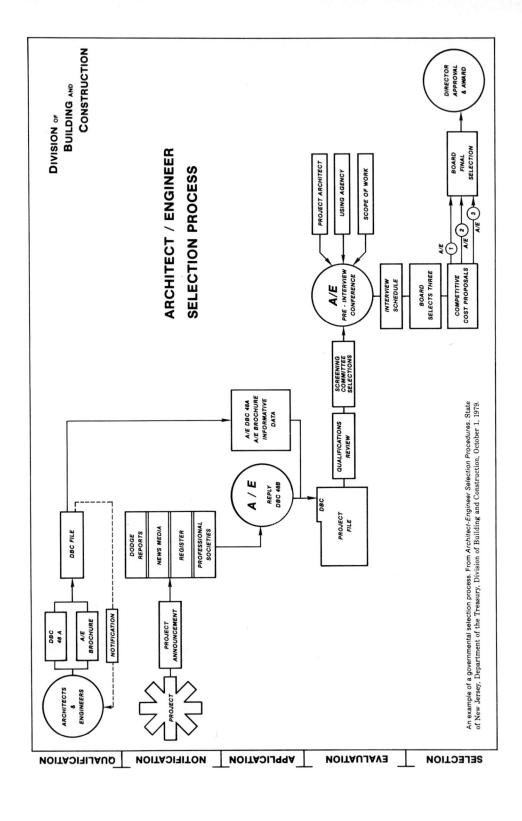

ARCHITECT / ENGINEER
SELECTION PROCESS

DIVISION OF BUILDING AND CONSTRUCTION

An example of a governmental selection process. From *Architect-Engineer Selection Procedures*, State of New Jersey, Department of the Treasury, Division of Building and Construction, October 1, 1979.

QUALIFICATION | NOTIFICATION | APPLICATION | EVALUATION | SELECTION description of professional services required for the proposed project, a deadline for the submission of the design proposal, and information as to how interested firms should apply for the award of the design contract. These invitations are advertised in government publications or the local news media. Interested design firms may be required to respond to the invitation with the submission of a current and accurate Federal Standard Form F254, Architect-Engineer and Related Services Questionnaire, and Federal Standard Form F255, Architect-Engineer and Related Services Questionnaire for Specific Projects.

Following the receipt of any information required under the invitation, interested design firms are reviewed. The selection committee then holds interviews with at least three firms that have responded to the invitation. The purpose of the interviews is to solicit any further information required by the selection committee so that the committee may fully acquaint itself with the relative qualifications of the interested firms.

The selection committee then evaluates each of the firms interviewed, taking into consideration (1) each firm's past performance; (2) the ability of the firm's professional personnel; (3) the capability of the firm to meet project time and project budget requirements; (4) the location of the firm and the location of the proposed project; (5) the recent, current, and projected workloads of the design firm; and (6) the firm's related experience on other projects similar in nature to the proposed project. Based on the committee's evaluations of the design firms, the selection committee then ranks each of the firms.

Information concerning the firm and the order of ranking is reported by the selection committee to its controlling body. The governmental agency then contacts the first ranked design firm, and negotiations toward a contract for design services are begun. If a design contract is not successfully negotiated with the first ranked design firm, then negotiations are commenced with each of the design firms in order of rank until a satisfactory contract is reached.

The federal government, in the Brooks Bill,[2] has prescribed the method and manner by which agencies of the federal government must select architects and engineers. Under the Brooks Bill it is declared to be the policy of the federal government to announce publicly all requirements for design services and to negotiate contracts for design services on the basis of demonstrated competence and qualifications for the type of professional services required and at fair and reasonable prices.

In procuring design services, a federal agency head is required to encourage design firms to furnish annual statements of qualifications and performance. For each proposed construction project, the federal agency head is required to evaluate the current statements of qualifica-

[2]40 U.S.C. §§ 541-544.

tions and performance data on file with the agency, along with statements furnished by other firms interested in the proposed project.

The agency head is then required to conduct interviews with no less than three firms concerning anticipated concepts and required services. After this step, the agency head is required to select three design firms and to rank those three firms in order of preference based on the criteria established for the project. Ranking is required to be in the order of the most highly qualified.

Once the ranking is accomplished, the agency head is then required to negotiate a contract with the highest ranked and most qualified firm for the desired design services at a rate of compensation that the agency head determines is fair and reasonable to the federal government. In making such a determination, the agency head is required by law to take into account (1) the estimated value of the services to be rendered; (2) the scope of the desired design services; (3) the complexity of the proposed design services; and (4) the professional requirements of the design services sought. If the agency head is unable to negotiate a contract with the firm considered to be and ranked as the most qualified at a price that the agency head has determined to be fair and reasonable, negotiations with that firm are formally terminated and the agency head undertakes negotiations with the next most qualified firm. If the agency head is unable to negotiate a satisfactory contract with any of the selected design firms, he can select additional firms in order of their competence and qualifications and continue negotiations with those firms until an agreement is reached.

To supplement the Brooks Bill, federal regulations define further the policies and procedures for obtaining professional architectural and engineering services for federal contracts.[3] The head of each federal agency is required to establish an architect-engineer evaluation board composed of highly qualified members of the agency who have experience in architecture, engineering, construction, and related procurement matters, and, if provided for in agency procedures, private individuals engaged in the practice of architecture, engineering, or related professions may also be appointed. The evaluation board collects and maintains data files on design firms. These files contain information on the qualifications of the members and employees of the design firms, the firms' key employees, and the firms' past experience on various types of construction projects. Information derived from clients, other members of the design profession, and managers or occupants of facilities previously designed by the firms may also be included in the files, as well as the procuring agency's assessments of the designs and design services by the firms on prior projects. When design services are needed, the architect-engineer evaluation board reviews the current data files on all eligible firms that have responded to the invitation for

[3] 41 C.F.R. § 1-4.10.

design proposals.

In evaluating the responding design firms, the evaluation board examines the following criteria:

(1) The specialized experience and technical competence of the design firms (including joint ventures or associations) with the type of services required;

(2) The capacity of the design firms to perform the work (including any specialized services) within the time limitations;

(3) The past record of performance on contracts with government agencies and with private industry with respect to such factors as control of costs, quality of work, and ability to meet schedules; and

(4) Familiarity with the area in which the project is located.

After making this review, the board then holds discussions with not less than three of the most qualified firms regarding anticipated concepts and the relative utility of alternative methods of approach for furnishing the required design services. Federal regulation specifically states that fees shall not be considered in these discussions.[4] The evaluation board then prepares a report for submission to the agency head recommending in order of preference no less than three firms that are considered most highly qualified to perform the required design services.

As stated earlier, negotiations are conducted initially with the design firm determined to be the most highly qualified. Contract negotiations are directed toward:

(1) Making certain that the design professional has a clear understanding of the essential requirements of the project;

(2) Determining that the design professional will make available the necessary personnel and facilities to accomplish the work within the required project time;

(3) Determining, where applicable, whether the design professional will provide a design that will permit construction of the project at a construction cost not to exceed the limit established for the project; and

(4) Reaching a mutual agreement on the provisions of the contract, including a fair and reasonable price for the required design work.

Federal regulations[5] specifically state that the amount of the fee that may be paid to a design firm under a cost reimbursement contract for the production and delivery of the designs, plans, drawings, and specifications may not exceed 6 percent of the estimated construction cost of the project, exclusive of the amount of the fee. The statutory limitation is applied on an individual basis and applies also to the fee paid to a design professional for the performance of design services under a fixed-price contract.

[4] 41 C.F.R. § 1-4.1004-2.
[5] 41 C.F.R. § 1-4.1005-1.

Before initiating contract negotiations, the federal agency is required to prepare an independent government estimate of the cost of the required design services. The selected design firm is then requested to submit its fee proposal together with supporting cost and pricing data.

The Model Procurement Code for state and local governments, which is a code providing for procurement of goods and services by state and local governments, contains, at section 5-501, a procedure for securing design services. Under the Model Procurement Code provisions, the chief procurement officer encourages design firms to submit a yearly statement of qualifications and performance data. For each proposed construction project, an architect-engineer selection committee is required. The selection committee evaluates the current statements of qualifications and performance data on file with the state or local government as well as data submitted by other design firms interested in the proposed contract. The selection committee conducts discussions with at least three design firms concerning the relative utility of alternative methods of approach for furnishing the required design services and, from the firms interviewed, selects in order of preference the three firms deemed to be the most qualified to provide the required services.

The chief procurement officer then attempts to negotiate a contract with the most qualified firm at a compensation determined by the procurement officer as being fair and reasonable. If a satisfactory contract cannot be negotiated with the design firm determined to be most qualified, then negotiations are formally terminated and negotiations are continued with the next most qualified firms in order of rank until a contract is successfully negotiated. The Model Procurement Code Commentary indicates:

(1) The principal reasons supporting this selection procedure for design services are the lack of definitive scope of work for such services at the time the selection is made and the importance of selecting the most qualified firm. In general, the design professional is engaged to represent the owner's interests and is, therefore, in a different relationship with the owner from that normally existing in a buyer-seller situation. For these reasons, the qualifications, competence, and availability of the three most qualified design firms are considered initially, and the price is negotiated later.

(2) It is considered more desirable to make the qualification selection first and then to discuss the price because both parties need to review in detail what is involved in the work (for example, estimates of worker-hours, personnel costs, and alternatives that the design professional should consider in depth). Once parameters have been fully discussed and understood and the design professional proposes a fee for the work, the recommended procedure requires the owner to make its own evaluation and judgment as to the reasonableness of the fee.

(3) If the fee is fair and reasonable, award is made without consideration of proposals and fees of other competing firms. If the fee cannot be negotiated to the satisfaction of the owner, negotiations with other qualified firms are initiated. Thus, price clearly is an important factor in the award of the design services contract under this procedure. The principal difference between the recommended procedure for design-

professional selection and the procedures used in most other competitive source selections is the point at which price is considered.

(4) If an enacting jurisdiction desires to use a different selection process, then it may consider the following language:

"The procurement officer shall negotiate with the most qualified firms for a contract for design services at compensation that the procurement officer determines in writing to be fair and reasonable to the owner. In making such a determination, the procurement officer shall take into account, in the following order of importance, the professional competence of offerors, the technical merits of offers, and the price for which the services are to be rendered."

PRIVATE-SECTOR SELECTION PROCEDURES

There are no requirements for the selection or evaluation of design professionals in the private sector. However, any private owner would be well advised to seek and consider data concerning the competence and experience of the design firm being considered, the qualifications of the design personnel to be assigned to the proposed project, the quality of the design proposal, and the client-design-professional relationship. Proposed fee arrangements or financial terms may also be an additional element to be considered. The owner may decide to approach a single firm of its own choice in securing design services, or it may consider inviting design proposals from three to six qualified and experienced firms and, through a suitable selection process, choosing a firm most appropriate for the proposed design. The owner would, of course, have to first determine the key objectives for the proposed project and the general scope of the design services sought. The principal steps in selecting the design professional might be as follows:

(1) The preparation and determination of the scope of the design services sought;

(2) The preparation of the proposed budget or estimated cost for the design project;

(3) The preparation of a list of design firms to be contacted;

(4) The determination of a selection procedure;

(5) The forwarding of a letter of invitation to design firms to submit a proposal;

(6) An evaluation of the responding design firms' proposals;

(7) The selection of a design firm for contract negotiation; and

(8) The negotiation of a design contract with the selected firm.

The scope of the design services will form an integral part of the design contract and will govern the work that the design firm is to perform. Therefore, the scope of the design services should be clear and precise. Normally, the statement of expected services or scope of services should contain the following:

(1) A precise and clear statement of the objectives of the owner for the proposed construction;

(2) The scope of design services sought and time required for their implementation;

(3) The information and assistance to be provided by the owner; and

(4) That which the owner requires of the design firm.

Prior to beginning negotiation of the contract, the design firm should clearly understand not only the owner's requirements for the project, but also the definition and depth of the services as dictated by the complexity of the project. The owner should clearly state whether or not detailed engineering and construction supervision is sought and whether the owner expects the design firm to prepare all of the contract documents in addition to final design documents.

Where design cost is to be taken into account in the selection of the design professional, this should be stated in the letter of invitation. In preparing a list of design firms to be considered, the owner should remember that the meaningful evaluation of numerous professional-services proposals is time consuming and may result in inadequate evaluation. It is strongly recommended that the list of firms have a lower limit of three and upper limit of six. The selection procedure and evaluation criteria used by the owner should be determined prior to inviting proposals, and this information should also be included in the letter of invitation.

Generally, there are two basic types of selection procedures. The first method relies solely on an evaluation of the technical competence of the firm, the personnel undertaking the design assignment, and the suitability of the professional-services proposal. The second method involves both a technical evaluation and the consideration of the proposed price for the professional services. Under a technical evaluation procedure, professional-services proposals are evaluated on the basis of the following:

(1) The design firm's general experience in the field of the proposed services sought;

(2) The adequacy of the proposed work plan and the firm's approach in responding to the owner's statement as to the scope of the services desired; and

(3) The qualifications and general competence of the design personnel proposed for the project.

The process of design-professional selection, with or without considerations of price, should always maintain quality of service as the fundamental requirement. Price or fee should not dominate the selection process to the detriment of quality design services. Examples of areas in which a comparable cost proposal might be used would be simple construction supervision services, seismic survey, topographic mapping, simple road design, and aerial survey. In other words, where the design services are of a clearly defined technical nature, comparative cost proposals may be effective. The extent to which price should be used as a factor in selecting the design professional depends on the technical complexity of the project. The more complex the proposed project, the less influence price should have on selection of the design professional.

The decision whether or not to take fee or price into consideration should be made prior to inviting proposals. Where price is to be taken into account, a two-stage procedure, in which the financial proposals are submitted separately from the professional-services proposals or in which the price proposals are submitted at a later date, is advisable. The evaluation of professional-services proposals should be completed before the price proposals are reviewed. This procedure is to ensure that the professional-services proposals are evaluated independently and free from the influence of fee or cost.

When the proposals have been received, the owner's primary objective is to evaluate them in order to choose the design firm that, through the quality of its proposal, is deemed to be the most qualified to furnish the design services for the proposed construction. The best method of evaluation is for the owner to establish an evaluation committee. The firm that is ranked the highest, taking all factors into consideration, should then be invited to negotiate a contract with the owner. Once a contract is successfully negotiated, the owner should notify other firms responding to the invitation that they were unsuccessful and the award of the design contract should be announced.

DEVELOPMENT OF A DESIGN PROGRAM

There are three types of owners—one-time builders, "occasional" builders, and "repeat" builders. The experienced "repeat" builder usually understands construction and what is expected from the participants. The other two types of owners often fail to understand or comprehend the services generally offered by a design professional.

Once the design professional has been selected and a contract negotiated, the design professional will develop a definite design program.

AIA Document B141, Standard Form of Agreement Between Owner and Architect, sets forth basic professional services to be performed by the design professional. The following services are not part of the design professional's basic services under the AIA contract and may either be provided for by a different agreement for an additional fee or remain the responsibility of the owner.

First, the owner must obtain a complete site survey and topographical map. The site survey should include the following: (1) property boundaries, public walks, and planting strips; (2) easements, rights-of-way, lampposts, electric-wire posts, fire hydrants, manholes, manhole covers, and catch basins with rim and invert elevators; (3) sewers, gas and water mains (indicating location, size, and depth); (4) water taps and water service stubs (indicating location, size, and depth); (5) interior roads, drives, walks, cultivated areas, walls, pits, fences, quarries, hedges, boulders, ditches, culverts, cisterns, and wells; (6) the location, size, and variety of trees within the site; (7) the elevations of tops of curbs, retaining walls, first floor and basement levels of buildings on or adjoining the site, tops and bottoms of all exterior steps and of the surface at the counterlines of roads and the ground at the base of the trees within the site; (8) the contour lines at specified intervals; (9) the location, thickness, height, and variation from plumb of party walls; (10) the establishment of a permanent benchmark for use during construction; (11) the establishment of all corners of the property with permanent stakes or monuments; (12) a record of subsoil investigations made by means of rock soundings at specified intervals in each direction, soil samples at specified locations; or test pits of size and locations as specified.

Second, the owner must consider customs, resources available, the local labor market, existing land use, the character of the neighborhood, local growth tendencies, transportation, and suitability of size and topography. Also considered by the owner, or at its request, the design professional, are such factors as land valuation, demand for space, the probable operating expenses, taxes, interest rates, expected rate of return, trends, and competitive buildings. Site conditions such as the character and condition of nearby buildings and party walls, drainage and surface conditions, the appearance and condition of trees and ground cover, views from the proposed construction, prevailing winds, location of wind breaks in minimum winter and maximum summer temperatures, and earthquake considerations must also be taken into account.

For the proposed construction, relying on the owner's statement of space needs, the design professional must determine the specific activities and functions of the proposed construction; parking, storage, service, and utility requirements; public and private space needs; circulation and functional relationships; special equipment requirements; area and volume; ceiling heights; orientation such as view, climate, sun control, and vegetation; topography to include drainage and horizontal and vertical displacements; foundation and structural requirements; electrical and mechanical demands; safety, security, and maintenance requirements; and finishes and colors. The design professional will also review state laws and codes, the requirements of local building codes, and zoning regulations.

Once these factors have been considered and the project budget established, the design professional will proceed with the preliminary drawings, which in the industry are termed schematic design documents. The design professional will make simple sketches and drawings and create a general description of the project. Following owner approval of these design development documents and the estimated construction cost, the design development phase commences. The design development documents more fully define the size and character of the proposed project and include in the site plan, plans and elevations for the project, outline specifications, and an additional updated Statement of Probable Construction Cost.

Once the owner gives approval of these documents, the construction documents phase commences. This is the phase when bidding and construction documents, such as the working plans and specifications that set forth in greater detail the requirements for the construction of the proposed project, are drafted.

The design professional may also prepare the bid documents or contract documents for use in establishing the contract between the owner and the contractor. Once the construction contract is negotiated or awarded, the construction phase of the project begins. The design professional may be retained to make periodic visits to the construction site, review job progress, inspect the quality of the work, and certify to the owner that the contractor is entitled to payment for the amount of work done.

In conclusion, the owner, whether public or private, should be aware that although it is a buyer's market, it is not an easy task to retain a design professional. Investigating and rating design professionals is a good practice, irrespective of the amount of effort that must be expended by the owner or the owner's selection committee. This investigation should go far beyond looking at the design professional's brochures and photographs of past projects.

At minimum, the owner should ask other designers for their opinions as to the work of the design firms being considered. Another source of information of the design professional's ability lies with the general contractors in the area that have worked with that design professional or that have knowledge of the designer's reputation and ability to work with the contract administration. In fact, when considering design professionals initially, general contractors could be consulted for their opinions about particular design professionals. General contractors could be asked if a certain design professional gets his work done on time, if meetings are well-run, and if the design professional is decisive on construction problems and disputes.

Additional inquiries about the design professional's financial situation should always be made. The question as to the amount of errors and omissions insurance coverage should always be directed to the design professional during the interview. Quite often, a design professional working on a multimillion-dollar project maintains little capital and only minimal errors and omissions coverage.

2 DESIGN-PROFESSIONAL CONTRACTS

The complexity of most construction projects, sound business practices and principles, and the possibility of costly legal liability preclude the use of oral contracts for any prospective construction. Written contracts are mandatory in today's construction industry. It is these contract documents that create and define the responsibilities and liabilities of each of the parties involved in the construction process—the design professional, the contractor, and the owner.

Early in the formative stages of project development, the owner, irrespective of whether it is a private corporation or a governmental entity, will usually retain a design professional under contract to advise the owner, to assist the owner in the definition of its needs and project requirements, and to plan and design the project. The design professional draws the plans and formulates the project specifications for the owner. The design professional may also be retained during actual project construction to make sure that the general contractor is adhering to the plans and specifications and performing the contract in a workmanlike manner.

The general contractor is hired by the owner on a competitive bid or negotiated contract basis to construct the project from the plans and specifications furnished by the design professional and the owner. Although there is no direct contractual relationship between the design professional and the general contractor, it is obvious that since each has a contract with the owner specifying certain complementary responsibilities, the terms and conditions of their respective contracts must be closely coordinated.

The owner may be sophisticated or unsophisticated, experienced or inexperienced in construction procedures. The failure of an inexperienced and unsophisticated owner to be aware of construction industry custom, usage, and language, coupled with a lack of understanding of the roles and requirements of each of the participants in the construction process, can be devastating. On the other hand, if the owner can coordinate all the necessary elements—the project's requirements of quality, quantity, cost and date of completion, the responsibilities of the design professional and the contractor, and the owner's own duties—the project will run smoothly.

Many owners have found, much to their chagrin, that under the American Institute of Architects (AIA) form contract, the design professional's responsibility and liability to the owner were sadly lacking. This lack of accountability for professional error accounts for a movement toward owner-drafted contracts. This chapter will discuss the commonly used AIA Document B141, Standard Form of Agreement Between Owner and Architect (1977 ed.), some of its problems, and suggested alterations. A sample owner-oriented contract form will be found in Appendix B.

SCOPE OF PROFESSIONAL SERVICES AND RESPONSIBILITIES

Article 1 of AIA Document B141 is entitled "Architect's Services and Responsibilities." This twelve-page contract covers an entire construction project from design through substantial completion and defines the design professional's services and the owner's responsibilities during the progress of the project. While this form covers only basic services, additional AIA forms detail everything an owner might want a design professional to do and provide for the pricing of additional services.

Although the design professional can be involved in the primary definition and analysis of project requirements with the owner and later retained to provide services to the owner following the issuance of the final Certificate for Payment or the Date of Substantial Completion, the AIA form contract generally divides the project into five phases. The phases are the schematic design phase, the design development phase, the construction documents phase, the bidding or negotiation phase, and the construction phase, which includes the administration of the construction contract. Generally, the first three phases are all considered part of a broad category of design. The bidding or negotiation phase has traditionally been treated as a part of the design phase because no construction work has actually begun; however, for some purposes the bidding or negotiation phase is treated as part of the construction phase. The last phase is the actual construction phase.

SCHEMATIC DESIGN PHASE

The schematic design phase under paragraph 1.1 of AIA Document B141 (1977 ed.) is the project phase during which the design professional and his consultants determine the owner's needs and requirements for the prospective project and then translate those needs and requirements into a fundamental conceptual design. This conceptual design should encompass the functional relationship between project space and special uses.

During the schematic design phase under the traditional AIA concept, the design professional is required to review the owner's program for the project and ascertain that his understanding of the requirements comports with the understanding of the owner. The design professional is further required to do a preliminary evaluation to make sure the program is in line with the project budget. However, under subparagraph 3.2.1, the design professional specifically does not warrant or represent to the owner that bids or prices will conform with the project budget or with any Statement of Probable Construction Cost prepared by the design professional. If bids exceed the owner's project budget, the design professional is only required to review with the owner alternative approaches to design and project construction. The design professional must then submit to the owner a Statement of Probable Construction Cost based on the schematic design documents.

All contracts should contain the requirement that owner approval of the documents and Statements of Probable Cosntruction Cost be in writing. This review and written approval, or the lack of such an approval, can be extremely helpful in the event that a subsequent dispute occurs over design or the recovery of design fees.

The general legal rule is that the owner is not liable to the design professional for the design professional's fee if the actual probable cost of construction substantially exceeds the agreed-to minimum cost. The owner should always provide the design professional with the project budget and require the design professional to conform the design to fit within that budget.

Illustrative Case

An automobile dealer sought an architect to design a new building and showroom for his automobile dealership. The requirements for the building were that it contain 40,000 square feet, that the construction begin immediately since the dealer's lease on his present showroom was expiring, and that the building not cost more than $250,000.

The architect furnished the owner with some preliminary drawings of prefabricated steel buildings to demonstrate possible floor plans and later drew some sketches and an elevation study. The owner and the architect signed an AIA Standard Form of Agreement Between Owner and Architect. The contract stated that the building was to be "a multiple purpose building suitable to the needs of the owner, at an approximate estimated cost of $250,000."

Bids were put out on both steel-frame and prestressed concrete types of construction. The bids for steel-frame construction were under $250,000, but the bids for prestressed concrete construction totaled $317,000.

The owner terminated the contract on the basis that the architect had agreed to design a building of prestressed concrete for $250,000 and that the bids had exceeded that amount. The architect filed a lawsuit for his fee, and testimony at trial substantiated the owner's contention that the building was to be constructed of prestressed concrete. The architect argued that the $250,000 was only an approximate estimate and not a guarantee.

The court found that, under the contract, the architect agreed to furnish plans and specifications for a prestressed concrete building at a cost not to exceed $250,000 and that, irrespective of the contract provision stating that the architect "does not guarantee the accuracy of any statements or estimates of probable construction cost," the architect was not entitled to any fee or compensation under the contract.[1]

To protect the owner, to forestall claims for fees by the design professional, and to ensure recovery by the owner of any fees already paid to the design professional should the bids for the construction exceed the owner's project budget, all contracts between owner and design professional should contain a statement of total funds available for construction of the project. This simple technique can save the owner both money and time. The design professional will be placed on notice that unless his design comes within the project budget, he must refund his fee, or that he must, at the owner's option, assume the cost of redesign in order to bring the project within the budget in a manner acceptable to the owner.

DESIGN DEVELOPMENT PHASE

Subparagraph 1.2.1 of AIA Document B141 (1977 ed.) states that, following approval by the owner of the schematic design documents, and after any owner-authorized adjustments to the project scope or budget, the design professional is required to submit another Statement of Probable Construction Cost to the owner under subparagraph 1.2.2. The owner's written approval of the design development documents and the Statement of Probable Construction Cost should be required prior to commencing the next phase of architectural services.

In the design development phase of the contract, the architect and his engineers, consultants, and advisers prepare the drawings and other documents to demonstrate how the project will appear. All structural, electrical, and mechanical systems are laid out and diagrammed, and the overall project design is firmly established. The AIA form contract contains eleven lines defining what is expected of the design professional during this phase. There is little to demonstrate what is to be furnished to the owner under the definition of design development documents.

At a minimum, the owner should specify that design development

[1]Stevens v. Fanning, 59 Ill. App. 2d 285, 207 N.E.2d 136, 20 A.L.R.3d 769 (1965).

documents are to include sufficient data, information, and material to define the scope of the project and to demonstrate the project's general design, specifically including the site and the character of all architectural, structural, mechanical, and electrical systems and materials, together with any other functional elements or systems necessary under the project scope and design.

CONSTRUCTION DOCUMENTS PHASE

Once the design development documents are approved and any changes in the project scope or budget are authorized by the owner, under subparagraph 1.3.1 of AIA Document B141 (1977 ed.), the design professional begins to prepare the construction documents. These documents should, at minimum, consist of complete drawings and specifications that detail the actual requirements for construction of the project. The construction documents should establish the specific criteria and material requirements for the actual project construction since these documents are the foundation for the owner's contracts with the general contractor. It is these specific documents that furnish the basis for the contractor's bid preparation. The construction documents are in fact the plans and specifications for the construction of the entire job.

The design professional is responsible, under subparagraph 1.3.2 of AIA Document B141 (1977 ed.), for assisting in the preparation of the bid documents, for assisting the owner in filing documents for construction permits, and in obtaining any necessary approvals from building departments and government agencies under subparagraph 1.3.4. The design professional is also required to advise the owner of any adjustments to previous Statements of Probable Construction Cost under subparagraph 1.3.3.

The design professional's standard liability for defective plans and specifications is one for deviation from the practices of other design professionals. It is important to note that in all but three states (South Carolina, Alabama, and Washington), the courts have routinely held that a design professional does not warrant or promise that the plans and specifications will be sufficient to accomplish their intended purpose.

Illustrative Case

The City of New Orleans hired a design firm to design and supervise the construction of a refuse incinerator with a daily capacity of 200 tons. The owner was required by contract to hire a soil expert. The design firm, however, supervised the subsoil investigation at the site. Only three soil borings were taken. Latent unstable soil conditions were later encountered during evacuation, and a large number of piles were displaced by a deep lateral movement in the soil. The contractor warned that the design for a floating slab was defective and that the slabs would settle if installed in accordance with the plans and specifications. The design professional ignored the contractor's warning and ordered the

Installation of the floating slabs without structural supports and in accordance with the plans and specifications.

The slabs began to settle immediately. The contractor sued the city for extra work and the city sued the designer who, after final inspection, had advised that the work had been satisfactorily completed. Experts agreed that the plans and specifications failed to show the soil conditions, that the site was the worst area for construction in New Orleans, that the designer had approved compaction under the slab, and that the designer had chosen to ignore the contractor's warning that if the slabs were installed as designed, costly settlement would occur. In spite of these facts, the court rule that the designer had performed his services in accordance with the skill usually exercised by other architects and engineers in the same general area and so was not liable to the owner for professional incompetency or negligence.[2]

This rule is highly unpleasant for the owner since the owner in all jurisdictions is held to guarantee or warrant the adequacy and sufficiency of the plans and specifications to the general contractor. If the plans are deficient and the contractor suffers an economic loss due to defective plans or project specifications, then the owner pays.

Bidding or Negotiation

Once the owner approves the construction documents and the adjusted Statement of Probable Construction Cost, the owner, with the designer's assistance, begins to negotiate proposals. In the private sector, the owner is relatively free to pick and choose the general contractor to construct the project. If the owner is a public agency bound by competitive bidding practices, it puts the project out for bids. The usual public bidding statutes or regulations commonly provide for award of the construction contract to the "lowest responsible bidder" who submits a "responsive" bid. A responsible bidder is generally one who has the ability to perform the contract requirements properly. A responsive bid is one that complies with the Invitation for Bids.

The design professional generally should be required to prepare the necessary bid documents and the Invitation for Bids, including all contractual addenda and terms and conditions required by the project. (A sample bond form for bids is included in Appendix C.) If the project is complex, the design professional should be required to prepare a pre-bid construction schedule and to hold a pre-bid conference. When proposals or bids are taken, the design professional should be required to assist the owner by receiving the bids or proposals. In addition, the design professional should be required to recommend those bidders whose bids are responsive and to review the qualifications of the apparent low bidders.

Whether or not a bid is responsive is determined by whether or not the bid complies with the requirements of the Invitation for Bids. If the bid does not comply with the Invitation for Bids, then the question becomes whether or not the lack of compliance is material. Under fed-

---

[2]Pittman Constr. Co. v. City of New Orleans, 248 La. 434, 178 So.2d 312 (1965).

eral regulations and standard Procurement Code Regulations, defects in the bid can generally be waived or corrected unless the error or deficiency could affect price, quality, quantity, or date of delivery of the goods and services, and if waiver or correction would not operate to the prejudice of other bidders. Other states without Model Procurement Code guidelines have adopted more stringent guidelines.

Illustrative Case

The Borough of Milford, New Jersey, put a garbage scavengers contract out for bids with a request for proposals for contracts of one, two, three, and five years' duration. The contractor submitting the lowest bid submitted proposed contracts for one, two, and three years, but neglected to submit a proposal for a five-year contract. The borough announced that it would enter into a three-year contract with the low bidder, waiving the nonconformity with the Invitation for Bids and Instructions to Bidders. Another bidder sued the borough, contesting the low bidder's status as "lowest responsive bidder."

The Supreme Court of New Jersey ruled that it was the policy of bidding laws to curtail the discretion of local public authorities by requiring strict compliance with public bidding guidelines, and that the failure to bid all contracts was a material irregularity that could not be waived by the borough.[3]

The design professional and the owner's attorney are best suited to determine the responsiveness of the bids. Local contracting officers should always seek legal advice prior to rejecting any bid.

Once a bid or proposal is established as being responsive, in order to determine whether or not the bidder is responsible, a determination must be reached as to that bidder's qualifications to do the job. Some states, such as New Jersey, prequalify all contractors, and a contractor cannot bid on a state project if that contractor is not determined to be responsible.

Other states, such as South Carolina, have adopted a Contractor's Qualification Questionnaire. A copy of this form is included in Appendix D. This questionnaire is a part of the bid package, but it is submitted in a separate sealed envelope that is not opened for examination unless the contractor is determined to be the apparent low bidder. The questionnaire contains inquiries such as the number of projects currently being done by the contractor, any delays in those projects, liquidated damages or delays assessed against the contractor during the last five-year period, names of design professionals and projects involving delays or claims against the contractor, and claims filed against the contractor in court, in arbitration, or with the contractor's bonding company. Based on this information, the design professional makes a determination as to the qualifications of the apparently successful bidder and makes the appropriate recommendation to the owner on the "responsibility" of the contractor. If the apparent low bidder is not determined to be responsible, the procedure of examining the question-

[3]Puccillo v. Mayor and Counsel of New Milford, 73 N.J. 349, 375 A.2d 602 (1977).

naire is repeated with the next apparent low bidder.

In complex and complicated construction, it is advisable for the owner to prequalify contractors and restrict bid solicitation to those contractors that are experienced and successful in their trades, that have done such type of construction in the past, that are financially capable of performing the work, and that are aware of the necessity for coordinating their work with other contractors. Public owners often cannot restrict bidders because of applicable small business setasides and minority-participation requirements. When multiple prime contracts are to be used, the design professional should become involved in the prequalification of bidders by soliciting the general contractor's data and documentation on personnel and financial resources and by reviewing the qualifications of personnel whom the contractor intends to use on the project.

Prequalification can be accomplished by publication of notice that bids will be solicited only from qualified bidders and by requiring potential bidders to submit specific information to the design professional. Those prospective bidders approved by the design professional should then be notified that they have been found qualified to bid, but the notice of qualification should stipulate that this qualification to bid is based solely on information submitted by the contractor and that the owner reserves the right to review the qualifications of the apparent low bidder based on the information furnished in the Contractor's Qualification Questionnaire. Prequalification and usage of the contractor's questionnaire to determine responsibility of the contractor can help eliminate the possibility of claims-oriented contractors and financially unsound bidders.

Once the contract bids are received, the problem of construction cost estimates often arises. As discussed earlier, AIA Document B141 (1977 ed.) refers to "Statements of Probable Construction Cost." A typical owner unknowledgeable in industry custom can readily assume that this cost-estimating device can be relied on. However, under the AIA contract the design professional is not responsible for inaccurate estimates, and legal decisions on this issue vary according to jurisdiction.

Subparagraph 3.2.2 of the AIA form contract requires that in order for a fixed limit of construction cost to be valid, it must be in writing and agreed to by both parties. If construction cost has a fixed limit, the design professional is permitted to include contingencies for alternate design and for bidding and price escalation and may determine what materials, equipment, component systems, and types of construction are to be used for the project. The design professional also retains the right to use alternate bids.

Under article 3 of the AIA form contract, if the project bids or the lowest negotiated proposal exceed the fixed limit of construction cost, the owner can approve an increase in the fixed limit; authorize rebidding or renegotiating the project; terminate the design professional's contract in accordance with paragraph 10.2, still paying the design professional's fee; or authorize the design professional to revise the project scope to reduce the construction cost. Note that unless there is a fixed limit on construction cost, under the AIA contract the owner will be required to pay for the modification and revision of the drawings and specifications necessary to bring the project within the owner's budget in addition to the already established design fee. This can easily be avoided by using a contract drafted to specify the owner's project budget or cost limitation.

CONSTRUCTION PHASE—ADMINISTRATION OF THE CONSTRUCTION CONTRACT

Traditionally, the design professional is responsible for administering the construction contract following award of the contract to the general contractor. The design professional acts as the owner's representative on the construction site, assisting in the construction process and acting as the contract administrator. The design professional serves as the liaison between the general contractor and the owner.

Under subparagraph 1.5.1 of the AIA form contract, the construction phase commences with the award of the construction contract to the general contractor and terminates when the final Certificate for Payment is due or sixty days after the Date of Substantial Completion, whichever occurs first. During the construction phase, the design professional serves as the agent of the owner and deals with the contractor for the owner. Subparagraph 1.5.3 states that "instructions to the contractor shall be forwarded through the architect." The scope of the agency, or the design professional's authority, must be spelled out in the contract between the owner and the design professional and in the contract between the owner and the general contractor.

Under subparagraph 1.5.4 of the AIA form contract, one of the primary functions of the design professional is site visitation. However, no specific number of site visits is required, and the design professional's obligation is only to become acquainted with the progress and quality of the work and to determine in general if the work is proceeding in accordance with the plans and specifications. The design professional is specifically not required to make continuous on-site inspections or to check the quality or quantity of the work. Subparagraph 1.5.5 of the contract states that the design professional is not responsible for any acts or omissions of the contractor or for the failure of the contractor to carry out work in accordance with the contract documents, but the design professional does have the authority, under subparagraph 1.5.12, to reject work that does not conform to the contract documents. The design professional's right to stop work was deleted from the standard-form contract after the 1968 edition. (This issue is discussed in "Design Services Contract—Problem Areas," later in this chapter.)

Another major responsibility of the design professional is the approval and certification of the general contractor's "Applications for Payment." (See Appendix E for a sample form.) Under subparagraph 1.5.7 of AIA Document B141, the design professional is required to determine the amounts owed to the contractor based on observations at the construction site. Under subparagraph 1.5.8, the issuance of a Certificate for Payment to the owner constitutes a representation by the design professional that the work has progressed to the point indicated on the contractor's application and that to the best of the design professional's knowledge, information, and belief, the work is in accordance with the contract documents. Thus the design professional is required to provide ongoing determinations as to whether or not the contractor is actually performing the construction work in a manner that meets the requirements of the plans and specifications and the contract documents.

While the design professional is not a guarantor of the general performance of the contract, he is required to use professional care and diligence to reach a determination as to the quality and quantity of work based on visits to the construction site. These site observations and the determination by the design professional as to the quality and quantity of the work in place form the basis on which the design professional approves the contractor's Applications for Payment and forwards them to the owner. One common area of liability for the design professional is negligent certification of the work.

The design professional's potential liability to the owner is governed by the obligations and authority assumed by the design professional under the contract. The basic duties during the construction phase services under the AIA form contract are

(1) Administration of the construction contract;

(2) Visitation at the construction site;

(3) Notification to the owner of the progress and quality of the work in place;

(4) Approval and certifications of the contractor's Applications for Payment;

(5) Interpretation of the contract documents;

(6) Impartial decisions concerning the performance of the owner and the general contractor;

(7) Decisions concerning disputes between the owner and the general contractor;

(8) Rejection of nonconforming work;

(9) Review and timely approval of shop drawings, product data, and samples;

(10) Preparation of change orders (see Appendix F) for the owner's approval;

(11) Determination of the Dates of Substantial Completion and Final Completion.

The AIA form contract makes it clear that the design professional is required through site inspections to check only the quality or quantity of the work and that the design professional is not responsible for construction means, methods, or techniques, for the acts or omissions of any contractor or subcontractor, or for any failure by the general contractor or the subcontractors to carry out work in accordance with the contract documents. These provisions reduce a design professional's exposure to liability for injury or damage not only to the owner, but also to third parties such as subcontractors or employees of the contractors. The owner should take care to require supervisory services and a minimum number of site visits for the specific purpose of guarding against deficiencies in the work of the general contractor.

Because the design professional is the owner's representative on the construction site, it is extremely important that the provisions in the design professional's contract with the owner be consistent and coordinated with the general conditions of the construction contract. The AIA Standard Form of Agreement Between Owner and Architect is correlated with Document A101, Standard Form of Agreement Between Owner and Contractor and A201, General Conditions of the Contract for Construction. In any contract adopted or drafted by an owner, care must be taken that all of the design professional's rights and responsibilities to the owner flow through into the General Conditions and the construction contract so that the general contractor will have notice of the design professional's authority in administering the construction contract.

Checklist for Construction Phase Services

In drafting a construction contract, the owner should always make it clear that the construction phase commences with the award of the construction contract and terminates only on final acceptance of the project by the owner. It should be clear that the design professional's obligation to provide basic services under any agreement does not terminate on his certification of substantial completion. These services should continue until final inspection at the end of the one-year construction warranty.

The design professional should be required to conduct job progress meetings and to monitor the construction schedule generated by the contractor. The design professional should also be required to visit the construction site as often as necessary during the course of construction.

On the basis of a required bi-weekly review of the general contractor's construction schedule, the design professional should be required to monitor the progress of the work and to submit a monthly report to the owner. In addition, the design professional, on discovering a delay, should be given the authority to place the general contractor on notice that the project must be brought back onto schedule and that a plan must be submitted to the design professional for having the project on schedule within a reasonable length of time.

In paragraphs dealing with the contractor's written request for payment, the design professional should be required to determine clearly the amount owing to the general contractor based on observations at the site and on review that the work in place was done in conformity with the contract documents. The design professional should be required to reject work not in conformity with the contract documents.

The design professional should be required to review and approve all shop drawings for conformance with the design concept of the project and the criteria set out in the contract documents. The design professional should also be required to return shop drawings to the general contractor within a reasonable time following their receipt so as not to delay the contractor, unless the design professional notifies the contractor in writing, setting forth the reason for the delay.

Following the design professional's review and analysis of all requests by the general contractor for change orders, the design professional should be required to prepare change orders and submit written recommendations to the owner along with the change-order requests.

If the owner chooses, the design professional may also be required to coordinate the sequence of work if multiple prime contractors are used. If multiple contracts are used, it should be clearly spelled out in the design contract that the design professional is solely responsible for enforcing the performance of the construction contract and is not relieved from this responsibility by the presence of representatives or employees of the owner on the job site.

The design professional should be required to arrange for all final inspections and to ensure that all work performed by the general contractor and any subcontractors is in accordance with the requirements of the contract documents. This obligation should include a final inspection at the end of the one-year warranty period.

In order to avoid delay disputes, the design professional should be required to make decisions within a reasonable time after the presentation of any claim or dispute. If claims are submitted to the owner, the design professional should be required to review the claims and to prepare a written report outlining the background and status of each and making recommendations to the owner as to their disposition.

The contract should require the design professional, upon completion of each inspection, to submit a written report to the owner. This same procedure should be repeated one month prior to the expiration of the general one-year warranty period for the project.

OWNER'S RESPONSIBILITIES

AIA Document B141, under article 2, lists the owner's responsibilities under the contract. Included under these subparagraphs is the owner's obligation to provide full information regarding requirements for the project. The owner is required to provide a property survey giving all information concerning restrictions, easements, and zoning; to furnish the services of soils engineers; and to provide the subsurface soils report. The owner is also required to furnish all structural, mechanical, chemical, and laboratory tests, inspections, and any other reports required for the project.

These subparagraphs are frequently a major source of dispute and litigation resulting in damage and loss to the owner. One way to avoid this type of loss is to transfer the responsibility for testing to the design professional and to require the design professional to obtain the information to be gathered under these subparagraphs.

Under the AIA standard-form documents, the design professional typically selects and hires the soils engineers and other engineering and testing experts in the owner's name. With this procedure, any errors on the part of the soils engineers or the testing engineers become the problem of the owner since these consultants are in fact working for the owner and not for the design professional. However, the typical owner has little, if any, knowledge of what is good engineering practice, of what is adequate testing procedure for subsurface conditions, or of the sufficiency and meaning of mechanical and electrical testing and chemical evaluations. If the owner requires the design professional to obtain these services in his own name, the design professional becomes responsible for the negligence of the engineers performing the tests and surveys and will be much more likely to require good testing procedures and adequate soil borings on the site. A typical contract clause would require that the design professional obtain a survey of building site conditions, a report on subsurface investigations, and all other tests deemed necessary by the design professional subsequent to the owner's approval of the costs.

The owner is required to designate a representative to act for it during the construction project, to examine documents, and to make decisions promptly so as to avoid delaying or interfering with the functions of the design professional. The owner is required under these paragraphs to make decisions and to take action on a variety of approvals and decisions arising during the construction of any project. When an owner's representative is required, a failure to act reasonably can give rise to delay claims and can invalidate any time schedule established by the owner. If the owner has knowledge of defects in the construction or of a lack of adherence to the plans and specifications and fails to take action, and if the work is rejected at a later date, the contractor may claim that the owner had knowledge of the work and accepted the work by not objecting in a timely manner.

PAYMENT PROVISIONS

Under AIA B141, the design professional is paid a fee for basic services listed in paragraphs 1.1 through 1.5, and for any other basic services listed in article 15. Additional services are listed under paragraph 1.7, and the owner is required to pay an additional fee if these additional services are required.

The fee for basic services furnished by the design professional has been most commonly computed on the basis of a percentage of construction cost. Some design firms prefer to be paid at an agreed-upon hourly rate. Irrespective of which method of payment is chosen, an owner concerned about excessive design fees should negotiate a "not-to-exceed" limit for compensation. A third payment method is a lump-sum fee. Again, as with the other two payment methods, it is important for the parties to establish the scope of the project and of the services expected to be performed for those fees. The owner will still be obligated to obtain additional services not contemplated as basic services at a separate rate.

The owner is typically obligated to pay to the design professional certain expenses that are called reimbursable expenses. A lack of definition of what comprises a reimbursable expense can lead to disputes between owner and design professional. These disputes can easily be avoided by addressing the issue under the contract. Article 5 of AIA Document B141 (1977 ed.) lists the most common types of reimbursable expenses, including transportation, living expenses, long-distance communication, permit fees, document copying, postage and handling expenses, data processing, photographic requirements, overtime work authorized by the owner, models and mockups requested by the owner, and the cost of any insurance coverage requested by the owner in excess of that normally carried by the design professional and his consultants. These expenses are considered by the design professional to be either directly related to the project or beyond normal office overhead. Paragraph 14.5 of the AIA form contract allows the design professional to "mark up" these expenses on submission to the owner for reimbursement. The owner may object to the markup since a standard multiple of 1.0 will be reimbursement for these expenses at cost.

Article 6 of AIA Document B141 deals with payments to the design professional, requiring an initial payment followed by monthly payments plus additional payments in proportion to services performed within each phase as set forth under article 14. The additional payments are made at the end of each phase of services rendered in accordance with a schedule that establishes the percentage of the total compensation to be paid for completion of each phase. This allows the design professional to bill the owner on a time-payment basis within each phase and permits an adjustment at the end of each phase. Under the AIA contract payment outline, the design professional may collect as much as 95 percent of his fee at the end of the bidding phase of the contract, leaving little monetary impetus to furnish adequate services during the construction phase of the project.

Design Professional's Accounting Records

Under article 7 of AIA Document B141 (1977 ed.), records of reimbursable expenses and expenses related to services performed on the basis of a multiple of direct personnel expense must be kept on a monthly basis under generally accepted accounting principles and made available to the owner. A great number of design professionals now base their compensation on costs of personnel time. Basing the design fee on a percentage of construction costs is no longer as popular in the construction industry as in past years; and even when the fee is computed as a percentage of construction cost, additional services furnished in the contract are usually computed on a time basis. The form contract under subparagraph 14.4.1 allows the design professional to list his employees at the employees' payment rate and to use a multiplier to cover overhead, personnel expense, and profit when computing compensation for additional services.

Article 4 of the form contract defines direct personnel expense as the direct salaries of all the design professional's personnel engaged on the project, together with the related portion of the cost of their mandatory and customary contributions and benefits, such as employment taxes, statutory employee benefits, insurance, sick leave, holidays, vacations, and pensions. Direct personnel expense thus includes payroll, FICA taxes, and other such expenses. The owner may wish to consider limiting personnel expense to direct payroll costs, or, in lieu of this, setting a dollar amount limiting direct personnel expense for the project.

ARBITRATION

The concept of arbitration as a method for dispute resolution in construction projects has been supported by the construction industry for years. Standard-form contracts published by the AIA contain broad-form arbitration clauses that incorporate by reference the Construction Industry Arbitration Rules of the American Arbitration Association. Article 9 of AIA Document B141 states that all claims, disputes, and other matters in question between the parties to the agreement arising out of or relating to the contract or any breach of the contract must be decided by arbitration. Article 9 specifically states that the owner may not consolidate with or join any other party, including the general contractor, except with the written consent of the design professional and the general contractor.

This type of arbitration clause puts the owner in the unenviable position of perhaps being required to arbitrate with the general contractor on a claim that flows through to the design professional. For instance, the general contractor could demand arbitration with the owner for losses incurred from defective drawings and specifications. The owner would be unable to consolidate in that arbitration a claim against the design professional for the defective drawings and specifications. The owner would instead be required to arbitrate first with the general contractor. If the contractor were successful in its claim against the owner, the owner would then be forced to begin an entirely new arbitration against the design professional for defective plans and specifications. Before a different panel the owner could quite possibly lose even though a prior panel had found that the plans and specifications were, in fact, defective.

This inequitable situation, plus the extreme cost to the owner of having to endure two separate arbitrations, is untenable. Therefore, many public and private owners have struck the arbitration clause entirely from their contracts. If arbitration is to be retained in the contract, the nonconsolidation provision should be removed. Note, however, that the American Arbitration Association will not compel consolidation of multiparty arbitration if any party objects. In court actions, some courts have ruled to compel consolidation of claims and joinder of parties, but this consolidation is ordered only in the absence of specific contract language prohibiting nonconsensual consolidation and joinder. A solution to the problem might be to limit arbitration to those claims and disputes that do not involve an amount in excess of $250,000 and to allow joinder of both design professional and contractor at the owner's option. The arbitration clause would merely say that if the amount in controversy exceeds the stated amount, then the arbitration panel is divested of jurisdiction.

There are other considerations for the owner to bear in mind. For example, under the AIA form contract the American Arbitration Association rules govern the proceedings. If the parties are not able to agree where the arbitration is to be held, then the American Arbitration Association may select the site for the hearing. If the parties are unable to agree on the panelists, the American Arbitration Association may select the panelists. The possibility of an inconvenient locale and of an undesirable panel should be considered.

In addition, as more and more states adopt Consolidated Procurement Code procedures for resolving disputes and claims, the need for arbitration in the public sector lessens. Under Procurement Code guidelines and regulations a board of contract appeals can be established, and all claims and disputes arising under bid solicitations, contract awards, and contract claims and disputes of any kind can be required to be heard by the panel as an exclusive remedy.

The owner should also keep in mind that in arbitration, not only is the owner required to secure legal counsel and to pay the cost of expert witnesses and the engineering tests and studies necessary to support its case, but also to pay a fee to the American Arbitration Association and to pay for the panelists' expenses during the duration of the hearings.

MISCELLANEOUS PROVISIONS

Governing Law

If AIA Document B141 (1977 ed.) is used as the contract between the owner and the design professional, it is governed by the law of the design professional's principal place of business. When the design professional and the owner are located in the same jurisdiction as the project locale, then this clause is feasible. However, if the owner is contracting with an out-of-state design professional, conflicts can arise. The owner should always stipulate that the laws of a specific jurisdiction, either that of the owner or that of the construction project location, should govern.

In selecting a specific jurisdiction, the owner should be certain to consider not only the advantages and disadvantages of location, but also the impact that the law of that jurisdiction may have on claims and disputes. States have varying laws concerning statutes of limitation, notice provisions, delay claims, hold harmless agreements, site exploration clauses, and general exculpatory clauses. Also, the states have varying laws concerning the right of the design professional to file a mechanic's lien against the project. Selection of a state with a short statute of limitations for claims against a design professional would, of course, be most beneficial to the design professional, while a jurisdiction with a long statute of limitations or one not permitting the filing of a lien against the building by a design professional would be most beneficial to the owner.

Successors and Assigns

Article 12 prevents the assignment of the contract by either the owner or the design professional without the written consent of other parties. If the owner is a developer, this clause may have to be deleted since the developer's lending institution may require the developer to include a provision permitting the financing institution's assumption under the contract in the event of the developer's default so that the lending institution may complete the construction project. The lending institution would obviously wish to keep the design professional contractually bound to continue performance.

Termination of Agreements

Article 10 of AIA Document B141 (1977 ed.) allows either the owner or the design professional to terminate the contract by giving seven days' written notice if the other party substantially fails to perform obligations under the contract and there is no fault on the side of the party initiating termination.

Paragraph 10.2 allows the owner to terminate the agreement on seven days' written notice to the design professional in the event that the construction project is permanently abandoned. This is a premature termination of the contract agreement and generally takes place when the owner decides not to continue the project. This type of termination is generally due to lack of funding or financial resources.

When the contract is terminated prior to completion of the project, the owner's two major considerations are the amount of payment owed to the design professional and the owner's rights to the design, drawings, and specifications prepared by the design professional prior to contract termination.

Under paragraph 10.3, which governs termination when the design professional is not at fault, the design professional must be compensated for all services performed up to the termination date, together with all reimbursable expenses due and all termination expenses that are set forth and defined under paragraph 10.4. The termination expenses clause states:

Termination Expenses include expenses directly attributable to termination for which the Architect is not otherwise compensated, plus an amount computed as a percentage of the total Basic and Additional Compensation earned to the time of termination, as follows:

(1) 20% if termination occurs during the Schematic Design Phase; or

(2) 10% if termination occurs during the Design Development Phase; or

(3) 5% if termination occurs during any subsequent phase.

Termination of the construction project by the owner often occurs when the owner has not begun construction but has received the plans and specifications for the project. If the owner is forced to terminate construction at the bidding phase on account of a substantial overage above the owner's budget in the lowest bids received for the project, then the owner is, in all likelihood, going to object to paying the design professional's fee. To protect against this possibility, the AIA has incorporated monthly payment provisions for the duration of the project into the standard contract. In addition, the project is divided into five phases, with a portion of the fee payable at the end of each phase. (See "Payment Provisions.")

Note that the termination-of-agreement clause contains no provision for termination of the design contract at the "convenience" of the owner. The AIA form contract seems only to contemplate termination due to a failure of performance by either the design professional or the owner or due to permanent abandonment of the project by the owner. Under the AIA form contract, an owner may terminate the contract only if the design professional has failed to substantially perform his obligations under the contract and the owner is not at fault in any manner, or if the owner permanently abandons the project. If the owner and design professional reach an impasse during the contract, there may be no remedy for escaping from the contract. If the owner terminates the project through no fault of the design professional, the design professional is to be compensated for all services performed up to the termination date, together with all reimbursable expenses due and subject to the payment provision in paragraph 10.4.

Any owner should incorporate into the design services contract a clause specifying that the owner may terminate the contract for any reason, including the convenience of the owner, by giving written notice to the design professional specifying the date of termination.

It is recommended that the paragraph governing termination expenses be removed from the contract because of the indefinite nature of the termination expenses provision. A better clause from the owner's perspective would state that if termination is not the fault of the design professional, the owner shall pay whatever compensation is due him for services properly performed prior to the effective date of termination and for any reasonable reimbursable expenses properly incurred.

Costly and time-consuming litigation may be avoided with a termination clause establishing that the agreement can be terminated by the owner if bids received are 10 percent in excess of the estimated construction cost or of the owner's budget, and that the design professional shall then be liable to the owner for the return of any fees paid to the design professional under the contract. If the owner is forced to litigate to recover that fee, the owner will have the burden of proving either that there was a minimum cost limitation in the contract or that the contract for design services contained an estimated cost figure. The basic rule is that the cost of construction must reasonably approach the cost stated in the estimate provided by the design professional unless the owner has ordered changes that increase the cost of construction.

OWNERSHIP OF DOCUMENTS

Article 8 of AIA Document B141 (1977 ed.) states that all drawings and specifications shall remain the property of the design professional whether the project is constructed or not, and that the plans and specifications shall not be used by the owner for completion of the project, for other projects, or for additions to the project unless the design professional agrees. If the contract between the owner and the design professional has been terminated, the ownership of the documents becomes a critical issue.

State and federal contracts often stipulate that the ownership of the documents is vested in the federal or state government. Owners should add into the contract a specific provision giving the owner unlimited rights to all drawings, designs, and specifications developed in the performance of the design agreement, including the right to use those plans and specifications, without additional cost.

ADDITIONAL SERVICES

Article 15 of AIA Document B141 (1977 ed.) is a blank page labeled "Other Conditions or Services." This article is for use by the owner and the design professional in describing additional services that are to be included under the scope of the contract. Under article 15, services not listed in the contract as basic services may be added to the contract as additional services to be provided by the design professional when authorized by the owner and when paid for by the owner in addition to the compensation or fee established for basic services. Paragraph 1.7 of the form contract sets forth twenty-two subparagraphs defining services that are in addition to services normally furnished under the AIA standard program for the five phases discussed earlier. These services are as follows:

Subparagraph 1.7.1. Furnishing analysis of the owner's needs and programming construction project requirements for the owner.

Subparagraph 1.7.2. Furnishing financial feasibility studies or other special duties.

Subparagraph 1.7.3. Furnishing planning surveys, site evaluations, and special studies and surveys necessary for the project.

Subparagraph 1.7.4. Furnishing services for facilities that are not to be constructed until a later date.

Subparagraph 1.7.5. Furnishing services for future facilities or to verify the accuracy of drawings or information furnished by the owner.

Subparagraph 1.7.6. Preparing documents for alternate, separate, or sequential bids or providing extra services for bidding negotiation or construction prior to completion of the construction documents phase as requested by the owner.

Subparagraph 1.7.7. Providing coordination of the work performed by multiple prime contractors or by the owner's own forces.

Subparagraph 1.7.8. Providing services in connection with the work of the construction manager or a separate consultant.

Subparagraph 1.7.9. Providing detailed estimates of construction costs and various analyses and surveys.

Subparagraph 1.7.10. Providing interior design services.

Subparagraph 1.7.11. Furnishing services for planning tenant or rental spaces.

Subparagraph 1.7.12. Making revisions in drawings, specifications, or other documents that differ from written approvals or instructions given by the owner or that are required by code revisions or changes to laws or regulations that occurred subsequent to the preparation of the contract documents or that are due to other causes not solely within the control of the design professional.

Subparagraph 1.7.13. Preparing drawings, specifications, and supporting data in connection with change orders where the adjustment in the basic compensation resulting from the adjustment in construction costs is not commensurate with the services already required of the design professional, provided such change orders are required by causes not solely within the control of the design professional.

Subparagraph 1.7.14. Furnishing any investigations, surveys, evaluations, or detailed appraisals of existing facilities and services required in connection with construction that has been performed by the owner.

Subparagraph 1.7.15. Providing consultation concerning replacement of work damaged by fire or any other cause and furnishing any services required in connection with replacement of such work.

Subparagraph 1.7.16. Providing services made necessary by the default of the contractor or by major business defects or deficiencies in the work of the contractor or by failure of performance by the owner or the contractor under the contract for construction.

Subparagraph 1.7.17. Preparing record drawings showing significant changes in the work during construction based on marked-up prints, drawings, and other data furnished by the contractor.

Subparagraph 1.7.18. Providing extensive assistance for operating equipment or systems incorporated into the new construction.

Subparagraph 1.7.19. Providing services to the owner after final Certificate for Payment or more than sixty days after Date of Substantial Completion of the work.

Subparagraph 1.7.20. Furnishing expert-witness service in connection with any hearing or proceeding.

Subparagraph 1.7.21. Furnishing consultant services for other than the normal architectural, structural, mechanical, and electrical engineering services required by the project.

Subparagraph 1.7.22. Providing services not otherwise included in this agreement and not customarily furnished in accordance with generally accepted design practice.

Under the AIA form contract, the owner must authorize the performance of these services in writing. This written confirmation is extremely important in any dispute resolution concerning the design professional's right to payment for services performed beyond the basic scope of the contract.

In the standard AIA form documents, if an owner elects to use one or more of the services described under paragraph 1.7, then the appropriate subparagraphs should be removed from paragraph 1.7 and listed under article 15. The professional fee would then be adjusted accordingly. *Note:* Carefully review subparagraph 1.7.3, which concerns site evaluation and planning surveys. As mentioned earlier, planning surveys, site evaluations, and soil investigation studies are not part of the basic services enumerated in the AIA form contract. Also, subparagraphs 1.7.12 and 1.7.13 entitle the design professional to an additional fee when he makes revisions in the plans and specifications and in the preparation of change-order documents when the revisions and change orders are required by causes *not solely* within his control. This language, in effect, requires the owner to assume the liability of an additional fee for revisions or changes that may partially be the fault of the design professional.

Subparagraph 1.7.16 requires the owner to pay an extra fee for design services made necessary by major defects or deficiencies in the work of the contractor. The owner should question liability for a design fee incurred by the design professional's failure to monitor the work of the contractor.

Subparagraph 1.7.19 requires the owner to pay extra for services rendered after substantial completion. Under AIA Document A201, General Conditions of the Contract for Construction (1976 ed.), subparagraph 13.2.2 establishes a one-year warranty from the Date of Substantial Completion for correction of defective work by the contractor. The one-year inspection is not, however, considered under AIA form B141 to be a basic service, but must be specifically required in addition to the basic services. The owner may well wish to consider requiring this one-year inspection and the furnishing of a "punch list" for correction of work by the contractor as a part of the services to be provided by the design professional. (A punch list is a list of things that need to be done before the project is completed.)

Subparagraph 1.7.17 states that the preparation of a set of record drawings showing significant changes in the work and based on marked-up prints and drawings and other data furnished by the contractor shall be an additional service entitling the design professional to an additional fee.

DESIGN SERVICES CONTRACT— PROBLEM AREAS

The relationship between the owner and the design professional is a contractual relationship, and the parameters of the design professional's duties, responsibilities, and liabilities must be specifically spelled out in the contract so that the owner is thoroughly protected from the negligence of the design professional. Below are listed several areas where problems frequently arise and which may be easily addressed by adequate contract provisions.

Insurance

AIA Document B141 (1977 ed.) is silent on the issue of professional liability insurance. In addition to ascertaining that errors and omissions coverage is carried by the design professional, the owner should additionally ask what type of professional liability insurance the design professional is carrying. Many owners have neglected this point much to their distress at a later date. A design firm generally has few, if any, tangible assets so the owner's only recourse in the event of professional negligence is to look to the design professional's errors and omissions insurer. The owner should always address the issue of professional liability insurance coverage prior to signing a contract with the design professional.

The design professional will probably have a "claims made" professional liability policy. The owner should keep in mind that a "claims made" policy covers the design professional only for claims that are filed while the policy is in effect, irrespective of when the basis for the claim occurs. In other words, a "claims made" policy insures the design professional for any negligent act claim, as long as the claim is filed while the policy is in effect, perhaps long after the actual construction has been concluded. A policy on an "occurrence" basis covers only claims that are based on acts occurring during the life of the policy. An "occurrence" policy gives coverage only if the policy was in effect when the errors or omissions in design occurred, but the policy still provides coverage long after any possible expiration of that policy. "Occurrence" policies are not generally available.

The owner should also be aware that all errors and omissions policies contain a specific deductible amount and that attorney's fees under some policies may be deducted from the amount of coverage furnished under the policy. Also, a design professional may have a half million dollars in coverage, but if a claim is filed prior to the present owner's claim against the design professional, the entire coverage may be consumed by the prior claim, leaving the present owner with little or no coverage at all. The way to address this problem, particularly for owners of large and complex projects that require substantial coverage, is to require project liability insurance for each specific project.

Subparagraph 5.1.6 of AIA Document B141 (1977 ed.) specifically states that the expense of additional insurance coverage, including professional liability insurance requested by the owner in excess of the amount normally carried by the design professional and his consultants, is to be treated as a reimbursable expense. The owner should be wary and avoid paying for the design professional's normal errors and omissions and professional liability insurance coverage. This professional liability coverage is a cost of doing business for the design professional, and that cost should be apportioned among all the design professional's clients, rather than borne by one owner.

Compliance with Applicable Laws, Codes, Regulations, and Industry Standards

AIA Document B141 (1977 ed.) does not address the planning, designing, and furnishing of specifications for the construction of the project in accordance with standard building codes or state, municipal, and federal regulations. This is an important omission, since an owner would obviously want the prospective construction project to comply with all applicable building-code regulations. In the absence of an express provision, the law will not hold a design professional responsible for failing to achieve compliance with codes and regulations. The design professional will only be required to conform to a standard of ordinary care in the performance of his professional services.

The design professional, by his professional training, should have a general familiarity with applicable codes and regulations and should be required to perform design services in a manner consistent with those codes and regulations. However, design professionals are hesitant to assume the liability that may be associated with a failure to comply with code and regulatory requirements. A failure to require this compliance can result in the owner paying additional fees to the design professional for redesign if the plans and specifications are discovered to be contrary to building code and state and federal requirements. It is therefore to the owner's benefit to insert a contract provision requiring the design professional to design the work in conformance and in strict compliance with all applicable laws, codes, and industry standards.

Time

AIA Document B141 (1977 ed.) provides as follows under subparagraph 1.8.1.:

The Architect shall perform Basic and Additional Services as expeditiously as is consistent with professional skill and care and the orderly progress of the Work. Upon request of the Owner, the Architect shall submit for the Owner's approval a schedule for the performance of the Architect's services which shall be adjusted as required as the Project proceeds and shall include allowances for periods of time required for the Owner's review and approval of submissions and for approvals of authorities having jurisdiction over the Project. This schedule, when approved by the Owner, shall not, except for reasonable cause, be exceeded by the Architect.

This statement requires the design professional to perform in an expeditious manner consistent with professional standards. Design professionals are reluctant to commit themselves by contract to a fixed time schedule, especially since the majority of professional liability insurance policies exclude claims by owners that are caused by a failure of the design professional to deliver documents on time, unless that failure is due to his professional negligence. There are, of course, many reasons a design professional may be delayed due to the negligence of others. However, if a consultant to the designer does not act and delays the designer, the designer would be able to look to the consultant for any delay damages.

The owner is protected the most by requiring the design professional to render interpretations and decisions within ten days of any written request and to return shop drawings to the contractor within fifteen days following their receipt. These time periods can be mitigated by language stating that if review and approval by the design professional are delayed, he may notify the contractor and owner in writing, stating the reason for the delay. A somewhat standard clause might require the design professional to make decisions promptly and that, in any event, the design professional shall respond within ten days after the presentation of the issuance of a change order or of a claim or complaint by any party to the construction contract.

Supervision

AIA Document B141 (1977 ed.) does not contain any reference to the word *supervision*. The design professional's duty to supervise is replaced by an obligation to make occasional on-site observations through which the design professional endeavors to guard the owner against defects and deficiencies in the work covered by the contract. It is the degree of supervision retained by the design professional during the construction of the project that determines the degree of liability for the design professional's negligence during contract administration. There is no cause of action by the owner for negligent supervision if the owner has not imposed a duty on the design professional to supervise the general contractor's work. Where the contract specifically states that the design professional is required to supervise the construction of the work and to require the contractor to comply with the contract documents, where the design professional is given the authority to reject the work of the contractor for nonconformity with the contract documents, and where the design professional has the right to stop the work of the general contractor whenever the design professional determines that it is necessary for the proper performance of the contract, then the owner has achieved substantial protection during the construction phase of the program.

Authority to Stop the Work

Under subparagraph 1.5.12 of AIA Document B141 (1977 ed.), the design professional is given the authority to reject work that does not conform to the contract documents. However, the design professional's authority to stop work was removed from the AIA contracts in all other editions published after 1967.

The general rule is that the duty to supervise construction creates an obligation on the part of the design professional to make sure that the building is constructed in accordance with the contract documents for the project. In 1967, an Illinois court found a design professional liable for injury to workers on a construction site when a roof collapsed.[4] Under the decision, a design professional will be found liable to workers injured on the construction site if the following circumstances exist:

(1) The design professional must have a contractual obligation to the owner to supervise the general contractor's work for compliance with the contract documents;

(2) The agreement between the owner and the general contractor must require the general contractor to observe safety precautions during construction;

[4]Miller v. Dewitt, 37 Ill. 2d 273, 266 N.E.2d 630 (1967).

(3) The dangerous condition causing the injury either must have been known or should have been known to the design professional; and

(4) The design professional must have had the authority to order the condition corrected or to stop the work and failed to do so.

Other cases impose liability on the design professional for injury to workers where there was no right to stop the work of the contractor.[5] These decisions do allude to supervisory duties.

However, in *Day v. National Radiator Corp.*, 241 La. 288, 128 So.2d 660 (1961), the court found that supervisory duties did not make the design professional liable for injuries to workers. This view has been followed in numerous cases where the design professional had the contractual authority to stop work.[6]

Because of the possibility of liability being imposed on design professionals, the AIA deleted supervision and the right to stop work from Document B141. For the owner's benefit, it is suggested that supervision and the authority of the design professional to stop work should be reinserted or drafted into any Owner-Architect Agreement and that the Owner-Contractor Agreement be modified to require the general contractor to be "solely responsible for initiating, maintaining, and supervising all safety precautions and programs in connection with the work."

Note: An owner-drafted contract should include provisions that

(1) require supervision of construction;

(2) require weekly site visits;

(3) impose a duty on the design professional to require contractor compliance with the contract documents;

(4) give the design professional the authority to stop the general contractor's work on account of a failure to comply with orders of the design professional, or a failure to remedy lack of compliance with the contract documents; and

(5) require that the design professional recommend termination of the general contractor for failure to comply materially with the construction contract documents.

Again, a coordination of clauses between the design professional's contract and the General Conditions of the contractor's contract is required.

FEE ALLOCATION

In the general compensation procedures established under the AIA standard forms, by the end of the bidding phase the design professional

---

[5]Loyland v. Stone Webster Eng'rs, 9 Wash. App. 682, 514 P.2d 184 (1973); Simon v. Omaha P.P. Dist., 189 Neb. 183, 202 N.W.2d 157 (1972).

[6]Baker v. Pidgeon Thomas Co., 411 F.2d 744 (6th Cir. 1970); Luterbach v. Mochor, 84 Wis.2d 1, 127 N.W.2d 13 (1978); Lewis v. Slifer, 577 P.2d 1092 (Colo. 1978).

has received the majority of his fee or compensation. The owner is advised to keep in mind that claims against design professionals arise most commonly because of

(1) underestimation by the design professional of the cost of construction;

(2) defective plans and specifications;

(3) improper certification of payment to the general contractor; and

(4) negligent supervision of construction.

A claim for breach of cost conditions by the owner arises during the bidding phase. Claims for improper certification of contractor payments, defective plans and specifications, and incompetent supervision arise only during the construction phase of the contract. If the owner pays the design professional the majority of the design fee or compensation prior to entering the construction phase, the owner has little means of convincing the design professional to proceed in a careful manner under the contract. It would be greatly to the owner's benefit to retain a larger portion of the design professional's compensation than is normally withheld, so that during the construction phase of the project the owner will have some financial leverage with the design professional should the designer neglect to comply with the responsibilities enumerated under the contract.

3 CONTRACTUAL ARRANGEMENTS

Once an owner decides to contract for construction, it must select the type of contract it will use. A wide variety of pricing arrangements is available, but the two main categories are fixed price and cost reimbursement. A fixed-price contract involves payment of a lump sum for performance of the contract, while a cost reimbursement contract involves payment made on the basis of the costs incurred in performance of the contract plus a fixed amount. Variations on the two arrangements can create a pricing arrangement that will work well for the owner and meet its specific needs.

In negotiating a pricing arrangement with the contractor, the owner must prioritize the objectives of cost, time, and quality because any pricing arrangement will usually result in a trade-off between objectives. For example, a fixed-price contract requires the contractor to perform the contract at a fixed price regardless of cost to the contractor. The contractor assumes the risk of increased costs unless the contract includes an escalation clause. However, a fixed-price contract generally takes longer to complete than a cost reimbursement contract, because the project plans and specifications must be much more detailed and complete before they are used.[1]

FIXED-PRICE CONTRACTS

Under a fixed-price contract, the contractor agrees to do the work described by the contract for the lump sum specified in the contract. The lump sum will generally remain the same even if the expenses of the project increase or decrease.

The fixed-price contract is generally considered to transfer the risk of increased costs to the contractor so that the contractor will be responsible for completing the project within the budget. However, this does not preclude the contractor from seeking an equitable adjustment to the

---

[1]The Business Roundtable. *Contractual Arrangements*, Report A-7, at 8 (October 1982).

contract in the event that its costs are increased by changes in the contract requirements, by unforeseen risks or delays, or by other acts of the owner or its agents. In any event, the owner has, by this method, transferred all of the risk of increased cost to the contractor. There are some important issues to consider before an owner adopts this method of payment.

One issue is the amount of planning required in developing contract documents. The owner must provide complete, detailed contract documents, including plans, drawings, and specifications that cover the entire scope of the proposed project. The contractor's price depends on the completeness of the documents because the contractor bears the risk of work that was unanticipated but is arguably covered by broadly drafted contract documents. The design phase is generally the longest when a fixed-price contract is involved because more careful preplanning on the part of the owner or its design professionals is required. This has its advantages because it can only result in a more efficient, well-run project. However, one disadvantage is that the contractor generally makes no contribution to the design or construction phase of the project. It is generally to the owner's advantage to involve contractors in discussions of design and constructability.

A second issue to consider is cost. Under a pure fixed-price contract, the contractor bears the full risk of almost anything that causes an increase in the cost of the contract. Although the advantage of this to the owner is clear, there is an inherent disadvantage. Because the contractor is required to bear the risk of many factors beyond its control, it will generally build a contingency in its price to cover all of the risks. Therefore, the owner will pay an increased amount whether any unforeseen contingencies arise or not. Requiring a contractor to indemnify an owner for risks over which the contractor has no control is really counterproductive. Changes and unforeseen conditions frequently result in disputes and delays in the project.

Unit-Price Contracts

A fixed-price contract, without modifying clauses, generally provides that the contractor is required to do "everything necessary" to construct the project. It does not generally address quantities of work to be performed, and the contractor, by the terms of the contract, assumes the risk of loss on the project. One variation of the fixed-price contract is the unit-price contract, whereby the owner assumes the risk of the amount of work required.

The unit-price contract divides the work into various quantities. Under unit pricing, a fixed amount is paid for each unit of work. Accordingly, the unit-price contract does not contemplate the payment of a fixed sum but rather payment for the amount of work actually performed. The critical factors are a definition of each "unit" and the designation of a final judge who will decide how many units of work are actually performed. Unless these are defined precisely in the contract, disputes as to how many units of work have been performed can easily arise.

The contract must state what the unit prices apply to, particularly if the contractor will be paid in accordance with normal customs of the trade. It is also good practice for a contractor to specify in the contract the normal customs of the trade to avoid any undue literal technical reading of the contract and to avoid having decisions made only on literal contract language. Customs and usage of a particular trade may be used to clarify the contractor's obligation or to clarify ambiguous provisions of the contract.

The owner bears the risk of variations in the quantity of work. However, the contractor bears the risk of increased costs in each work unit. Since certain fixed expenses like overhead will generally be apportioned among the anticipated number of units, if the number of units is substantially decreased or increased, the cost per unit may not cover fixed expenses. The contract may provide that unit prices may be renegotiated if actual quantities overrun or underrun the estimate by more than a set percentage. Such a provision reduces the contractor's risk of bidding too low on a work item that proves to be much smaller in quantity than the design professional's estimate. Likewise, it reduces the owner's risk of paying a high unit price for a work item that is far in excess of the quantity estimated by the design professional.

Many contracts provide the owner with the right to add work at the unit prices agreed upon. The harshness of this clause can be tempered by one providing for renegotiation when there is a significant increase or decrease in the quantity of work. For example, the Armed Services Procurement Regulation[2] provides a clause that can be used in construction contracts containing estimated quantities. The clause provides that where the actual quantity varies by more than 15 percent above or below the estimated quantity, the parties may request an equitable adjustment to the original contract unit price.

Escalation Clauses

In a fixed-price contract, "escalation clauses" can be used to eliminate some of the risks of increased unit costs. An escalation clause will automatically adjust the contract price in the case of some specific event. In this way, escalation clauses shift the full risk or part of the risk of price increases to the owner. Although there are many variations of escalation clauses, three basic types are day-one—dollar-one escalation clauses, significant-increase escalation clauses, and delay escalation clauses.

Day-one—dollar-one escalation clauses reimburse the contractor for the costs of any price increases that occur after the signing of the con-

[2]32 C.F.R. § 7-603.27 (1973).

tract or another specified date. The owner pays the difference in the cost of materials, equipment, and in some cases, labor, between the date of the contract or another specified date and the time of installation. Under a day-one—dollar-one escalation clause, each dollar increase in materials or equipment is reimbursed from the first day of the contract or the date specified in the contract. A typical day-one—dollar-one escalation clause applied to materials or equipment is as follows:

Illustrative Example

The prices of materials or equipment contained in this contract are those in effect as of _____ (date); the contractor shall be reimbursed for all increases in the cost of materials or equipment as of the date of installation, plus _____ for overhead and profit.

Significant-increase escalation clauses are only intended to reimburse the contractor for large price increases that occur between the tender or contract date and the date of installation. The contractor still bears the burden of any small price increases, but the risk of significant price increases is shifted to the owner. A typical significant-increase clause is as follows:

Illustrative Example

In the event of significant delay or of price increase in material, equipment, or energy occurring during the performance of the contract through no fault of the contractor, the contract sum, time of completion, or contract requirements shall be equitably adjusted in accordance with the procedures set forth in the contract documents. A change in price of an item of material, equipment, or energy will be considered significant when the price increases _____ percent between the date of this contract and the date of installation.

A delay escalation clause seeks to reimburse the contractor for price increases and extra expenses that arise during a period of delay. It generally provides for a fixed price for a limited period of time, but allows the contractor to receive increases resulting from delays beyond a given date. A typical delay escalation clause is as follows:

Illustrative Example

It is contemplated that the performance of the contractor's work will be completed by _____ (date). In the event that the contractor's work is not completed by that date, through no fault of the contractor, the contractor shall be reimbursed for all increases in the cost of labor, material, equipment, and energy by reason of said delay, including reimbursement for extended on-site supervision and overhead plus _____ for overhead and profit.

An owner contemplating the inclusion of an escalation clause may want to consider making it applicable to a downward adjustment in the contract price as well as to increases. In this way, the owner would not only bear the risk of increases in price, but also would gain the benefit of any decreases. The term *escalation* by itself connotes only an upward adjustment. An intention to cover both increases and decreases would need to be made very clear by contract language.

Illustrative Case

A subcontract contained a provision that the parties agree to escalate prices according to indexing formulas for labor and transportion. The general contractor attempted to make a deduction for negative indexing, while the subcontractor contested the validity of the deduction on grounds that the provisions of the contract would result only in an upward adjustment for the index. The subcontract provided "The parties agree to index prices by applying each month the indexing formula as per Annex 5, use certain indexes, in particular labor for unskilled, skilled, and foremen, for transportation costs, price of gasoline and oil, and for loss of concrete aggregates on the local market."

The arbitrators ruled that the parties contemplated only upward adjustments since the annex referred only to "escalations." The memorandum inviting tenders and the tender also referred to escalation. In the absence of any specific contractual provisions stating that the index adjustment should be downward as well as upward, the arbitrators ruled that escalations were only upward. They further ruled that before making any unilateral downward adjustments, the general contractor should have consulted with the subcontractor and should have submitted evidence justifying its position. The arbitrators characterized the general contractor's election to make a unilateral deduction a set-off from the progress payment as an unusual interpretation of the indexing formula because the general contractor's failure to pay the subcontractor the amount due under the subcontract justified the subcontractor's termination of the contract.[3]

The advantage of an escalation clause to an owner is that it still provides the contractor with an incentive to control costs and keep them within the budget; yet at the same time it greatly reduces the contractor's risk of unanticipated increases in price. If contractors do not have to assume the risk of increases in cost, owners will generally receive better and more competitive offers and will only have to pay for the net increases that actually occur. The owner must be very careful to define the mechanism for measuring and paying escalation costs. The escalation clause may be based on actual increases in the contractor's costs or on index formulas.

COST REIMBURSEMENT CONTRACTS

In a cost reimbursement contract, the owner pays the contractor for all necessary and reasonable expenses incurred in the construction plus some other amount intended to cover the contractor's overhead and profit. These cost contracts are often accompanied by a "target" or "upset" figure beyond which no additional fee will be payable to the contractor. The advantage to the contractor is obvious: the owner assumes almost all the risk of increased costs. This decrease in degree

[3] I.C.C. Case No. 3267 (1979).

of risk will allow the contractor to accept a smaller margin of profit.

This type of contract is generally useful when an owner wants to start a project immediately, without waiting for detailed, complete plans and specifications. In addition, it is useful where the performance of the contract for some reason implies such uncertainties that no contractor would assume the risk of a fixed-price contract. The contractor can begin work, and the scope and extent of the work can be determined afterward by arrangements that are fair to both the owner and the contractor. The owner also has the flexibility to make changes as desired at their actual cost.

Cost reimbursement contracts require, by their very nature, that the owner take an active role in the actual construction process. The owner provides administrative and supervisor personnel to oversee the construction and to monitor costs.

Of critical concern in cost reimbursement contracts is the definition of reimbursable and nonreimbursable costs. Detailed schedules need to be drafted to define what expenditures will be classified as "costs" and what are to be included in the fee or percentage and cannot be charged as reimbursable costs. Reimbursable costs are those necessarily incurred in the proper performance of the work: wages, payroll, fringe benefits; cost of all materials, supplies, and equipment incorporated in the work, including rental and maintenance charges for all necessary equipment; transportation charges and duties or tariffs therefor; payments to subcontractors; salaries of the contractor's employees stationed at the field office or elsewhere while expediting production or transportation of materials or equipment; proration of reasonable travel, meals, and hotel expenses directly incurred with the work by officers or employees of the contractor; premiums on all bonds and insurance, seals, and use taxes related to the work; permit fees; minor expenses, such as telephone and telegraph costs; cost of temporary site facilities, and removal of debris; and losses and expenses not compensated by insurance that result from causes other than the fault or negligence of the contractor.

Typically, costs that are not reimbursable are stipulated as salaries or other compensation for the contractor's officers and employees while working at the contractor's main office or branch offices; expenses of the contractor's principal or branch offices other than the field office; any capital expenses, including interest on the contractor's capital and any additional capital required to perform the work; all general overhead expenses; and costs due to negligence of the contractor, subcontractors, or anyone directly employed by the contractor.

Unfortunately, disputes frequently arise over the status of items such as overhead, taxes, insurance, casualty expenses, and the salaries of the contractor's managerial employees. It is not sufficient to say the price will be the cost of construction plus a specified fee. The owner must also take care to eliminate discount and profit elements from the contractor's cost so that the owner is only reimbursing the actual costs incurred.

The other element involved in a cost reimbursement contract is an amount intended to provide the contractor with reimbursement of a portion of general office overhead attributable to the job and with a profit for performance of the contract. This amount may be fixed as a percentage of the cost of the work or may be set as a specific lump-sum amount.

Since the owner assumes the burden of increased costs under a cost reimbursement contract, the owner may desire to include incentives that encourage the contractor to minimize costs. Many owners may feel that a cost reimbursement arrangement can result in a large increase in the cost of construction because the contractor has no real incentive to try to control costs. For this reason, many owners will negotiate modifications that combine a pure cost reimbursement with a fixed fee. A maximum price for which the owner will reimburse the contractor may be placed on total costs. Often the parties will negotiate provisions in the contract providing that the contractor will be paid bonuses or a share of cost saving below the maximum price.

A shared savings provision is an agreement that if the contractor completes the work below the fixed price, then the savings are to be shared between the contractor and the owner at an agreed-upon proportion. This type of provision requires that a clear definition of costs be included in the determination of savings. The contractors thus have an identity of interest with the owner and have an incentive for keeping costs under control. Generally, the owner and the contractor can develop a more amicable working relationship geared to the accomplishment of the same goal when a cost reimbursement contract is modified by an incentive clause.

4 GENERAL CONDITIONS OF THE CONSTRUCTION CONTRACT

Once the design professional has produced a final set of plans and specifications for the proposed project, the owner is ready to enter into a construction contract. The construction industry today uses several sets of standard-form contract documents, the most popular of which are the American Institute of Architects standard-form contract agreements. However, modification of the standard-form documents can be excessively risky if coordinated clauses contain discrepancies following alteration. As a result, some owners, both public and private, have begun to draft and use their own contract documents in recent years.

The construction contract is not a simple sheet or two of paper with which the general contractor agrees to construct the owner's project for a stipulated sum payable by the owner at the completion of construction. Typically, the construction contract documents consist of the agreement between the parties; a document referred to as the General Conditions of the Contract for Construction, which defines the duties, rights, and responsibilities of the owner, the design professional, and the contractor during the construction process; Supplemental General Conditions that individualize the General Conditions for a particular project; addenda and modifications; and the drawings, plans, and specifications. In addition, the contract documents often incorporate by reference other documents. Examples of an Owner-Architect Agreement and General Conditions are included in Appendixes G and H.

Well-written contracts are the owner's best means of ensuring that construction will proceed smoothly and will not result in disputes or claims. For this reason, the owner should initially consider the risks commonly incurred during construction and should seek legal advice as to how to best avoid exposure to those risks through utilization of a carefully prepared set of construction contract documents. The inclusion of standard clauses known in the construction industry as exculpatory clauses or disclaimers can protect the owner from common areas of loss by shifting the risk to the other party. The owner should be aware of these clauses, but should also be aware that a contract that is equitable and reasonable is less likely to be disputed and more likely to be enforced as written.

A CONTRACTOR QUESTIONNAIRE

AIA Document A305, the Contractor's Qualification Statement, may be a useful tool for the owner inviting contract bids for construction. As an alternative, the owner's attorney can prepare a questionnaire for general contractors bidding on the proposed project. Appendix D includes a form from South Carolina. A typical questionnaire might include the following:

(1) How long has the general contractor been in business?

(2) Has the general contractor been in business under other corporate titles?

(3) If the general contractor is a corporation, require the contractor to list the date of incorporation, state of incorporation, president's name, and vice-president's name.

(4) If the general contractor is an individual or partnership, have the contractor list the date of organization and the names and addresses of all partners.

(5) If the general contractor is other than a corporation or partnership, have the contractor name the principals and describe the organization.

(6) Require the contractor to list its registration or licensing numbers by state or licensure.

(7) Have the contractor list the types of work normally and usually performed by its own work forces.

(8) Ask if the general contractor has ever failed to complete any work on any project awarded to it. If the answer is affirmative, require the contractor to state the name and location of the project, the project owner, the project designer, the date of the project, and reasons for the failure to complete the work.

(9) Have the contractor state whether or not an officer or partner in the firm has failed to complete any construction contract within the last five years. If the answer is affirmative, have the contractor state the name and location of the project, the project owner, the project designer, the date of the project, and reasons for the failure to complete the construction contract.

(10) Have the general contractor list all major construction projects in progress, giving the names and locations of the projects, the names and addresses of the project owners and designers, the contract amounts, the amounts of work completed, and the scheduled completion dates.

(11) Require the general contractor to list major projects completed within the last five years, giving the names and locations of the project, the names and addresses of the project owners and designers, the contract amounts, the dates of completion, the percentage of the work performed with the contractor's own forces, and the percentage of the construction cost paid for the contractor's services.

(12) Have the general contractor give the general construction experience of the key individuals in the firm.

(13) Require the general contractor to list five references.

(14) Require the general contractor to list bank references.

(15) Require the general contractor to give the name of its bonding company and the name and address of its agent.

(16) Require the general contractor to list any notice of default filed with its bonding company and to state the date of that default, the name and location of the project, the name and address of the project owner, the name and address of the design professional for that project, and the reason for the contractor default.

(17) Require the general contractor to furnish a certified financial statement.

THE CONSTRUCTION CONTRACT

Whatever method of construction the owner chooses to utilize, there are a number of questions that must be addressed prior to bidding or negotiating a construction contract. These key issues are as follows:

(1) Is there a definitive statement and definition of the scope of work under the contract?

(2) What is to be the method of compensation for the general contractor—fixed price, cost reimbursement, or a variation of either?

(3) Who is to assume the responsibility for the construction schedule—the design professional, the general contractor, or the construction manager?

(4) Who is to be responsible for delays in construction, and should a "no-damages-for-delay" clause be incorporated into the contract?

(5) Who is to be responsible for compliance with local building codes and for obtaining building permits?

(6) How are progress payments and final payments to be handled?

(7) Is arbitration to be left in the contract?

(8) Who is to assume the liability for subsurface soil conditions?

(9) Have all insurance requirements for the construction been handled correctly?

(10) Have performance and payment bond forms been drafted to protect the owner adequately?

AIA General Conditions

AIA Document A201, the standard form of General Conditions of the Contract for Construction (1976 ed.), is the traditional and most commonly used form of General Conditions for the construction contract. The General Conditions basically enumerate the responsibility of the owner, the design professional, and the contractor and contain fourteen articles.

The following pages will briefly comment on this document and suggest amendments if the form is to be used.

Contract Documents

Subparagraph 1.1.1 of the General Conditions of the Contract for Construction (AIA Document A201, 1976 ed.) lists the contract documents: the Owner-Contractor Agreement; the General, Supplementary, and other conditions for the contract; the drawings and specifications; and all contract addenda and modifications. Modifications can be written amendments to the contract, change orders, interpretations of the contract in writing by the design professional, or written orders for minor changes in the work not involving an adjustment in the contract sum or an extension of the contract time. The contract documents in the AIA form specifically do not include the bid documents such as the Advertisement and the Invitation for Bids, Instructions to Bidders, sample forms, the contractor's bid, or any other bid documents.

In order to clarify the contract and to avoid possible disputes, it is advisable for the owner to modify the definition of contract documents to include not only the executed contract, the General Conditions, and all special conditions, but also Instructions to Bidders; proposals; specifications and drawings, including all modifications, addenda and change orders; the required certificates of insurance; the labor and material payment bonds; the performance bond; the notice to proceed; and the critical path or construction schedule, together with updates and any authorized time changes in those updates.

By including the bid documents such as the Invitation for Bids, the Instructions to Bidders, and the contractor's bid form, together with any addenda relating to the bid in the contract documents, the owner ensures that the information contained in these documents will not be barred from consideration by a court if the scope of the work is later disputed. Subparagraph 1.1.2 of the AIA standard form of General Conditions states that the contract supersedes all prior representations and agreements.

The Design Professional's Role

Article 2 of the General Conditions (AIA Document 201, 1976 ed.) provides that the design professional will administer the contract for construction and will be the owner's representative during construction, but is given the authority to act on behalf of the owner only to the extent provided in the contract documents. However, the contract documents do not include the owner's agreement with the design professional. If the owner has, by agreement with the design professional, conferred greater authority on him than is normally found in the AIA contract, that authority will be worthless as far as the construction contract is concerned unless that authority is also specifically stated in the General Conditions.

Under the AIA General Conditions, the design professional is required to visit the construction site at intervals so as to familiarize himself with the work. Subparagraph 2.2.3 of the General Conditions is identical to subparagraph 1.5.4 of AIA Standard Form of Agreement Between Owner and Architect (Document B141, 1977 ed.); so that if one paragraph is modified to provide for weekly visits, then the other paragraphs must be modified also.

Subparagraph 2.2.4 of the AIA General Conditions specifically states that the design professional will not be responsible for any acts or omissions of the contractor. This is the identical paragraph found under subparagraph 1.5.5 of AIA Document B141, the Owner-Architect Agreement. These two paragraphs inform the contractor that the design professional will not make regular site inspections and will not be responsible for any inadequacies in the contractor's work. Both subparagraphs should be subjected to thoughtful scrutiny by an owner.

An additional important topic is found under subparagraph 2.2.6 of the AIA General Conditions. This subparagraph establishes the design professional's obligation to determine amounts owing to the contractor and to issue Certificates for Payment. The clause coordinates with subparagraphs 1.5.7 and 1.5.8 of AIA Document B141, the Owner-Architect Agreement (1977 ed.). The standard Application and Certificate for Payment, AIA Document G702, requires the design professional to certify to the owner that the work has progressed to the point indicated by the contractor in the payment application; that the quality of the work is in accordance with the contract documents to the best of the design professional's knowledge, information, and belief; and that the contractor is entitled to payment of the amount certified. The owner may wish to require a payment certificate from the design professional containing a statement that the quality of the work is in accordance with the contract documents and with sound construction practices.

Subparagraph 2.2.12 of the AIA General Conditions establishes that any claim or dispute arising between the owner and the contractor is subject to arbitration. If the owner does not intend that the contract contain an arbitration provision, this subparagraph should be deleted along with paragraph 7.9, which is discussed in "Arbitration" later in this chapter. If the owner desires an arbitration provision, it is in its best interest to modify this provision and the design professional's contract to require joinder of parties and the consolidation of claims.

Under subparagraph 2.2.13, the design professional is given the authority to reject work performed by the general contractor that is not in accordance with the contract documents.

Under subparagraph 2.2.14, the design profesional is required to review and take action on contractor submittals such as shop drawing data and product samples with reasonable promptness so as to cause no delay to the project. Subparagraph 2.2.15 allows the design professional to prepare change orders, and subparagraph 2.2.16 requires the design professional to conduct inspections to determine the Dates of Substantial Completion and Final Completion.

The Owner's Role

Article 3 of AIA Document A201 (1976 ed.) specifies the obligations of the owner during construction of the project. Subparagraph 3.2.2 requires the owner to furnish all surveys, describing the physical characteristics, legal limitations, and utility locations for the project site, together with a legal description of the property. Subparagraph 3.2.3 requires the owner to pay for and to secure all approvals, easements, assessments, and charges required for the construction. Subparagraph 3.2.6 specifically requires that the owner forward all instructions to the general contractor through the design professional. These same requirements are imposed on the owner in AIA Document B141, the Owner-Architect Agreement.

Attention is directed to subparagraph 3.3.1, which details the owner's right to stop the work if the contractor fails to correct defective work or fails to carry out the work in accordance with the contract documents. In the past, the design professional was given the authority to stop the work under AIA Document B141, but this authority is no longer included in the document. This shifting of authority from the design professional to the owner may be viewed as an attempt to shift liability from the design professional, since the right to stop work for defects or for a failure to perform the work in accordance with the plans and specifications implies the obligation to stop the work under these circumstances. If there is no obligation to stop defective work, there can be no liability on the part of the design professional for a failure to halt the work because of the contractor's failure to adhere to the plans and specifications. However, the design professional's authority to reject nonconforming work may actually have the same effect.

Subparagraph 3.4.1 specifies the owner's right to carry out the work should the contractor default or fail to perform the work in accordance with the contract documents. This right becomes operative if the contractor fails to remedy the work after receiving written notice from the owner to correct the default or defects. The owner may, seven days following receipt by the general contractor of the first written notice, forward a second written notice and proceed to correct any deficiencies in the work. The cost of correcting the work may be deducted from the contract price by change order.

The Contractor's Role

Under subparagraph 4.2.1, the general contractor is required to study the contract documents and to report any error in consistency or omission.

There is an implied warranty in construction contracts that a contractor's work will be done in a workmanlike manner, and the contractor's obligation to advise the owner of defects or problems in construction is viewed as part of this implied warranty. If the contractor has superior knowledge or expertise and fails to warn the owner of potential defects in the construction, the contractor may be held liable and required to put the owner in as good a position as the owner would have been in if the warning had been given.[1]

Paragraphs 4.3 and 4.4 require the contractor to direct the work attentively, to use its best skill, and to be directly responsible for payment of all labor, materials, equipment, tools, construction equipment, and anything else necessary for the execution and completion of the work.

Under subparagraph 4.5.1, the general contractor warrants to the owner and the design professional that all materials and equipment furnished under this contract will be new, unless otherwise specified, and that all work will be of good quality, free from faults and defects, and in conformance with the contract documents. Work not conforming to these requirements may be considered defective. While the general rule has been that there is no implied warranty of fitness for a building,[2] this rule is crumbling; there are holdings in a growing number of jurisdictions that when a new building is sold, an implied warranty of fitness for its intended use springs from the sale itself.[3]

If the general contractor fails to follow the contract documents (that is, the drawings and specifications), it is held to guarantee the sufficiency and suitability of the work. This is true even if the drawings and specifications are found to be defective.

Subparagraph 4.9.1 states that the general contractor will employ a competent superintendent to represent the contractor during the progress of the work. Many construction problems are caused by lack of supervision and coordination of the work by the general contractor. The owner should ascertain prior to signing the contract with the general contractor the name of the superintendent proposed, the qualifications of that person, and, if possible, his track record. The owner may also wish to provide in the contract or General Conditions that a superintendent may not be removed or substituted without the design professional's consent.

The Progress Schedule

Subparagraph 4.10.1 requires the contractor, following the contract award, to prepare and submit an estimated progress schedule for the work. The owner should require that the progress schedule indicate the dates for starting and completing the various stages of construction, and should also require monthly revisions and updates of the schedule.

[1]Lewis v. Anchorage Asphalt Paving Co., 73 Alaska 3d 796, 535 P.2d 1188 (1975); Cooperative C. Stor. Builders, Inc. v. Arcadia Foods, Inc., 291 So.2d 403 (La. App. 1974). See also Annot. 73 A.L.R.3d 1213 (1976).

[2]See 61 A.L.R.3d 792 (1975).

[3]Lane v. Trenholm Bldg. Co., 267 S.C. 497, 229 S.E.2d 728 (1976).

A better contract provision would require the general contractor to submit to the design professional a schedule showing the rate of progress that the general contractor agrees to maintain during the job and the order in which the general contractor proposes to carry out the various phases of the work. The construction schedule should show the percentage of work to be completed on a biweekly basis and the owner's anticipated monthly payments to the general contractor. If the design professional is required in his contract to make a biweekly review of the contractor's performance on the basis of the schedule, then whenever the design professional discovers that the work is behind the contractor's projected schedule, he may be given the authority to require the contractor to submit a revised schedule at the next two-week period, showing either that the work is back on schedule or that reasonable attempts are being made to bring the work up to date. If the work is not back on schedule, the design professional may be given the authority to allow the contractor to proceed, to withhold payment, to stop work, or to recommend termination, depending on the severity of the delay. To be effective, any authority placed in the General Conditions must also be placed in the design professional's contract.

Site Investigation

As a general rule, where the bid documents and contract documents indicate that certain subsoil conditions are to be expected, and the general contractor relies on this information in preparing the bid, if the soil conditions actually encountered are substantially different from those indicated, the general contractor is entitled to compensation for any extra work required by the site conditions. The owner may avoid responsibility for unforeseen site conditions by placing a disclaimer in the contract, placing the responsibility on the contractor. The disclaimer must be carefully drafted, however, since a court may refuse to allow the provision to stand. If the contract requires the general contractor to examine the site prior to bidding and if adverse soil conditions are discovered, the fact that soil conditions are not depicted accurately in the contract documents will not render an owner liable for losses suffered by a general contractor.

Arbitration

Paragraph 7.9 of the AIA General Conditions deals with arbitration. If the owner does not wish the contract to be subject to arbitration, this entire paragraph should be eliminated. Arbitration is strictly contractual in nature, and an owner cannot be forced into arbitration unless there is an arbitration provision in the contract. Subparagraph 7.9.1 states:

No arbitration arising out of or relating to the contract documents shall include by consolidation, joinder or in any other manner, the architect, his employees, or consultants, except by written consent containing a specific reference to the Owner-Contractor Agreement and signed by the architect, the owner, the contractor and any other persons sought to be joined. No arbitration shall include by consolidation, joinder or in any other manner parties other than the owner, the contractor and any other persons substantially involved in a common question of law whose presence is required if complete relief is to be accorded in the arbitration. No person other than the owner or contractor shall be included as an original third party or additional third party to an arbitration whose interest or responsibility is insubstantial. Any consent to arbitration involving an additional person or persons shall not constitute consent to arbitration of any dispute not described therein or with any person not named or described therein.

It is greatly to the owner's advantage to consolidate arbitration claims. This avoids both excessive legal fees and the duplication of time-consuming hearings and expert-witness costs. Immediate resolution of smaller claims using expedited procedures may be provided by contract. In addition to requiring consolidation of claims, the owner may well wish to add language to the arbitration clause to the effect that should the contractor be terminated under article 14 of the General Conditions, the termination and any disputes arising out of the termination specifically including allegations of a wrongful termination by the general contractor will not be subject to arbitration, but shall be settled in a court of law.

Time

All construction contracts should require a written notice to proceed as evidence of the date of commencement of the contract time. The contract time under the AIA General Conditions runs from the date of commencement of the work to the Date of Substantial Completion. The Date of Substantial Completion is designated as the date certified by the design professional when construction is sufficiently complete for the owner to utilize the work. Although jurisdictional definitions vary, substantial completion is generally held to be the date when the work is fit for its intended use, irrespective of whether or not the design professional has certified the building or construction as being substantially complete.

A construction contract may not be held to be one in which time is of the essence unless that language is inserted into the contract. Subparagraph 8.2.1 of the General Conditions does state that all time limits stated in the contract documents are of the essence of the contract. It is still advisable to print this language on the signature page of the contract.

Delays and Extensions of Time

Subparagraph 8.3.1 of the AIA General Conditions A201 states that if the general contractor is delayed in the progress of the work by any act or neglect of the owner or the design professional or by any separate contractor employed by the owner; by changes in the work; or by labor disputes, transportation delays, adverse weather conditions, unavoidable casualties, any other causes beyond the contractor's control; or any other cause by which the design professional justifies the delay, then the contract time shall be extended by change order for such reasonable time as the design professional may determine. In order to validate an extension of time, a claim must be made in writing to the design professional not more than twenty days after the commencement of the delay. If the general contractor fails to make a written claim within twenty days, the claim is held under the contract to be waived. Some legal jurisdictions have held that if actual notice of the delay is received by the owner, that is sufficient. Under the AIA contract, an extension of time does not exclude the recovery of monetary damages for delay.

While there are many arguments on the subject, the owner should consider whether or not to include a no-damages-for-delay clause in the contract. The basic content of such a clause is that if the contractor cannot proceed at any time to perform the work on account of the act or negligence of the owner, unusually severe and unanticipated weather, changes in the work, labor disputes, delays authorized or caused by the owner, or delays caused by casualties or causes beyond the contractor's control, then the time of completion may be extended by change order at the contractor's request, but no payment or monetary compensation of any kind will be made to the general contractor for damages. Such a clause should also state that an extension of time shall be the contractor's sole remedy.

Although the result may seem harsh, this type of clause will force the general contractor to accurately bid or negotiate a contract for the construction of a prospective project because it will no longer be able to pad the contract amount through claims based on change orders and delays. Any claims provisions should also require that the contractor make a request for time extension in writing to the design professional, complete with supporting data, within a specified number of days after the commencement of the delay, and that any failure to file a timely written claim will be a waiver of such a claim by the general contractor.

Payments and Completion

Subparagraph 9.3.2 allows the contractor to submit an Application for Payment for materials or equipment delivered and stored at the job site but not incorporated into the work. The owner may wish to delete or modify this clause since the effect of this provision is to allow the general contractor to load the site with unnecessary materials and equipment long before those items are needed in order to collect payment. Much expensive casework and costly carpeting has been lost following the default of the contractor because the general contractor ordered these materials far in advance of the building's readiness for their installation. However, there is another side to the issue. Long-lead-time items have to be ordered in time so that the project is not delayed. If they are shipped early and stored at the site, some handling and carrying charges, and the possibility of delay to the project, may be eliminated.

Although subparagraph 9.5.5 does state that no Certificate for Payment, progress payment, or any partial or entire use or occupancy of the project by the owner will constitute an acceptance of any work not in accordance with the contract documents, the owner may wish to insert a provision stating that the owner may withhold or nullify in whole or in part any Certificate for Payment as may be necessary to protect the owner because of defective work, a failure by the contractor to perform its contractual obligations, a failure to maintain the agreed-upon time schedule, or reasonable evidence indicating the probable filing of claims.

Substantial Completion

Subparagraph 9.8.1 deals with substantial completion and requires the design professional to determine when the work is substantially complete and thereafter to prepare a Certificate of Substantial Completion. Warranties required by the contract documents under this provision commence on the Date of Substantial Completion of the work. It is in the owner's better interest to have all warranties begin to run from the Date of Final Completion as evidenced by the date final payment is due. It may be months after substantial completion before the project is finally complete.

Another requirement of this subparagraph is that at the Date of Substantial Completion, the owner is obligated to make payment to the general contractor. The owner may well wish to modify the substantial completion clause to state that only the certificate is binding on the owner since this date is frequently at issue.

The contract should also provide that substantial completion does not relieve the contractor of any obligations concerning final completion. In addition, the costs and expenses of the owner that are incurred if work is not substantially complete when due can be imposed upon the contractor.

Changes in the Work

Under subparagraph 12.1.1 of AIA Document A201, a change order is defined as follows:

A change order is a written order to the contractor signed by the owner and the architect, issued after execution of the contract, authorizing a change in the work or an adjustment in the contract sum or the contract time. The contract sum and the contract time may be changed only by change order. A change order signed by the contractor indicates his agreement therewith, including the adjustment in the contract sum or the contract time. The owner must be allowed by contract to make modifications in the work, and it is essential that the contractor be required to proceed with the work regardless of whether price and time adjustments have been agreed upon. However, changes that are beyond the general scope of the contract are cardinal changes and do give the contractor the right to refuse to perform the work. If a price and time adjustment for a cardinal change can be agreed upon in advance, the owner may be able to avoid any disruption in the project.

It is suggested that any adjustment in the contract price for the authorized changes should approximate an acceptable unit price or lump sum or should be on a cost-plus-fixed-fee (percentage) basis with the maximum cost set so as not to exceed a certain figure. In determining the cost or credit to the owner resulting from the change order, the typical allowance for overhead and profit above actual cost would be 15 percent for the prime contractor or subcontractor. When the work is performed by a subcontractor, it receives 7 percent of the amount. The cost includes such expenses as labor, materials, and insurance costs. It is also suggested that a contractor be required to file a claim for extra costs incurred pursuant to a change order. The contractor should be required to give the owner written notice of a claim within fourteen working days after receiving the change order, or the claim will be waived.

Termination of the Contract

Article 14 of the AIA General Conditions deals with the procedures by which the contractor or the owner may terminate the construction contract. Since there is no termination-for-convenience clause under the subparagraphs dealing with termination by the owner, the owner may wish to include such a clause in the contract. A termination-for-convenience clause generally provides that the owner may terminate the contract in whole or in part at any time it determines that its best interest will be served by doing so. The contractor must immediately stop work, and the owner shall pay the contractor its termination costs.

SPECIAL AREAS OF CONCERN

Owner's Duty to Disclose

The courts imply a duty that an owner must disclose to the general contractor all information in the owner's possession that may affect construction. Generally, the rule is that any information that could possibly affect the work and that is peculiarly within the knowledge of the owner must be disclosed to the general contractor.

Bonding

Problems may arise under the standard AIA Performance Bond forms. Under the bond contract, if the owner declares the general contractor to be in default or terminates the general contractor, the bonding company may still refuse to rectify the default or complete the project by alleging that its obligation under the bond does not become active until such time as all claims and defenses of the general contractor have been litigated or decided. Using this rationale, the bonding company may be able to refuse to assist the owner for years until the owner's claims against the general contractor are settled. A bond more favorable to the owner is included in Appendix I.

No-Damages-for-Delay Clauses

No-damages-for-delay clauses are frequently construed very strictly and narrowly or struck down. In order for the no-damages-for-delay clause to be upheld, courts ruled that the delay must be reasonably contemplated by the parties. The court may attempt to find that the delay was not contemplated by the parties, or that the delay was equivalent to an abandonment of the contract, or that the delay was caused by the bad faith of the owner and was, therefore, unenforceable. No-damages-for-delay clauses have been ruled unenforceable where the delay was the result of active interference by the owner. In addition, there has been legislative activity declaring that a no-damages-for-delay provision is unlawful when included in a construction contract. However, no-damages-for-delay clauses have also been upheld. In New York, at least, the trend seems to be toward upholding such clauses.[4]

Notice Provisions

A construction contract should always require that the general contractor give the owner notice of any events that the general contractor alleges have delayed its progress in the work. This notice is held to be a condition of the general contractor's right to claim extra compensation because it permits the owner to change conditions or requirements in response to conditions that have occurred, thereby protecting the owner. Notice requirements should always mandate that actual notice be given in writing to the owner, although it has been held that the test is whether or not the owner has had actual notice. Also, notice to one of the owner's agents or representatives may be sufficient to find that the owner had actual notice. The owner's conduct may waive the notice requirements.

Joint Arbitration

Where both the Owner-Architect Agreement and the Owner-Contractor Agreement contain arbitration clauses and the owner has claims against both the design professional and the general contractor, the

---

[4]Kalisch-Jarcho, Inc. v. City of New York, 461 N.Y. 52d 746, 58 N.Y. 2d 377, 448 N.E. 2d 413 (1983).

design professional can be required to participate and be joined in the arbitration of all disputes among the parties only where neither contract prohibits joint arbitration.

Illustrative Case

Episcopal Housing Corporation filed suit against its design professional and general contractor alleging negligence in design and construction. Both the design professional and the general contractor filed a motion to stay the litigation pending arbitration. Neither the Owner-Architect Agreement nor the Owner-Contractor Agreement contained clauses prohibiting joint or consolidated arbitration. The South Carolina Supreme Court upheld the owner's motion for consolidation of the arbitration proceedings.[5]

---

[5]Episcopal Hous. Corp. v. Federal Ins. Co., 273 S.C. 181, 255 S.E.2d 451 (1959).

5 MULTIPLE PRIME CONTRACTS

The building construction industry has changed greatly from the time when the general contractor was the master builder who directly hired employees of various crafts to construct a building. Today the general contractor performs almost no construction work directly with its own forces, but subcontracts practically all the work to subcontractors or specialty contractors that actually perform the construction. The general contractor has become, in effect, a middleman taking general contracts and brokering subcontracts, a middleman administering the flow of funds, a middleman arranging for bonding, and a middleman managing the actual performance of the work by subcontractors.

Recently, the role of the general contractor has further evolved to that of a consultant employed by an owner to act as construction manager on a project. A construction manager is directly employed by the owner to manage a construction program from concept through construction in a manner that contributes to the control of time, cost, and quality. To that end, the construction manager works together with the owner and designer as a team dedicated to best serving the owner's interests. The construction manager provides expert advice to the owner on the design, plans, and specifications of the project, and evaluates cost projections and construction feasibility, as well as the time, labor, materials, services, and methods needed to construct the project. A construction manager also schedules, supervises, and coordinates the work of specialty contractors during the building of the project.

Several large general contractor brokers have espoused the view that the function of the general contractor acting as a construction manager is the same as that of the traditional general contractor, but that the construction manager receives a fee for providing construction management advice to the owner. The general contractor acts as a middleman in brokering out subcontracts and, at the same time, has a confidential relationship with the owner because of its construction management function. While on the one hand the general contractor manages the project on behalf of the owner, on the other hand it has an adversarial relationship with the owner; that is, it is in the general contractor's interest to maximize reimbursement and minimize the scope and cost of construction in order to maximize its own profits. It is clear that this setup creates an obvious conflict of interest.

The system of construction management that works best is one in which the owner deals directly with subcontractors and uses a construction manager as an agent. When the construction manager is actually an agent for the owner, instead of a general contractor acting as a middleman, many of the problems that plague specialty contractors and owners are solved. A major advantage is that construction management may ultimately lower the cost of construction.

Subcontract bids ultimately determine the cost of construction since general contractors merely add competitive percentages for their overhead and profit to the subcontractors' prices. In addition, where subcontractors are unable to deal directly with the owner, they usually add extra costs into their bids. Subcontractors that have questions about some general contractors' sharp practices add healthy contingencies to their prices to cover the frequent problems and high risks encountered with greedy general contractors. These extra costs are over and above competitive construction costs.

There has been a history of sharply lower construction costs in states that require separate bids from general contractors and subcontractors on public works contracts. In New Jersey, for example, general contractors bid for the total general contract and also on a separate general contractors' package that includes supervision and coordination. The major subcontractors submit separate specialty prime bids. A ten-year study comparing these prices, compiled by the Mechanical Contracting Industry Council of New Jersey, shows that the separate bids reflected a 10.4 percent savings to the owner on 254 jobs amounting to over $500 million in construction and a dollar savings of $55 million. The separate bid prices included the general-contract coordination function as a requirement of the general contractor. Therefore, the 10.4 percent savings was a clear savings with no offsetting costs to the State of New Jersey.

There are many pros and cons to letting multiple specialty contracts rather than acting through one general contractor, and this method is not right for every project. The following sections discuss the advantages of using a construction management approach and compare them to the traditional general-contract approach. In this discussion, the construction management method is one in which specialty contractors deal directly with owners employing a construction manager as an agent or consultant.

THE OWNER RECEIVES THE SPECIALTY CONTRACTORS' REAL PRICES ON THE BID DATE

It is the policy of most governmental owners, and many private owners, to base procurement on a competitive bidding system in which the lowest responsible bidder on the bid date prevails. However, under the traditional general-contract approach, the owner may *not* receive the benefit of competitive specialty-contractor prices on the bid date. In order to calculate a bid to the owner, the general contractor takes bids from subcontractors just prior to the bid time and uses these prices, along with other costs of construction, in making its bid to the owner. Once the bid is made, the cost to the owner is firmly established. Should the successful general contractor subsequently be able to reduce its subcontract costs by bid shopping, the general contractor alone gets the benefit of the price reductions. It is well known that many subcontractors submit arbitrary prices to general contractors on bid dates in anticipation of such bid shopping.

Indeed, the contractor may have anticipated bid shopping and computed its bid on prices lower than those actually received. In such a situation, the general contractor's bid price may approximate what it will actually have to pay out to subcontractors, and the general contractor will enjoy no resulting "windfall profits." Some general contractors go further and defend bid shopping as a form of vigorous price competition. It should be pointed out, however, that the practical results of the procedure generally impair the efficiency of the bidding system as a means of market competition.

The price agreed upon after all the shopping is over is purely an arbitrary amount and may or may not approach the subcontractor's best price. Whether the final amount is above or below the subcontractor's best price, the owner has been victimized by what is essentially an inefficient system. If the ultimate price is too high, it simply means that the owner is paying more than it should for the particular work. If the ultimate price is below a fair subcontract price, the loss may be greater because substandard workmanship may accompany the low price.

Even if the general contractor, in anticipation of bid shopping, bases a bid on the prices that are ultimately anticipated, this method of pricing is arbitrary and rarely represents the subcontractor's real price based upon the estimated cost of labor and materials plus a reasonable markup for overhead and profit. Negotiations for bid shopping and bid peddling, which may go on for days, weeks, and even months after the owner's bid date, effectively mitigate against realistic competitive bidding on the bid date and are often a cause for project delays.

Construction management is a practical approach that solicits a subcontractor's ultimate price on the bid date and ensures that the subcontractors' real price will be passed on to the owner at the time of the bid. This may result in substantial savings to the owner because it will benefit by receiving realistic subcontractor prices instead of fictitious arbitrary prices submitted in anticipation of bid shopping or bid peddling. Separate contracts will also save some of the general contractor's markup on portions of the job that are actually performed by subcontractors.

DOUBLE PAYMENT FOR BONDING AND INSURANCE IS AVOIDED BY THE OWNER

In the traditional construction situation, the general contractor must furnish surety bonds to the owner guaranteeing performance and payment to subcontractors and suppliers under the contract. (See Appendixes I and J for samples.) In turn, the general contractor often requires most of its subcontractors to obtain payment and performance bonds so that the general contractor can receive the same assurances as the owner. Under this system the subcontractors include the cost of bonds in their bids, and the general contractor includes the cost of bond premiums in its bid, both of which are ultimately paid by the owner. Therefore, on a typical job that uses a general contractor, but in which subcontractors do the work, the owner may pay double the amount of bond premiums and could even pay more if sub-subcontractors are used.

The owner may also pay double for insurance. General contractors will obtain liability insurance and then require the subcontractor to obtain a similar liability insurance policy, which may result in duplicate insurance. In a construction management situation, the general contractors' tier of insurance and bonding is eliminated, and therefore, the owner saves approximately one-half of the money on bonding and substantial sums on insurance.

MIDDLEMAN FINANCIAL ABUSES ARE AVOIDED

Subcontractors on traditional general-contract jobs are not only faced with the provisions imposed on them by the general contract, but they are also often faced with extremely harsh provisions in subcontract forms that are loaded to give the general contractor unnecessary legal and practical advantages. These inequitable subcontract forms have become increasingly long and complicated, and they are deliberately drafted by general contractors' attorneys to benefit the general contractors at the expense of subcontractors. Obviously, any extra expenses imposed on subcontractors are ultimately passed on to owners as increases in subcontract prices.

Many such abuses occur because the general contractor is a middleman in the flow of funds. Progress payments, retention (amounts withheld from progress payments to be released at some future time), and final payments are often collected by general contractors who delay payments to subcontractors. This creates a float available for diversion as operating capital or for other uses by the general contractor. Advance payments and retention reductions may be received by general contractors but are rarely passed on to the subcontractors involved in the project.

General contractors support their delay of payments by including a "contingent payment clause" in the subcontract. Subcontract forms presented by general contractors typically have "contingent payment clauses" providing that subcontractors will not be paid until the general contractor is paid by the owner. As a practical matter, this means the general contractor shifts the risk of nonpayment by the owner to the subcontractor. Many things can happen to cause delays in payment by the owner or delays in or denial of certification by the design professional. Often they are totally beyond the control or responsibility of the subcontractor; however, the general contractor can use the contingent payment clause to keep from paying a subcontractor if the owner does not pay the general contractor. This forces subcontractors to consider the "general contractor factor" in their prices in anticipation of not being paid promptly. Under the construction management concept, subcontractors are paid directly by the owner, and the need for this contingency is eliminated.

The general contractor may also hold retention payments due the subcontractor. Under a general contract, a subcontractor will not receive retention until after the entire general contract is completed, even though the subcontractor's own work has been completed for months and even years. Holding retention on each subcontract until after the entire general-contract work is completed increases the cost of the building to the owner. Subcontractors must pay for their labor, materials, and indirect costs on a current basis and, therefore, must fund any retention held for a long duration either out of working capital, borrowed funds, or by increasing their subcontract prices. Subcontractors simply do not have sufficient working capital to fund the amounts to be held until completion of the entire general contract, nor do they have the capacity to borrow these amounts. Therefore, most subcontractors fund a portion of the retention by increasing their contract prices. A survey by the American Subcontractors Association of some 1200 subcontractors throughout the United States indicated that the average increase in a subcontractor's price is 3.7 percent of the subcontract price, or more than one-third of the 10 percent retention. This is a capital cost, and the immediate tax effect on a 50 percent tax-bracket owner is an increase in after-tax cost of 7.4 percent. Paying retention as each specialty contractor completes its work eliminates the subcontractor's need to increase the price in order to fund the retention over a long period of time.

Holding retention on subcontractors until the general contractor finishes the entire building actually delays completion because the subcontractors are not financially motivated to finish their punch-list items rapidly. For example, if a subcontractor has punch-list work to complete and if it makes a maximum effort to complete the punch list rapidly, the subcontractor will not benefit because its retention will not be paid until all other work is completed. However, a subcontractor doing work as a specialty prime contractor knows that retention will be paid as soon as the punch list is completed on that portion of the work, so the subcontractor will complete the punch list as rapidly as possible in order to receive the retention. Each specialty prime contractor, in turn, will be similarly motivated to complete its work so that it can receive its retention, and therefore, the entire building will be completed far more rapidly.

CONSTRUCTION MANAGEMENT COORDINATES SCHEDULING AND CONSTRUCTION OF THE WORK FROM DESIGN TO COMPLETION

A construction manager may be assigned to perform the coordination function, or the coordination responsibility may be put into the general-contract package as one of the separate prime contracts. Similarly, the construction manager can provide the temporary facilities that are common to all contractors on the job site, or the separate general-contract package may require the general contractor to provide these temporary facilities. This question of who is responsible for facilities used in common has been a very troublesome area that has led to myriad disputed backcharges by general contractors against subcontractors. The best way for the owner to remove uncertainties is to make the construction manager or a designated prime contractor responsible for each of the facilities. Construction management not only solves the problem of temporary facilities better than the general-contract approach, but it may also save the owner money. General contractors and subcontractors include money in their bids for these facilities.

One of the most important functions to be assigned in a construction contract is that of establishing a job progress schedule and the final date by which the work is to be substantially completed. Under the traditional general-contract approach, a detailed construction schedule is prepared by the general contractor after the award of the contract. Under the construction management approach, in which the construction manager is retained for the design phase as well as the construction phase, detailed scheduling can be considered during the design phase so that early planning, such as site preparation, can start before the final building systems are completed. This involves detailed coordination of the design plans and separate prime contract work by the construction manager. But without construction management, there is often a lack of realistic scheduling. Even if the owner stipulates in a contract that the building must be completed by a set date, the schedule set by the owner or the owner's design professionals may be unrealistically short. This results in either unexpected delays in completion of the building or acceleration costs in order to complete the construction on time. Advice from an expert construction manager can provide optimum scheduling in the initial design stage and through project performance to substantial completion.

THE COST OF CHANGES CAN BE MINIMIZED
UNDER CONSTRUCTION MANAGEMENT

As construction technology develops and becomes more advanced and complex, the problem of making changes in projects becomes more complicated and costly to the owners and to the specialty contractors who perform the work. Ideally, changes can be minimized if a knowledgeable construction manager can take the time to develop, review, and check original drawings and specifications. Close cooperation between owners and design professionals during the design phase is an absolute must in the complex arena of modern-day construction.

When an owner requests a change, the specialty contractor performing the work must evaluate the scope of the change and determine the various costs associated with it. In a traditional general-contract situation, the general contractor adds an additional markup for overhead and profit to the subcontractors' prices for changes. Obviously, in construction management the general contractor's markup is eliminated. But more fundamentally, the review by the construction manager during the design phase should minimize the need for changes. Also, the construction manager can fairly evaluate proposed changes. General contractors have an inherent conflict of interest because they profit from extras.

In sum, the interests of specialty contractors and owners run parallel in a construction management system. Under construction management, the owner deals directly with the specialty contractors who actually build the building. The owner saves the general contractor's markup on the specialty contractors' work, avoids the specialty contractors' allowances for the "general contractor factor," and avoids bid shopping by securing solid, competitive bids. The specialty contractors are paid directly by the owner, so there is no chance for a general contractor to float payments or manipulate finances. The owner does not pay double for bonding by both the general contractor and subcontractors because the owner receives assurances of performance in the form of bonding directly from the specialty contractors or selectively omits bonding for proven performance. In addition, a construction management system provides coordination of scheduling from design to completion and supplies meaningful input as to constructability. As a result,

the owner obtains a higher-quality product as well as quicker completion and maintains better control than is the case with the general-
contract approach.

6 CONSTRUCTION MANAGEMENT

What is construction management? The answer to that question is never simple. Generally, the definition is determined by the particular project in which these services are used. Construction management is basically a program or project strategy through which an owner purchases management services for the construction of a proposed project separate and apart from design services and from the actual construction services. The general contractor is replaced by the construction manager who plans, schedules, coordinates, and manages a construction project. The construction manager provides value engineering, cost estimating, cost control, time control, and overall supervision and coordination of multiple construction contracts. (Value engineering is the analysis of the requirements of systems to achieve the best results at the lowest total cost.)

SELECTION OF THE CONSTRUCTION MANAGER

Construction management may be treated as a professional service under which the fee is negotiated or bid upon. Construction management is generally furnished for either a percentage or lump-sum fee, at the owner's option, together with reimbursable costs. The contract should specify the maximum amount available for reimbursable costs.

The owner should select a construction management firm by evaluating its capability. The owner should review the construction management firm's past work and interview the firm's past clients. The individual to be used on the project should be specifically identified and his past reputation and performance investigated.

When considering the use of the construction management approach, the owner should publish or issue a "Request for Proposals" (RFP) in which the owner clearly states its requirements and objectives for the proposed project. As part of this RFP, the owner should define the services expected from the construction management firm, such as project feasibility studies, cost analysis, and value engineering.

In interviewing and evaluating construction management firms, the owner should determine

(1) Is the construction management firm familiar with local contractors?

(2) Is the construction management firm familiar with the availability of materials, and is the firm acquainted with local material suppliers?

(3) Has the construction management firm been involved in the construction of any projects similar in scope and size to the owner's proposed construction project?

(4) How many projects has the construction management firm handled?

(5) How many projects is the construction management firm involved in at present?

(6) How many projects will the construction management firm be involved in during the time period in which the owner plans to design and construct its project?

(7) Does the construction management firm have architectural and engineering expertise and staff with general contracting experience?

(8) Does the construction management firm offer both architectural and engineering services and construction management services?

(9) Does the construction management firm offer both contracting services and construction management services?

(10) Has the construction management firm previously only served as an architectural firm?

(11) Has the construction management firm previously only served as a general contractor?

(12) Does the construction management firm understand the desires and requirements of the owner? Does its proposal clearly define the design and construction parameters of the owner's proposed project, and are its statement of methods to be utilized and anticipated end results in furtherance of the owner's objectives?

(13) Has the construction management firm "custom tailored" a program for the owner to include the owner's requirements and objectives, or has the construction management firm merely furnished a standard proposal?

(14) Has the construction management firm clearly defined its organization and identified the people to be used on the project, furnishing résumés including the past experience and previous training of each individual?

(15) Does the proposal submitted by the construction management firm contain "hidden costs" such as unlimited or undefined reimbursable expenses, extra costs, or fees for change orders or cost overruns; does it contain a statement of intention or ability to furnish design services on the construction or to furnish actual construction services on the project?

(16) If the construction management firm has included profit incentives in its proposal, are these areas clearly defined and limited, or does it appear that these profit incentives are vaguely stated and contrary to the owner's interests?

(17) Does the construction management firm have a good working relationship with design professionals and contractors?

(18) Does the construction management firm appear willing to give the owner a firm guarantee as to costs and time limitations?

(19) Does the construction management firm address the requirements of the owner as stated in the owner's "Request for Proposals"?

Construction Management Services

A construction manager can be employed just for the construction phase of a project to deal with the administrative tasks that were traditionally handled by a general contractor. However, to be totally effective, the construction manager should be employed at the commencement of the project to handle the design phase as well. He should be on hand to plan, schedule, coordinate, and manage a construction program from the initial "concept phase" through completed construction.

Construction management services may be divided into two phases: design phase services and construction phase services. In the design phase, the construction manager should assist the owner by identifying the owner's needs, conducting the initial feasibility study, giving advice on securing financing if necessary, completing marketing studies where needed, providing value engineering so far as the design is concerned, scheduling the design, preparing the bid package, identifying long-lead-time items that will be required, specifying operating procedures, managing the budget and making detailed cost estimates, assisting in awarding the contracts, analyzing the labor market, and handling the paperwork for the project from the first day.

During the construction phase, the construction manager should provide detailed scheduling and on-site management, along with inspections and quality control on the project. The construction manager should be in charge of change orders and the administration of prime contracts. He should handle all estimating, operating procedures, paperwork, cost and time control, and process the contractor payments.

Both the general contractor and the construction manager, acting as contract brokers, provide a major service through the coordination function. The owner, at the initial stage of the project, must determine whether or not the coordination will be better served by a general contractor or by a construction manager.

CONSTRUCTION MANAGEMENT CONTRACTS

Whether or not the construction manager is to serve as the owner's agent throughout the project or as an independent contractor is a decision for each owner and its attorney in each particular situation. The prime purpose of construction management is to fulfill the owner's objectives. A clear and comprehensive construction management contract is mandatory and essential to the successful utilization of construction management on any project.

A construction management contract should clearly define the relationship of the parties and should address the problems likely to arise during performance of the contract. While the construction management contract should be adapted and structured for each individual project, certain areas should always be covered. The most important of these areas are as follows:

(1) What are the rights and responsibilities of the construction manager, the owner, the design professional, and the prime contractor?

(2) Who is to be responsible for supervising construction, coordinating multiple contracts, and managing the construction process?

(3) Who is to be responsible for defects in the work?

(4) Who is to be responsible for delays and disruption during construction of the project?

(5) How is the construction management fee or cost to be calculated?

(6) How are disputes between the owner and the construction manager to be handled?

(7) How may the contract be terminated?

This is a minimal checklist of the topics that every construction management contract should address. It should be kept in mind that the construction manager directs a wide spectrum of management services that complement and augment the services furnished by the design professional. Of greatest benefit to the owner is when the construction management services commence prior to or at the time of the design professional's services. While design is under way, the construction manager may provide the following services that should also be included in the construction management contract:

(1) Review of the conceptual design, plans, and specifications to ensure that the design and construction of a project are adequate for the owner's needs and value engineering;

(2) Cost control and the evaluation of the design from a cost viewpoint;

(3) Recommending and arranging for all material and equipment purchase contracts for long-lead-time items;

(4) Review of the design and construction contract for interface problems;

(5) Scheduling and expediting of the design work; and

(6) Review of the General Conditions and bid documents to ensure consistency with construction needs and requirements.

Appendix K contains a sample contract for construction management.

An Owner-Oriented Construction Management Contract

In construction management, as in other contractual situations, no form contract is sufficient unto itself. Any contract is drafted for the benefit of the party originating the document and should be modified for the particular project in which it is to be used.

Of prime importance to the owner in any construction management contract is the inclusion of a clause requiring the construction manager to furnish all management activities necessary to plan, schedule, coordinate, and manage both the design and construction of the project in such a manner as to ensure the control of time, cost, and quality of construction.

While the construction manager should of course be required to cooperate with the design professional through the design and construction of the project, it should be clear under the contract that the construction manager's first duty is to guard the interests of the owner so that the construction project will be most advantageous and cost effective to the owner and within the owner's budget.

The contract also should require the construction manager not only to protect and guard the owner against errors and omissions in the performance of the design professional but also to supervise the construction of the work so that the multiple prime contractors comply with the contract documents. The construction manager should also be required to adhere strictly to all building codes and industry standards in his own work and to ensure that all contractors strictly comply with all applicable laws, codes, regulations, and industry standards in performing their separate contracts.

The construction management contract is most easily drafted if the construction manager's responsibilities and basic services are divided into a design phase and a construction phase. Within the design phase, the work should be divided as follows:

(1) Schematic design phase;

(2) Design development phase;

(3) Construction documents phase; and

(4) Bidding and bid award phase.

In the schematic design phase, the construction manager should be required to review with both the owner and the design professional the owner's needs and requirements for the proposed project. The construction manager should be required to prepare a project budget for the owner's written approval, and to advise the owner and the design professional immediately if the design appears to exceed the budget. The construction manager should analyze the systems, materials, and equipment proposed for use and should provide the owner and the design professional with a written statement of recommendations for alternative designs or construction materials together with a Statement of Probable Construction Cost.

During the design development phase, the construction manager should advise and assist the architect in the preparation of the schematic design documents. These documents define the scope of the project and delineate the general design, including the size and character of the project as to architectural, structural, mechanical, and electrical systems, materials, and any other appropriate project elements. Again, prior to entering the construction documents phase of the project, the construction manager should provide the owner and the design professional with a written set of recommendations for any alternative design or use of construction materials together with a revised Statement of Probable Construction Cost.

During the construction documents phase, the construction manager should assist the design professional in preparing the construction documents and should prepare a preliminary construction schedule reflecting the sequence of the work and the probable construction time for the project. The construction manager should also consult with the design professional on costs during the entire life of the project. Prior to entering into the bidding phase, the construction manager should again review the plans and specifications and make written recommendations concerning alternative design. Based on the drawings and specifications, the construction manager then prepares another revised Statement of Probable Construction Cost for submission to the owner and design professional. If this Statement of Probable Construction Cost shows that the project budget is likely to be exceeded, the construction manager should make written recommendations to the design professional and the owner for corrective action.

During the bidding and bid award phase, the construction manager should advise the owner on the best method for the award of contracts and the selection of contractors either through bidding or negotiation. At this point the construction manager should review the plans and specifications carefully to ascertain that they are adequate and sufficient to construct the project, that the plans and specifications include all work necessary for the completion of the proposed project, that all codes, regulations, and industry standards have been complied with, and that the multiple contracts method of construction is the method most advantageous to the owner.

The construction manager should also be required to expedite the purchase and storage of long-lead-time items and should advise the owner and the design professional in writing as to the types and quantity of labor required for construction of the project. The construction manager should be responsible for assembling all documents necessary for obtaining bids and should prepare the Invitation for Bids for the owner if necessary.

Once the bid documents and bid packages have been prepared, the construction manager should draft a pre-bid construction schedule and should prepare prequalification criteria for the contractors. If bids are let, the construction manager should hold a pre-bid conference and assist the owner in receiving, recording, and evaluating the bids. If the project is competitively bid, the construction manager should also review the bids with the owner and the design professional and make recommendations to them.

Once the design process is completed and contractors are selected, the construction phase begins. The emphasis now is on successfully completing construction of the project on time and within budget. The construction manager must be given the authority and responsibility to accomplish this end. The construction manager should hold preconstruction conferences to define and delineate the parties' responsibilities and should conduct job progress meetings on a regular basis so as to monitor the progress of the work and so that all parties are aware of what is going on. The construction manager should be required to take written notes of all meetings for distribution to the owner, design professional, and contractors.

The construction manager should be specifically required to plan, direct, coordinate, manage, schedule, supervise, and monitor the progress and the work of the multiple prime contractors so as to meet the progress schedule and to ensure the completion of the work in a timely manner and in accordance with the plans and specifications.

Therefore, the construction manager should be required to review the construction schedule periodically. This review should be on a biweekly basis, and the construction manager should be required to submit a written monthly report to the owner and the design professional on the progress of the work. If any contractor falls behind the construction schedule, the construction manager should be required to advise the owner and the design professional.

The construction manager should also be required to guard the owner against defects and deficiencies in the work of the contractors and to advise the owner and the design professional in writing whenever a contractor fails to comply with the contract document or fails to carry out the work in accordance with the documents. It should be noted that under the AIA Standard Form of Agreement Between Owner and Construction Manager (Document B801), subparagraph 1.1.12 and paragraph 6.2, the construction manager does not assume any responsibility for defects in the work or for delays in completion of the project. The owner should include paragraphs placing some responsibility on the construction manager. Where the contract documents are not complied with, the construction manager should be given the authority to recommend that payment be withheld from the contractor, that work be decertified, that that contractor be terminated, or that any other reasonable actions be taken.

The construction manager should be required to review all shop drawings promptly and to approve those shop drawings promptly if they are in full conformance with the design of the project and comply with the requirements of the plans and specifications.

The construction manager should be required to assist the design professional in determining the amount owing to the contractor under its written request for payment. This determination should be based on the contractor's compliance with the project schedule and the assurance that all work complies with the plans and specifications, with all codes, regulations, and industry standards, and with good construction practice.

The construction manager should also be required to review all requests for change orders and should make written recommendations to the owner and the design professional. The construction manager should draft change orders approved by the owner.

In addition to the biweekly report, the construction manager should be required to maintain a daily diary of all events occurring on the job. On the basis of this daily diary, the construction manager can monitor construction progress. The manager should be required to advise the owner and the design professional in writing immediately if a delay in the completion of the project appears likely.

The construction manager should be required to assist the design professional in arranging for inspections during the course of the project. It should be clear from this clause that all work monitored by the construction manager must be performed in compliance with the requirements of the plans and specifications.

At the end of the project the construction manager should assist the design professional in implementing a closeout program for the project and should ensure that record drawings are maintained accurately.

When a contractor asserts that its work is substantially completed, the construction manager should then prepare a schedule for the correction and completion of the remaining items. The manager should be required to supervise the correction and completion of the work to ensure compliance with the contract documents and with the instructions of the design professional. The construction manager should be required to prepare for the design professional a list of incomplete or unsatisfactory items.

At final completion the construction manager should be required to give written notice to the design professional and the owner that the work is ready for final inspection. The construction manager should transmit to the design professional all required guarantees, affidavits, releases, bonds, and waivers, as well as all keys, manuals, and record drawings.

Where a general one-year warranty period is incorporated into the construction contract, the construction manager should be required to assist the design professional in inspecting the project for any defects or deficiencies one month prior to the expiration of the warranty period at no cost to the owner. On completion of this inspection, the construction manager should be required to draft a written report for submission to the owner and the design professional listing the deficiences to be corrected under the warranty.

The construction manager should be required to file with the owner a certificate of insurance pertaining to the owner's project only.

The careful owner will also require that the construction management contract contain an "indemnification" clause through which the construction manager will be required to defend and indemnify the owner from any losses due to any acts or omissions occasioned by the construction manager or his agents or consultants. This should extend to the payment of the owner's attorney's fees, witness costs, consultant costs, and any other costs incurred.

The construction manager should further be required to maintain a competent full-time supervision staff at the job site under the direction of a licensed individual. Key personnel should be named and assigned to the project, and it should be agreed that these personnel will not be transferred or substituted without the prior consent of the owner.

In preparing the construction schedule it should be clearly spelled out that the construction manager is to obtain construction schedules from the contractors and their subcontractors so as to prepare one schedule for the construction of the entire project within the project time.

It should be specifically stated in the construction management contract that the owner will not be held responsible for any costs or damages due to any acts, omissions, or delays caused by the construction manager, the design professional, or any contractor, and that the construction manager's sole remedy for any delay caused by the owner shall be an extension of time.

The public owner may wish to include a termination-for-convenience clause since these are frequently of great usefulness.

The construction management contract is the tool best suited to ensure that the owner is fully protected; however, because there are as many kinds of construction management as there are owners and construction management projects, the form contract is rarely, if ever, advisable. Every contract should be modified for, or adapted to, the particular owner and the particular project. Not only is a well-drafted contract necessary, but this contract must be interfaced with the design professional's contract, the General Conditions of the construction contract, and the construction contract itself. A failure to coordinate contracts can only lead to disaster for the owner.

Construction Management Fees

Because of the variety in projects and in the breadth and depth of construction management services required on a particular project, a number of different fee-structure arrangements have been used. Several of these are as follows:

(1) A lump-sum fee arrangement covering a clearly defined scope of services;

(2) A fee computed as a percentage of construction costs. This should be used only

where the scope of services is precisely defined, and it should be clearly stated that the cost of construction management is not to be considered in computing the cost of construction;

(3) An hourly fee for actual time spent on the project plus reimbursement for actual costs;

(4) A lump-sum fee including the expenses of the project manager, the construction manager, and the office engineering staff, plus reimbursement of costs including overhead for field and office staff; and

(5) Cost plus negotiated fixed fee for services rendered. Reimbursement is made for the actual cost including salaries, overhead, and certain defined expenses plus a fixed amount for contingencies. In other words, cost is defined as payroll cost plus overhead plus reimbursable expenses.

The question of the fee to be paid to the construction management firm must always be addressed in the construction management contract. Typically the basic fee includes the following:

(1) Compensation of principals and officers in the construction management firm;

(2) Salaries of home-office staff, including construction, accounting, purchasing, estimating, and cost-evaluation staff;

(3) Payroll taxes, pensions, and health and life insurance;

(4) Home-office staff engineers' salaries, including payroll taxes, pensions, and health and life insurance;

(5) Salaries of the general supervisory employees who devote some time to the project, including payroll taxes, pensions, and health and life insurance;

(6) Professional fees, including accounting and legal fees and bookkeeping expenses;

(7) The expenses generated by home-office overhead, including heat, light, water, rent, insurance maintained on the premises, telephone, sales, printing, stationery, and postage;

(8) Salaries of the field inspection staff and supervisors, including payroll taxes, pensions, and health and life insurance;

(9) All travel expenses plus taxes, interest, advertising, dues, subscriptions, contributions, recruiting costs; and, of course,

(10) Profit.

On some public contracts, reimbursable costs are computed exclusive of profits and general office overhead and may include

(1) The cost of the project manager, construction manager, and assistant construction manager;

(2) The cost of the secretary and clerk typists;

(3) The cost of the actual office trailer;

(4) Subsistence;

(5) Utilities and fuel;

(6) Telephone and telegraph;

(7) Office supplies;

(8) Data processing;

(9) Photocopier rental;

(10) Furniture and office equipment rental;

(11) Travel;

(12) Testing, surveys, and borings;

(13) General insurance;

(14) Miscellaneous supplies and sundries;

(15) Office trailer setup and move out;

(16) Personnel move in and out;

(17) Professional liability insurance;

(18) Reproduction of plans and specifications; and

(19) Permits, licenses, and fees where required.

Rights and Responsibilities of the Owner

Generally, under standard forms of agreement between the owner and construction manager, such as the AIA standard form, the owner's responsibilities include the following:

(1) Designating a representative with decision-making powers;

(2) Retaining an architect for the purpose of designing and preparing construction documents;

(3) Furnishing necessary site information, including surveys, soil reports, the results of subsurface investigations, and a legal description of the site;

(4) Securing necessary approvals, easements, and permits; and

(5) Furnishing the construction manager with a sufficient quantity of construction documents.

Liability and Insurance

Owners considering the use of construction management should carefully consider its greater risk of liability.

When construction management services are furnished as an extension of design-professional services, then liability is little changed from that of the typical design professional. The owner should carefully check as to the amount of errors and omissions coverage carried by the construction management firm, and, just as with the design professional, should require project insurance from the firm. Also, if the construction management services are being furnished by a design professional, the owner should require the design professional to furnish a statement from its insurer that the policy in fact covers the construction management services contemplated under the contract.

7 DESIGN-BUILD CONTRACTS

The basic concept behind a design-build construction contract can best be understood by comparing it to the traditional construction contract. The typical contract involves a tripartite arrangement between an owner, design professional, and contractor. The owner hires a design professional to design the structure and then a contractor to construct the project according to the plans. In so doing, the owner warrants the sufficiency of the plans and assumes any liability for defects in them. The contractor is then responsible for defective construction and workmanship, but is free from any liability for design defects.

By contrast, in a design-build contract the owner enters into a single agreement by which the contractor agrees to perform both the design and construction of the project. In some instances, the contractor may also agree to be responsible for acquiring land, financing the project, and leasing the finished structure. This arrangement is termed a "turnkey contract." In either a design-build or turnkey arrangement, the contractor's objective is to satisfy the owner's broad performance specifications rather than to adhere rigidly to the architect's blueprints. As well as being responsible for faulty workmanship in construction, the contractor is liable for any defects or deficiencies in design.

Illustrative Case

Mobile Housing Environments filed suit against Barton and Barton, a contractor, to recover damages that resulted from the improper construction of a mobile home park. Barton and Barton had contracted for a "turnkey" construction job. Before a complete trial on the issue of liability was held, both sides asked the court to resolve the meaning of the contract term "turnkey construction job." The court ruled that the use of this term required the contractor to furnish both the design and construction of the project and to assume any responsibility for design deficiencies or defects.[1]

[1]Mobile Hous. Environments v. Barton & Barton, 432 F. Supp. 1343 (D. Col. 1977).

DISTINCTIONS BETWEEN GENERAL CONSTRUCTION CONTRACTS AND DESIGN-BUILD CONTRACTS

A design-build contract between the owner and contractor will include many of the same provisions contained in general construction contracts involving owner, design professional, and contractor. Both types of contracts define the relative responsibilities of the owner and the contractor. The contract price, schedule of work, and method of compensating the contractor are also included in each agreement. Provisions pertaining to subcontracting, changes in the project, and termination of the contract are commonly included in both design-build and general construction contracts. In addition, both contracts establish who is to provide what type of insurance coverage for specified activities.

The main reason a design-build contract differs from a general construction contract is that a design-build contractor agrees to design, as well as build, a structure. As a result, the two contracts differ in the following ways:

General Construction Contract	Design-Build Contract
Contains a provision pertaining to the design professional's function as the owner's representative.	Does not contain a similar clause since the contractor, rather than the owner, hires the design professional.
Drawings, plans, and specifications remain property of design professionals.	Drawings, plans, and specifications remain property of contractor.
Design professional interprets plans and specifications.	Design professional continues to be interpreter of plans and specifications.
Contractor not liable for material errors in contract documents, including plans and specifications.	Contractor liable for errors and deficiencies in plans and specifications.
Contractor need only comply with laws, ordinances, and regulations pertaining to actual construction of the work.	Owner should include contract provision requiring contractor to warrant that design, as well as construction, accords with applicable laws, ordinances, and regulations.
Design professional agrees to inform owner about defects and deficiencies in contractor's work.	Design professional hired by contractor has no such obligation.

While the design-build contract must include these modifications, there is also a major area of concern because the design professional does not function as the owner's agent. In a general construction contract, the design professional often determines the valuation schedule for various portions of the work and the means of establishing that they have been completed. The design professional also issues Certificates for

Payment to the owner and establishes the Date of Substantial Completion of the project. Since these determinations can have important legal ramifications, the owner should specify in the design-build contract that the design professional will use his own objective criteria, rather than those of the contractor, in making these decisions.

The contract should also require the contractor to ensure that any design professional who is hired has professional malpractice insurance to cover design errors and omissions. This is a necessary precaution since a contractor's liability insurance does not cover damage resulting from design deficiencies.

It is strongly suggested that the design-build contract require the contractor to employ only licensed personnel to carry out those aspects of the project that must be performed by licensed personnel. In this way, the contract cannot be voided because of a failure to comply with applicable state licensing requirements. In addition, lengthy delays resulting from enforcement of these licensing statutes can be avoided.

A significant feature that is unique to a design-build contract is that the owner and contractor will work together to develop a design phase schedule. The contractor's design professional will prepare a schematic design study to determine the feasibility of the owner's project. If this schematic design is approved by the owner, the design professional progresses to the design development phase, which establishes the size and character of the project. Next, the detailed drawings and specifications are prepared based upon the design development documents. Finally, the project proceeds to the construction phase, in which the structure is built in accordance with the plans and specifications.

It is vital that the owner and contractor communicate openly and frequently, especially during the design phase. This is necessary in order to determine the most efficient contract time schedule and to establish a fair guaranteed maximum price for the entire project.

Changed Role of the Design Professional In a Design-Build Contract

In the traditional tripartite construction contract, the design professional often acts as the owner's representative. The design professional observes and inspects the contractor's work to ensure that the plans and specifications are being followed and that the owner's interests are protected.

In contrast, the owner and the design professional occupy a different relationship in a design-build contract. In this form of contractual arrangement, the contractor and the design professional either work together as a team in a joint venture agreement or the design professional is a subcontractor hired by the contractor. Thus, the design professional is not subject to the owner's direct control and does not seek to place the owner's interests above those of the contractor. The owner should be aware of this changed relationship in a design-build contract; some states even require that the owner be informed of it.

Even though the design professional does not act as the owner's agent in a design-build contract, the owner is given some measure of protection to ensure that the contract will be performed in a workmanlike manner. Courts have ruled that there is an implied warranty regarding the performance of construction contracts. Unless the contractor has expressly disclaimed this implied warranty, the contractor is required to both design and construct the project in a manner that ensures the structure to be free of defects. If the contractor breaches this warranty, the owner can recover for the damages resulting from the breach.

Illustrative Cases

Robertson Lumber Company contracted to construct a storage facility for Stephen Farmers Cooperative. The co-op had not given the lumber company any plans or specifications to follow; it had merely indicated that it desired to have a general type of building. Soon after completion the building collapsed. The co-op alleged that the lumber company had breached an implied warranty of fitness that the storage bin would be fit for the purpose of storing grain. The trial court found that faulty design work and the builder's selection of inappropriate material had caused the collapse. The Minnesota Supreme Court upheld the lower court's finding that the lumber company had breached the implied warranty of fitness; therefore, the co-op was entitled to recover damages. The court ruled that an implied warranty of fitness exists in a construction contract if the contractor holds itself out as competent to perform the contract and if the owner (1) has no particular expertise in the specified work; (2) has furnished no plans, specifications, or designs; and (3) has indicated its reliance upon the contractor's skill and experience after its specific needs have been communicated to the builder.[2]

The parents of Lawrence J. Schipper brought an action against Levitt & Sons, Inc., a mass developer of homes, to recover for injuries to their son resulting from defective design of a water heating system. Levitt had both designed and constructed the house in which the plaintiff's injury occurred. The New Jersey Supreme Court reversed and remanded the trial court's dismissal of the complaint, stating that the plaintiffs had a cause of action if they could show that Levitt had breached an implied warranty of workmanship and habitability.[3]

ADVANTAGES OF A DESIGN-BUILD CONTRACT
FROM THE OWNER'S PERSPECTIVE

The aspect of a design-build contract perhaps most advantageous to an owner is that it provides a single source of responsibility. The contractor has singular responsibility for both construction and design defects. The owner can recover directly from the contractor for deficiencies in either design or construction of the project; so the owner need not determine initially whether the defect was caused by an error in design or in construction. In a more traditional construction contract, this issue must be resolved so that the owner can determine whether the design professional or contractor is at fault.

[2]Robertson Lumber Co., v. Stephen Farmers Coop. Elevator Co., 143 N.W.2d 622 (Minn. 1966).

[3]Schipper v. Levitt & Sons, Inc., 44 N.J. 70, 207 A.2d 314 (1965).

Another feature favorable to the owner is that the contractor bears any additional costs that may occur as a result of using defective or inadequate plans. Because the owner warrants the sufficiency of the plans in a typical construction contract, it is liable for any increased costs because of defective or inadequate plans. In a design-build contract, the contractor is responsible for design as well as construction and agrees to meet the owner's performance specifications rather than merely build the structure. Thus, if the plans are inadequately designed, the contractor is unable to look to the owner for additional compensation.

A third advantage of a design-build contract is that the project can be completed within a shorter period of time than with a traditional tripartite arrangement since construction can begin before the entire plans and specifications are completed. This time savings results from designing the project in phases so that the contractor can begin work on the initial phases of the project while the later phases are being designed. No corresponding time savings occur in a tripartite contractual arrangement because the contractor does not even bid, much less begin work, until the design professional has finalized the plans.

Still another advantage is that the contractor's increased control over a design-build project may result in lower overall costs. Since a design-build project can be designed and constructed in phases, the contractor is able to order necessary materials for subsequent phases ahead of time, perhaps at a reduced cost. In addition, its control over design details allows the contractor to use familiar methods and processes in building the structure, with the result of much more efficient construction. The savings ultimately benefit the owner.

DISADVANTAGES OF A DESIGN-BUILD CONTRACT FROM THE OWNER'S PERSPECTIVE

The owner will likely find it difficult to effectively compare the various preliminary design proposals submitted by contractors. The designs will probably not be uniform because there are usually many different methods of satisfying the owner's general needs and performance specifications. In addition, the owner's input on the detailed design of the structure will be limited because the contractor, rather than the owner, is responsible for furnishing the design work. As a result, the finished structure may not be exactly as the owner envisioned. However, the owner should be able to alleviate this situation by selecting a preliminary design. If the structure's appearance and detail are of prime importance to the owner, the owner may really want to forego a design-build arrangement and hire a design professional to do the design work.

Another disadvantage is that the owner may not obtain the lowest cost on a project since a design-build contract is usually entered into by negotiation rather than competitive bidding. The owner may also find it difficult to induce contractors to produce preliminary designs unless they are compensated for their costs. To guard against the danger of not receiving any payment if the owner does not accept the proposal, a contractor will require that a formal payment arrangement be agreed upon before submitting a preliminary design.

OWNERSHIP OF THE PLANS AND DRAWINGS

The initial step in the design-build contract is the preparation of a set of preliminary plans that will fulfill the owner's performance requirements. The plans are then submitted to the owner for a determination of whether they satisfy its needs. At this stage, however, the owner is under no obligation to proceed with the final design and construction of the project. To compensate for the time and effort involved in preparing this preliminary design, many contractors will require the owner to enter into a preliminary design-build agreement whereby the owner agrees to pay the contractor's costs plus a reasonable profit. In this way, the contractor is assured of being compensated for this phase of the work if the owner chooses to scrap the proposed project or selects another contractor's design.

The preliminary design-build agreement will likely contain a provision stipulating that the drawings and specifications shall remain the property of the contractor and will not be used by the owner on other projects without the contractor's express written consent. This clause is intended to prevent the owner from selecting one contractor's design and then hiring a different contractor to perform the actual construction of the first contractor's design. The agreement may also contain a provision that allows the contractor to obtain an injunction against unauthorized use of the plans, liquidated damages, and the payment of attorney's fees by the breaching owner.

The owner should keep in mind that any agreement should be the product of bargained-for negotiation between the parties. Thus, the owner is free to negotiate the amount of compensation the contractor is to receive for preparing a preliminary design as well as the ownership of the plans.

In the absence of any contractual agreement, the contractor has the exclusive right to use the plans if they have been copyrighted. Any unauthorized attempt to construct a building based upon the contractor's submitted design will subject the owner to legal liability for copyright infringement.

Illustrative Case

Imperial Homes Corporation, a builder-designer, developed and copyrighted plans for a residential dwelling it named "Chateau." As part of its marketing efforts, Imperial prepared and distributed to the public an advertising brochure that contained the floor plan of the copyrighted architectural drawings. After obtaining a copy of the brochure and inspecting one of Imperial's model homes, the defendants, Mr. and Mrs. Lamont, constructed a home that was intended to be substantially similar to Imperial's "Chateau" model home. Imperial then brought suit against the Lamonts, alleging that its copyright had been infringed. The district court dismissed the claim by reasoning that Imperial's publication of the floor plan of the copyrighted drawings in the advertising brochure had constituted a waiver and abandonment of its statutory copyright. The appellate court reversed this decision, holding that any entire or partial imitation or transcription of the copyrighted architectural drawings would constitute an infringement.[4]

The illustrative case is based upon the statutory framework that existed prior to the current copyright laws. The copyright laws currently in effect continue to provide protection for technical plans and drawings.[5] It is important to note, however, that only the plans themselves are given full protection under the copyright laws. The structure depicted by the plans is entitled to only limited protection. An owner would be prohibited from copying the nonfunctional artistic or decorative features contained in a copyrighted set of plans, but could imitate the nonpatented functional and utilitarian features presented in the drawings. The bottom line is that an owner can construct a building similar to the one depicted in a set of plans, but cannot copy, imitate, or reproduce the plans of another without the consent of the originator.

An owner who infringes upon copyrighted plans or designs is legally liable for damages. The originator of the plans may recover actual damages or the profit to the infringer that resulted from the unauthorized use of the plans. If damages or profits cannot be proved with the requisite certainty, the originator can recover statutory damages of not less than $250 nor more than $10,000, as determined by the court. If it can be shown that a deliberate infringement has occurred, the maximum recovery is increased to $50,000.[6] In addition, the court is empowered to allow the originator to recover costs and attorney's fees from the infringer if an infringement can be shown.[7]

An owner who induces a contractor to submit a preliminary design in anticipation of being awarded a design-build contract should not use the plans if that particular contractor is not selected to build the structure. Doing so without the contractor's express authorization will likely result in a copyright infringement that will subject the owner to legal liability. The amount of liability is likely to be equal to at least the contractor's cost of formulating the plans.

STATE LICENSING REQUIREMENTS

Even though a general contractor can enter into an agreement to perform both the design and construction of a building, it must comply

[4]Imperial Homes Corp. v. Lamont, 458 F.2d 895 (5th Cir. 1972).

[5]17 U.S.C.A. §§ 101—102 (1977).

[6]17 U.S.C.A. § 504 (1977).

[7]17 U.S.C.A. § 505 (1977).

with state licensing statutes that require certain aspects of the work to be performed by licensed personnel. All states have enacted legislation mandating that design professionals be licensed in order to engage lawfully in their professions within the state. The purpose of these regulations is to protect the lives, health, and safety of residents.

Design-professional contracts that violate licensing statutes are generally unenforceable. A contract entered into by an unlicensed party to perform services for which a license is required will be invalidated because either the licensing statute so provides, or in the absence of such an express provision, the statute is a regulation stating that the unlicensed practice of a profession or business is illegal.

Illustrative Case

Harry Clark brought a breach-of-contract action against James Moore, seeking to recover $1000 for engineering services rendered in connection with the building of a naval base in Virginia. Clark had a civil engineering degree and a significant amount of experience but was not licensed to practice his profession in Virginia. Moore defended on the basis that the contract was void for illegality since Virginia law prohibited the practice of engineering without a license. The trial court entered a judgment in favor of Moore. The appellate court affirmed by reasoning that the violation of a licensing statute prohibiting a person from practicing without a license made the contract void and unenforceable.[8]

While contracts to perform unlicensed services are void, agreements to furnish services have been upheld by courts. In these contracts, the general contractor agrees to hire a licensed design professional to perform the work that must be performed by a licensed professional.

Illustrative Case

Medicenters, a licensed general contractor, filed suit against Seaview Hospital to recover money due it for architectural and engineering services provided pursuant to a turnkey contract. At the time of the execution and performance of the contract, none of Medicenter's employees were licensed to practice either architecture or engineering. However, all of the required architectural or engineering work was actually performed by firms hired by Medicenters and whose members were duly licensed to practice architecture and engineering.

Seaview sought to avoid liability under the contract by alleging that the contract was void because it violated the Texas licensing statute. The appellate court affirmed the trial court's determination that the Texas law that invalidated contracts performed by unlicensed parties did not void contracts that merely required the contractor to furnish architectural and engineering services by hiring personnel licensed to do so.[9]

If an owner enters into a design-build contract with a corporate contractor, the contract must clearly specify that the contractor is to furnish, rather than perform, the necessary design-professional services.

[8]Clark v. Moore, 196 Va. 878, 86 S.E.2d 37 (1955).

[9]Seaview Hosp., Inc. v. Medicenters of America, Inc., 570 S.W.2d 35 (Tex. Civ. App. 1978).

This is important because some states do not allow corporations to obtain a professional license to perform services because they cannot satisfy the character and fitness requirements.

Illustrative Case

T. R. Ray, Inc., entered into a contract with the West Baton Rouge Parish School Board to perform the architectural services necessary to erect a new high school building. After the architect who had been in charge of the corporation left the firm, the school board sought to terminate the contract. T. R. Ray attempted to submit the claim to arbitration as required by the contract. The school board brought suit to have T. R. Ray enjoined from doing so on the ground that the contract was void since the corporation was not licensed to practice architecture as required by Louisiana law.

In upholding the trial court and reversing the intermediate appellate court, the state supreme court ruled that the corporation had entered into a contract to perform, rather than merely furnish, architectural services and had invalidated the contract. In its opinion, the court noted that it would be legally impossible for the corporation to obtain the requisite license since a licensee must pass a test and possess various legal, moral, and educational qualifications.[10]

Other states will allow a corporation to perform design-professional services even if the corporation itself is unable to obtain a license, provided that a managing agent of the corporation is a licensed design professional who will plan and supervise the work.

Illustrative Case

Hattis Associates, a corporate architectural firm, sought to foreclose on a mechanic's lien filed as a result of Metro Sports' breach of contract. Metro Sports raised the defense that the execution and performance of the agreement to provide architectural services violated the Illinois Architectural Act and was, therefore, illegal. The appellate court upheld the trial court's dismissal of this defense, ruling that the statute had been complied with since the head of Hattis's architectural division was a licensed architect who had both planned and supervised the architectural work needed for the project.[11]

In a tripartite construction contract, the design professional usually has supervisory duties regarding construction of the building. Ordinarily, the design professional acts as the owner's agent and ensures that the contractor fully complies with the plans and specifications. However, in a design-build contract, the design professional is either employed by the contractor or is engaged in a joint venture with the contractor. Therefore, the design professional may have a diminished supervisory function. Nevertheless, it is likely that a licensed design professional will be required by law to be in charge of any design work.

Illustrative Case

Food Management, Inc., an Ohio corporation, entered into a turnkey contract in which it agreed to design and supervise construction of a meat-packing plant in Iowa for Blue

---

[10]West Baton Rouge School Bd. v. T.R. Ray, Inc., 367 So. 2d 332 (La. 1979).

[11]Hattis Assoc., Inc. v. Metro Sports, Inc., 34 Ill. App. 3d 125, 339 N.E.2d 270 (1975).

Ribbon Beef Pack, Inc. Because Food Management was not licensed to practice either architecture or engineering in Iowa, it hired Johnson Jamerson, a licensed firm, to perform the required engineering and architectural services. As a result of a dispute concerning the project's cost limitations and Blue Ribbon's subsequent refusal to make any further payments to it, Food Management brought a breach-of-contract action. Blue Ribbon defended on the ground that the contract was void because Food Management had engaged in the unauthorized practice of architecture and professional engineering. The Eighth Circuit affirmed the district court's determination that Food Management had violated the Iowa licensing statute, and that the contract was, therefore, void. The court found that Food Management's act of gathering cost data constituted a part of the practice of architecture or engineering. Since this work was not done by or under the responsible supervision of a licensed architect, Food Management had violated Iowa law. The court further reasoned that simply because a licensed subcontractor had been hired to perform the work required to be done by a licensed architect or engineer, that did not mean the general contractor was not also engaging in the practice of architecture or engineering. The court held that Food Management could not recover any payments due for rendering engineering and architectural services.[12]

However, not every aspect of the construction project must be performed under the responsible supervision of a licensed design professional. The contractor is able to purchase materials, hire laborers and mechanics, and let subcontractors without the need for consulting with, or obtaining the approval of, the project's design professional.

Illustrative Case

A building contractor agreed to design and erect an apartment building for the defendant. The contractor hired a licensed architect to prepare the necessary plans and specifications, but retained the authority to purchase materials, hire workers, and sublet contracts. After the defendant's abandonment of the project, the contractor sued to recover the money due it under the contract. The defendant contended that the contract was unenforceable since the contractor had entered into the unauthorized practice of architecture by rendering the aforementioned services without the responsible supervision of the architect. The Wisconsin Supreme Court upheld the trial court's finding that the plaintiff had not engaged in the practice of architecture and upheld the validity of the contract. The court reasoned that the statute was intended to encompass only those activities ordinarily done by an architect, such as determining whether the materials used are of the required quality and whether the work is performed in accordance with the plans and specifications.[13]

In addition, at least two states, Massachusetts and New York, exempt a contractor's administration of a construction contract from the operation of the state's licensing laws pertaining to architects.[14] However, neither of these statutes provides a definition of what constitutes administration of the contract. An owner needs to scrutinize the language and delineation of responsibilities in a design-build contract to ensure that the contractor does not engage in the unauthorized practice of engineer-

[12]Food Management, Inc. v. Blue Ribbon Beef Pack. Inc., 413 F.2d 716 (8th Cir. 1969).

[13]Wahlstrom v. Hill, 213 Wis. 539, 252 N.W. 339 (1934).

[14]MASS. GEN. LAWS ANN. ch. 112, § 60L(3) (West Supp. 1983); N.Y. EDUCATION LAW § 7302(g) (McKinney Supp. 1982).

ing or architecture. In this way, the owner does not risk having the contract invalidated or the project stopped by a public attorney.

CONTRACTOR'S LIABILITY INSURANCE

It is important for the owner to understand the extent of coverage provided by the contractor's liability insurance policy. Even if the owner can prove that an imperfection in the finished project resulted from a design or construction defect, the owner may be unable to recover anything if neither the contractor's assets nor its insurance coverage is sufficient to compensate the owner for the resulting damage.

In a design-build contract, the contractor is liable for both design and construction (workmanship and installation) defects. Thus, most contractors carry comprehensive general liability insurance to cover any damage claims resulting from its negligence. Note that some policies exclude coverage for property damage caused by the contractor's breach of the implied warranty that the construction of the project will be performed in a workmanlike manner. A wise owner will obtain a copy of the contractor's liability insurance policy and consult with an attorney to determine whether the policy will provide coverage for defective construction.

An important consideration for the owner is that almost all contractor's general liability insurance policies do not cover property damage to the structure itself that is caused by defective designs, plans, and specifications.

Illustrative Case

Bowerman Brothers, Inc., a construction company, and its "umbrella" insurance carrier sought a declaratory judgment that Bowerman's policy with its liability insurer covered damages that had been caused by Bowerman's negligent design of a floor plan. Bowerman's recommended design changes had failed to achieve its objective of preventing the floor from settling in a cost-efficient manner. The First Circuit upheld the district court's ruling that the policy expressly excluded design defects from coverage and that an active malfunctioning exception to this exclusion did not apply. The court reasoned that the design error had resulted in a mere passive failure to discharge the intended function of the design rather than having created an active harm.[15]

Even though design errors that cause harm to the structure itself are excluded from coverage under the contractor's policy, design errors causing active harms that are considered to be extraordinary are exempted from the operation of this exclusion.

Illustrative Example

Smith, a contractor, changed the design specifications of a floor plan by substituting a less expensive type of concrete. This modification was made so that the basement could

---

[15]American Employers' Ins. Co. v. Maryland Cas. Co., 509 F.2d 128 (1st Cir. 1975).

be constructed at a cheaper cost while still providing an adequate means of support. The modification accomplished its intended objective, but the concrete used in implementing the change emitted a noxious vapor that rendered the basement unusable. A court would likely hold that any damage to the basement that was caused by the design change would constitute an active malfunction that would not be excluded from coverage under the contractor's liability insurance.[16]

Thus, the owner may only look to the contractor's liability policy to recover for those damages that result from the active malfunction of a defectively designed structure.

In the more typical construction project, in which the design professional hired by the owner provides the plans and specifications, the design professional's malpractice insurance covers any design errors and omissions. However, a general contractor does not usually carry malpractice insurance. In fact, a contractor may have a difficult time obtaining liability insurance to cover design defects even if it has a registered design professional on its staff or in an affiliated organization. Therefore, an owner may have a substantial amount of difficulty in looking to the contractor's effective insurance coverage to recover for damages caused by design defects.

GOVERNMENT USE OF TURNKEY CONTRACTING

Various governmental bodies have utilized the turnkey construction method in recent years. A turnkey contract is a more extensive type of design-build contract in which the contractor agrees to acquire the needed land and finance the project, as well as to design and build the structure.

The government must follow the relevant procurement regulations in entering into a turnkey contract. These regulations will usually require the government to contract by means of a two-step advertising procedure. In some instances, the regulations allow the government to enter into a contract by competitive negotiation. Competitive negotiation can generally be used only if an exception to the regulations requiring two-step advertising applies, or if this method of procurement generates the most effective price competition.

At least three federal government agencies have used turnkey contracting. The Department of Housing and Urban Development was able to procure low-income housing by means of this method, but the use of turnkey contracting ended soon after the practice of revenue sharing began in the early 1970s. The Department of Defense has also utilized turnkey contracting for constructing military housing. In fact, the General Accounting Office has generally approved the Defense Department's use of competitive negotiation to enter into turnkey con-

[16]Based on a hypothetical contained in American Employers' Ins. Co. v. Maryland Cas. Co., 509 F.2d 128, 131 (1st Cir. 1975).

tracts and has also used turnkey contracting. This method was once used to construct five Social Security district office buildings. However, it does not appear likely that the General Services Administration will use turnkey contracting again because of its belief that the disadvantages of doing so outweigh the advantages.

In addition, New York has entered into turnkey construction contracts. The state's dormitory authority has used this contracting method with success on some of its projects.

8 CONTROLLING CASH FLOW

The cash-flow needs of most contractors require that they vigorously pursue their right to payment. It is the nature of construction work that contractors require dollar volumes many times in excess of their working capital. The subcontractors and those general contractors that actually perform work must pay for their labor weekly and for their materials and overhead on a current basis. If they are unable to collect payments on time, they have immediate cash-flow problems. Therefore, it is important for contractors to ensure immediate collection of money for work performed. Moreover, when contractors are not paid immediately and cannot meet their own costs, the owner will ultimately have to pay higher construction costs. If procedures can be introduced to ensure that payments reach the subcontractor or supplier for whom they are intended, this will cut the costs of construction.

The general contractor must have an adequate amount of money due and payable at the proper time to enable it to finance the work of each subcontractor as well as the work that the general contractor will perform directly. For this reason, the contract must therefore specify the amount, method, and time of payments to be made by the owner to the general contractor and the percentage of retention (if any) to be withheld from progress payments by the owner. The general contract must also specify accurately the scope of the work to be performed and the time within which the work must be completed. In addition, provisions are necessary to establish fair and precise procedures for handling changes in the work to be performed.

THE CONTRACT PROVIDES THE PAYMENT TERMS

Owners should pay special attention to the payment clauses that control the contractors' cash flow. It is very expensive for the owner not to pay adequate attention to the payment clauses because they may inadvertently put the project contractors in the "banking business." That is, if payments are not received by a contractor in time to actually finance the labor and materials, it will have to pay out of pocket for expenses and wait to be reimbursed. In essence, the contractor will be financing the construction.

The contract must answer two questions in the payment clauses: "How much is the contractor to be paid?" and "When is the contractor paid?" In answer to the question "How much is the contractor to be paid?" the general contract must specify the total amount of payment in return for the performance of the construction. Although there are variations in payment clauses, there are two basic ways of calculating the compensation that the contractor will receive under the contract: by fixed price (lump sum) and by cost reimbursement (cost plus a fee). Chapter 3 discusses these payment arrangements in detail.

The construction work required to be performed under the scope-of-work provision of the general contract is the other side of the payment coin since payment and scope of work depend on each other. Thus, an owner must pay as much attention to the scope-of-work provision as it does to those provisions concerning payment.

The question "When is the contractor paid?" involves progress payments, retention, and final payment. These payment terms govern whether the contractor will have an adequate amount of cash flow to cover certain costs and expenses during construction. Contracts should specify a certain date on which payment is to be made each month, and the owner should attempt to make the payment on that date.

The contract should clarify whether the progress payment provision includes payment for materials and equipment suitably stored at the site or at a suitable off-site location as well as for completion of the work in place. It is to the owner's advantage to provide that progress payment clauses in the contract include payment for stored materials and equipment. Otherwise, the contractor may have a serious cash-flow problem that will translate into extra costs for the owner as well as scheduling and completion problems.

THE CONVENTIONAL PAYMENT SYSTEM

The traditional methods of payment evolved during earlier periods when general contractors performed the vast majority of their own work and received payments in a timely and correct fashion. Currently, however, the conventional payment system has some basic weaknesses. On most construction projects the funds advanced for progress payments go through many hands before reaching the parties for whom they were intended—the trade contractors who actually perform the job-site work and the suppliers of material and equipment. The parties in between may include owners, developers, construction managers, general contractors, prime specialty trade contractors, and upper-tier subcontractors. At each point along the way the funds may well be used for purposes other than compensation to the firms entitled to payment.

The temptation for diversion or for slow payment has been increased by spiraling interest rates and the far greater use of specialty trade subcontractors to perform work previously accomplished by the contractors' own work forces. Another problem is that subcontractors and suppliers have only limited opportunities for determining the amount of money advanced to cover their payment requisitions. The specialty trade firms have no contractual relationship with the owner or lending institution for the construction project and therefore cannot easily obtain information on the flow of payments.

The net result is that construction subcontractors and suppliers are often paid at a slower rate than that at which lending institutions advance funds for a project. This in turn causes unnecessary job delays, disruptions, and liens. The lender may even have to pay twice for the same work if funds are diverted by a party who becomes insolvent.

Considering the serious nature of these problems, particularly in a high-interest-rate economy, it is evident that a more practical payment system is needed if the construction industry is to function effectively. As discussed below, there are alternative approaches that provide a more direct payment link between those supplying construction funds and those providing material and labor for the construction.

ALTERNATIVE PAYMENT SYSTEMS

One method that would result in greater efficiency and lower costs on most construction projects is the use of direct contracts between owners and individual trade firms. The owner and major specialty trade contractors can have a direct contractual relationship or the owner can be represented by a construction manager acting as agent. Such direct contracts have the obvious advantage of shortening the gap between the owner and the trades. These contracts also allow the trade firms to extend credit on the strength of a solid owner in those cases where a marginally financed general contractor is involved. Still, this method does not completely overcome the dependence of owners on the integrity of those to whom money is paid, particularly where there are numerous tiers of subtrades and subsidiary suppliers.

Another payment method that might correct some of the abuses of the present system provides for the disbursement of construction funds via a title company. This method is suitable for use whether there is one prime contractor or many contractors. Using the title-company disbursement arrangement, each contractor continues to submit periodic requisitions for approval in much the same way as under the conventional system. The title-company method essentially differs from the conventional payment system by eliminating general contractors, construction managers, and prime contractors as payment agents to the various specialty trade and major supply firms. The funds advanced for the project actually flow directly to the contractors that are performing the work. In doing so, the system also provides for a more professional exchange of partial final lien waivers at the time of payment.

RETENTION

In order to facilitate the flow of cash to subcontractors and trades that are actually performing the work and to avoid disruptions, delays, and liens, owners should consider the elimination of retention. Many private owners have eliminated retention, and major governmental agencies have eliminated retention entirely or reduced it substantially. Because a portion of progress payment is withheld from contractors and subcontractors, it places often severe financial burdens on them. The elimination of retention from contract payments improves the contractors' cash flow and in turn reduces the owners' overall cost of building, as well as improving the incentive for both subcontractors and general contractors to finish their work within the time limits specified in the contract. The elimination of retention also benefits the owner by reducing contract prices, since subcontractors and general contractors no longer have to increase their prices to cover themselves against substantially deferred payments on retained money.

Historically, retention of about 10 percent has been withheld from progress payments for several reasons: to provide partial financial security to the owner if work is not completed in accordance with the contract; to provide practical leverage against the contractor to ensure that the contract is fully performed; to discourage financially irresponsible construction contractors from attempting to perform a contract; and to save the owner the cost of paying interest on the amounts retained. Retention is generally withheld by providing in the general contract that only 90 percent of each progress payment due to the general contractor will be paid.

With the introduction of surety bonding, retention became unnecessary. Surety bonds guarantee full contract performance and provide a 100 percent guarantee of financial security to the owner. In the underwriting process, the surety companies also weed out financially unstable contractors. However, even after the advent of surety bonding, the retention system continued. Thus, under the present system, which requires both bonds and the withholding of retention to ensure performance, an owner has the double protection of a 100 percent surety-bond guarantee and a 10 percent guarantee in the form of a retention holdback. In addition, there are express and implied warranties required under the contract documents. It is clear that this overlapping protection is not needed to ensure completion because the owner has recourse against the bonding company in the event of a default by the contractor; moreover, retention is inequitable to the contractors that perform work with their own forces and in turn is unduly costly to the owner.

Subcontractors ultimately add an extra amount to cover retention into their contract price. In pricing their work, the subcontractors ultimately determine the owner's cost of building. General contractors who supervise and coordinate do little work with their own forces and add a competitive percentage for overhead and profit to the subcontractors' prices for the major portion of the work. Contractors and subcontractors must pay for their labor weekly and their materials monthly or even more frequently to obtain vendors' cash discounts. They also have current indirect costs that must be covered with an overhead and profit markup. The contingencies added to the contract price by subcontractors often indicate whether an owner can realize an economic saving on the cost of the construction.

If the owner holds back a 10 percent retention in the general contract, the general contractor will normally hold back the same percentage retention from the subcontractors. However, contractors and subcontractors must fund 100 percent of their current costs each month. Therefore, they must cover the 10 percent retention holdback either by increasing their prices to compensate for all or a portion of the retention holdback, borrowing the money from financial sources to replace the retention, or funding the retention out of working capital.

The cost of construction has become so enormous that most subcontractors simply do not have the working capital to fund the 10 percent retention. The use of working capital to fund retention results in a continuing withdrawal of the working capital because as each contract is performed and the retention is paid to the appropriate contractor, another contract will normally take its place with a similar or greater amount of retention. The end result is the withdrawal of an amount to cover retention from the effective working capital of the contractor performing the work. Borrowing the money from banks to cover retention is often impractical because the interest rate is usually far above the prime rate and funds are not available in sufficient quantity to finance the large amounts retained. Thus, subcontractors must increase their subcontract prices to fund a substantial portion of the 10 percent retention. The practice of withholding retention from progress payments becomes progressively burdensome as the project advances. The effect is particularly acute after a subcontractor has completed its work.

The magnitude of the problem is shown by the results of a survey by the American Subcontractors Association in 1974, which showed that, on the average, each subcontractor had to cover approximately $200,000 in outstanding retainage. The financial burden of retention is particularly heavy in the case of subcontractors that finish their contract work in the early phases of a construction project, for example, grading, foundation, steel erection, and roofing. These subcontractors must endure a 10 percent retention until the entire general contract is completed; they sometimes wait one or two years for their retention. Because they cannot wait so long, they often calculate their prices by providing for overhead and profit that will be paid currently out of the

90 percent progress payments, and substantially discount the retention that they will not receive until a year or two after their work is completed. Although the subcontractors that perform work over the entire length of the general contract do not have to wait as long after finishing their portion of the contract to receive retention, the effect is still quite severe because they must fund the 10 percent holdback progressively over the entire length of the contract.

Owners could obtain substantially lower contract prices if no retention is withheld on general construction contracts. The previously cited survey by the American Subcontractors Association in 1974 showed that owners would realize an average cost savings of 3.7 percent if the subcontractors had no retention to consider in establishing their prices. Thus, the owner would be in a better position to save on the contract by eliminating retention than by withholding retention and collecting interest on it. The General Services Administration has found that by eliminating any retention, it has been able to save substantially on contract prices and still obtain good job results. Other agencies of the United States government, including the Department of Defense, have recently eliminated retention.

Eliminating retention can reduce not only construction costs but also construction time. The argument that retention is a necessary club for the owner to wield in order to get punch-list items finished and the building completed is illusory. Retention has just the opposite effect. When list items are to be completed by the general contractor and all subcontractors, individual subcontractors simply are not motivated to finish the work quickly because they know that the work of the other contractors will delay payment of retention for an indefinite period. However, if the subcontractors know that final payment of their retention will be made when they complete their individual punch lists, they have a strong incentive to complete the work as quickly as possible.

An alternative to eliminating retention is to reduce it on a graduated scale based on a percentage of completion as long as the contract progresses satisfactorily. When the project nears 50 percent completion, a significant reduction may be made in retention by one of three basic methods: (1) holding the full percentage retention until the total work reaches 50 percent completion, then paying one-half of the retention to the general contractor, and cutting retention on future progress payments to one-half of the original percentage; (2) holding the full percentage retention until the work reaches 50 percent completion and then eliminating withholding of further retention from progress payments for the rest of the general contract; and (3) holding the full percentage retention for each work category performed by the subcontractors and reducing the retention as each subcontract work category reaches 50 percent completion.

In the *Guide for Supplemental Conditions* published by the American Institute of Architects (Document A511, 1973 ed.), options are provided for the reduction of retention where the work project is 50 percent completed. This can have the inequitable result of retaining a full percentage with early-finishing subcontractors and a reduced percentage with later-finishing subcontractors. If the basic retention percentage is 10 percent, the reduction in payment upon completion of 50 percent of the general contract would be 5 percent. On all subsequent progress payments, a 5 percent retention would be withheld. The clause providing for this type of retention reduction at 50 percent completion is stated as follows in the *Guide for Supplemental Conditions:*

Until the Work is 50 percent complete, the Owner will pay _____ percent of the amount due the Contractor on account of progress payments. At the time the Work is 50 percent complete and thereafter, if the manner of completion of the Work and its progress are and remain satisfactory to the Architect, and in the absence of other good and sufficient reasons, the Architect shall (on presentation by the Contractor of Consent of Surety for each Application) authorize any remaining partial payments to be paid in full.

The interests of the owners, general contractors, and subcontractors actually run parallel on the elimination or reduction of retention because the owner may save substantial sums of the principal project costs and because the contractors that perform the work may eliminate the negative cash flow created by the 10 percent retention holdback. It is also in the interest of all parties to complete the building and punch lists as quickly as possible and receive final payment.

The modern method of reducing and paying retention is to reduce it equally in all subcontract work categories, to reduce it as each subcontractor satisfactorily completes 50 percent of its work, and to release retention when the work category is completed. The general contractor is paid the retention reduction to be passed on to each subcontractor as the subcontract work category reaches 50 percent completion, and the full retention is paid upon completion of the subcontractor's work. This is known as "line-item payment" of the retention. The retention withheld from subcontractors that finish their work early in the life of the project is released by the owner upon completion of that work. Language similar to the following will provide line-item reduction and payment retention:

If the manner and completion of work and its progress are and remain satisfactory to the design professional, in the absence of other good and sufficient reasons, for each work category shown to be 50 percent or more complete in an Application for Payment, the design professional shall, without reduction of previous retention, certify any other remaining progress payments for each work category to be paid in full.

When the work in each work category has been substantially completed and is satisfactory to the design professional, in the absence of other good and sufficient reasons, all funds previously retained for each work category shall be paid in full to the contractor, which shall make payment of retention to the subcontractor performing such work category less the amount determined by the design professional to be equal to one and one-half times the cost of completing or correcting any items not completed in accordance with the contract documents.

A system of line-item reduction of retention in which the 10 percent retention for each work category is reduced after 50 percent completion and in which retention is paid in full upon completion of work in each work category benefits owners because buildings are completed faster at a reduced cost.

Some contend that it is impractical to ascertain when each trade has substantially completed its individual portion of a project. For example, there are inherent difficulties involved in determining that a steel contractor has fully complied with the plans and specifications until other trades have completed their work at a later time. In such a case, it may be necessary to delay confirmation of completion for a short while, but there is absolutely no reason to hold back the final payment until the grass is mowed twice and the structural steel cannot even be seen to be inspected.

AIA Document A201, General Conditions of the Contract for Construction (1976 ed.), provides that final payment constitutes a waiver of all claims by the owner except unsettled liens, faulty or defective work appearing after substantial completion, failure of the work to comply with the contract documents, or the terms of any special warranties. Conversely, the acceptance of final payment by the contractor under the AIA General Conditions constitutes a waiver of all claims by the contractor except those previously made in writing and identified by the contractor as unsettled at the time of the final Application for Payment. Those claims that are not reasonably discoverable until after final payment may usually be made after final payment.

An important concept related to final completion and final payment is that of substantial completion. When a contractor has not completed, and even refused to complete, every detail of the contract, the contractor is entitled to a final payment of a reduced amount. This generally means the contract price reduced by an amount necessary to account for the difference between what the owner got by actual performance as compared to what was bargained for.

Even after making final payment upon completion or upon substantial completion, the owner is normally protected by the contractor's warranties that all work is of good quality, free from faults and defects, and in conformance with the contract documents. For equipment and building systems requiring maintenance, specialty contractors normally provide a guarantee as well as maintenance and callback service during a prescribed period following the date on which the equipment is placed into operation.

The contractor has a right to receive the retained percentage when it completes the project and complies with the contract procedures for obtaining final payment. However, most courts have construed retention to be for the purpose of protecting or indemnifying the owner, and therefore, the owner may not permanently retain amounts beyond the extent of its damages.

9 MANAGING CHANGES TO THE CONTRACT

It is the rare construction contract that does not need to be changed at some time during construction. The ideal situation is to eliminate as many changes as possible before construction begins. It is much less costly to make changes during the design phase than during construction. This is why it is so important for an owner to select a good, competent design professional. Changes become incredibly expensive once construction has begun since they affect the actual construction of the project. However, it is not always possible to avoid making changes to the contract during construction. Events occur, ambiguities are discovered, owners change their requirements. The contract documents need to provide for these eventualities.

The construction contract documents define and determine the extent of the parties' original obligations and must also provide the terms and conditions for any changes that need to be made to those obligations. It is essential that a workable procedure to make changes be written into the contract. Without such a procedure, an owner would be tied into a contract that could not be changed except at the risk of a breach-of-contract action. In addition, if there were no procedure for changing the contract, contractors normally would bid the contract at a higher price to avoid bearing the risk of any changed conditions or differing site conditions. A changes clause gives the owner the flexibility to make changes and places the cost of a changed condition on the owner only in the event of the occurrence of a condition that actually does increase the cost of performance.

The changes clause must specify the extent to which an owner may order changes in the original contract requirements, who may order changes, the procedures that must be followed to change the requirements, and methods for pricing changes and for calculating an appropriate extension of time for the impact of the changes. The owner must ascertain that it can live with the procedures specified in the contract documents. If the terms are not practical and workable, the processing of changes will interrupt the smooth flow of the project.

A contractor has the right to additional compensation under three different circumstances: a formal change by the owner or design professional, a constructive change, or changed or differing site conditions. The contract documents should provide for each of these categories of changes.

FORMAL CHANGES

Construction contract documents should contain a clause providing that an owner may change the contract requirements (within limits) by issuing a change order to the contractor. An owner must reserve the right to change the contract by change order, in such a case allowing an equitable adjustment to the contract price and a time extension for the additional time necessary to perform the work. Otherwise, the owner has absolutely no flexibility. For example, the AIA General Conditions (Document A201) provide the owner with the right to order changes in the work:

12.1.1 A Change Order is a written order to the Contractor signed by the Owner and the Architect, issued after the execution of the Contract, authorizing a change in the Work or an adjustment in the Contract Sum or the Contract Time. The Contract Sum and the Contract Time may be changed only by Change Order. A Change Order signed by the Contractor indicates his agreement therewith, including the adjustment in the Contract Sum or the Contract Time.

12.1.2 The Owner, without invalidating the Contract, may order changes in the Work within the general scope of the Contract consisting of additions, deletions or other revisions, the Contract Sum and the Contract Time being adjusted accordingly. All such changes in the Work shall be authorized by Change Order, and shall be performed under the applicable conditions of the Contract Documents.

The federal government provides a procedure for changes in the work in Standard Form 23-A:

3. CHANGES

(a) The Contracting Officer may, at any time, without notice to the sureties, by written order, make any change in the work within the general scope of the contract, including but not limited to changes:
   (1) In the specifications (including drawings and designs);
   (2) In the method or manner of performance of the work;
   (3) In the Government-furnished facilities, equipment, materials, services, or site; or
   (4) Directing acceleration in the performance of the work....
(c) Except as herein provided, no order, statement, or conduct of the Contracting Officer shall be treated as a change under this clause or entitle the Contractor to an equitable adjustment hereunder.

Authority to Order Changes

An owner of a construction project needs to make certain that the contract documents specify who has authority to order changes in the work. An owner must retain control over changes to the contract. The owner does not want to be liable for changes that were ordered by someone who had no authority to do so.

In government contracts, if the person ordering changes is not authorized to do so, the contractor may not be allowed recovery for performing a change. A change to a government contract must generally be ordered by the contracting officer or an authorized representative. Government inspectors and agents other than the contracting officer do not generally have the authority to order changes, and any changes ordered by other government employees do not normally bind the government. Parties contracting with the government are assumed to know the extent of the authority of government employees.

Illustrative Case

C.D. Spangler Construction Company entered into a contract for the construction of housing units at Warner Robins Air Force Base in Georgia. Spangler then entered into a subcontract with a heating and cooling subcontractor. Submittals were made by the subcontractor to the contracting officer. Evidence showed that submittals and approvals were haphazard and inconclusive. The contractor relied on a meeting at which time the representative of the architect was alleged to have made an oral agreement to change the contract requirements. However, the contractor and the subcontractor were fully aware that the representative of the architect did not have authority to amend the contract and that any changes had to be made through the contracting officer. The board held that in view of the "strict requirement of contract that changes be accomplished in writing by authorized personnel we conclude there was no change in the contract requirement...."[1]

However, an owner needs to be aware that authority to make changes has, under certain circumstances, been implied from the language of the contract or from the circumstances surrounding the situation.

To protect itself, the owner should include a contract provision requiring that an authorization for extra work must be given by the owner in writing or that extra work claims will not be recognized without a written agreement between the parties prior to the contractor's performance of the extra work. The requirement that extra work be ordered in writing gives the owner an opportunity to clarify, define, or rescind any orders for extra work before the contractor performs it. The owner can demand technical compliance with a requirement that change orders be in writing.

Illustrative Case

Wilkerson entered into a subcontract with McDonald to do subcontracting work on housing units at Cannon Air Force Base, New Mexico. The subcontract contained a clause that provided: "Extras—No claim for additional compensation, whether on account of extra labor or materials furnished, or otherwise, shall be made or paid unless the same is

[1]Appeal of C.D. Spangler Constr. Co., ASBCA 6877, 1963 B.C.A. ¶ 3840 (1963), *reconsideration denied*, 1964 B.C.A. ¶ 4011 (1964).

furnished under a written order signed by the Contractor prior to the furnishing of the same and unless Subcontractor shall submit to Contractor within thirty days after the last of such labor or materials was furnished an invoice or invoices covering the same."

Wilkerson and the subcontractors on the project erected some model buildings to work out the various problems that usually arose in these kinds of housing projects. As a result, Wilkerson and McDonald amended their subcontract in writing to compensate McDonald for the extra work required to build the units. McDonald finished the contract without making any other claims or requests for adjustment and then asserted a claim for extra compensation. The court held that the subcontractor was barred by the terms of the written contract as to all claims for extra work that were not agreed to in writing.[2]

Note that a contractual requirement that extra work must be ordered in writing may be waived. Literal compliance with a contract provision requiring a signed order will not be required where the owner is aware that extra work is being done without the proper authorization, yet stands by and allows the work to continue without making a protest.

Illustrative Case

Geigy Chemical Corporation contracted with Fanning & Doorley Construction Company to construct a new system of underground piping at its plant in Cranston, Rhode Island. Fanning & Doorley had no experience laying chemical stoneware pipe; however, it was done under the direction and supervision of the resident engineer. As leakages occurred in the various joints and the contractor encountered difficulties in repairing them, the resident engineer directed new and different procedures. The Fanning & Doorley contract was terminated by Geigy. Thereafter, Fanning & Doorley brought an action to recover the balance due under the contract and an additional sum as excess costs. Geigy defended against the excess costs on the grounds that the contract provided that "no extra work shall be paid for unless specifically ordered as such in writing by the Engineer" and that the express terms had not been complied with. The court held that although there was no compliance with the contract, the resident engineer was aware of the extra work and in fact had directed that it be done. The court stated that the "conduct of a contractee clearly evidencing an acceptance of extra work by a contractor coupled with an inference of payment is a clear waiver of express contract provisions to the contrary."[3]

CONSTRUCTIVE CHANGES

A formal change order is generally issued in writing by the owner or by an authorized representative of the owner and is acknowledged by everyone to be a change to the contract. A constructive change arises from informal acts or omissions of the owner or the owner's representative that change the requirements of the contract. Such actions or omissions cause the contractor to perform beyond that required by the contract, increase the cost of performance by the contractor, and entitle the contractor to an extension of time. Any oral or written act or omission by the owner or its authorized representative that in practical effect

[2]United States ex rel. McDonald v. Barney Wilkerson Constr. Co., 321 F. Supp. 1294 (D.N.M. 1971).

[3]Fanning & Doorley Constr. Co. v. Geigy Chemical Corp., 305 F. Supp. 650 (D.R.I. 1969).

requires the contractor to perform work in a different manner than originally specified in the contract may create a constructive change order. A constructive change order may be implied where additional or different work is done with the owner's knowledge and approval, even though no actual direction to do the work is made by the owner or its authorized agent.

The most common types of conditions that result in a claim by the contractor that the owner has made a constructive change are defective specifications, or specifications that contain an ambiguity, a direction to change the method of performance, rejection of "or equal" substitutions, defective materials, overinspection, and rejection of conforming work.

Defective Specifications

An owner that provides plans and specifications for use on a project is held to give an implied warranty that if the plans and specifications are followed, the work will meet the performance requirements of the contract. The owner is held to have breached that warranty if the plans and specifications prove to be defective. The contractor is generally allowed to recover any increased costs incurred in attempting to perform under defective specifications. Error is one of several ways defective specifications may cause a compensable constructive change. Inadequate detail in the specifications may also be compensable if the contractor is forced to incur more costs than were expected under the original contract.

Although the general rule is that a contractor fully complies with contractual obligations by following the plans and specifications, the owner does have various defenses against a claim of defective specifications.

Generally, specifications are defective if they establish unattainable performance requirements. But if performance is possible, and if the work is covered by the contract and the specifications are not otherwise defective, the general rule is that the contractor cannot recover for difficulties encountered in doing the work. Furthermore, if no particular materials or methods are specified in the contract, the general contractor may be required to select a material or method that will produce the result required by the contract.[4] Similarly, if the contract does not require performance of a particular part of the work necessary to accomplish the desired result, the contractor may be required to perform that work, especially if it had received some notification outside the contract that the work had to be done.[5]

[4]Cannon v. Hunt, 116 Ga. 452 (1902).

[5]Eastern Iowa Light & Power Coop. v. McKenzie, 296 F.2d 295 (8th Cir. 1961); Economy Fuse & Mfg. Co. v. Raymond Concrete Pile Co., 111 F.2d 875 (7th Cir. 1940).

Ambiguous Specifications

If there is an ambiguity in the contract or the specifications, the specifications may be considered defective because they are not clear. In this case, if the contractor interprets the contract to require certain performance requirements and the contractor's reading of the contract is reasonable, the contractor is entitled to relief for the increased cost of performance. The contractor has a right to read the contract as any reasonable person would and is not deemed to have knowledge of any other interpretation that could be placed on the contract. Ambiguities are generally construed against the owner because the owner drafted the agreement.

The contractor cannot convert its interpretation of specifications into a compensable change if the owner's interpretation is reasonable and the contractor's is not. To determine whose interpretation is the more reasonable, the courts choose the meaning of the words in the contract that would be attached to the writing by reasonably intelligent persons acquainted with all the operative usages and customs of the trade and knowing all the facts and circumstances prior to and at the time of the making of the contract. Sometimes the application of this general rule will be sufficient to decide the case. For example, if one of the proposed interpretations is inconsistent, illogical, or absurd, or produces an impractical or unjust result, it will be disregarded. On the other hand, if one of the proposed interpretations is clearly the logical and natural meaning of the words, the court's analysis need go no further.

A contractor has a duty to seek clarification of any major patent discrepancy, obvious omission, or drastic conflict in the provisions of the contract. There is no duty to seek clarification where a contractor innocently construes a subtle ambiguity in its favor, but a contractor that deliberately seeks to profit from an ambiguity in the contract that it knows is the drafter's error may not recover for a constructive change if the contractor has not sought clarification from the owner. If clarification of an ambiguity is sought from but is not provided by the owner, the owner will be held to have waived any right to complain of the contractor's interpretation of the contract.

Illustrative Case

Ed Goetz Painting Company was under contract to sandblast a steel bridge to achieve the "appearance of cast aluminum" in preparation for painting. The inspector rejected the job completed by the contractor. The contractor argued that the term "appearance of cast aluminum" was not a standard normally used and that, in fact, the appearance of blasted steel differs from that of aluminum. The Board of Contract Appeals held that the contractor had a duty to inquire about the ambiguous standard in the contract, and its failure to do so resulted in the interpretation of the specifications in favor of the government.[6]

[6]Appeal of Ed Goetz Painting Co., 80-2 B.C.A. ¶14554 (1980).

A contractor may not claim a compensable constructive change when, in the absence of a direction by the owner and without protesting, the contractor ultimately performs the work according to an interpretation of the contract that is more costly than another possible interpretation. The contractor's voluntary performance may be taken to show that both parties intended that the contract be interpreted to require the more costly performance.

Illustrative Case

A contract between the government and Marinell & Campbell, Inc., provided that certain enamel and varnished surfaces were to be repainted but did not specify the type of paints to be used. During the early stages of contract performance, the contractor used enamel paint on the enameled surfaces and varnish on the varnished surfaces without protest and without directions from the government to use these paints. Subsequently, Marinell & Campbell asserted that the contract required only a latex emulsion paint and, there-fore, the contractor claimed an adjustment to the contract price for the difference in price between the latex emulsion paint and the enamel and varnish used. The Board of Contract Appeals disallowed this claim because it found that Marinell & Campbell's actions in proceeding without protest and without directions from the government showed that at the time of the contract both parties intended enamel to be used on surfaces that had previously been enameled and varnish to be used on surfaces that had previously been varnished.[7]

Change in Manner or Method of Performance

The contractor has the right to choose the method of performance when no particular method of performance is specified in the contract or when two or more optional methods are specified. The contractor has the right to choose the least expensive method. If the owner directs that the work be performed in a manner that is more expensive to the con-tractor, it has ordered a constructive change entitling the contractor to recover for the increase in cost of performance by the more expensive method plus the cost of any modification of work completed under the least expensive method.

Illustrative Case

A contract for the recovering of roofs provided that where fire walls protruded through the roof, bituminous flashings would be "returned and sealed or capped and sealed to waterproof edges and ends." The roofing contractor, L.F. Still, chose to cap and seal the flashings, but the government demanded that the work be redone by the return-and-seal method, which was more expensive. The court held that the government had no right to demand a more expensive method because the contract unambiguously provided that either method would be acceptable. The roofing contractor was allowed to recover the difference between the cost of returning and sealing the flashings and the cost of the cheaper method as well as the cost of modifying the work already completed.[8]

[7]Appeal of Marinell & Campbell, Inc., 1963 B.C.A. ¶ 3948 (1963).
[8]United Pacific Ins. Co. v. United States, 497 F.2d 1402 (Ct. Cl. 1974).

A contractor may not recover if the owner reserves the option of choosing one particular procedure or method of performance over another.

A constructive change may also occur when the owner requires the contractor to change the sequence of work, thereby increasing the cost of performance of the contractor's work. In order to recover for a constructive change because of the use of a more expensive alternative method of performance, there must be a direction by the owner or its authorized representative designating the more expensive method of performance. If the contractor voluntarily selects the more expensive method, the contractor cannot recover. Some courts have made it an exception to the rule for constructive changes that no actual direction is necessary if the extra work is done with the owner's knowledge and approval.[9] Mere acceptance by the contractor of a suggestion by the owner may not constitute a constructive change.

Illustrative Case

Orndorff Construction Company contended that under the sequence charts that had been prepared, work was to proceed to completion upon the Gettysburg Cyclorama Building before work was commenced on a neighboring office building. The contractor contended that the government ordered it to change that sequence and to begin work on the office building before completion of work on Cyclorama. It was held that even though the contractor was encouraged to start work early on the office building, it was not directed to do so and, in fact, changed the sequence voluntarily for its own convenience.[10]

In addition to showing that it was directed to use a more expensive alternative method of performance, the contractor must show that the owner's direction to use the alternative method was, in fact, the cause of the increased cost of performance. If some other condition for which the contractor is responsible caused the increased cost, the contractor cannot recover.

Illustrative Case

Balze International, Inc., a contractor that had agreed to resurface airport runways in Korea, claimed that the contract allowed the bags of cement to be stored in large piles. The government required the contractor to stack the bags of cement in rows with spaces in between for inspection purposes. Subsequently, the cement became hydrated and useless. Balze sought compensation for the useless cement, claiming that it became hydrated because the method of storing the bags in rows exposed more surface area for hydration. It was held, however, that the hydration was caused not by storing the cement

[9]Chris Berg, Inc. v. United States, 455 F.2d 1037 (Ct. Cl. 1972).
[10]Appeal of Orndorff Constr. Co., 67-2 B.C.A. ¶ 6665 (1967).

in rows, but by the inadequate covering material that was placed over the bags of cement. The contractor did not recover because covering the bags was its responsibility.[11]

Overinspection

Overinspection by the owner or the owner's representative may also create a constructive change order. Overinspection may take the form of changing the scheduling or frequency of inspections or continuously nitpicking so as to require a higher standard of performance than is normally required in the trade. However, the owner does have the right to demand strict compliance with the contract requirements. A contractor cannot complain of overinspection merely because the inspector is requiring full compliance with the contract requirements.

Rejection of Conforming Work

A constructive change order can arise when the owner or its authorized representative unjustifiably rejects the contractor's work and requires the contractor to perform certain rework. However, the contractor will not be compensated for additional costs incurred in redoing work to meet standards required by the contract. The owner must properly carry out the inspection procedures required by the contract before rejecting the contractor's work.

Illustrative Case

Carlin Construction Company, a contractor, completed work on a concrete wall using good workmanship and following the specifications in the contract. The work was rejected, however, because of discoloration of the concrete called "sand-streaking." The government required the contractor to perform work not authorized by the contract to eliminate this discoloration, and this was held to be a compensable constructive change.[12]

Not only are the standards of performance governed by the contract and the specifications, but they are also measured by the customs and practices of the particular trade. If the contractor has performed the work under the contract according to the normal customs and practices of the trade, the rejection of work that conforms to the standard of the trade constitutes a constructive change entitling the contractor to an equitable adjustment of the contract price for the costs and a reasonable profit to redo the rejected work.

A contract will often require the contractor to follow the specifications using "first-class workmanship," which has been interpreted to mean skillful, average work conforming to industry standards. The

[11]Appeal of Baize Int'l, Inc., 1963 B.C.A. ¶3963 (1963).

[12]Carlin Constr. Co. v. United States, 92 Ct. Cl. 280 (1941).

determination of whether work was performed in a first-class manner may be influenced by whether or not the contractor followed the manufacturer's recommendations in working with the materials. If there is no standard of workmanship expressly stated in the contract, a promise by the contractor to carry out the specifications using good workmanship is implied.

Illustrative Case

Healy Tibbitts Construction Company, a contractor installing pumps at a salt-water pumping station for the government, did not apply epoxy to the screw threads at the juncture between the steel piping and the bronze pump bowl. After testing in salt water, the government observed that corrosion had occurred at the juncture between the piping and the bronze bowl that would not have occurred had epoxy been applied to the screw threads. The specifications did not expressly require that the screw threads be coated with epoxy, but it was held that the installation was not done in a workmanlike manner. That is, by the standard of workmanship in the trade, the contractor should have known that epoxy had to be used on the screw threads. Therefore, Healy Tibbitts was not compensated for recoating the pipe with epoxy and reinstalling the pumps.[13]

Rejection of "Or Equal" Substitutions

Private owners and developers have every right to demand the use of a single name-brand item in construction of their projects. It is perfectly within their contract rights to draft the contract documents to make that demand, and in such a case the contractor will be bound by the contract's language. In public contracts, however, competitive bidding is often mandated by statute. A demand by a public owner that the contractor use one particular item would circumvent competitive bidding. Thus the specifications on public projects generally provide for "or equal" substitutions; that is, the contractor is entitled to make a substitution of materials or equipment that is equivalent or equal to the materials or equipment specified in the contract. The refusal to approve an "equal" substitution constitutes a constructive change in the contract specifications and entitles the contractor to an equitable adjustment in the contract to cover the increased costs of procuring the more expensive product.[14] The courts interpret an "or equal" clause in a construction contract as creating a valuable contract right for the contractor.

The word *equal* as used in "or equal" clauses does not mean that to be approved the substitution must be identical in every respect to the brand named as the standard of quality. The substitution may be "equal" and at the same time have a somewhat different design; equality is to be defined by the quality, performance, and design of the substitution compared to the brand name specified. But "equality" does not

[13]Appeal of Healy Tibbitts Constr. Co., 73-1 B.C.A. ¶ 9912 (1973).

[14]Appeal of Lehigh Chem. Co., 1963 B.C.A. ¶ 3749 (1963); Davies v. Kahn, 251 F.2d 324 (4th Cir. 1958).

mean "identity." If the preferred substitution functions as well as the specified material or equipment, it should be accepted by the owner as satisfying the "or equal" clause. The owner does have the right to demand that the substitution function as well as the brand named in the contract and is not required to approve a product merely because it is cheaper for the contractor. The contractor has the right to an honest judgment by the owner or the owner's representative of the quality of the proposed substitution in relation to the brand-name standard.

Defective Owner-Furnished Property

A compensable constructive change also can arise from additional work required of the contractor because of defective property, equipment, or materials furnished by the owner to the contractor under the contract. The contractor can therefore recover for the increased cost of performance occasioned by defective property furnished by the owner.

The owner that contractually agrees to furnish property must furnish property suitable for its intended use under the contract, which means that the property supplied by the owner must be adequate for the performance of work contemplated by the parties at the time they enter into the contract. If the property furnished is not suitable, then the contractor is entitled to an increase in the contract price for the higher cost of performance incurred in procuring suitable property or for its expenditures. The same rule applies to defective models or patterns, erroneous data or information, or erroneously marked parts. The burden of showing the unsuitability of the property is on the contractor.

In purchasing property and equipment for use on a construction project, the owner should make sure to obtain warranties that reimburse any costs incurred by a contractor's claim of defective materials.

Impossibility of Performance

When for some reason it is impossible for a contractor to meet the requirements of the plans and specifications, it may have a right to some relief in attempting to perform the contract. If there is, in fact, an impossibility of performance under the plans and specifications, the contractor may be relieved of the obligation to perform and can recover the costs actually incurred in attempting to comply with the impossible requirements plus a reasonable profit. If the contractor is required to perform under new contractual terms or designs that result from the impossibility, the contractor may be able to recover the additional costs incurred on its changed performance plus a reasonable profit.

Practical impossibility (commercial impracticability) exists when performance would cause such extreme and unreasonable difficulty and expense that performance is not practicable within the existing commercial circumstances and basic terms of the contract. Merely because performance is made harder or more costly than what the contractor had planned on is not enough to excuse performance or entitle the contractor to recover the additional cost of performance. The courts will generally hold that, barring extremely unusual circumstances, the promise to perform the contract is not conditional and the contractor must either perform or be responsible for the consequences of the breach.

Illustrative Case

Blount Brothers Construction Company was to construct and precisely align a circular rail as a part of a ship-model testing facility for the government. Blount Brothers claimed that because of an inherent flaw in the design, the foundation was unsteady and the rail would not retain alignment. Thus, Blount Brothers sought to recover the cost of attempting permanent alignment after the government allegedly relaxed the specification for precision in alignment by accepting the work. The Board of Contract Appeals denied the claim, holding that the rail was capable of permanent alignment and that the contractor simply had to go to more expense than anticipated to accomplish it. The expense was not recoverable.[15]

To be entitled to relief for impossibility of performance, the contractor must prove that performance of the contract was, in fact, either actually or practically impossible. Actual impossibility means that the contract could not be performed by any contractor. It is usually the result of erroneous specifications or a performance requirement that cannot be met with the equipment specified in the contract.

The basis on which a contractor may obtain relief when performance is impossible rests upon the doctrine of implied warranty by the owner of its plans and specifications. When the owner furnishes plans and specifications, it implicitly warrants that those plans and specifications are workable, that they will satisfactorily produce the result called for in the contract, and that the prescribed performance requirements can be achieved. A contractor has the right to rely on those plans and specifications without making an independent evaluation that the requirements can be feasibly met. There are some exceptions. The contractor cannot rely upon the doctrine of impossibility of performance when the contractor has originated the specifications or design, or where under the circumstances the contractor may be deemed to have assumed the risk of impossibility. The contractor can expressly agree to assume the risk if the contract provides for the accomplishment of a goal of performance without setting out specifications indicating how the contract should be performed, or if the risk of impossibility is obvious.

[15]Appeal of Blount Bros. Constr. Co., 1963 B.C.A. ¶ 3760 (1963).

Illustrative Case

A.D. and G.D. Fox contracted to build a road for a national forest in Oregon. They claimed that the clearing requirement in the contract was economically impossible to accomplish according to the method of disposal specified. The Board of Contract Appeals found the Foxes to be experienced contractors on notice as to the difficulty of the job prior to award of the contract. Thus, they assumed the risk of performance and were denied additional expense.[16]

CHANGED OR DIFFERING SITE CONDITIONS

One of the major risks inherent in undertaking any construction project is that of encountering unusual or unexpected conditions on the site. In the past the contractor assumed the risk of unexpected costs and problems that might be encountered in performing the project, but this meant increasing its estimate to compensate for conditions other than normal that might be encountered and that might increase the cost of performance. However, the problem was that the owner paid the increased price even if site conditions subsequently proved to be normal.

A "changed conditions" or "differing-site-conditions" clause is now included in contracts to take the gamble of subsurface conditions out of bidding. These clauses entitle the contractor to an increase in the contract price if physical conditions encountered at the site differ from those either normally encountered or originally contemplated in the contract documents. When there is a changed conditions or differing-site-conditions clause in the contract, the bidder knows that a contingency price need no longer be included in the bid. As a result, the owner benefits from lower bids and pays for difficult subsurface work only when it is encountered.[17]

A typical changed conditions clause is found in the AIA General Conditions (Document A201, 1976 ed.):

Article 12.2.1   Should concealed conditions encountered in the performance of the work below the surface of the ground or should concealed or unknown conditions in an existing structure be at variance with the conditions indicated by the Contract Documents, or should unknown physical conditions below the surface of the ground or should concealed or unknown conditions in an existing structure of an unusual nature, differing materially from those ordinarily encountered and generally recognized as inherent work of the character provided for in this Contract, be encountered, the Contract Sum shall be equitably adjusted by Change Order upon claim by either party made within twenty days after the first observance of the conditions.

The typical government differing-site-conditions clause is found in Federal Procurement Regulations section 1-7.602-4 (1976) and in Standard Form 23-A, section 4. It provides:

[16]Appeal of A.D. & G.D. Fox, 80-2 B.C.A. ¶ 14,788 (1980).

[17]Foster Constr. C.A. v. United States (15 C.C.F. ¶ 84,163), 193 Ct. Cl. 587 (1970).

(a) The contractor shall promptly, and before such conditions are disturbed, notify the Contracting Officer in writing of: (1) subsurface or latent physical conditions at the site differing materially from those indicated in this contract, or (2) unknown physical conditions at the site, of an unusual nature, differing materially from those ordinarily encountered and generally recognized as inhering in work of the character provided for in this contract. The Contracting Officer shall promptly investigate the conditions, and if he finds that such conditions do materially so differ and cause an increase or decrease in the contractor's cost of, or the time required for, performance of any part of the work under this contract, whether or not changed as a result of such conditions, an equitable adjustment shall be made and the contract modified in writing accordingly.

(b) No claim of the Contractor under this clause shall be allowed unless the Contractor has given the notice requirement in (a) above; provided, however, the time prescribed therefor may be extended by the Government.

(c) No claim by the Contractor for an equitable adjustment hereunder shall be allowed if asserted after final payment under this contract.

There are two types of changed conditions. The "category one" changed condition entitles the contractor to an increase in the contract price if the contractor encounters "subsurface or latent physical conditions at the site differing materially from those indicated in th[e] contract." The contract documents must necessarily indicate what subsurface conditions the contractor should be expected to encounter for a "category one" changed conditions claim.[18]

The "category two" changed condition is more complex and does not involve any specific contract documents. A "category two" clause entitles the contractor to an increase in the contract price if the contractor encounters "unknown physical conditions at the site, of an unusual nature, differing materially from those ordinarily encountered and generally recognized as inhering in work of the character provided for in th[e] contract." In a "category two" changed conditions claim, the contractor must demonstrate that it has encountered something materially different from the known and the usual. The AIA and government clauses provide coverage for both kinds of unknown physical conditions.

Site Inspections

A differing site condition is one that the contractor could not reasonably have expected from examining the site or the specifications. Conditions differing from those ordinarily encountered on the job site that may not conflict with the contract documents but nevertheless are of an unusual nature are generally recognized as changed conditions. The contractor must demonstrate that the condition is an unknown physical condition that differs from the conditions ordinarily encountered in

[18]Hardeman-Monier-Hutcherson v. United States, 458 F.2d 1364 (Ct. Cl. 1972).

normal situations.[19] Recovery may not be awarded if examinations would normally disclose the condition and the contractor fails to inspect the site. The contractor's expectations must be reasonable under all the circumstances.

Illustrative Case

Academy Construction and Home Remodeling, Inc., contracted with the Federal Aviation Administration (FAA) for the construction of eleven flight aid systems at seven Missouri airports. Academy allegedly was required to remove between 140 and 175 tons of rock as part of the operation, and claimed that this was extra work since the contract was based on the belief that no more than four to five tons of rock would have to be removed. The Board of Contract Appeals found that Academy failed to demonstrate that its expectation was a reasonable one, stating that there was no basis for finding that the amount of rock to be removed constituted either a differing site condition or extra work. The special specifications stated that "unused excavated material shall be removed from the site immediately and disposed of." Since there was no limitation placed on the volume of unused material and it was reasonable to have expected the volume involved, Academy was denied compensation.[20]

The definition of an unusual condition under the differing-site-conditions clause varies and will depend upon the facts of each case. Generally, a site condition is considered unusual in nature if it could not reasonably be anticipated by the contractor from the examination of the contract documents, site inspection, or any personal experience as a contractor working in the area.

Illustrative Case

An excavating contractor, Promacs, Inc., claimed an equitable adjustment for extra work when it encountered permafrost in McKinley National Park in Alaska. There was no indication of permafrost in the contract specifications. The contractor's claim was dismissed because "[t]he basic concept underlying the Changed Conditions clause is that the long-term interest of the Government, in attempting to eliminate excessive contingency allowances from bid prices, justified the Government in assuming a portion of the risk concerning subsurface conditions. . . . [T]he Government assumes the risk . . . that the subsurface conditions will conform to those described in the contract, or, if not there described, to normal conditions for the area involved."

The contractor should have known that permafrost is prevalent throughout Alaska, and so it was not an "unknown" condition.[21]

Exculpatory Clauses

Specifications may contain exculpatory language stating that the contractor shall make its own thorough site investigation, shall make its own test borings and its own engineering measurements, and should not

[19]Urban Constr. Corp., ASBCA 8792, 1964 B.C.A. ¶ 4082 (1964).
[20]Academy Constr. & Home Remodeling, Inc., DOT CAB No. 1153, 82-1 B.C.A. ¶ 15,482 (1982).
[21]Appeal of Promacs, Inc., 1964 B.C.A. ¶ 4016 (1964).

rely on the data submitted by the owner. An owner should consider the use of exculpatory language to try to avoid risks that might otherwise fairly be placed on the contractor. A site investigation clause requires the contractor to make a reasonable inspection of the site before bidding and shifts the risks of those things the contractor ought to be reasonably knowledgeable of back to the contractor.

However, an owner needs to be aware that most courts strictly construe such exculpatory language. If the contract contains a broad exculpatory clause, a construction contractor may still be granted recovery for a differing site condition if an independent site inspection was not feasible and the contractor was thereby compelled to rely upon the owner's representations. In view of specific warnings and provisions, however, the court may uphold such a clause where it finds that the owner went to great effort to avoid making representations that would make it liable and drafted the contract to effectuate that purpose.

Illustrative Case

James McHugh Construction Company, a tunnel contractor, brought an action to recover additional expenses incurred as a result of difficulties encountered in driving subway tunnels through rock. McHugh's contract was with the Washington Metropolitan Area Transit Authority (WMATA) to construct a rapid transit system. WMATA moved to dismiss the appeal for failure to state a claim under the contract. The contract contained exclusions and disclaimers in the "differing-site-conditions" clauses, which disclaimed any liability on the part of WMATA for unknown subsurface rock conditions. The Board of Contract Appeals held that the exclusions and disclaimers barred McHugh's claim for additional costs of "moling" a tunnel because it knew of the clauses when it contracted for the project and thereby assumed a contingency of unpredictable proportions. The board found that although the trend in government contract cases is that certain risks, such as the risk of differing site conditions that construction contractors at common law were once subject to, are now to be borne by the government, WMATA made it clear that it would not be responsible for rock conditions and openly exempted itself from responsibility. Since McHugh had entered into the contract freely and assumed a contingency that WMATA itself was unwilling to risk, McHugh, therefore, must assume the additional costs.[22]

A disclaimer, however, would never protect a party in the event of a deliberate or intentional misrepresentation.

Notice Requirements

Changed conditions clauses or differing-site-conditions clauses normally include the requirement that a contractor must notify the owner or design professional or both prior to disturbing a discovered subsurface condition or a latent condition at a site differing from those indicated in the contract. It is particularly important that a contractor encountering a subsurface changed condition comply with the notice requirements of

---

[22]James McHugh Constr. Corp., ENG B.C.A. No. 4600, 82-1 B.C.A. ¶ 15,682 (1982).

the changed conditions clause. If a contractor proceeds with performance of the work affected by the changed condition and does not comply with the notification requirement, then the contractor may have waived the right to obtain a change and an equitable adjustment. If the owner is not notified of a changed condition, the owner may have been prejudiced because the right to inspect the alleged changed condition as it originally existed would be lost. As an example, if rock was encountered and the contractor proceeded to remove the rock without notifying the owner, then the owner would have lost the opportunity to verify the quantity of rock.

Illustrative Case

Coleman Electric Company claimed compensation under the changed conditions clause for the excavation of 7500 cubic yards of earth beyond the volume specified in the contract. The contractor had waited to inform the government until the extra work had been done so that it could present an accurate claim. The claim was denied because the government was not notified "before such conditions [were] disturbed" so that the government had no opportunity to determine whether the conditions were, in fact, changed.[23]

However, if a contractor fails to give the required notice, it is still possible that its claim may not have been lost if the owner or design professional is fully aware of the changed conditions and of the difficulty experienced by the contractor and no prejudice is otherwise shown by the failure to give timely notification.

[23]Appeal of Coleman Elec. Co., 58-2 B.C.A. ¶ 1928 (1958).

10 MANAGING THE SCHEDULE

Few elements in construction are of greater importance than the time factor. Proper control of the time factor is essential to the successful completion of almost all construction projects, while lack of control can result in financial disaster. The ideal situation is to spot the problems that could cause the schedule to be delayed or disrupted. Trend reports between the owner and the contractor may be very helpful in keeping the schedule on track. It is important for all parties involved in a construction project to be aware of the schedule.

The project schedule is probably the owner's single most important tool for ensuring a successful project. A schedule that is designed for a particular project and that is updated and revised as construction progresses is vital in monitoring the construction and also in controlling the progress of the project to ensure completion on time. In addition to its role in planning, the project schedule is extremely important in claims situations. A project schedule that is skillfully prepared and updated will show how the planned schedule of construction was affected by various delays and changes.

At the outset of the project, the owner needs to determine the scheduling requirements to be included in the contract. The contract should specify who is to prepare the schedule and when it is to be prepared. The owner may either specify a scheduling technique or may merely impose certain minimum requirements. The scheduling provision should specify whether or not the schedule is to be updated, who is responsible for updating it, and when and how often it is to be reviewed. In considering the kind of clause to be included in the contract, the owner should keep in mind that scheduling requirements should be tailored to the needs of the particular project. If the owner imposes scheduling requirements that are more detailed or complex than the project warrants, the owner will ultimately bear the contractor's higher cost of maintaining the schedule. Complex scheduling requirements will also generally impose specific requirements and duties for which the owner will be responsible. There are various scheduling techniques available; each has its own benefits and its own limitations.

SCHEDULING TECHNIQUES

Bar Charts

The bar chart was once the most popular method of scheduling construction projects. The bar chart contains a series of bars that demonstrate the start and end dates of various work activities. The schedule can be made more detailed by breaking down the activities into component parts, designating where the activities are to be carried out, assigning projected costs to the activities, and indicating manpower requirements. The bar chart can then be updated by using contrasting bars to show actual time of performance, actual costs, and actual manpower information.

Bar charts are beneficial because they are easy to read and relatively simple to revise and update. At the same time, however, they suffer from their simplicity because they do not show the interrelationship between tasks and so they cannot be used to demonstrate the causes of delays.[1]

Network Scheduling

Network scheduling techniques were developed in response to the limitations of the bar chart. Network scheduling demonstrates the interrelationship between the various work activities and their sequence. Network scheduling allows the project to be broken down into parts and to be planned in terms of work sequence. Two methods of network scheduling are the most generally accepted scheduling techniques used by the construction industry: CPM and PERT.

Critical Path Method (CPM)

The critical path method of scheduling has been used in both large and small projects to achieve significant success in project planning and pursuing delay claims. CPM illustrates a breakdown of the entire project into various individual tasks and analyzes the time needed for performance of each task. CPM identifies the most critical sequence of performance and schedules the remainder of the work around this "critical path" of the sequence to achieve the most efficient work schedule in terms of time and cost. Delay of any activity along the critical path results in delayed completion of the entire project.

The CPM is intimately connected with the issue of "float time," which is the amount of extra time in the schedule that can be used without delaying the entire project. It is created by the sequence of work that can be completed in less time than is maximally available before its delay will affect work on the critical path. In substance, the issue is who

---

[1]Appeal of Minmar Builders, Inc., ASBCA 3430, 72-2 B.C.A. ¶ 9599 (1972).

owns the float time. The cases are developing rapidly on this point.

When a delay occurs, a computer can recalculate the CPM schedule to show the precise effect of the delay on work progress. The computer can also work out the net effect on the project of two interrelated time delays. The maintenance of an up-to-date critical path schedule throughout the course of construction provides ready-made documentation of the history of the project, which the courts accept as persuasive evidence of the effects of delay. This history also provides a good negotiation tool for settlement discussions, and, if resort to the courts is necessary, it may provide convincing evidence that the project would have been completed on schedule but for the excusable delays. However, to be effective, a CPM schedule must be constantly updated and carefully followed. The failure to update and maintain the integrity of the CPM schedule will render it useless for consideration as evidence in proving scheduling claims.

The existence of sophisticated scheduling analysis techniques such as CPM has made it possible to accurately separate the impact of concurrent owner and contractor delays. The courts will not charge the contractor for inexcusable delays that occur simultaneously with delays caused by the owner; but by the same token, where the concurrent delay of the owner exceeds that of the contractor or vice versa, the court may allocate responsibility to the party responsible for the excess impact.[2] Use of the CPM in obtaining damages where concurrent delays are involved may be extremely important in light of the older rule that where concurrent delays occur neither party may recover damages, even though one party may be more responsible for the delay than the other.[3]

Program Evaluation Review Techniques (PERT)

The PERT system is more often used in the area of systems and supply procurement than in actual construction. The PERT system requires that the sequence of individual activities be identified and the time for performance calculated. Three time estimates are prepared: (1) the most pessimistic, (2) the most probable, and (3) the most optimistic. The statistical average of the estimates is calculated and used as the expected time of completion. Costing information can also be added into a PERT schedule to illustrate the costs of construction.

Sophisticated schedules can also provide a means of determining when to make progress payments. Costing information can be built into some schedules so that a check against the schedule to determine the amount to be paid will provide a fairly accurate measure of the value of

[2]Blackhawk Heating & Plumbing Co., GSBCA, 2432, 76-1 B.C.A. ¶ 11649.

[3]*See id.;* J.A. Jones Constr. Co. v. Greenbriar Shopping Center, 332 F. Supp. 1336 (N.D. Ga. 1971).

the work performed. This also imposes a somewhat stringent require-ment on the owner to make progress payments as reflected by the schedule.

The result of using a project schedule is the creation of a number of rights and duties involving timing and scheduling, including a duty not to delay others, a duty not to hinder or interfere with construction, and a duty to cooperate. The contract generally will outline what constitutes an excusable delay. The party asserting the delay must prove the facts that caused the delay and that the delay actually caused increased costs. It is therefore important to maintain the types of records that may be required later to prove why the project failed to proceed on schedule and the time in which the work would have been completed if it had not been delayed.

DELAYS

Only an excusable delay will allow the contractor to deviate from the project schedule. Two types of delays are excusable. The first is the non-compensable delay. Noncompensable delays generally arise from events that are beyond the control of the contractor or the owner, but that nevertheless delay the contractor's timely completion of the project. A noncompensable delay may be excusable in that it justifies the contrac-tor's deviation from the project schedule and avoids the imposition of a penalty on the contractor for not completing the project on time; how-ever, it does not allow the contractor to collect additional compensation for any extra costs. Noncompensable delays include such things as labor disputes, unusually severe weather conditions, unusual delays in trans-portation, vandalism, and delays caused by suppliers and second-tier subcontractors.

The second type of excusable delay is the compensable delay. Com-pensable delays are those caused by the owner or the owner's represen-tatives. A compensable delay not only gives the contractor a right to an extension of contract time, but also provides a right to collect additional compensation. In order for the contractor to recover damages for a delay, it must show that the delay was caused by the owner or that the owner somehow disrupted or interfered with the contract and that the contractor thereby incurred additional costs. Some owners, particularly the United States government, expressly provide in their contracts that if their representatives suspend, delay, or interrupt the contract, the contractors will be entitled to extra compensation. Some private con-tracts also have suspension-of-work clauses that allow the contractor to collect additional compensation for delays caused by the owner.

These basic categories of legal liability for delays on a construction project may be modified by special contractual terms, such as liqui-dated damages and no-damages-for-delay clauses. A liquidated damages clause represents an agreement by the parties that certain amounts of damages will be recoverable for a breach of contract. The liquidated damages clause is usually written to provide compensation to the owner for delays caused by the contractor. Liquidated damages clauses seldom provide for the payment of liquidated damages to the contractor upon default or delay by the owner.

A no-damages-for-delay clause generally provides that a contractor is entitled to an extension of time as a result of a delay but is not entitled to receive any additional compensation because of the delay. Generally such clauses will be strictly construed because of their harshness; however, when it is clear that a particular situation falls within the language of the clause, the clause will almost invariably be upheld. However, a no-damages-for-delay clause will not be enforced when the owner has actively or fraudulently interfered with the performance of the contract or when, for some reason, the delay is totally unreasonable.

Excusable Delays

There must be a clause in the contract or in the General Conditions in order to ensure an extension of the contract time for an excusable delay. In the absence of an excusable delay (or force majeure) clause, the common-law rule is that a contractor that undertakes a contractual obligation containing a time limitation that is of the essence must perform the obligation on time unless it is rendered impossible by an act of God, law, or the other contracting party. The General Conditions of most construction contracts, which may also be incorporated by reference into the subcontract documents, contain clauses to allow extensions of time when the contractor encounters excusable delays.

The excusable delay clause in the AIA General Conditions (Document A201, 1976 ed.) is contained in subparagraph 8.3.1, which states

If the Contractor is delayed at any time in the progress of the Work by any act of neglect of the Owner or the Architect, or by any employee of either, or by any separate contractor employed by the Owner, or by changes ordered in the Work, or by labor disputes, fire, unusual delay in transportation, adverse weather conditions not reasonably anticipatable, unavoidable casualties, or any causes beyond the Contractor's control or by delay authorized by the Owner pending arbitration, or by any other cause which the Architect determines may justify the delay, then the Contract Time shall be extended by Change Order for such reasonable time as the Architect may determine.

This excusable delay clause aims to cover delays that are the fault of neither party to the contract as well as delays caused by the owner. The clause serves to grant an extension of the time set for performance.

Technical Requirements for Asserting an Excusable Delay

Construction contracts typically set forth two basic prerequisites to the successful assertion of a claim for scheduling relief. The most common requirement is that the contractor advise the owner in writing within a specified number of days after the delaying event that performance of the work has been or potentially might be delayed. A less common requirement is that the contractor submit, within a specified number of days, a statement of the magnitude of the delay and of any additional costs occasioned by the delay.

Subparagraph 8.3.2 of the AIA General Conditions (Document A201, 1976 ed.) provides that

> Any claim for extension of time shall be made in writing to the Architect not more than twenty days after the commencement of the delay; otherwise it shall be waived. In the case of a continuing delay only one claim is necessary. The Contractor shall provide an estimate of the probable effect of such delay on the progress of the Work.

The rationale behind this notice provision is that by apprising the owner that a delay is occurring or that some other basis for a claim has arisen through no fault of the contractor, the owner has sufficient opportunity to take available corrective action.

Courts have established certain exceptions to the notice requirements in order to eliminate harsh and unjust outcomes of the contractor's failure to give notice. Substantial compliance with the requirement of timely written notice has been held to be sufficient where there was some written indication that the contractor was experiencing difficulty. Informal communications that give enough information to apprise the owner of the nature and extent of the delay may amount to substantial compliance with the requirement of timely written notice.

Illustrative Case

Hoel-Steffen Construction Company submitted a claim to the Interior Department's Board of Contract Appeals for an increase in the contract sum under the suspension-of-work clause of the standard federal government construction contract. The basis of Hoel-Steffen's claim was that the government had unjustifiably interfered with its work on the St. Louis Gateway Arch by giving other contractors priority of access to the work space. The board dismissed the case because of the contractor's failure to give notice within the twenty-day limitation set forth in the contract. On appeal, the Court of Claims reversed the board's decision. The rationale for the court's holding was that the notice provisions were for the benefit of the government to permit officials to collect data and evaluate the desirability of continuing the delay-causing conduct. The court found that the proper officials had sufficient notice of the problem, albeit not the specific written notice required by the contract. The court held that the contractor was entitled to recover its extra costs because "notice provisions in contract-adjustment clauses [should] not be applied too technically and illiberally where the Government is quite aware of the operative facts." Although the case deals with a compensable delay, it is illustrative of the tolerance shown by courts in applying contractual notice requirements.[4]

Since the purpose of the notice requirement is to enable the owner to investigate the alleged causes of delay while the evidence is fresh and

---

[4]Hoel-Steffen Constr. Co. v. United States, 456 F.2d 760, 768 (Ct. Cl. 1972).

there is still time to correct the situation, the owner's actual knowledge of the delay situation renders the notice requirement superfluous. This is particularly true when delay of the work is caused by actions of the owner.

Illustrative Case

John H. Maxwell & Company was required by subcontract to erect three fuel tanks on a foundation to be provided by Macri Construction Company, the general contractor. Maxwell experienced delays caused by defects in the foundation but failed to give written notice to Macri in accordance with a provision of the subcontract that required timely written notice of the causes of delays. Macri, however, was aware of the defects and tried to remedy them, finally ordering Maxwell to proceed. The court held that the notice requirement had been waived by Macri, and that Maxwell was not liable for liquidated damages. The court said: "Under the circumstances equity does not permit Macri to assert surprise and prejudice."[5]

Where the owner has not been injured by a lack of notice, the failure of the contractor to give the required notice is not always fatal to the contractor's attempt to establish an excusable delay.[6] In addition, the owner may be deemed to have waived the technical requirement of timely written notice by considering a claim for excusable delay on its merits.[7] Accordingly, the owner's actions in response to the delay may result in a waiver of the requirement for timely written notice.

Proof of the Extent of an Excusable Delay

A contractor must prove not only that an event within the definition of the excusable delay clause occurred, but also that the event caused an actual delay in the contractor's performance. The effect of a delay in a single phase of performance can be extremely complex to determine because it may alter the schedule for all subcontracts yet to be completed. Work may be shifted into a season in which the weather will extend performance times, or seasonal activity may make it more difficult to find certain tradesworkers. Along with time changes, there may be increases in costs of performance and overhead. If the delay is compensable, the courts may not accept as proof of damages the difference between the contract price and the contractor's actual cost; the contractor must prove that the extra cost caused by an excusable delay was reasonable and, in fact, was caused by a compensable delay rather than by the contractor.

[5]Macri v. United States *ex rel.* John H. Maxwell & Co., 353 F.2d 804 (9th Cir. 1965).

[6]Appeal of Hansel-Phelps Constr. Co., 71-1 B.C.A. ¶ 8652 (1970).

[7]Dirtmore-Freimith Corp. v. United States, 390 F.2d 664 (Ct. Cl. 1968); Callahan Constr. Co. v. United States, 91 Ct. Cl. 538 (1940).

Compensable Delays

An excusable delay clause provides for an extension of the contract time if the contractor is delayed at any time during the progress of the work by general conditions beyond the control of the parties. Such delays are not generally compensable in damages. However, delays attributable to the owner are compensable. They entitle the contractor not only to an extension of the contract time, but also to damages for the increased cost of performance occasioned by such delays because the owner has an implied obligation of cooperation with the contractor.

There are numerous ways in which the owner can delay a contractor. The most common owner-attributed delay arises from inadequate or incorrect plans and specifications. The owner that furnishes plans or specifications warrants to the contractor that they are satisfactory for their intended purpose. Therefore, any delay resulting from reliance on that warranty is attributable to the owner and excuses the contractor.

Illustrative Case

The contractor, Industrial Controls Company, Inc., was performing space alterations on a government building when it was delayed by a specification in the government's plans that incorrectly placed a wooden pocket for folding partitions. New partitions that would attach to the wall had to be ordered, and the contractor was entitled to an equitable adjustment of the contract time and compensation for additional costs incurred.[8]

Another common excusable delay attributable to the owner results from the owner's right to make changes from time to time that interrupt and aggravate performance of the work, extend the time of performance, and make performance more costly. In addition, the owner may issue conflicting changes that delay the completion of performance. The contractor can usually receive an extension of the contract time and recover additional compensation for such delays even if the owner's actions do not directly delay the activities of the contractor. For example, the owner's actions may delay a subcontractor whose work is prerequisite to the contractor's.

Illustrative Case

The government ordered a change in the size of concrete blocks from 8 inches to 12 inches. Several months later the government changed the specifications back to 8-inch block. The next day it requested that the contractor return to 12-inch block. The Board of Contract Appeals found that the government's indecisiveness caused a subcontractor's delay in installing reinforcement bars that were needed before the contractor could proceed further. The contractor was granted an adjustment in the contract amount.[9]

[8]Appeal of Industrial Controls Co., GSBCA 5391, 79-2 B.C.A. ¶14171 (1979).
[9]Appeal of Ray I. Strate, ASBCA 19914, 78-1 B.C.A. ¶13128 (1978).

Owner-attributed delays may also occur when the contractor is waiting to obtain access to the job site, a notice to proceed, inspections, decisions or approvals of the owner or the design professional, and decisions about changes.

The AIA General Conditions (Document A201, 1976 ed.) in subparagraph 8.3.1, allow for an extension of time in the excusable delay clause and also state, in subparagraph 8.3.4, that an extension of the contract time does not preclude recovery for damages due to delay. Subparagraph 8.3.4 provides as follows:

> This Paragraph 8.3 [relating to an extension of the contract time for delays] does not exclude the recovery of damages for delay by either party under other provisions of the Contract Documents.

The AIA General Conditions recognize the right of the contractor to claim additional costs (including damages for delays) in subparagraph 12.3.1, which provides as follows:

> If the Contractor wishes to make a claim for an increase in the Contract Sum, he shall give the Architect written notice thereof within twenty days after the occurrence of the event giving rise to such claim. This notice shall be given by the Contractor before proceeding to execute the Work, except in an emergency endangering life or property in which case the Contractor shall proceed in accordance with Paragraph 10.3. No such claim shall be valid unless so made. If the Owner and the Contractor cannot agree on the amount of the adjustment in the Contract Sum, it shall be determined by the Architect. Any change in the Contract Sum resulting from such claim shall be authorized by Change Order.

As with the required notice under the excusable delay clause, there may be certain exceptions that allow a contractor to obtain damages for delays in spite of failing to give the required notice. When the owner has actual knowledge of the situation and is not prejudiced by the lack of written notice, the notice requirement may be deemed satisfied.

Courts have historically held that the parties to a contract have a duty not to delay, hinder, or interfere with the other parties in the performance of their contractual obligations. This duty results from the covenant implied in every contract that the parties act in good faith toward one another and in a manner of fair dealing. The duty to cooperate is implicit in this covenant, and in a construction contract it imposes on the owner and the owner's agent an obligation to cooperate fully with the contractor to expedite the work. This means cooperating by providing information, clarifying ambiguities in contract documents, providing services or equipment as required by the contract, and making progress payments according to the contract, all with reasonable promptness so as not to delay or interfere with the ordinary progress of work.

Not only do the owner and the general contractor have a duty to cooperate, but so do the general contractor and subcontractors, as well as the multiple prime contractors and all subcontractors. The design professional, as the owner's agent, is subject to the same implied covenant of good faith and fair dealing that binds the actual parties to the contract. Thus, the duty to cooperate is at the heart of the construction contract and affects all parties. A breach of this duty will subject the breaching party to liability for resulting damages.

There are many situations in which the contractor is entitled to damages for delays caused by owner interference. Some of the situations that have allowed the contractor to collect damages for owner-caused delays are as follows:

- A formal or constructive change order that directs the performance of extra work and necessarily extends the time of performance.
- The owner's failure to provide adequate and accurate specifications, or the owner's misinterpretation of the specifications, resulting in delay for correction of the specifications or in replacement of work done pursuant to the faulty instructions.
- An unreasonable delay in the owner's approval of drawings or of a subcontractor, resulting in delay of the contractor's performance.
- An unreasonable delay for inspection or testing by the owner, or the owner's failure to give notice of an inspection, thereby causing delay.
- The owner's failure to make the site available on time or to obtain title to a right-of-way when promised, or denial of access to the site by another contractor whose work must precede the work of the complaining contractor.
- Delay in receipt of owner-furnished materials or replacement of defective materials provided by the owner.
- When the owner allows another contractor to disrupt the work.
- When the owner directs the contractor to give priority to work under another contract.
- When the owner directs that the work be done in a less efficient sequence or suspends the work.
- When the owner directs that a less efficient method of performance be used.
- An unreasonable delay in paying the contractor, which results in delay or disruption of the contractor's work.

Any delay in the performance of a construction contract can have a ripple effect on the cost of the work remaining to be done. When owner-caused delays force the contractor into more costly operations, the owner is liable for damages for the resulting additional outlays. The possible extent of the additional expense caused by an owner-caused delay is demonstrated by the following case.

Illustrative Case

The government provided faulty specifications to J.D. Hedin Construction Company, a contractor engaged in building a Veteran's Administration hospital. Substantial delay was caused by the faulty specifications and the government's failure to correct them within a reasonable time. These delays extended the work into bad weather; the exterior work would otherwise have been completed sooner. A strike occurred, seventeen days of which would have been after completion of the work but for the government's delays.

Hedin was forced to maintain temporary roads for a longer period at additional cost. The extension into bad weather brought increased costs for heating and snow removal. The delay extension was a period of higher wages for laborers under their collective bargaining agreement. The contractor was forced to take over the work of a subcontractor that did not perform because of the delay. The Court of Claims held that all these effects were caused by the government's delays with respect to its faulty specifications and awarded damages plus job and home-office overhead to the contractor. The final damage figure recovered by Hedin was $518,000.[10]

DISRUPTION

The owner can disrupt the contractor's performance without delaying it, but disruptions can be extremely expensive since they impede the contractor's ability to attain job momentum and productivity. An owner-caused disruption is a breach of the owner's implied obligation of cooperation. If the disruption causes the contractor extra costs, it is entitled to the damages that flow from the disruptive conduct of the owner. Even though the contract may be completed on time, a disruption entitles the contractor to damages.

ACCELERATION

When performance on a project is accelerated, the contractor will almost inevitably accrue additional costs. Some causes of acceleration entitle the contractor to additional compensation; others do not. When the owner or its authorized representative directs a contractor to accelerate performance in order to finish prior to the contract completion date, the contractor is entitled to recover under the change clause for the increased cost of accelerated performance. Acceleration also occurs when the owner requires a contractor to complete work by the original contract date despite the occurrence of an excusable delay entitling the contractor to an extension of the original contract time. Such an occurrence is a constructive change order, or a constructive acceleration, and entitles the contractor to an equitable adjustment in the contract price.

Courts require a showing of certain key elements before allowing relief on a claim for a constructive acceleration. There must be an excusable delay for which the contractor is entitled to an extension of time. The contractor must have requested an extension of time, and the owner must have failed or refused to grant the extension to which the contractor is entitled. The contractor must have been required, either expressly or implicitly by the owner or its representatives, to complete the contract without an extension, and the contractor must have completed the contract on time and actually incurred extra cost.

A broad range of acceleration costs are recoverable. An obvious example

[10]J.D. Hedin Constr. Co. v. United States, 347 F.2d 235 (Ct. Cl. 1965).

is the extra cost of overtime wages that would not have been paid otherwise.

The costs of scheduled overtime may even be higher than anyone anticipated. Owners must be very careful to consider all of the costs when requiring a contractor to schedule overtime. In a November 1980 report by the Business Roundtable, *Scheduled Overtime Effect on Construction Projects*, the conclusion was threefold:

- Placing field construction operations on a scheduled overtime basis disrupts the economy of the affected area, magnifies any apparent labor shortage, reduces labor productivity, and creates excessive inflation of construction labor costs without material benefit to the completion schedule.

- Where a work schedule of sixty or more hours per week is continued longer than about two months, the cumulative effects of decreased productivity will cause a delay in the completion date beyond that which could have been realized with the same crew size on a forty-hour week.

- Where overtime operations are deemed necessary despite productivity losses, for example, on remote construction projects where bachelor housing is provided at the job site and on maintenance turnarounds, proper management can minimize the inflationary effects. Management actions to be considered include the use of an additional shift and periodic shutdown of the work for a Sunday or weekend.

It is clear that there are many indirect costs involved in the use of overtime. If the owner is responsible for the costs of acceleration in a certain instance, this will include the costs of wages for actual overtime work. Any other direct costs incurred by a contractor in a reasonable effort to comply with an order to accelerate may be recoverable.

If the contractor causes inexcusable delays and the owner directs the contractor to accelerate to the extent necessary to finish by the original completion date, the contractor is not entitled to any additional compensation. The contractor is also not entitled to any additional compensation if acceleration is taken on voluntarily merely in order to finish ahead of schedule.

SUSPENSION OF WORK

A suspension of work occurs when the owner either expressly or constructively causes the contractor to suspend any part of the work. Suspension of work is most relevant in government construction contracts, which often contain a standard suspension-of-work clause aimed at allowing the contracting officer to suspend or delay work for a reasonable period of time at no additional expense, while allowing the contractor the right to recover additional costs caused by any unreasonable suspension, delay, or interruption caused by the government.

The Federal Conditions, Standard Form 23A, contain the usual suspension-of-work clause, which reads as follows:

SUSPENSION OF WORK (1968 FEB)

(a) The Contracting Officer may order the Contractor in writing to suspend, delay, or interrupt all or any part of the work for such period of time as he may determine to be appropriate for the convenience of the Government.

(b) If the performance of all or any part of the work is, for an unreasonable period of time, suspended, delayed, or interrupted by an act of the Contracting Officer in the administration of this contract, or by his failure to act within the time specified in this contract (or if no time is specified, within a reasonable time), an adjustment shall be made for any increase in the cost of performance of this contract (excluding profit) necessarily caused by such unreasonable suspension, delay, or interruption and the contract modified in writing accordingly. However, no adjustment shall be made under this clause for any suspension, delay, or interruption to the extent: (1) that performance would have been so suspended, delayed, or interrupted by any other cause, including the fault or negligence of the Contractor; or (2) for which an equitable adjustment is provided for or excluded under any other provision of this contract.

The importance of the suspension-of-work clause in government contracts is that it gives the contractor the express right to collect extra monies for costs incurred as a result of unreasonable delays by the government that would otherwise constitute a breach of the contract. Traditionally the clause has been used to extend the authority of government appeals boards to grant a contractor's claim for damages in excess of the liquidated damages. However, the Contract Disputes Act of 1978 now grants jurisdiction over such claims to the appropriate administrative board regardless of the existence of a suspension-of-work clause.

Similarly, in a private construction contract the suspension-of-work clause allows the contractor to collect money for unreasonable delays caused by the owner. The effect of this clause in settling scheduling claims may be quite important in that it represents an express agreement between the parties that, in accordance with the contract provisions regarding the settlement of claims, damages for delays can be granted in addition to time extensions where unreasonable owner delays are involved. This creates a contractual mechanism for the parties to deal with delays that would otherwise be construed as a breach of the contract. Most important, it allows the owner to cause reasonable delays with no liability for damages, while protecting the contractor from unreasonably extended delays.

When a suspension of work occurs, the contractor once again will be bound by technical notice requirements in the contract. Federal Conditions, Standard Form 23A, contain a specific notice requirement applicable when a suspension of work occurs:

(c) No claim under this clause shall be allowed (1) for any costs incurred more than 20 days before the Contractor shall have notified the Contracting Officer in writing of the act or failure to act involved (but this requirement shall not apply as to a claim resulting from a suspension order), and (2) unless the claim, in an amount stated, is asserted in writing as soon as practicable after the termination of such suspension, delay, or interruption, but not later than the date of final payment under the contract.[11]

The notice requirement in this clause applies to all suspensions except those caused by an express suspension order of the government. Suspensions that are not expressly ordered by the government or owner are constructive or de facto suspensions. Such suspensions occur primarily when the contractor is forced to wait for an owner's decision on a proposed course of action or method of performance proposed by the contractor. The fact that the owner ultimately may agree to the contractor's proposed method has no bearing on whether the delay was a reasonable one.[12]

In order to recover additional monies under a suspension-of-work clause, the contractor must show that the suspension was of unreasonable duration, that additional expense or loss was incurred as a result, and that a reasonable dollar amount can be calculated for that expense or loss. The unreasonableness of the delay must usually be proven by showing that the lack of action by the owner was unreasonable *under the circumstances*. In addition, there are some delays that are *per se* unreasonable, in which case the contractor does not bear the burden of showing that the delay was unreasonable, but rather the owner has the burden of showing that it acted reasonably. A delay due to defective government plans or specifications where the defects were not obvious to the contractor is *per se* unreasonable. Where the delay is not *per se* unreasonable, there is no formula for determining whether a delay is unreasonable. The duration of the delay may be irrelevant if the event causing the delay was so obviously contrary to the circumstances contemplated by the contract that any delay was unreasonable.

Illustrative Case

Liburn Construction Company contracted to construct drainage trenches beside runways at an Air Force base. The contract contained detailed provisions for the Air Force's use of the runways during the course of the work so that the work crews could avoid dangerous conditions that might be caused by planes landing on runways close to the work site. The Board of Contract Appeals ruled that a delay of one day was an unreasonable delay within the suspension-of-work clause, since the delay was caused by an aircraft on a runway that was exclusively scheduled that day for construction work. The contractor was awarded $1000.[13]

The owner may order the contractor to stop work, without liability for damages, if the contractor's work is defective or persistently contrary to

[11]ASPR § 7-602.46.

[12]Appeal of United Contractors, ASBCA 6142, 1962 B.C.A. ¶3314 (1962).

[13]Appeal of Liburn Constr. Co., ASBCA 11582, 68-1 B.C.A. ¶ 7035 (1968).

the terms of the contract. With regard to the owner's right to stop work, the AIA General Conditions, Document 201, subparagraph 3.3.1, state:

If the Contractor fails to correct defective Work as required by Paragraph 13.2 or persistently fails to carry out the Work in accordance with the Contract Documents, the Owner, by a written order signed personally or by an agent specifically so empowered by the Owner in writing, may order the Contractor to stop the Work, or any portion thereof, until the cause of such order has been eliminated; however, this right of the Owner to stop the work shall not give rise to any duty on the part of the Owner to exercise this right for the benefit of the Contractor or any other person or entity, except to the extent required by Subparagraph 6.1.3.

The owner must, of course, carefully exercise the authority given under this article. The owner has no power to order the contractor to needlessly stop work due to defects that the contractor could have corrected while continuing with the job. Such a suspension will constitute an unreasonable delay for which the contractor can recover damages.

A suspension of work by the owner due to a lack of funds to meet progress payments shows bad faith and may constitute a breach of the contract.[14] Likewise, a suspension of work when followed by a failure to give timely notice to proceed again with the work when the cause of suspension has been cured may be seen as a breach of the contract.

[14]Edgarton v. United States, 117 F. Supp. 193 (Ct. Cl, 1954).

11 CONTROLLING QUALITY

Quality control is concerned with ascertaining that the materials, equipment, and workmanship of the contractor conform to the quality required by the contract. If the contract documents do not specify a standard of quality, the contractor is deemed to have guaranteed that the materials will be new and free from defects and that the workmanship will conform to industry standards.

Generally, quality control is not addressed by any of the contract documents, so the owner must make an affirmative assignment of the responsibility for quality control.

THE DUTIES OF THE DESIGN PROFESSIONAL

The responsibilities of the design professional are determined by the written obligations incorporated in the contract. If the design professional is retained to administer the construction contract, then one of the primary functions should be the supervision of the contractor's performance with respect to adherence to the plans and specifications, good construction practices, applicable building codes and regulations, and time requirements. This is accomplished through inspection of the work. Of critical importance in the contract is the requirement of inspection and a definition of exactly what is expected.

Webster's Ninth New Collegiate Dictionary defines the word *inspect* as "to view closely in critical appraisal." However, the only reference to inspection duties found in the AIA Owner-Architect Agreement (Document B141, 1977 ed.) is located in subparagraph 1.5.15:

The Architect shall conduct inspections to determine the Dates of Substantial Completion and final completion, shall receive and forward to the Owner for the Owner's review written warranties and related documents required by the Contract Documents and assembled by the Contractor, and shall issue a final Certificate for Payment.

That no other duty of inspection exists is clarified in subparagraph 1.5.4:

The Architect shall visit the site at intervals appropriate to the stage of construction or as otherwise agreed by the Architect in writing to become generally familiar with the progress and quality of the Work and to determine in general if the Work is proceeding in accordance with the Contract Documents. However, the Architect shall not be required to make exhaustive or continuous on-site inspections to check the quality or quantity of the Work. On the basis of such on-site observations as an architect, the Architect shall keep the Owner informed of the progress and quality of the Work, and shall endeavor to guard the Owner against defects and deficiencies in the Work of the Contractor.

Under the American Institute of Architects contract documents, the design professional's duty is one of observation and not inspection, with the exception of the duty to inspect in order to determine the Dates of Substantial Completion and Final Completion.

There is no duty to inspect in the absence of specific contractual provisions. Subparagraph 1.5.5 states that the design professional is not responsible for the acts or omissions of the contractor or for the contractor's failure to carry out the work as required by the plans and specifications.

Illustrative Case

The architectural services contract required that the architect would only be responsible for general supervisory functions and that a resident inspector would be used on the job. The architectural services contract also stated that the architect would not be liable for the failure of the general contractor to carry out the contract in accordance with the plans and specifications. Following completion of the building, the roof was blown off during a windstorm. It was alleged that the failure of the roof was due to the general contractor's failure to attach the roof as required in the plans and specifications. The court found that the owner had no legal recourse against the architect because the architectural contract specifically exempted the architect from liability for the acts or omissions of the general contractor in failing to carry out the construction in accordance with the contract documents.[1]

In the glossary of construction industry terms included in the *Architect's Handbook of Professional Practice*, the American Institute of Architects defines "inspection" at page 10 as follows:

INSPECTION: Examination of work completed or in progress to determine its compliance with contract requirements. The architect ordinarily makes only two inspections of a construction project, one to determine substantial completion, and the other to determine final completion. These inspections should be distinguished from the more general observations made by the architect on his periodic visits to the site during the progress of the work. The term is also used to mean examination of the work by a public official, owner's representative, or others.

"Observation of the work" is defined at page 12 as follows:

OBSERVATION OF THE WORK: A function of the architect in the construction phase, during his periodic visits to the site, to familiarize himself generally with the progress and

---

[1]Mountainview Independent School District #621 v. Buetow & Associates, Inc., 253 N.W.2d 836 (Minn. 1977).

quality of the work and to determine in general if the work is proceeding in accordance with the contract documents.

While observation of the work is an important component of contract administration, more than mere observation during some indeterminate number of periodic visits to the construction site is desirable from the owner's point of view.

The design contract should be drafted to ensure control of the quality of construction, the quality of materials, and the quality of workmanship.

An owner's representative may be retained, preferably as a part of the design professional's work force, to conduct daily inspections to ascertain that the work is being done in accordance with the plans and specifications. However, the design professional should be required to make weekly or biweekly visits to the construction site not only for the purpose of conducting inspections to determine the adequacy of the construction and compliance with the contract documents, but also to be able to foresee future problems.

The role of inspection in construction contract administration can be defined as follows:

(1) To ensure the construction contractor's adherence to the plans and specifications.

(2) To ensure compliance with all applicable codes and regulations and good construction practices.

(3) To monitor the progress of the work so as to ensure compliance with the contract time and to take whatever steps are required to maintain the project schedule.

(4) To provide timely interpretation of the plans and specifications where questions arise and to suggest solutions to contract disputes.

(5) To monitor, coordinate, and implement approvals of shop drawings and work reviews.

(6) To schedule observations of tests required by the contract specifications.

(7) To reject all work that fails to meet contract specifications or industry standards.

(8) To stop the work when the work does not comply with industry standards or good construction practices and the contractor has failed to remedy the defective work within a reasonable time.

(9) To approve in a timely fashion all materials, samples, and shop drawings submitted by the construction contractor under the contract requirements.

(10) To ensure that the work claimed to have been completed in the contractor's Application for Payment is actually in place and is of good quality and workmanship.

In the Statement of the Architect's Services, AIA Document B551 (June 19, 1972 ed.), at pages 6 and 7, the American Institute of Architects considers the duties of the design professional during administration of the construction contract to generally include the following:

(1) Preparation of supplementary drawings;

(2) Review of the contractor's detailed cost breakdown of materials and building trades;

(3) Review of the fabricators; review of suppliers' shop drawings, samples of materials, equipment, and any other required submissions;

(4) General administration of the construction contract or contracts including periodic visits to the construction site to review the progress of the work, to review the quality of the work, and to determine if the work is proceeding in accordance with the contract documents;

(5) Review of the contractor's Applications for Payment and determination of the amount owed to the contractor;

(6) Issuance of Certificates for Payment for the amount due;

(7) Preparation of change orders authorizing changes in the work;

(8) Determination of the Dates of Substantial Completion and Final Completion;

(9) The receipt and forwarding to the owner of all written guarantees required to be furnished by the contractor; and

(10) Issuance of the Final Certificate for Payment.

The American Institute of Architects makes the following statement in its Statement of the Architect's Services, AIA Document B551 (June 19, 1972 ed.), at page 7:

During construction the architect, by on-site observations, endeavors to guard the owner against defects and deficiencies in the work of the contractor, but the architect does not supervise construction. The contractor, and not the architect, is solely responsible for construction means, methods, techniques, sequence, and procedures and for safety precautions and programs in connection with the work. The architect likewise is not responsible for the contractor's failure to carry out the work in accordance with the contract documents, but he does have a responsibility to notify the owner of any such failure or unsatisfactory performance about which he becomes aware.

The American Institute of Architects does state in the *Architect's Handbook of Professional Practice* (1973 ed.), chapter 18, "Construction Contract Administration," at page 4, that general observations of the following should be made at suitable times during the progress of work:

SPECIFIC DUTIES—General observations of the following should be made at suitable times during the progress of the work:

1. Bench marks and building layout

2. Dimensions and grades

3. Excavations

4. Soil under footings

5. Public utility connections

6. Foundation sizes and reinforcing

7. Pile driving

8. Caisson work

9. Concrete work

10. Concrete forms

11. Concrete tests

12. Structural frame

13. Floor openings, sleeves and hangers

14. Quality and placing of concrete

15. Weather precautions

16. Masonry layout, materials, bonding, anchorage and flashings

17. Setting of frames and prefabricated elements

18. Partition layout

19. Temporary enclosures, heat and light

20. Protection of finished work

21. Setting of bucks

22. Partition construction

23. Plaster grounds

24. Tile work

25. Electrical conduits, wiring, accessories and connections

26. Duct work, piping, valves

27. Special equipment

28. Elevators

29. Furring and lathing

30. Setting of fixtures

31. Cabinet work

32. Finishes

33. Paint and painting

34. Hardware

35. Plumbing tests

36. Mechanical equipment tests

37. Inspections by public authorities

The owner who desires more from the design professional than the general observation of the work for the purpose of endeavoring to guard the owner's interest is well advised to address this in the design services contract, requiring the design professional to inspect the work on a weekly or biweekly basis for the purpose of ascertaining that the construction is proceeding in accordance with the contract documents.

If the owner attempts to amend the AIA documents in this respect, it should modify the language of subparagraphs such as 1.5.4 and 1.5.5 in AIA Document B141.

QUALITY ASSURANCE/QUALITY CONTROL PROGRAMS

Quality assurance is a plan to ensure that the construction will conform to established requirements. Quality control is the implementation of the planned action to conform to established requirements. Quality assurance and quality control should complement each other.

Owners have traditionally not been interested in quality assurance (QA)/quality control (QC) programs, although they would benefit the most from any increased attention to quality because they are the ones that end up with the product. Increased attention to quality results in lower costs, increased productivity, and better facilities. Owners must take responsibility for QA and QC in order to ensure quality on their projects.

In its 1982 study on quality assurance,[2] the Business Roundtable concluded that owners that have adopted innovative management techniques for QA/QC programs seem to consistently obtain the highest-quality construction. Among its recommendations to owners were the following:

(1) Clearly define the level of quality assurance required on the project;

(2) Require designers, constructors, and vendors to have formal QA/QC programs and procedures as one prequalification for bidding or negotiating work;

(3) Require pre-job meetings to review and clarify all QA/QC requirements and define how they will be monitored;

(4) Have the operational executive (preferably the plant manager) become more active in the planning and execution of QA/QC efforts;

(5) Establish an autonomous quality assurance group within the company to (a) analyze and approve programs and procedures that are submitted; and (b) ensure that the programs are in fact put to use during design and construction;

(6) Place the responsibility for the control of quality directly upon the organization performing the work and under the day-to-day direction of the manager responsible for execution of the work;

(7) Establish a regular post-project quality review to assess the effectiveness of the QA/QC effort. The results of the review should be documented for use in future project planning; and

(8) Track the cost of critical items over the entire life of the facility in order to assess more precisely the results of the quality level achieved during design and construction.

A contractor must of course perform the construction according to what is expected, following plans and specifications in a first-class and

---

[2]The Business Roundtable, *Modern Management Systems*, Report A-6, November 1982.

workmanlike manner. To accomplish this, the contractor should implement a QA/QC program with written procedures, including provisions for inspecting materials to ensure that the materials are of the quality established in the contract. Such a program can be cost-effective and beneficial when compared to the costs of rework and downtime. Contractors that do not take measures to ensure that the work is done right the first time may have to take time to redo the job.

Perhaps the most important means of controlling quality is through the employer-employee relationship. Pride runs deep in construction work. Having employees rip out their work and redo it can destroy morale and motivation. With proper QA/QC planning, rework can be eliminated and motivation maintained. Therefore, the contractor should instill a prideful attitude in employees—an attitude that focuses on detail and quality. This starts with the reading and comprehension of the plans and specifications and with ensuring compliance with them as each stage of the construction progresses. The construction should be constantly monitored and coordinated to achieve the contractual level of quality; and the goal should be a "zero punch list."

The Business Roundtable's *Construction Labor Motivation* report explains that both blue- and white-collar workers are motivated by seeing the end result of their labor; that is, witnessing the completion of the structure. Consequently, construction employees should be aware of the progress on each stage of the project. Quite often, on large industrial projects, only minimal information about the project is released. Duplication of effort, numerous modifications to plans, and schedules that constantly slip also make it difficult to keep employee motivation high.

In addition, materials should be available before workers are assigned to an area, so that workers do not start in one location only to be shifted to another. Such efficiency improves worker motivation and productivity and helps promote a high level of accomplishment.

In sum, owners can obtain the highest-quality construction if contractors pursue an effective QA/QC program. The owner is therefore well advised to require the contractor to

(1) Establish a separate quality-control group.

(2) Institute a formal, documented QA/QC program.

(3) Compare its program with those of other contractors. This will help detect where improvements can be made.

(4) Use data processing more extensively to measure quality control's role in cost control.

(5) Establish a formal, post-project evaluation procedure, including a review of QA/QC efforts during construction.

(6) Explore how motivational techniques can be used to improve the quality of construction. This includes the use of quality circles, innovative labor relations, and employee participation.

12 CLAIMS MANAGEMENT

Many construction attorneys preach about the need for a management system of processing claims for which a contractor is entitled to payment. Such a procedure is really too late: the owner that is always defending a claim after it arises may not be in business for long. However, the owner that spots the driving forces leading to cost overruns and that communicates with the contractor and design people to avoid those driving forces will have a successful and efficient project.

This approach is called claims management. Effective claims management means controlling the costs of a contract to avoid overruns and minimizing the driving forces that tend to lead to claims by a contractor. Effective construction professionals view claims management as proactive and primarily seek to prevent the conditions that cause claims to arise in the first place.

MINIMIZING CLAIMS

Claims are not as inevitable as people might think. In reality, claims are a result of management-control problems; therefore, the way to minimize claims is to solve management-control problems. Even the most complex construction project can be performed on time, within the budget, and with a minimal amount of disputes and changes if the owner and the contractor, as well as the design professional, reasonably manage the construction from design through the final construction punch list.

One of the most important ways to minimize claims is by taking appropriate steps during the design process. A poor design will cost the owner, the design professional, and the contractor an inordinate amount of time and expense. The design stage should therefore include a review of the plans and specifications by both the contractors and subcontractors in terms of value engineering, constructability, and job-site coordination. In addition, it is important to investigate similar construction projects to see what problems have occurred on them. Cutting corners during the design stage and not obtaining practical feedback are big mistakes; if changes are left to be worked out while the building is being built, the result will be increased costs of performance.

To ensure thorough and accurate design and specifications, owners are well advised to choose design professionals carefully, not only on the basis of their design ability but also on their ability to manage the construction process with a minimum of disputes, within the contract time, and within the budget. Design professionals often focus on the owners' design requirements and not on the often fundamental responsibility of administering the contract in the owners' interests. To determine whether a design professional has sufficient management expertise, the owner should check references.

In addition, the design professional should receive fair compensation for his work. An owner will often interfere with the design professional's ability to manage the contract efficiently by cutting back on his professional fees to a point where the design professional cannot afford to coordinate and manage the construction effectively. Trying to cut design-professional fees may not really be cost-effective for an owner. If design professionals are compensated adequately, they can afford to take the time to develop plans and specifications that are well thought-out, coordinated for constructability, and value engineered, as well as to manage the construction process effectively.

Ambiguities should be worked out of the contract before construction begins. Many claims arise because of conflicts over the standard of quality. It is extremely important that the owner, the design professional, and all of the contractors have an understanding as to what standard of quality is required. It is best to solve these conflicts at the outset by stipulating a standard of quality in the contract specifications. A first-class job or a workmanlike manner is generally defined by the custom of the trade, and reference can be made to industry standards, such as voluntary codes, to define the standard of quality more specifically.

Illustrative Example

Government employees performed the inspection of a large government building in Washington, D.C., to find defects in construction. The specifications stated that a marble joint would be exactly 3/8 inch. The government inspectors interpreted this to require exactly 3/8 inch with no deviation and tolerances. The inspectors obtained a steel slug that had been ground within a 1/1000-inch tolerance to test the marble joints. The normal custom of the trade was to permit 1/8-inch tolerance in this marble size. The overinspection sharply interfered with the productivity of the contractor, which decreased from ten pieces per day being set by each crew to three pieces per day being set by each crew. A meeting with the authorized contracting officer for the government solved this problem and restored the normal custom-and-trade tolerances. The government would otherwise have faced a multimillion-dollar claim by the contractor.

Owners who cut corners will often incur more costs during construction by not having their design professionals perform inspections. Owner-hired nonprofessional inspectors tend to be more technical and more disruptive in their administration than design-professional inspectors. This is especially true of government-hired inspectors who have to justify their jobs by nitpicking and finding minor faults. Design-professional inspectors realize that there is a range of acceptable performance by contractors.

DEFINE THE RESPONSIBILITIES

Also important in minimizing claims is the working relationship of the owner, the design professional, and the contractor. Of critical importance is the pre-bid and preconstruction conference where all aspects of the project should be coordinated and all responsibilities delineated, divided, and reinforced. A list delineating the various areas of performance, such as planning, design, contract preparation, contract review and finalization, bidding and award, construction, coordination and administration of various programs, and post-construction activities, should be prepared.

The responsibility for coordination is then shifted to the contractor. If there is only one prime contractor, it has the responsibility for the overall coordination of its work and that of its subcontractors after commencement of construction. A survey of experienced superintendents or project managers would show that smooth coordination can make all the difference between a project that operates within budget and one with huge cost overruns.

Illustrative Example

A large national specialty contractor continually had problems with one or two large construction projects getting out of control each year and resulting in large cost overruns. These overruns caused massive million-dollar claims once or twice a year and severe cash-flow drains on the contractor. As a result, the contractor formed a corporate control group at the corporate-headquarters level to oversee initially the setup and start-up of all construction projects that were over $2 million. The contractor selectively picked a team consisting of its best superintendent, its best construction-cost engineer, its best labor and personnel coordinator, and its best construction administrator. This team had the responsibility to control and coordinate the commencement of major projects, while the branch offices continued to manage the construction projects as a whole. After the four-person team was formed, the contractor had virtually no large cost overruns.

If the owner is using multiple prime contractors, the owner retains the responsibility for coordinating the work on the project. However, too often the owner's attitude is that once all the contractors and subcontractors are on the project they will coordinate with one another, but it doesn't work that way. More likely such lack of coordination will lead to claims since the subcontractors and general contractors will probably have cost overruns. A miscoordinated project will be delayed and the owner may very well face claims for delay damages. To avoid these problems, the owner must make sure that the coordination responsibility is handled by someone. The owner may expressly delegate that responsibility to the design professional. In addition, it is important to maintain excellent communication between the general contractors and the subcontractors orally as well as by memos and to hold periodic meetings to provide for coordination and anticipation of problems and adverse trends that may occur.

An effective meeting might include a discussion of material problems encountered on the project, drawing problems, any claims that might arise or that have arisen since the last meeting, labor or union problems, an updated project schedule, any additional instructions from the owner or design professional, scheduling instructions, and any new or anticipated problems that need discussion in order to coordinate the project so it will run smoothly.

CHANGE PROCEDURES MUST BE PRACTICAL

Contractors, owners, and design professionals make critical mistakes by deferring negotiations on claims and disputed items until the end of the contract. It is to everyone's advantage to settle a dispute about a change before any work is performed to execute the change. It is to the owner's advantage to get the disputed item settled quickly so that the project can progress on schedule and so that the owner can ascertain before the work is performed exactly what the change is going to cost. The contractor definitely benefits from pricing a change before the work is performed because then it has greater control over costs and cash flow. The contract documents must therefore be written in such a way that it is practical to make changes.

Construction contracts are meant to be changed, and they are often meant to be changed unilaterally by the owner or the owner's design-professional representatives. For this reason, a change-order procedure must be built into the construction contract so that counter-performances can be easily determined. The change procedure should be reviewed not only for its protection of the owner but also for practicality.

One example of an impractical procedure is a provision requiring that all changes be approved in writing by a designated officer of the owner when that officer is not often readily available on the site. Some job-site authority should be given so that representatives of the owner can make the decisions that will enable the contractor to proceed efficiently with construction.

Illustrative Example

A large hospital in New England was being constructed by a state building authority. The change procedure required that every change order exceeding $500 be in writing and authorized by the head of the agency. However, the agency head was not often available, and the project required many changes that disrupted and stopped construction in certain areas for months while the crews awaited the official change-order paperwork. The direct labor of the contractors dramatically increased because of the disruptions and inability to maintain job momentum as the work had to be "hopscotched" around to avoid the areas where changes were pending. Completion of the building was delayed two years, and the contractor and subcontractors claimed massive claims that exceeded the original construction price of the building. The claims tied up the owner, contractor, and subcontractors for years in litigation.

Not only must there be a fair and practical procedure for making changes in the contract, but the parties must be psychologically committed at the preconstruction meeting to understanding and using the procedure. It is very important that the procedure be reviewed and reinforced by the job personnel of the owner, design professional, contractor, and subcontractors so that everyone understands the procedure and can handle changes routinely.

Construction contracts are often written to protect the owner. However, unrealistic, impractical contract-change provisions can actually be counterproductive to the owner. For example, it makes no sense to place on the contractor the responsibility to make a subsurface investigation that cannot be realistically done by the contractor as part of a pre-bid inspection. A provision that the contractor is responsible for any underground conditions encountered is not very practical for the owner because the contractor is going to estimate the job with substantially more costs for uncertain soil conditions than are probably going to be encountered. A practical approach for all parties would be to include a changed conditions clause in the contract that allows pricing flexibility if underground conditions are different from those indicated in the plans and specifications or if conditions turn out to be different from those generally encountered. A contract that attempts to shift all the responsibility onto the contractor while the owner is responsible for nothing will ultimately lead to claims.

The typical construction-contract change clause contains a requirement that the contractor give written notice of a change or extra work within a specified time. The failure of the contractor to give this written notice may bar the contractor from claiming additional compensation under the contract. The owner should not hesitate to require compliance with these requirements because they were formulated for the owner's protection. (See Chapter 9, "Managing Changes to the Contract.")

RECORD KEEPING

Keeping documentation merely as a means of defending against a claim may be very self-defeating; the key in preventing a claim is a system of documentation for the effective management of the project. If the owner maintains a system of documentation that keeps track of the trends and progress on the job, the owner will minimize the driving forces leading to claims and there will be enough documentation to protect against a claim should one arise. An effective system of documentation includes management records of all aspects of the project.

One of the most basic documentation needs is to keep track of the current plans and specifications. The owner, design professional, and contractor should each maintain a current and constantly updated set of plans and specifications. This should include a complete running account of approved and unapproved changes. Change orders should be processed routinely. Everyone should know which forms are to be filled out, collected, and submitted. They should be processed currently by the contractor and approved currently by the owner. Accumulation of unprocessed change orders necessarily leads to large and out-of-control construction problems, and therefore large and out-of-control claims.

The owner should also maintain a complete schedule of shop drawings including submission dates and approval dates. The contract should contemplate that both parties have timely responsibilities for the processing and approval of shop drawings. Owners should be aware that they must get the approvals back on time, and contractors should be aware that they must submit coordinated shop drawings well in advance in order to receive approvals back on time. Followups must be made immediately. Both parties should keep track of incoming and outgoing correspondence and of the replies that have been made.

Another of the most basic documentation needs is the maintenance of a project schedule. An accurate, updated project schedule will reflect not only the scheduling of the work on the project, but also will reflect the actual progress of the work and any changes affecting the schedule. Since there are a number of different scheduling techniques available, it is extremely important to select the method that is right for the particular project (see Chapter 10). Then if the schedule is systematically and accurately updated, it will provide an important management tool and a document to protect against claims.

Job-site records are vital in any claim situation. Of course, job-site personnel should keep logs of what was scheduled to be done, what was done and not done, what the weather was like, what changes were requested, and what interferences arose. What is important is to record in the job-site records what actually happened on the job. Progress photographs are also useful in many jobs and can be a valuable management aid in measuring and proving productivity as well as providing evidence in claims.

It is also extremely important for the owner and the contractor to keep each other informed about everything that is happening on the project. The owner should schedule frequent meetings during the course of construction. Minutes should be prepared after each meeting and sent to all of the parties. If none of the parties objects to the minutes, whatever is contained in them will provide evidence of the understanding and agreement of the parties.

Trend reports, sometimes called status reports, should inform the parties of the status of the project and of any adverse trends that appear to be developing. If the parties know early on that an adverse trend is likely to develop, management on both sides can take steps to minimize the impact; but if they are unaware of the problem until it has already developed, the impact may be overwhelming and result in cost overruns and claims. If the contractor is slipping behind, the owner should tell the contractor about the slippage in periodic reports. The contractor should also inform the owner of delay trends so that the owner will not be surprised and can plan for the possible delays. This is particularly important if there is going to be a late material or equipment delivery or if there is a necessary delay caused by the other party.

A management documentation system must be simple enough so that it can be effectively maintained and used by management and field personnel to supervise the progress of the job. It does not do any good to set up a complex system that is not going to be followed during the job. For example, it does not do any good to establish a complex critical-path schedule at the start of the job unless it is going to be constantly modified and updated throughout the job. A documentation system is only effective if it is used.

CLAIMS RECOGNITION

Although it is not possible to supply a comprehensive list, there are some recurring problems that typically result in claims by contractors. Owners and design professionals must be aware of their actions or omissions that may result in a valid claim by the contractor.

The first thing any owner must do in order to recognize a potential claim is to become familiar with the contract documents. Contract provisions typically define and explain the occurrences that will entitle a contractor to extra compensation.

Disruptions and delays caused by the owner or the owner's representative might include

- Delay in providing access to the site;
- Delay caused by the actions of the owner's separate contractors;
- Errors in plans and specifications;
- Delay in inspection or overinspection;
- Failure to approve shop drawings;
- Failure to make payments when required.

Other causes of delays are possible. Extensions of time may also be granted for actions that delay the project that are not the fault of the owner. (See Chapter 10, "Managing the Schedule.")

Once events that could lead to claims occur, both parties should immediately attempt to resolve the issues quickly. Deferring the resolution of a claim normally results in a larger claim down the road. In order to defend against a claim successfully, the owner must (1) recognize the claim; (2) confront it directly and immediately; and (3) respond one way or another to the claim. The owner of a construction project must have a workable procedure for handling claims. There must be a system ensuring that the claim is processed through all the proper channels and that all of the parties involved have recorded an opinion of the causes and the relationships among the events leading to the claim. The owner should get opinions from all of the experts involved in the various aspects of the project: design professionals, accountants, schedulers, on-site personnel, and, if it would prove helpful, an expert in analysis of construction claims.

When a claim arises, the owner should request that the contractor provide as much information as is available so that the claim can be resolved quickly. The owner should request that the contractor supply facts to establish the actions causing injury, to show that under the contract the contractor is entitled to additional compensation, and to prove the amount of additional compensation requested. The contractor should be informed that once both parties have equal access to the information and have become well educated as to the facts of the claim, the bargaining instead becomes mutual cooperation in settling the claim. When a contractor without a valid claim is pressed for information sufficient to prove the claim, it will probably back down at that point.

NEGOTIATION

The majority of claims can be settled by negotiation. Only if one of the parties is out of touch with contractual realities, is acting in bad faith, or has not been adequately informed will the claim have to go farther to administrative remedies, arbitration, or litigation. Many construction companies and owners never let a single claim get so out of control that it necessitates litigation. They are professionals in controlling their business, and they are the ones that have long-term survival.

Negotiating the resolution of a dispute has numerous benefits for all of the parties. Negotiation avoids delays in construction, enables the contractor to restore cash flow, provides reimbursement for the costs of performing changes, and avoids the adversary relationship that is so damaging to business relations. Negotiation also preserves reputations and preserves the dispute as a private matter that does not set a precedent for later claims. Even if negotiations fail, the discussions provide a good look at the other side's position and strategy for future litigation. A thorough negotiation attempt tends to prevent a surprise during the litigation phase.

The starting point for negotiation is for the owner to know its own objectives. The owner must have realistic objectives for the negotiations. Once these objectives have been formulated, it is possible to develop a negotiating strategy. Just as when the contractor decides the initial request for additional compensation, the owner must know the facts and be able to communicate those facts persuasively to the other side. There is no substitute for having a clear definition of your objectives and interests. Proceeding on an ill-defined theory will not convince the other side of the weakness of its claim.

A key in managing claims is trust. The construction process necessarily involves a continuing, trusting relationship between the parties from the pre-bid conference through the performance of the final punch list, and this is especially true in negotiation. As evidence of this trust, it is therefore important to avoid an adversary relationship in negotiations. A mutual spirit of cooperation and communication is necessary if the parties are to reach an agreement that is satisfactory to both. Both parties should realize that although they are in dispute, they should be able to disagree amicably, negotiate their differences, and emerge as a stronger cooperative team.

It should go without saying that a positive, objective attitude will achieve better results than one that puts the other side on the defensive. Unflattering and unprofessional emotionalism should be avoided in negotiations, as well as trying to embarrass the other side or cause them to lose face. When an objection is raised, the other party should try to understand the objection and negotiate its settlement rather than simply ignore it. With extremely negative opposition, it may well be necessary to become a politician and win over the person who is not voting for you. Tension and conflict are often unavoidable in negotiations, but how that tension and conflict are handled will differ depending on the parties' relationship and on the experience they bring to the negotiations.

It is also important to determine the other side's position and have some empathy with it. A negotiating position is always stronger if there is an understanding of the other party's interests and objectives in the dispute. Once each party's interests are established, it is much easier to reach common ground. The negotiating process can thus be used to meet both the needs of the contractor and the needs of the owner.

Perhaps one of the best techniques is to select issues on which the parties can agree right away and leave the difficult issues until last, or at least agree to the points not in dispute and so leave fewer issues to be settled by subsequent negotiations. Once both parties realize that they can reach an agreement, the way is paved for the more difficult issues.

One way to proceed is to ask questions during negotiations, rather than to confront the contractor with declaratory statements. Questions often lead the other side to discover the answers. However, it is important not to ask the final question — "What will you settle for?" — first. This merely polarizes positions and tends to make both parties defensive. The important thing is to ask questions that relate to the facts of the claim. Once the other side is committed to the basic facts, it is much easier to negotiate the actual claim. If the owner can establish a logical chain leading from the events that actually occurred to the claim, the contractor will have a difficult time denying the conclusion.

Setting deadlines for the settlement of claims is particularly important and requires the owner to establish a procedure for handling changes, establishing meetings, and insisting upon the deadlines. Of course, the owner must know when to make a concession and when to reach a settlement. Avoid giving concessions without receiving meaningful concessions or offers from the other side. Negotiation studies have shown that the party giving the first concession is normally the loser. And, of course, the party giving the largest concessions is certain to emerge the loser.

At some point one of the parties will inevitably consider litigation or arbitration, whichever is provided in the contract. Because the threat of power can be more powerful than the actual power, the threat of arbitration or litigation may be more powerful in bringing the other party to a settlement than actually going to arbitration or litigation. However, any desire of a party to pursue a claim through arbitration or litigation must be tempered by its high costs. Before proceeding, therefore, the owner must weigh this alternative against management objectives, costs, delays in construction, and the probable risks and results. In any case, there is no need for haste; there is time to litigate if all else fails.

To avoid such measures, the owner must realize at the outset that the negotiation business is basic human engineering. The goal is to make the other side want to settle, and that goal is reached by satisfying some of the needs of each party. There should be no winners and no losers; all of the parties should come away from the negotiation table thinking that a fair deal was struck and that no one really lost. In the final analysis, a fair settlement of a claim is far better than a good lawsuit.

13 CLAIMS BY OWNERS

Construction disputes between an owner and a contractor usually arise when the contractor claims additional expenses caused by delays, change orders, and extra work; but the owner may also suffer damages due to actions or omissions of the contractor. In order to avoid unnecessary problems, the owner should consider potential problem areas before drafting the contract. If a dispute does occur, however, the owner must know what claims, counterclaims, and defenses are available. The owner's effective use of these methods is a powerful tool in effectuating a settlement with the contractor, or in the event of actual litigation, in assessing liability and damages.

When negotiation and arbitration are not successful, the owner should be prepared to enforce the protections granted by the contract. If court action is necessary, the owner should assert all its legal rights and valid claims against the contractor in order to prove that the owner is not liable, to collect damages on a counterclaim, or to limit the amount of the contractor's recovery. Frequent sources of litigation between parties to construction contracts are those provisions dealing with change orders, design professionals' certificates, and the need for written notice. Interpretation and enforceability of liquidated damages and indemnity clauses have also been vigorously litigated.

There are really two aspects to "claims by owners." The first is to defeat any claims brought by a contractor against the owner. The second is the assertion of an affirmative claim against the contractor to recover for losses incurred. If a dispute should occur, the owner should be prepared to pursue both aspects of its claim. An old maxim states that "the best defense is a good offense," and it is true that the successful combination of a defense against a claim and the pursuit of an affirmative recovery will provide the owner with the best possible position in case of a dispute.

A common characteristic of the claims and defenses available to an owner is that if they are not provided for in the contract, they may not be available. The contract language controls the rights and duties of the parties to the contract. Careful thought and preparation by the owner must go into the drafting of the contract. Not only must the contract be drafted so that unnecessary problems are avoided, but also so that rights and liabilities are clearly delineated and defined.

Drafting and then checking the contract for legal pitfalls is the first and most important stage of avoiding a claim. A systematic definition of contract performance is vital in determining that both parties have met all the necessary requirements.

LIQUIDATED DAMAGES

Generally, it is in the best interest of the owner and general contractor to settle their differences amicably under the contract without having to resort to legal redress. Settlement is preferable because it avoids the costly delays of arbitration or litigation. One way of avoiding legal proceedings is through a contract provision stating the amount of damages that will be assessed in the event of a delay. A liquidated damages provision stipulates the amount that the contractor will pay in damages for every calendar day of delay for which the contractor is responsible. Owners normally use liquidated damages clauses in construction contracts to ensure that the contractor will complete performance on time. Both parties decide in advance the amount to be paid and thereby alleviate further dispute on the amount to be awarded. This is advantageous because the parties are familiar with the work and are better able to evaluate the appropriate amount than a court or arbiter unfamiliar with the particular circumstances involved.

Some jurisdictions hold that the liquidated damages clause applies to delays in completion of a project whether the contractor finishes the job or whether the contractor totally abandons performance of the contract and the owner must find another contractor to complete it.[1] Other jurisdictions hold that the liquidated damages clause applies only to delays in completion of the work and is void if the contractor totally abandons performance.

Illustrative Case

Six Companies of California brought suit against Joint Highway District No. 13 to recover the reasonable value of materials and labor furnished under a contract. Six Companies had attempted to rescind the contract on account of an alleged breach by Joint Highway District No. 13 and had stopped work. Joint Highway District No. 13 counterclaimed for damages resulting from Six Companies' alleged wrongful abandonment of the contract. The contract contained a liquidated damages clause in case of delay in completion. The district court found against the contractor and awarded $142,000 as liquidated damages to Joint Highway District No. 13.

The circuit court affirmed the decision. The Supreme Court reversed and remanded. The Court held that under the law of California the clause providing for liquidated dam-

[1]Southern Pacific Co. v. Goble Indemnity Co., 30 F.2d 580 (2d Cir. 1919); City of Reading v. Fidelity & Guaranty Corp., 19 F. Supp. 350 (E.D. Pa. 1937).

ages did not apply to delay that occurred after the abandonment of the work by the contractor and that liquidated damages should not have been applied.[2]

The owner cannot assess the contractor liquidated damages for delays that fall within the scope of an excusable delay clause. That is, if the contract contains a clause, such as article 8.3.1 of the AIA General Conditions (Document A201, 1976 ed.), excusing delays caused by the owner, formal change orders, labor disputes, fire, unusual delays in transportation, unanticipated adverse weather conditions, unavoidable casualties, or any causes beyond the contractor's control, the contractor will receive an extension of the contract time and will not be liable for liquidated damages.

If the contract does not contain an excusable delay clause, the contractor assumes the risk of delays that are the fault of neither the contractor nor the owner. If the delay is caused by the owner, most courts will not assess damages.[3] However, an increasingly large number of courts will allow damages to be apportioned when both parties are found to be at fault.

Illustrative Case

Butte-Meade Sanitary Water District contracted with J.F. Brunken and Sons, Inc., to complete two contracts. Aetna Casualty and Surety Co., the bonding agent for Brunken, brought an action to recover payments retained by Butte-Meade. Butte-Meade counterclaimed for liquidated damages for failure of Brunken to timely complete the project.

Butte-Meade claimed that completion of both contracts was delayed over 1000 days each and that various acts of Brunken and the surety caused the delay in completing the projects. Brunken alleged that a good portion of the delay was caused by the defendant's actions.

The court held that although both Brunken and Butte-Meade were at least in part responsible for delaying the completion of construction, apportionment of fault for delay would be made; the fact that the owner was partially at fault did not preclude Butte-Meade from recovering liquidated damages under the contract.[4]

Where the causes of the delay can be apportioned, the court is free to assess liquidated damages on this basis, unless the court finds that the contract would have been completed on time but for the delays caused by the party claiming liquidated damages.

The courts will generally refuse to enforce a liquidated damages provision where the effect is to enforce a penalty on the defaulting party. Some factors that have been used by the courts in determining whether or not a liquidated damages clause acts as a penalty are

(1) Was the clause valid when adopted?

[2]Six Co. v. Joint Highway Dist. No. 13, 311 U.S. 180 (1941).

[3]United States v. Kanter, 137 F.2d 828 (8th Cir. 1943).

[4]Aetna Casualty & Sur. Co. v. Butte-Meade Sanitary Water Dist., 500 F. Supp. 193 (D.S.D. 1980).

(2) Is the stipulated sum reasonable, and are actual damages difficult, if not impossible, to assess?

(3) Did the delayed performance actually cause harm to the owner?

(4) Do the circumstances of the delay nullify the clause (that is, was the delay due, at least in part, to the owner, or did the contractor abandon the contract)?

The applicable jurisdiction's interpretation of liquidated damages-clause requirements should be checked and followed. If the provision is found to be a penalty, the owner will be required to demonstrate the amount of actual damages incurred as a result of the contractor's delay. If the owner is successful in arguing that the provision is not a penalty, the right to liquidated damages will be upheld.

Illustrative Case

Bethlehem Steel Corporation brought suit against the City of Chicago to recover an amount that had been withheld as liquidated damages for delay in furnishing, erecting, and painting structural steel for a portion of a superhighway. Bethlehem was granted a total of 63 days' additional time within which to perform its contract. However, actual completion by Bethlehem was 52 days after the extended date. The city assessed $1000 per day ($52,000) for this period of delay. The court of appeals held that the parties were free to contract for the amount of damages to be assessed in case of delay and that since the extent of the loss resulting from the delay was uncertain, the liquidated damages provision was valid.[5]

Liquidated damages clauses are a useful weapon for the owner as they provide the contractor with an incentive to complete the contract on time. The owner may withhold payment until the contract is completed and wait for the contractor to file suit before deciding whether to arbitrate or litigate, to determine whether or not the assessment of liquidated damages was appropriate.

WARRANTIES

Most construction contracts provide for some guarantee of the work, and these contract provisions generally are valid and will be enforced by the courts. Construction contracts typically give the owner an express warranty of the quality of the materials used or the workmanship performed. In certain circumstances, warranties may be implied in the construction contract. A warranty clause distributes between the parties the risk of any defects that may arise in the work.

The risks that the contractor assumes may vary greatly according to the scope of the warranty clause. A typical warranty provision is found in paragraph 4.5 of the AIA General Conditions (Document A201, 1976 ed.):

---

[5]Bethlehem Steel Corp. v. City of Chicago, 350 F.2d 649 (7th Cir. 1965).

4.5   Warranty

4.5.1   The Contractor warrants to the Owner and the Architect that all materials and equipment furnished under this Contract will be new unless otherwise specified, and that

all work will be of good quality, free from faults and defects in conformance with the Contract Documents. All work not so conforming to these standards may be considered defective. If required by the Architect, the Contractor shall furnish satisfactory evidence as to the kind and quality of materials and equipment.

The AIA warranty provides a comprehensive guarantee of all labor, materials, and equipment incorporated into the construction.

Regardless of their scope, warranty provisions generally designate the time during which the warranty period will run. For example, construction contracts generally contain provisions that the contractor will repair any damages due to faulty work or materials within a period of one year following completion and final acceptance of the project by the owner. Subparagraph 13.2.2 of the AIA General Conditions (Document A201, 1976 ed.) provides:

If, within one year after the Date of Substantial Completion or within such longer period of time as may be prescribed by law . . . any of the Work is found to be defective or not in accordance with the Contract Documents, the Contractor shall correct it promptly after receipt of a written notice.

However, an express warranty to correct defects appearing within one year does not apply to defects that existed at the time of acceptance and that the owner should have discovered by a reasonable inspection. Final payment will generally operate as a final bar to all claims between the parties, except defects discovered within one year after acceptance.

Illustrative Case

Independent Consolidated School District No. 24 sued Carlstrom Construction Company for damages caused by defects in the construction work it had done on a school. The floors in the building began to settle five and a half years after Carlstrom had completed the project.

The Supreme Court of Minnesota held that the construction contract provision limiting liability for faulty workmanship to one year after completion and acceptance was reasonable and not against public policy. The court held that the action was barred by the contract provision and denied recovery.[6]

In most express warranty clauses the contractor guarantees the work only against defects and does not guarantee that the work will survive normal wear and tear for the duration of the warranty period. Some contracts provide for the maintenance of the work and guarantee that

[6]Independent Consol. School Dist. No. 24 v. Carlstrom Const. Co, 277 Minn. 117, 151 N.W.2d 784 (Minn. 1967).

the work will perform for the period of the warranty. However, the cost of assuming the risk of wear and tear should be included in the contract price.

The owner need only demonstrate the existence of a defect in materials or workmanship to establish a claim under an express warranty. The owner must follow the notice requirements of the contract and give the contractor sufficient notice of the defect. The owner must also give the contractor a chance to correct the defect before instituting a suit. Then, if the owner gives the contractor prompt notice of the discovery of the defect, the owner will have the normal period of the statute of limitations allowed for any breach-of-contract action in which to bring suit.

IMPLIED WARRANTIES

The contractor must not only comply with the express warranties contained in the contract, but it will also be liable for warranties *implied* by law. Implied warranties may have a greater scope and a longer duration than express warranties. It is an implied warranty in all construction contracts that the general contractor is required to perform the work in a careful and workmanlike manner.[7] Disputes concerning implied warranties of workmanlike performance generally arise in cases where the contract involved does not contain an indemnity provision.

The law requires that the contractor must exercise the ordinary care and skill of its particular trade in performance of the contract. The owner has a right to insist upon precise performance of the contract, and the contractor is not justified in deviating from the precise execution of the terms of the contract. When the contractor makes a promise to perform under the contract, the contractor implies that the work will be done with skill conforming to industry standards.

Illustrative Case

National Fire Insurance Company of Hartford, a subrogated fire insurer, brought an action against Westgate Construction Company for the alleged negligence of an independent contractor that built a fireplace in Mr. and Mrs. Jamieson's home. Shortly after the Jamiesons moved into their home, it caught fire around the rear of the fireplace and was seriously damaged. National paid the loss and brought an action as a subrogee.

The district court held that under Delaware law, Westgate Construction had a nondelegable duty to do work in a careful and workmanlike manner and could be held liable in tort for the alleged negligence of Antonini, the independent contractor that built the fireplace. The court reasoned that it would be indefensible to permit Westgate to shrug off its contractual duties by shifting the blame to the independent contractor.[8]

[7]17A C.J.S. CONTRACTS § 329 (1963) at 293.

[8]National Fire Ins. Co. v. Westgate Constr. Co., 227 F. Supp. 835 (E.D. Ky. 1964).

The owner must be extremely careful not to waive any of its rights pursuant to implied warranties. If the owner inspects the work or has a reasonable opportunity to inspect the work, it is deemed to waive the right to complain about any patent defects that should have been discoverable upon a reasonable inspection.[9] However, the owner does not waive any rights with respect to latent defects that could not have been discovered upon an inspection.[10]

Notwithstanding the time limitation on express warranties, implied warranties are subject only to the statute of limitations. The AIA General Conditions do not prevent the owner from recovering against the contractor beyond one year if the contractor did not comply with the plans and specifications. That is because compliance with the plans and specifications is part of a warranty implied by law.

DISCLAIMERS

The law allows parties to decide who will bear the risks of defects in construction. An owner may agree to allow a contractor to disclaim implied warranties. The Uniform Commercial Code (U.C.C.) has established specific requirements for disclaimers of warranties to ensure an element of fairness. The U.C.C. requires that an effective disclaimer of an implied warranty of fitness be conspicuous, in writing, and mention the word *merchantability* in order to be enforced. Such limitation of liability may also preclude recovery for losses resulting from negligence.[11]

However, since construction contractors furnish services as well as goods to the owner, their contracts do not fall strictly within the U.C.C. The courts of some states have taken the precedents and theories of the U.C.C. and applied them to the construction contract situation. Other states have explicitly rejected application of the U.C.C. to construction contracts.[12] Those states giving the U.C.C. precedential weight have allowed disclaimers by contractors if certain requirements are followed. It is a sound policy for parties to follow the U.C.C. requirements even if the project is in a state that has not applied the U.C.C. to construction contracts.

The presence or absence of a disclaimer of implied warranties may have a significant effect on the time within which the owner may bring suit against the contractor for a defect in the work. If implied warranties are excluded, the owner may bring suit against the contractor only for those defects appearing during the one-year period specified by the express warranty. The state statutes of limitations that control suits based on implied warranties are typically from four to eight years.

[9]Barnard v. Kellogg, 77 U.S. 383 (1870).

[10]Langley v. Helms, 12 N.C. App. 620, 184 S.E.2d 393 (1971).

[11]Southwest Forest Indus., Inc. v. Westinghouse Elec. Corp., 422 F.2d 1013 (9th Cir. 1970).

[12]Tison v. Eskew, 114 Ga. App. 550, 151 S.E.2d 901 (1966).

When the owner inspects the contractor's work or has a reasonable opportunity to inspect and accepts the contract as completed, the owner may be precluded from suing the contractor for patent defects that should have been discovered. The owner is considered to have actual or imputed knowledge of these defects, and final payment by the owner will constitute a waiver of its claim against the contractor for defective performance. However, unless the right to sue the contractor for defective performance is reserved, the owner may not be prevented from holding its surety responsible for damages due to latent defects unknown to either party. Moreover, acceptance of payment does not operate as a waiver of the owner's remedy under implied warranties with respect to latent defects in the work. Final payment is not deemed to be acceptance of defects in the work; but some courts have held that final payment acts as a waiver for claims of defects if the owner has actual knowledge of the condition.

Illustrative Case

Elliott Consolidated School District sued John G. Busbroom, a general contractor, and his surety for defects found in a roof constructed by Nebraska Sheet Metal Contractors, Inc. The school district alleged it was required to replace the roof at a cost of $15,000. The district court held that where the contract provided that payment or certificate was *not* acceptance of defects in workmanship or of failure to comply with the plans and specifications, the school district was entitled to recover.[13]

Prior to 1973 a builder generally made no implied warranty against latent defects in materials used in construction nor was the builder held responsible for latent defects in the materials when acting in good faith and exercising reasonable care and skill. A builder was always held to be liable, however, upon any express warranty of fitness contained in the contract.

Illustrative Case

Wood-Hopkins Construction Company was the general contractor for the construction of an apartment building in Atlanta, Georgia. Wood-Hopkins entered into a contract with Masonry Contractors, Inc., by which Masonry Contractors agreed to furnish all necessary labor and materials for the construction of the building. Masonry Contractors was required to follow the plans and specifications, which called for the use of Miami Stone brick. After the masonry work was substantially completed, it was discovered that because of a latent defect in the Miami Stone brick, Masonry Contractors was required to waterproof the exterior walls of the building to correct the defect. Wood-Hopkins withheld $12,255, the cost of waterproofing the walls, from the final payment due Masonry. The district court held that Masonry was not liable for latent defects since it had purchased and installed the brick according to Wood-Hopkins specifications. The court found that the defect was not discernible, was not known to Masonry, and was not the fault of Masonry, and that Masonry should not be liable for the cost of correction.[14]

---

[13]Elliott Consol. School Dist. v. Busbroom, 227 F. Supp. 858 (S.D. Iowa, 1964).

[14]Wood-Hopkins Contracting Co. v. Masonry Contractors, Inc., 235 So. 2d 548 (Fla. App. 1970).

One jurisdiction has held that the contractor is liable for latent defects upon an implied warranty-of-fitness theory.[15] The builder cannot base its defense on a latent defect.

Illustrative Case

The owners of a new house, Mr. and Mrs. Frank Smith, brought an action against the builder, Old Warson Development Company, to recover for damage caused by allegedly abnormal settling of the concrete slab on which part of their house rested. There was no dispute that the slab settled or sank and resulted in cracks in the walls and space between the baseboard and floor. The Smiths claimed that the settling of the slab was due to improper and unworkmanlike compaction of the soil under the slab. Old Warson Development Company contended that no implied warranty exists in the sale of real estate, and that if it did, the sales contract expressly excluded such a warranty.

The Supreme Court of Missouri, en banc, found that no determination of the defect could have been made by the Smiths without ripping out the slab that settled, and that since the house was a newly manufactured "product" and purchased from the company that built it, the lower court had erred in granting Old Warson's motion for summary judgment. The court stated that purchasers of new homes are desirous of the same protection as "purchasers of a new car, or a gas stove, or a sump pump, or a ladder."[16]

NEGLIGENCE

An owner may be able to sue the contractor in tort as well as for breach of contract for defective performance. There is implied in every contract for work or services a duty on the part of the contractor to perform work skillfully, carefully, diligently, and in a workmanlike manner. The contractor's negligence in failing to observe any of these conditions is a tort. Generally, the contractor is held to a standard of ordinary care and skill and will not be held liable for latent defects unknown and not reasonably discoverable.[17] Some courts have ignored latency and knowledge and instead base the contractor's liability upon negligence. The vendor's or manufacturer's knowledge of a defect is not required where recovery is sought under implied warranty or strict liability.[18]

Illustrative Case

The school district of Mountain View, Oklahoma, entered into two contracts, one for the construction of a school building and one for the installation of a heating and ventilating system. Lisle had a contract for the construction of the building and was required to furnish all material to do the work, except that it was not responsible for the installation of the heating and ventilation system. Lewis & Kitchens had the contract to install the heating and ventilating system.

After Lisle had finished its work in the attic but before it had fully completed the build-

[15]Clark v. Campbell, 492 S.W.2d 7 (Mo. App. 1973).

[16]Smith v. Old Warson Dev. Co., 479 S.W.2d 795 (Mo. 1972).

[17]See Wood-Hopkins Contracting Co. v. Masonry Contractors, Inc., 235 So. 2d 548 (Fla. App. 1970).

[18]Keener v. Dayton Elec. Mfg. Co., 445 S.W.2d 362 (Mo. 1969).

ing, Lewis & Kitchens placed part of the heating system upon joists placed by the defendants. One of the joists broke and one of the workers was injured. The Supreme Court of Oklahoma stated that "one engaged in construction of a building certainly owes to another engaged in the same work and exercising due care for his own safety the duty of exercising care to do his work in such a way as not to negligently injure the other." The court held that in the instant case, Lisle was aware that the joists were to be used to support heating and ventilating equipment and violated the duty it owed to Lewis & Kitchens to exercise ordinary care in the selection of the bolts. The court affirmed the lower court's award of $3000 to Lewis & Kitchens.[19]

If the construction contractor enters into a contract with the owner for construction of a building, there may arise a cause of action in tort for negligent construction.[20] A subcontractor may also be liable to an owner for negligence even though there is no contract between the two parties. A contractor is liable for negligence causing injury or damage during performance of the contract. The modern trend is to hold a building contractor liable for injuries to third persons arising from negligent construction even though such injuries occur after completion of the work and acceptance by the owner. A contractor is therefore held to the standard of reasonable care for the protection of anyone who may foreseeably be endangered by negligence "even after acceptance of the work."[21] Damages due to faulty construction are available whether the negligence results in personal injury or property damage. The courts have held that, as between the owner (purchaser) and the builder, it is more equitable that the builder bear the loss resulting from negligent construction in a case of a latent defect.

Illustrative Case

Mr. and Mrs. Richard C. Fisher brought an action against Mr. and Mrs. Donald E. Simon to recover damages incurred in repairing the basement floor of their house. The Fishers' claim was based on two causes of action, negligence and implied warranty. The Fishers asserted that within one year after purchasing the house from the Simons, the basement floor cracked because of the Simons' negligent construction.

The circuit court overruled a demurrer to the Fishers' cause of action based on negligence, and the Simons appealed. The Supreme Court of Wisconsin held that the Smiths, who had constructed the house, could be held liable for the cost of repairing the allegedly latent defects that were the result of negligent construction, even though the purchasers had accepted the premises.[22]

The responsibility for damages resulting from product failure is often difficult to ascertain. Building-failure claims by owners are very complicated because the contractor will generally blame the design professional for defective design, and the design professional will in turn

[19]Lisle v. Anderson, 159 P. 278 (Okla. 1916).
[20]Colton v. Foulkes, 259 Wis. 142, 47 N.W.2d 901 (1951).
[21]See PROSSER ON TORTS, § 99, at 695 (1964).
[22]Fisher v. Simon, 15 Wis.2d 207, 112 N.W.2d 705 (1961).

blame the contractor for defective performance or defective materials. In some circumstances, the owner cannot sue both parties in one action. The owner may be unable to sue one party because of disclaimer provisions or provisions limiting a party's rights or remedies. The owner may consequently find itself caught in a triangle where sole responsibility cannot be determined. To avoid intricate suits involving interventions and third-party practice, the owner may choose to sue only one party. Careful consideration should be made as to the jurisdiction of the court to hear the case and the privity of contract between the owner and the party being sued. Most important, the owner must be able to prove a causal connection between the alleged liability of the party and the resulting damages.

RIGHT TO TERMINATE

Construction contracts often contain provisions that authorize the owner to terminate the performance of the contractor and take over the completion of the work using the contractor's materials. Under these provisions, the owner is generally required to obtain a certificate from the design professional stating that termination is justified, and the owner must give the contractor and its surety written notice of intention to terminate. Subparagraph 14.2.1 of the AIA General Conditions (Document A201, 1976 ed.) permits the owner to terminate the contractor's employment upon the occurrence of certain events. Subparagraph 14.2.1 provides:

If the Contractor is adjudged a bankrupt..., or if he persistently or repeatedly refuses or fails, except in cases for which extension of time is provided, to supply enough properly skilled workmen or proper materials, or if he fails to make prompt payment to Subcontractors or for materials or labor, or persistently disregards laws, ordinances, rules, regulations or orders of any public authority having jurisdiction, or otherwise is guilty of a substantial violation of a provision of the Contract Documents, then the Owner, upon certification by the Architect that sufficient cause exists to justify such action, may, without prejudice to any right or remedy and after giving the Contractor and his surety, if any, seven days' written notice, terminate the employment of the Contractor and take possession of the site and of all materials, equipment, tools, construction equipment and machinery thereon owned by the Contractor and may finish the Work by whatever method he may deem expedient. In such case the Contractor shall not be entitled to receive any further payment until the Work is finished.

Termination of the contractor by the owner for breach of contract is a drastic remedy. Therefore, the owner must establish that the contractor's breach is so material or fundamental that it goes to the "heart" of the contract. For example, a delay in completing the project is not in itself considered a substantial breach unless the contract contains a provision that "time is of the essence." If the contract contains such a provision, then whatever the reason the contractor cannot perform, the owner will usually have the option of terminating the contract or attempting to hold the contractor to continued performance and compliance with the contract requirements.

The owner must weigh all factors before electing termination, and it should only be used as a last resort. Consideration must be given to the difficulty, time, and expense involved in substituting another contractor. The exercise by the owner of the right to terminate employment dissolves the contractual relationship completely and should only be exercised when the breach is material and the economic factors demand it. The owner is normally better off attempting to obtain continued compliance, since it will normally cost the owner more to finish the job with another contractor, and the owner normally cannot obtain full compensation from the contractor or its surety.

If the contractor defaults or wrongfully abandons the project, the owner may recover whatever damages were reasonably contemplated by the parties at the time of contracting.

For a breach by the contractor, there are basically two alternative theories of recovery by the owner, the "result-of-cost rule" and the "diminution-in-value rule."[23] Assuming the contractor is at fault, some courts would hold that the owner is entitled to deduct from the amount due the contractor the amount it would have cost the owner to complete the work properly (result-of-cost rule). Other courts hold that the proper measure of recovery is the difference between the value of the structure left by the contractor and the value if completed according to the requirements of the contract (diminution-in-value rule).

As a general rule, when there has been substantial performance or when a particular defect can be remedied at a reasonable expense, the cost rule is applied. The diminution-in-value rule is generally utilized if it would be unjust to allow the owner to retain the benefits of the contractor's performance without paying for them and the defects cannot be remedied practically.

Illustrative Cases

Lee & Brothers built a house for Mrs. Small. Lee & Brothers did not fully comply with the plans and specifications, and ended up with rooms of smaller dimensions than planned. Mrs. Small refused to pay for the work. Lee & Brothers brought suit against Mrs. Small to collect the balance due on its contract.

The court concluded that application of the rule allowing the owner to demand compliance with the plans and specifications before payment would be unjust "where there has been substantial compliance of the contractor with the terms of the contract and the house as built was practically suited to its intended use, there being only a slight deviation in finishing the house . . . and the owner receives and retains the house, and gets the benefits of the labor and materials of the contractor." Thus, the court held that Lee & Brothers could recover the contract price less the damages on account of such defect.[24]

[23]RESTATEMENT (FIRST) OF CONTRACTS § 346 (1932).

[24]Small v. Lee & Bros., 4 Ga. App. 395, 61 S.E. 831 (1908).

Trainor Company conveyed property to Copley Homes, Inc., to carry out construction of a number of houses. On the date of completion, Copley had finished twenty-four of the fifty-two houses contemplated by the contract. The remaining twenty-eight houses were not considered complete under the requirements of the plans and specifications. Trainor Company elected not to complete the project but rather to sue for money damages. The project was ultimately completed by Sun Mortgage Company, holder of the first mortgage. The district court held that the damages recoverable by Trainor for breach of the building contract was the "difference between the value of the uncompleted buildings at the time of the breach and value, if completed, sufficient to bring mortgage up to face value."[25]

The contractor orally agreed to furnish labor and materials to build two porches, raise the garage, and build a cement floor at the owner's home. The garage floor sloped, and the owner refused to pay the contractor the balance due on the contract. The contractor had used poured concrete, although the plans and specifications had called for cement blocks. The court, applying the result-of-cost rule, held that the contractor's claim must be reduced for these defects and for the cost of replacing the foundation with poured concrete.[26]

B. L. Dollar Company brought an action against Mr. and Mrs. Kizziar to recover amounts due on its contract to construct a building. The lower court found that the air conditioning system installed by Dollar was inadequate to cool the building properly. The court of appeals held that Dollar was entitled to additional costs to provide a central system sufficient to heat and cool the building, not only the additional cost of installing window air conditioners to overcome the deficiency.[27]

The owner would normally prefer the result-of-cost rule because it gives the owner the benefit of its contract. But under certain circumstances, if the contractor can show that the cost rule would create unnecessary economic waste, as where the cost of completion or reconstruction is grossly excessive and disproportionate, the owner's measure of recovery will be based on the diminution-in-value rule.

CALCULATION OF DAMAGES

Where the owner is injured, it should be able to recover fully for its losses. While owner claims are relatively few in number compared to claims by contractors, the owner should be aware of the amount and extent of damages that are recoverable on counterclaims. Section 331 of the RESTATEMENT OF CONTRACTS (1932) sets forth the following rules:

(1) Damages are recoverable for losses caused or for profits and other gains prevented by the breach only to the extent that the evidence affords a sufficient basis for estimating their amount in money, with reasonable certainty.

(2) Where the evidence does not afford a sufficient basis for a direct estimation of profits, but the breach is one that prevents the use and operation of the property from which

[25]Trainor Co. v. Aetna Cas. & Sur. Co., 49 F.2d 769 (E.D. Pa. 1931).

[26]Huffman v. Hill, 245 Iowa 935, 65 N.W.2d 205 (1954).

[27]Kizziar v. B.L. Dollar Co., 268 F.2d 914 (10th Cir.), cert. denied, 361 U.S. 914 (1959).

profits would have been made, damages may be measured by the rental value of the property or by interest on the value of the property.

The following calculations should be made by the owner to measure the amount of damages to be assessed against the contractor for delays, defective performance, breach, abandonment, and claims.

(1) *Liquidated Damages*
   Daily rate assessed for delays:
   days of delay × daily rate = claim

(2) *Actual Delay Damages*
   If no applicable liquidated damages clause, the following costs may be recoverable by the owner:
   (a) Loss of rental
   (b) Financing costs
   (c) Overhead
   (d) Labor wages and supervision-personnel salaries
   (e) Special damages (if contemplated by the parties at time of contracting)

(3) *Defective Performance*
   (a) Cost of completion—difference between adjusted contract price and actual cost for repair or replacement incurred in completing the project
   (b) Diminution in value

(4) *Breach and Abandonment*
   (a) Cost of completion
   (b) Consequential damages

(5) *Special Damages*

(6) *Miscellaneous*
   (a) Interest
   (b) Professional fees (attorney's and expert's fees) generally not recoverable

INDEMNIFICATION

Normally, the owner has two options in contracting with a contractor with respect to the allocation of the risk of loss. First, the owner can transfer responsibility for the construction project to the contractor. The general contractor will then be required to acquire the necessary insurance coverage to protect against loss. The general contractor will assume the risk of damage to the building as well as all possible legal contingencies (that is, injury to the public). Second, the owner may choose to retain full responsibility for the risk of loss and reflect this obligation in the contract price.

Assuming the owner prefers to transfer the risk of loss to the contractor, the owner can seek damages from the contractor for indemnification if the contractor performs improperly. Construction contracts typically require that the contractor indemnify and hold harmless the owner against all claims, damages, losses, and expenses arising out of performance of the project. Paragraph 4.18 of the AIA General Conditions (Document A201, 1976 ed.) reads as follows:

4.18   Indemnification

4.18.1   To the fullest extent permitted by law, the Contractor shall indemnify and hold harmless the Owner and the Architect and their agents and employees from and against all claims, damages, losses and expenses, including but not limited to attorneys' fees, arising out of or resulting from the performance of the Work, provided that any such claim, damage, loss or expense (1) is attributable to bodily injury, sickness, disease, or death, or to injury to or destruction of tangible property (other than the Work itself) including the loss of use resulting therefrom, and (2) is caused in whole or in part by any negligent act or omission of the Contractor, any Subcontractor, anyone directly or indirectly employed by any of them or anyone for whose acts any of them may be liable, regardless of whether or not it is caused in part by a party indemnified hereunder. Such obligation shall not be construed to negate, abridge, or otherwise reduce any other right or obligation of indemnity which would otherwise exist as to any party or person described in this Paragraph 4.18.

4.18.2 In any and all claims against the Owner or the Architect or any of their agents or employees by any employee of the Contractor, any Subcontractor, anyone directly or indirectly employed by any of them or anyone for whose acts any of them may be liable, the indemnification obligation under this Paragraph 4.18 shall not be limited in any way by any limitation on the amount or type of damages, compensation or benefits payable by or for the Contractor or any Subcontractor under workers' or workmen's compensation acts, disability benefit acts or other employee benefit acts.

4.18.3 The obligations of the Contractor under this Paragraph 4.18 shall not extend to the liability of the Architect, his agents or employees, arising out of (1) the preparation or approval of maps, drawings, opinions, reports, surveys, change orders, designs or specifications, or (2) the giving of or the failure to give directions or instructions by the Architect, his agents or employees providing such giving or failure to give is the primary cause of the injury or damage.

Although hold harmless clauses are far from uniform and difficult to classify precisely, they do seem to fall within three general categories. The first type, a limited-form hold harmless clause, covers indemnification of the contractor's own negligence. Under such a clause the contractor is bound to cover the costs of defending any claims and paying any judgments against the owner arising solely from negligent acts or omissions of the contractor. A second type of clause is the intermediate form, which provides that the contractor must indemnify the owner for damages arising from the joint negligence of the contractor and owner. The contractor is bound to cover the costs of a claim whenever the owner is chargeable with any portion of the negligence that led to the injury. Only if the injury is solely due to the negligence of the owner is the contractor relieved of financial responsibility. The hold harmless clause contained in AIA Document A201 (1976 ed.) is an intermediate-form hold harmless clause. The third type is a broad-form indemnification under which the contractor agrees to indemnify the owner even when the owner is solely responsible for the loss. The contractor must bear the entire burden of all claims arising out of the work.

Generally, express agreements limiting damages recoverable for breach of contact are valid, and courts see no harm in the parties' limiting the damages to be recoverable for breach of contract.[28] Exceptions, however, are allowed for contracts of the adhesion type, in which the bargaining power of one party is extremely restricted to the point that the limitation becomes unconscionable. The courts have found this rule particularly applicable when an owner attempts to force a broad-form hold harmless clause on a contractor. Many states have laws invalidating broad-form hold harmless clauses in the construction industry because they are considered unconscionable. The owner's safest course is to provide either a limited-form or an intermediate-form hold harmless clause in the contract so that the courts do not entirely invalidate all hold harmless rights of the owner.

[28] *See* 5 CORBIN ON CONTRACTS, § 1068, at 386 (1960).

174 CONSTRUCTION LAW FOR OWNERS AND BUILDERS

14 CLAIMS AGAINST DESIGN PROFESSIONALS

Design professionals participate in every phase of the work on most construction projects, from the initial planning and design to the certification that the work has been completed and the contractor should be paid. Architects and engineers assume a wide range of responsibilities that establish their potential liability to the many parties involved in a project.

The design professional usually becomes involved in a project via a contract with the owner that expressly defines the role of the design professional in the project. The contract may also create implied duties for the design professional with responsibility to parties other than the owner. Furthermore, the design professional accepts a duty to perform according to a professional standard, so that a breach of that duty may give rise to a claim against the design professional. Claims may be based on the contract or they may be tort claims based on negligence. Since the measure of damages allowed by the courts, as well as the time within which a claim must be brought (statute of limitations), will differ depending on whether relief is granted on the basis of the contract or on negligence, the claimant should always consider the type of claims available to determine the manner in which the court is likely to handle the dispute.

The services of architects and engineers are interrelated and overlapping, so it is often difficult to characterize any activity as exclusively within the domain of one or the other. Although delineating the responsibilities of design professionals may be quite complex, the purpose of this chapter is to point out the general varieties of claims that might be made against design professionals and the extent of their potential liability.

CLAIMS BY OWNERS

The relationship between the owner and the design professional is both contractual and fiduciary. The owner contracts with the design professional at the outset of the project for the benefit of the design professional's skills and experience. For a fee, the design professional promises to work in the owner's best interest as its representative in dealing with the other parties involved in the project and as an advisor and consultant to the owner.

Usually, the owner has only an image of the project in mind. The design professional is charged with transferring that image into reality. The result may nonetheless conflict with the owner's expectations for the project or its cost. When that occurs, the courts may award the owner damages measured by the amount of out-of-pocket expenses incurred by the owner as a result of the design professional's defective performance. Underestimation, defective plans, improper certification, and incompetent supervision are among the most common reasons for owner claims against design professionals.

Underestimated Cost of Construction

At the outset, the owner seldom has any more than a vague idea of the probable cost of the project. The design professional is engaged to provide initial consultation with the owner as to the owner's needs and how they can be satisfied within its budget. This leads to the drawing of schematic design documents and, after owner approval, detailed drawings, plans, and specifications.

When the terms of the contract between the owner and the design professional do not specify a fixed maximum cost of construction and a project budget, or require the design professional to submit project cost estimates, the majority of courts have held that the design professional has no duty to offer an estimate of cost to the owner.[1] However, when the owner is trying to keep within a budget, it is incumbent upon the design professional to strive for accuracy when submitting estimates of the probable cost of construction. An accurate estimate is often considered a professional duty that the owner bargains for when hiring a design professional. Breach of that duty may give rise to a claim for breach of contract by the owner.

Illustrative Case

Edward Malo, an architect, verbally agreed with Arnold Gilman, the owner, that construction costs for Gilman's building could be kept below $20 per square foot. They later included this provision in their contract, which stated that the estimated project cost would be $70,000. When the lowest bid submitted was $105,000. Gilman abandoned the project and sold the land.

Malo sued for payment of his fee ($9132.60), while Gilman counterclaimed for the return of $500 already paid as fees to the architect. The court found that the conduct of the parties evidenced an expected maximum cost for the project and that Malo breached

[1]Baylor Univ. v. Carlander, 316 S.W.2d 277 (Tex. Civ. App. 1958). *See also* Moore v. Bolton, 480 S.W.2d 805 (Tex. Civ. App. 1972).

the contract when he designed a building that could not be built within Gilman's budget. Gilman was awarded the $500.[2]

The AIA Standard Form of Agreement Between Owner and Architect (Document B141, 1977 ed.) provides that the design professional submit statements of probable construction cost but also that the design professional need not warrant the accuracy of the estimates. The courts have sometimes found that the exculpatory clause protects the design professional by guaranteeing payment by the owner even when the lowest bid on the project is substantially higher than the design professional's estimate. Payment may even be required when bids on the project are so high that the owner must actually abandon the project. The relevant AIA clause, subparagraph 3.2.1, states:

Evaluation of the Owner's Project budget, Statements of Probable Construction Cost and Detailed Estimates of Construction Cost, if any, prepared by the Architect, present the Architect's best judgment as a design professional familiar with the construction industry. It is recognized, however, that neither the Architect nor the Owner has control over the cost of labor, materials or equipment, over the Contractor's methods of determining bid prices, or over competitive bidding, market or negotiating conditions. Accordingly, the Architect cannot and does not warrant or represent that bids or negotiated prices will not vary from the Project budget proposed, established or approved by the Owner, if any, or from any Statement of Probable Construction Cost or other cost estimate or evaluation prepared by the Architect.

The AIA agreement further provides that if the parties want to establish a fixed limit of construction costs, it must be established in writing. The incorporation of this additional clause in the contract prevents the parties from introducing evidence of oral agreements placing budgetary constraints on the project. Subparagraph 3.2.2 states:

No fixed limit of Construction Cost shall be established as a condition of this Agreement by the furnishing, proposal or establishment of a Project budget under Subparagraph 1.1.2 or Paragraph 2.2 or otherwise, unless such fixed limit has been agreed upon in writing and signed by the parties hereto. If such a fixed limit has been established, the Architect shall be permitted to include contingencies for design, bidding and price escalation, to determine what materials, equipment, component systems and types of construction are to be included in the Contract Documents, to make reasonable adjustments in the scope of the Project and to include in the Contract Documents alternate bids to adjust the Construction Cost to the fixed limit. Any such fixed limit shall be increased in the amount of any increase in the Contract Sum occurring after execution of the Contract for Construction.

If the project designed by the design professional will cost more than the fixed limit (as evidenced by the bids received for construction of the building), the owner may approve the increase or authorize rebidding on the project. Alternatively, the owner may allow the design profes-

[2]Malo v. Gilman, 379 N.E.2d 554 (Ind. 1978).

sional to modify the design to bring it within the fixed cost limit. (AIA Owner-Architect Agreement, subparagraph 3.2.4.) If the owner abandons the project before allowing the design professional the opportunity to correct the design, the AIA contract specifies that in the event of such termination, the owner must still pay the design fee. However, if the design professional is unsuccessful in redesigning the project so that costs are within the previously agreed-upon fixed limit, the owner may abandon the project without paying the design fee. When the design professional succeeds at modifying the project so that it falls within the fixed limit, the owner must pay the design fee even if the owner subsequently abandons the project.

As stated earlier, the AIA Owner-Architect Agreement in its present form prevents a claim by the owner for underestimation unless the owner and the design professional expressly agree to a fixed limit in writing. The standard by which the accuracy of the design professional's estimate is gauged is the same as at common law. Historically, courts have held the design professional to at least a standard of substantial accuracy in estimating cost where there is an agreed maximum. In addition, at common law the agreed maximum may be an oral agreement and need not be written to create a duty for the design professional. Since, as a practical matter, most owners instruct design professionals on budget, it is likely that owner claims (demanding refund of fees or refusing to pay fees) caused by unreasonable estimates will be upheld where the building designed by the design professional is impossible to build within the owner's budget. However, it is in the owner's best interest to have the design professional agree to any budgetary constraints in writing.

Illustrative Case

Aesculapius Corp., a group of doctors, hired Griswold, an architect, to design additions to their clinic to accommodate more doctors. The contract documents prepared by Griswold established a project budget of approximately $300,000. Later, the owner requested an enlargement of many of the proposed additions. The architect altered the design in compliance, and the lowest bid on the new building was $413,037. Griswold then determined what modifications could be made to bring the project within the original $300,000 budget. Aesculapius abandoned the project and claimed Griswold owed the return of over $12,000 in prepaid fees.

The court denied Aesculapius's claim, finding that the excess cost was due to changes requested by the owner, and that the architect had made reasonable proposals to bring the building within budget. The court also noted that the contract documents did not characterize the $300,000 as a guaranteed fixed limit.[3]

The design professional will only be held to a duty to provide accurate estimates if there is some agreement, either written or oral, that stipu-

---

[3]Griswold & Rauma, Architects, Inc. v. Aesculapius Corp., 301 Minn. 121, 221 N.W.2d 556 (1974).

lates the owner's budget. Where an oral agreement contradicts a contract provision requiring a written agreement, most courts will follow the parol evidence rule and discount the oral agreement. For example, an oral agreement as to maximum cost would normally not be binding on a design professional if the design contract contained the AIA provision requiring fixed limits on contract cost to be established in writing. Design professionals' attorneys should be aware, however, that the parol evidence rule is in disrepute in some jurisdictions, and that the design professional may have to show that the AIA clause and other similar exculpatory clauses are not merely boilerplate, but rather represent a meaningful agreement between the parties. A showing that the oral understanding was not a guarantee, but rather a mere estimate, will tend to protect the design professional.

The rationale that allows the owner not to pay the design professional's fee in cases such as those previously discussed is simply that the plans designed by the design professional are of no use to the owner if the project is unaffordable; in other words, having derived no benefit, the owner should be brought back to a precontract position. However, if the design professional can show that it would be impossible to build the project within the owner's budget, the design professional may be compensated for the reasonable value of the service rendered to the owner (quantum meruit), since the owner has derived benefit by learning that it is impossible to construct the project within the budget. This would also dispose of a claim by the owner that the design professional's underestimation was caused by negligence.

Having completed the design and assisted the owner in obtaining bids and awarding contracts for construction, the design professional's primary responsibility becomes the administration of the construction phase of the project. The design professional assumes a wide variety of duties in this context, and several things might occur that may give rise to a claim by the owner, which will be described in the next sections.

Defective Plans and Designs

A more common source of owner claims against design professionals is a defect in the project. The design professional does not warrant that designs and plans will be free from defects; however, a claim against a design professional for defective plans will be successful if the plans did not adhere to the standards of common knowledge in the profession at the time of construction.

While design professionals are not expected to be infallible, they do have a duty during construction to detect and disclose obvious errors, whether the errors are in the design or in deviations from the contract documents.

Illustrative Case

Virginia Military Institute brought suit against Edwin H. King, *et al.*, an architectural firm, alleging that damages in a building were caused by King's negligence in design, breach of warranties, and negligence in supervision and inspection. The damage involved deterioration of limestone and flagstone on terraces, stairs, walls, and piers; and the evidence demonstrated that architectural design deficiencies caused the stonework deterioration. The court stated that the VMI architects undertook to perform in good faith and with reasonable care and competence the service for which they were engaged. The Supreme Court of Virginia reversed the trial court's dismissal of a suit against King by finding there had been negligence in failing to observe and disclose design defects during the course of construction.[4]

The reasoning underlying the limited liability of design professionals to those situations in which the design professional is negligent is that these professionals deal in somewhat inexact sciences and are continually required to exercise their skilled judgment in order to anticipate and provide for random factors that are incapable of precise calculation. The indeterminate nature of these factors makes it impossible for professional service people to gauge them with complete accuracy in all situations. Because of the inescapable possibility of error inherent in these services, not perfect results but rather the exercise of that skill and judgment that can be reasonably expected from similarly situated professionals is required.[5]

Defective plans and specifications prepared by a design professional often will result in delay and additional expense to the contractor. The contractor can then make a claim against the owner, since the design professional was acting as the owner's representative. However, the owner may make a claim against the design professional to recover the damages paid to the contractor resulting from the design professional's negligence.

Illustrative Case

John McDonald, an architect, was engaged without a written contract by the General Trading Corporation to restore and remodel a burned-out building in St. Croix. Because of the area's historic value, no building was allowed to be constructed or reconstructed in the area without the approval of the Virgin Islands planning board. McDonald prepared plans and specifications for the project, and the contractor began construction.

Soon after, the planning board refused to approve the plan and gave McDonald a sample drawing of an appropate modification. McDonald modified the design by merely tracing the planning board's sketch and ambiguously specifying changes as "as required." Further work to make the modification was later unacceptable to the planning board.

The contractor sued the owner and architect for additional expenses required to make the building acceptable. The court said that the contractor could recover against the

---

[4]Comptroller of Virginia, *ex rel.* Virginia Military Inst. v. King, 217 Va. 751, 232 S.E.2d 895 (1977).
[5]City of Eveleth v. Ruble, 302 Minn. 249, 255 N.W.2d 521 (1974).

owner and that the owner could counterclaim against the architect for any losses caused by the architect's negligence.[6]

The illustrative case also shows that, although no written agreement between the owner and design professional may exist, the design professional's actions as the owner's representative may be formally viewed by the court as creating a contractual relationship designating the design professional as the owner's agent.

Improper Certification of Payment

The design professional is usually required by the contract with the owner to certify that the work is progressing according to the contract documents and to issue certificates entitling the contractor to be paid by the owner. Subparagraph 1.5.7 of the AIA Owner-Architect Agreement (Document B141, 1977 ed.) states:

The Architect shall determine the amounts owing to the Contractor based on observations at the site and on evaluations of the Contractor's Applications for Payment, and shall issue Certificates for Payment in such amounts, as provided in the Contract Documents.

When the design professional wrongfully issues a payment certificate, the owner can make a claim against him. The design professional can be held liable for failure to use the reasonable care of one skilled in the profession. Of course, the fraudulent issuance of a certificate will also give the owner a valid claim. Since the design professional's role is to protect the owner from making payments for work not done, any out-of-pocket expenses incurred by the owner as a result of an improper certification can be charged to the design professional.

Illustrative Case

The architect issued Certificates for Payment without first checking whether the contractor had paid his subcontractor and middlemen so as to insulate the owner from their potential liens. The court found the architect negligent, saying that he should have protected the owner by making sure all bills were paid or by obtaining releases from the subcontractors in accordance with his contractual duties and professional standards.[7]

Strict Liability

The traditional rule is that the design professional is liable only for rendering services in a reasonably competent manner as evidenced by the standards established in the profession for similar projects. As an outgrowth of products liability cases, recent efforts have been made to

[6]General Trading Corp. v. Burnup & Sims, 523 F.2d 98 (3d Cir. 1975).

[7]Palmer v. Brown, 127 Cal. 2d 344, 273 P.2d 306 (1954).

hold architects and engineers strictly liable for defects in the structures they design. The argument asserted for strict liability is based on the theory that the design professional, by his undertaking, impliedly warrants that the fruits of his work will be reasonably suitable for the uses and purposes intended. Efforts to hold design professionals liable even if it cannot be shown that they were negligent have usually been unsuccessful.

Illustrative Case

The City of Mounds View retained Kenneth H. Walijarvi, an architect, to design an addition to the city hall. Plans were prepared, and after construction commenced, the city expressed concern over possible water seepage into the basement of the new structure. Despite Walijarvi's assurance to the contrary, serious moisture problems were encountered. The city sued Walijarvi, alleging negligence and the breach of both express and implied warranties. The Supreme Court of Minnesota found that adoption of the city's implied warranty theory would in effect impose strict liability on architects for latent defects in the structures they design. The court stated that "until the random element is eliminated in the application of architectural services, we think it fairer that the purchaser of the architect's services bear the risk of such unforeseeable difficulties" and declined to impose implied warranty/strict liability on vendors of professional services.[8]

Dispute Resolution

The AIA Owner-Architect Agreement (Document B141, 1977 ed.) provides that claims by owners against design professionals shall be settled by arbitration unless it is waived by the parties. Article 9 of the AIA agreement provides that

All claims, disputes and other matters in question between the parties to this Agreement, arising out of or relating to this Agreement or the breach thereof, shall be decided by arbitration in accordance with the Construction Industry Arbitration Rules of the American Arbitration Association then obtaining unless the parties mutually agree otherwise....

Recent editions of the AIA Owner-Architect Agreement and General Conditions have been modified to prevent the design professional from being forced to join multiple-party arbitration. The owner may be required to initiate separate proceedings against the design professional and contractor even where the claim is based on the same set of circumstances. Insulating the design professional in these situations will result in more expensive proceedings and inconsistency, and has resulted in limiting the scope of the design professional's tort liability.

The design professional has no immunity from suit by the owner when the owner's claims relate to the design professional's activities in his professional capacity, but not when they relate to his judicial role as

[8]City of Mounds View v. Walijarvi, 263 N.W.2d 420 (Minn. 1978).

the arbiter of disputes arising from the owner's contract with the contractor. In essence, almost all owner claims against design professionals are based on the theory that the design professional did not perform in accordance with the skill of the profession at the time in question and thus violated the terms of the contract between the owner and the design professional.

Because the owner's claims against the design professional are based on the design professional's professional conduct, the use of experts in proving the owner's claims is indispensable and often required. The courts require adequate expert testimony to support a claim of malpractice unless the alleged act of malpractice can be competently evaluated by a lay jury. In circumstances where a lay jury cannot evaluate the facts of the case without expert testimony, absent a standard of competent architectural practice or expert testimony, it is difficult, if not impossible, for the jury to form a reasoned opinion.

CODES AND STATUTES AFFECTING CLAIMS AGAINST DESIGN PROFESSIONALS

Building codes, licensing requirements, and other local codes and statutes may all be of significant importance in claims against design professionals. The failure of a design professional to meet requirements of a local building code is usually viewed by the courts as constituting negligence per se where the injured party is one whom the code requirement might have been designed to protect. The effect of this is to make claims against design professionals easier, since actual negligence need not be proven by the claimant. By the same token, compliance with the building code may serve as a defense against a claim that the design professional did not perform in accordance with generally accepted standards. For example, a new section has recently been added to Chapter 43-03 of the North Dakota Century Code relating to liability of the design professional. The new law provides that unless a design professional assumes reponsibility by contract or by its conduct, the design professional is not liable for the construction-site safety of persons or property, or for contractors' or material suppliers' procedures or errors.

Chapter 43-03-23 provides:

Architect not liable for contractor's fault unless responsibility assumed — Liability for own negligence. An architect shall not be liable for the safety of persons or property on or about a construction project site, or for the construction techniques, procedures, sequences and schedules, or for the conduct, action, errors or omissions of any construction contractor, subcontractor or material supplier, their agents or employees, unless he assumes responsibility therefor by contract or by his actual conduct. Nothing herein shall be construed to relieve an architect from liability from his negligence, whether in his design work or otherwise.[9]

[9]Approved March 15, 1979.

Licensing statutes also create requirements that must be met by design professionals. An unlicensed architect or engineer cannot usually collect fees through a lawsuit, since the courts will not enforce the design professional's contract. Thus, the courts will not force claimants to pay fees to unlicensed design professionals unless they knew the design professional was unlicensed and unless they withheld payment in bad faith. In addition, these statutes may require that the design professional adhere to certain standards, the violation of which may be relevant in establishing burden of proof in a claim against the design professional.

"Safe place" statutes are statutes that create standards to which design professionals must adhere in the design of facilities to be used by the public. "Scaffold Acts" serve to create liability for workers' safety. Laws like these are often of key importance to the liability of design professionals, so claimants should always completely research the law in the area to find out to what duties the design professional might be held that are not contained in the contract or in the relationship between the parties.

Investigation of the applicable statute of limitations is the first step in evaluating whether a claim against a design professional might be successful. Claims against design professionals will simply not be heard if the statute of limitations has run. Whether the action against the design professional lies in tort or breach of contract may decide whether the claim will be heard or immediately thrown out of court. The time when the claimant's cause of action accrued is most important in determining when a claim exists. The action may accrue when the negligent act took place, when damages occurred, when the claimant discovered the injury, or upon completion of the project.

The Supreme Court has recently addressed the history of statutes of limitations and the accrual of causes of actions in *United States v. Kubrick*, 440 U.S. 906 (1979). The Court held that "the punitive malpractice plaintiff must determine within the period of limitations whether to sue or not" and that if the plaintiff fails to bring suit, because of incompetence or mistake, the claim will not be heard. Although *Kubrick* involved medical malpractice and the interpretation of the Federal Tort Claims Act, the design professional may be able to assert a statute-of-limitations defense based on this case.

Cases involving statutes of limitations for design professionals vary from jurisdiction to jurisdiction depending upon the period provided for the commencement of the statutory period. For example, in Colorado, the period begins "upon completion of construction."[10] In California the period begins upon substantial completion of the project.[11] Other jurisdictions follow "upon completion of professional services" (Louisiana);

[10]*See* Housing Auth. of Limon v. Leo A. Daly Co., 35 Colo. App. 244, 533 P.2d 937 (1975).

[11]Liptak v. Diane Apartments, Inc., 109 Cal. App. 3d 887, 167 Cal. Rptr. 440 (1980).

"upon performance of the allegedly negligent work" or "upon breach of legal duty" (Oregon); and "at time of completion of the project and the consequent termination of the professional relationship" (New York).

Illustrative Case

In an action against an architect by an owner alleging professional malpractice, the New York court held that the cause of action accrues on completion of the construction project and the consequent termination of the professional relationship between the parties. Construction had been completed in April 1973, and final payment was received pursuant to the contract by December 1973; however, a final payment certificate exhibiting actual acceptance was not received until June 1976. The lower court found that a final certificate served merely as an administrative act and, therefore, not the date on which the statute of limitations began to run. However, the appeals court held that where a construction contract required the architect to conduct inspections and supervise the construction, a cause of action against him did not accrue until the final Certificate of Payment was issued.[12]

Certain contingencies that may toll the statute from running can occur after the cause of action has arisen, thus allowing the claimant additional time in which to initiate the action. For example, allegations of fraud or knowledge on the part of the design professional of dangerous defects have been held sufficient to prevent the assertion of the statute-of-limitations defense.

Illustrative Case

Thirteen and one-half years after the architect had given his Certificate of Substantial Completion, the owner observed cracks in the exterior structural concrete of its building. Tests of the concrete later indicated the presence of calcium chloride, which causes it to "set up" faster than normal in cold water. The owner brought an action against the architect two years after discovery, alleging breach of warranty, negligent supervision, breach of contract, and fraud. The architect and contractor asserted that the six-year South Dakota statute of limitations for actions based on deficiencies in building construction barred the action.

The district court held that the existence of a clause in the architect's contract calling for him to supervise construction made him an agent of the owner and created a fiduciary relationship between the architect and owner. The architect's failure to disclose constituted a fraudulent concealment that served to toll the statute of limitations until the cause of action was discovered or might have been discovered by exercise of diligence. The federal court denied the architect's motion for summary judgment.[13]

Some states have enacted special statutes of limitations pertaining to design professionals' liability. For example, a special statute was enacted in Michigan to limit architects' and engineers' liability to "relieve them of the potential burden of defending claims brought long after completion of the improvement and thereby limit the impact of

[12]Tri-Valley Central School Dist. v. Celotex Corp., 451 N.Y.S.2d 290 (Sup. Ct. 1982).

[13]Canton Lutheran Church v. Sovik Mathre, Sathrum & Quanbeck, 507 F. Supp. 873 (D.S.D. 1981).

recent changes in the law upon the liability or cost of the services they provide."[14] The courts have reasoned that limiting the ability of plaintiffs to bring tort actions against design professionals does not violate due process. Where suits against architects and engineers may be maintained within six years from time of occupancy, use, or acceptance of an improvement, sufficient time is allowed for most meticulous claims to accrue and would permit suit against those guilty of malpractice.

Illustrative Case

The Tennessee statute barred actions for injuries suffered by the plaintiffs twelve years after completion of the original structures and five years after the completion of an addition. An employee died from chemical burns caused when escaping fumes from the refrigeration system leaked into the water drainage system. The architect had been involved in the design, construction, and installation of the refrigeration system, all of which were completed more than four years before the accident.

The Supreme Court of Tennessee affirmed the application of the state's four-year special statute of limitations for actions arising out of defects in the design and construction of improvements to real property.[15] The court found that the plaintiffs were not deprived of due process and upheld the constitutionality of the special statute.[16]

[14]Bouser v. City of Unicorn Park, 83 Mich. App. 167, 268 N.W.2d 332 (1978).

[15]TENN. CODE ANN. §§ 28-3-201 to 28-3-205.

[16]Harmon v. Angus R. Jessup Associates, 619 S.W.2d 522 (Tenn. 1981).

15 RESOLVING DISPUTES

Disputes almost invariably arise in the construction of any project, but the owner and contractor can resolve the majority of disputes without resorting to formal procedures for resolution. Neither party should underestimate the use of negotiation in resolving disputes. The main pitfall in negotiating a dispute is that an owner and a contractor are often carried away by emotions because both parties have a substantial interest in the outcome.

ADMINISTRATIVE PROCEDURES

Most construction contracts provide an administrative procedure that is to be followed in the resolution of disputes. Particularly in the public sphere, the administrative procedure must be followed before the contractor can take any other steps toward resolving the dispute.

Federal government contracts provide that claims for an equitable adjustment to a contract must be submitted to the contracting officer for a decision. The decision by the contracting officer is final and binding unless a timely appeal is made. The contractor has the option of appealing to a board of contract appeals or directly to a claims court.

State- and local-government contracts generally provide similar procedures for resolving disputes. A claim must usually be submitted to a particular government official before any other steps may be taken. After this, state- and local-government contracts generally require the submission of a dispute to some appeals board. The American Bar Association, in its Model Procurement Code for State and Local Governments, provides for the establishment of a procurement appeals board to provide "informal, expeditious, and inexpensive procedures for the resolution of controversies."[1] Alternatively, appeals may be taken to a court.

A great number of construction contract disputes can be resolved through negotiations between the parties involved. However, should negotiations fail, the injured party must seek other means of redress.

[1]American Bar Association Model Procurement Code for State and Local Governments, § 9.501, (2d printing, February 1979).

Among the alternatives available are arbitration and litigation. The decision to arbitrate or litigate must be carefully considered.

Arbitration and litigation each have particular advantages and disadvantages. An arbitrator can award virtually any type of remedy a court can award. An arbitration may be concluded in six months, whereas litigation seldom is completed in less than twelve months. However, given the size of most construction disputes and the fact that the arbitrator is paid by the parties on a daily or hourly basis, arbitration may not really be less expensive than litigation. These costs, together with the length of the hearing if there has been no discovery, tend to offset the expense of discovery. (Discovery is the process by which information about the case is gathered from other parties.) Nevertheless, the postponement of any cash award during the process of a trial and then through possible appeals may sometimes be of crucial importance to the parties involved.

Another important consideration is that many construction arbitrators have technical expertise in the area at issue. It is common for contractors, architects, and engineers to serve as arbitrators, and in technical construction matters it certainly is helpful to have people with expertise determining the issues. Moreover, there is little chance for procedural delays with arbitration because there are no court dockets to postpone the proceeding. The informality of arbitration is very conducive to getting the facts of the case without unnecessary delay or hindrance by technical evidentiary arguments.

On the other hand, an arbitration panel often has little or no legal expertise and may tend to look to the equitable rather than the legal side of a case. As a result, an individual may be defeated in an arbitration proceeding even though he has technically complied with his legal obligations. Unlike the courts, arbitrators are not bound by any legal precedents. Thus, if the contract or the legalities of the contract clearly favor one side, that party is better off taking the issue to the courts.

Some parties may find privacy to be an important advantage of arbitration. If a dispute is taken to litigation, it is made public and the court's decision will be precedent for future resolution of factually similar situations. The moving party should consider whether the outcome—an outcome that at commencement cannot be predicted— should be public knowledge and possibly become the standard for future lawsuits.

It is obvious, however, that there are situations where court action is the best and perhaps the only avenue to resolving a dispute. An advantage to court action is the availability of discovery procedures: depositions of involved parties, interrogatories, and motions to compel production of essential documents. The litigants also have the right to subpoena witnesses, documents, and records. Such legal procedures may well result in a more thorough uncovering of essential facts and a better base for decision. Whether this additional investigation is necessary depends, of course, on the particular facts involved in the case.

Another advantage to litigation is that all of the parties involved in the dispute can be brought into one lawsuit. The goal of modern court procedure under the Federal Rules of Civil Procedure and similar state court rules is to settle all the controversies between all the persons involved in a dispute in the same court proceeding. The person bringing the suit may therefore join as defendants all persons who may be liable to the plaintiff with respect to a single transaction or occurrence if any question of law or fact common to all the defendants will arise in the suit. Defendants may bring into the suit third-party defendants, that is, those who may be liable to the defendant for all or part of the plaintiff's claim against the defendant.

Court action also carries with it an efficient and certain means of enforcement. The judgment makes unequivocally clear which parties are bound and to what extent. In contrast, the enforcement of an arbitration clause or award against a nonwilling party can be trying and difficult. Whether it is advantageous to submit a dispute for resolution by arbitration or through litigation ultimately depends on the nature of the particular dispute.

ARBITRATION

Agreements to Arbitrate Future Disputes

The decision to arbitrate is generally reached by two different avenues. The contract between the parties may contain an agreement to arbitrate future disputes, or an agreement to arbitrate can be reached after the dispute arises. An example of an agreement to arbitrate future disputes is found in paragraph 7.9 of the AIA General Conditions (Document A201, 1976 ed.):

7.9   Arbitration

7.9.1 All claims, disputes and other matters in question between the Contractor and the Owner arising out of, or relating to, the Contract Documents or the breach thereof, except as provided in Subparagraph 2.2.11 with respect to the Architect's decisions on matters relating to artistic effect and except for claims which have been waived by the making or acceptance of final payment as provided in Subparagraphs 9.9.4 and 9.9.5, shall be decided by arbitration in accordance with the Construction Industry Arbitration Rules of the American Arbitration Association then pertaining unless the parties mutually agree otherwise. . . . The foregoing agreement to arbitrate and any other agreement to arbitrate with an additional person or persons duly consented to by the parties to the Owner-Contractor Agreement shall be specifically enforceable under the prevailing arbitration law. The award rendered by the arbitrators shall be final, and judgment may be entered upon it in accordance with applicable law in any court having jurisdiction thereof.

7.9.2 Notice of demand for arbitration shall be filed in writing with the other party to the Owner-Contractor Agreement and with the American Arbitration Association, and a copy shall be filed with the Architect. The demand for arbitration shall be made within the time limits specified in Subparagraph 2.2.12 where applicable, and in all other cases within a reasonable time after the claim, dispute or other matter in question has arisen, and in no event shall it be made after the date when institution of legal or equitable proceedings based on such claim, dispute or other matter in question would be barred by the applicable statute of limitations.

7.9.3 Unless otherwise agreed in writing, the Contractor shall carry on the work and maintain its progress during any arbitration proceedings, and the Owner shall continue to make payments to the Contractor in accordance with the Contract Documents.

Federal law supports the duty to arbitrate when a contract provides for arbitration. The Federal Arbitration Act[2] provides that a written agreement to arbitrate in a contract evidencing a transaction involving interstate commerce is valid and enforceable.

Illustrative Case

Lafaye Associates, Inc., and McCrory-Sumwalt Construction Company entered into general contracts with the Episcopal Housing Corporation for the construction of housing projects for the elderly. After construction was completed, Lafaye and McCrory were advised by the Episcopal Housing Corporation that water was discovered leaking into the building, and negotiations among all three parties in an effort to resolve the problem broke down.

Lafaye and McCrory demanded arbitration with the Episcopal Housing Corporation in accordance with the Construction Industry Rules of the American Arbitration Association. When the Episcopal Housing Corporation refused to arbitrate, Lafaye and McCrory filed proceedings in court to compel arbitration. The South Carolina Supreme Court held that although agreements to arbitrate are unenforceable under South Carolina law, the supremacy clause of the United States Constitution recognizes that federal statutes are the supreme law of the land. The Federal Arbitration Act was enacted pursuant to the commerce clause of the U.S. Constitution, thereby superseding South Carolina common and statutory law. The court found that there was a valid arbitration agreement and that the transaction involved interstate commerce in that equipment and materials were to be furnished to the project from outside South Carolina. Accordingly, the Federal Arbitration Act was applicable and the parties were ordered to arbitrate in accordance with their agreement.[3]

Diversity jurisdiction alone is not sufficient to make federal law applicable; the transaction must also have an interstate commerce aspect. In other words, it is not enough that the parties are from different states; there must be issues presented in the case that concern federal law. However, as a practical matter, most construction cases affect interstate commerce in some way. A contract between the parties that contains an arbitration clause as a matter of federal policy will be construed liberally. Courts have found that such clauses cover disputes reasonably contemplated by the language of the contract, usually resolving doubts in favor of arbitration.

[2]9 U.S.C. §§ 1–14 (1947).

[3]Episcopal Housing Corp. v. Federal Ins. Co., 269 S.C. 631, 239 S.E.2d 647 (1977).

Agreements to Arbitrate Existing Disputes

A written agreement to submit an existing dispute to arbitration is enforceable in almost every state and, in cases involving interstate or foreign commerce, is enforceable under the Federal Arbitration Act.[4] This kind of agreement is called a submission agreement and typically should identify the parties, describe the issues in dispute, state the relief sought, and provide for administration under specific rules.

Some states also have additional requirements for a submission agreement to be binding. They may require that a submission agreement be signed by the parties, be acknowledged in some particular manner, be filed with the court, or contain the names of the arbitrators. To be binding at all, the arbitration agreement must be binding on both parties and cannot be seen as giving one party the option to arbitrate or litigate.

Illustrative Case

A plastering contractor followed specifications for plastering a section of a transcript vaulted ceiling of a large church. The contractor contended that the plaster failed to adhere to the ceiling because of a defective specification in the mix of the plaster specified by the architect. The architect, who was the representative of the owner, contended that the contractor guaranteed the performance and that the plaster specifications were not defective and ordered the contractor to replaster the section of the ceiling. When no agreement between the owner and the plastering contractor could be reached on the cost of replastering the ceiling, the parties agreed to submit the dispute to private arbitration under the rules of the American Arbitration Association. The plastering contractor prevailed in the arbitration. However, both parties prevailed in getting the dispute settled privately and expeditiously without having to go to court, which is what both the owner and contractor wanted.[5]

Waiver of the Right to Arbitrate

A party who takes action that is inconsistent with arbitration may be seen as waiving the right to arbitration. The filing of an action at law is generally held to constitute a waiver of the right to arbitrate.[6] However, some courts have held that filing an action at law does not constitute a waiver unless the other party was prejudiced by the action.[7]

Illustrative Case

Capital Distributing Company appealed a judgment of the district court for the Southern District of New York that confirmed the award by three arbitrators in favor of Ballantine

---

[4] 9 U.S.C. §§ 1—14 (1947).

[5] Unpublished arbitration case.

[6] Cornell & Co. v. Barber & Ross Co., 360 F.2d 512 (D.C. Cir. 1966).

[7] Carich v. Reder: A/B Nordie, 389 F.2d 692 (2d Cir. 1968).

Books, Inc., for $151,143.84. Pursuant to the Federal Arbitration Act,[8] the proceeding was brought in the district court by Ballantine, a New York corporation, against Capital, a Connecticut corporation.

Capital claimed that the federal court lacked jurisdiction since the New York courts had previously taken jurisdiction by reason of Capital's motion there to disqualify the chairman of the arbitration board. The court of appeals affirmed the district court's ruling that it had jurisdiction to pass upon the award and found no basis for Capital's claim. Since the federal court had jurisdiction under the Federal Arbitration Act,[9] the arbitration clause was unquestionably part of a "contract evidencing a transaction involving commerce," and the diversity of the parties' citizenship gave the independent federal jurisdiction that is required under the act.[10]

A mere delay in demanding arbitration has been considered insufficient to constitute a waiver. Much more must be shown to demonstrate waiver. A defense of waiver has been sustained by the courts where the party seeking arbitration has filed an answer to an action at law on the merits or a motion for cross-claim, participated in discovery, failed to move for a stay of the action at law, or participated in a trial on the merits.[11] The most obvious situation in which a party can demonstrate a waiver is where the other party has filed an answer on the merits.[12]

In some cases, even where parties have participated in litigation they have been held not to have waived their right to arbitrate.[13] In addition, section 47 of the Construction Industry Arbitration Rules provides that "[n]o judicial proceedings by a party relating to the subject matter of the arbitration shall be deemed a waiver of the party's right to arbitrate." Some recent state court decisions have followed this rule. However, when one of the parties to an agreement to arbitrate brings an action at law, in order to preserve the right to arbitrate, the other party should move to stay that action and compel arbitration. Generally, the only issue to be decided by the court at this point is whether the parties did agree to submit the dispute to arbitration. If there was such an agreement, the court proceeding should be stayed. While the issue of arbitrability is being determined, both parties may be able to use discovery devices not available in arbitration without being deemed to have waived the right to arbitrate.

Illustrative Case

The Board of Education of the Willow Springs School District advertised plans and specifications for the construction of an elementary school. Delisi Construction Company was the low bidder and received notification that its proposal was approved and that con-

[8] 9 U.S.C. §§ 1-14 (1947).

[9] Id.

[10] Ballantine Books, Inc. v. Capital Distrib. Co., 302 F.2d 17 (2d Cir. 1962).

[11] Demsey & Assoc. v. S.S. Sea Star, 461 F.2d 1009 (2d Cir. 1972).

[12] Chatham Shipping Co. v. Fertex S.S. Corp., 352 F.2d 291 (2d Cir. 1965).

[13] Hilti, Inc. v. Oldach, 392 F.2d 368 (1st Cir. 1968).

tracts would be forthcoming. Later, the school board notified Delisi that the notification was being rescinded and awarded the contract to another contractor.

Delisi claimed breach of contract and filed an action for damages. In its answer, the school board denied the existence of a contract and demanded a trial by jury. A hearing was held at which the court determined that there was a contract and that the school board had breached it. At that point, the school board requested that the question of damages be submitted to arbitration according to the contract and applied for a stay of further proceedings pending arbitration. The stay was denied.

The school board appealed from that order. The company claimed that the school board had waived its right to arbitrate because it participated in the breach trial and had engaged in extensive pretrial activity. The court found that the fact that the school board had engaged in extensive pretrial activity did not constitute a waiver of the right to arbitrate because the issue of whether there actually was a contract was an issue determinable only by the court, and that until a contract was found, the arbitration provision could not be invoked.[14]

Administration of Arbitration

The procedure for arbitrating can be as varied as the participants themselves. Probably the most frequently used procedure is that used by the American Arbitration Association (AAA). The AAA is a public-service, nonprofit organization whose sole function is to resolve disputes through the use of arbitration. The rules of the association are incorporated into the AIA General Conditions and Standard Subcontract Form A401 and are particularly suited for the settlement of disputes in the construction industry.

Often the arbitration agreement itself will specify the method of designating arbitrators and the number of arbitrators to be used. In cases involving substantial sums of money, the agreement often provides that the panel consist of three arbitrators. Usually, each party selects its preferred arbitrator, and the two arbitrators select a third arbitrator. In the event that the two cannot agree on a third, the agreement usually provides for selection of a third arbitrator by a justice of a court or some other designated person. If the matter to be arbitrated is relatively simple, the designation of a single arbitrator may be preferable. The AAA provides a list that the parties use to rank potential arbitrators, and the AAA then selects a panel of three. The AAA also provides for the appointment of one arbitrator for smaller disputes.

At the same time arbitrators are being selected, the AAA requests the parties to specify when they will be available to arbitrate the dispute. From the dates commonly preferred by both parties, the AAA selects the arbitration date (or dates). If the parties agree to discovery or if the arbitrators allow discovery, the date for the hearing generally will be postponed until discovery is completed. After the arbitrators are selected, the postponement or selection of a hearing date is within the discretion of the arbitrators rather than the administrative personnel of the AAA. One of the greatest advantages of arbitration is that it is

[14]People ex rel. Delisi Constr. Co. v. Bd. of Educ., 26 Ill. App. 3d 893, 326 N.E.2d 55 (1975).

generally scheduled for a particular day and time not too far in the future.

Multiparty Practice

Arbitration does not normally permit joinder under the AAA rules, and the arbitration clause in AIA documents expressly forbids joinder of the design professional in the same case with the contractor. For example, the AIA General Conditions (Document A201, 1976 ed.) states in sub-paragraph 7.9.1:

No arbitration arising out of or relating to the Contract Documents shall include, by consolidation, joinder or in any other manner, the Architect, his employees or consul-tants except by written consent containing a specific reference to the Owner-Contractor Agreement and signed by the Architect, the Owner, the Contractor and any other person sought to be joined. No arbitration shall include, by consolidation, joinder or in any other manner, parties other than the Owner, the Contractor and any other persons substan-tially involved in a common question of fact or law, whose presence is required if com-plete relief is to be accorded in the arbitration. No person other than the Owner or Con-tractor shall be included as an original third party or additional third party to an arbitration whose interest or responsibility is insubstantial. Any consent to arbitration involving an additional person or persons shall not constitute consent to arbitration of any dispute not described therein or with any person not named or described therein.

Discovery

Arbitration is intended to be a method of dispute resolution that avoids the endless, time-consuming process of litigating a case. The discovery stage of the litigation process is expensive and lengthy, and until recently it generally was not allowed in connection with arbitration. There is, however, a recent trend toward allowing more expansive dis-covery in the arbitration process.

While arbitrators have the discretion to permit discovery in a particu-lar case, they may not have available the normal sanctions under the Federal Rules of Civil Procedure for failure to take part in discovery proceedings. The arbitrators may be able, however, to devise sanctions if they find that one of the parties has impeded or complicated their task by refusing to cooperate in pretrial disclosure of relevant matters.

Discovery in arbitration proceedings is a highly complex area. The parties can specify the limits and reaches of discovery by agreement, and then discovery is controlled by the terms of that agreement. In the absence of such an agreement, state and federal statutes generally pro-vide for limited discovery.

The Hearing

The arbitration hearing resembles a court proceeding. Witnesses are usually, though not always, sworn, and the arbitrators sit as judges.

Unlike courts of law, however, the rules of evidence are relaxed or not applied at all; the panel of arbitrators has broad discretion to allow any testimony it believes to be relevant or of probative value, including hearsay. The moving party first presents its case and is followed by the opposing party. At the end of the proceeding, each party generally is allowed a closing statement, which resembles the closing argument in a court of law.

The Award

After all closing arguments, either oral or written, are submitted and the record is closed, the arbitrators enter their decision. Under the rules of the AAA, the decision must be rendered within thirty days; however, the arbitrators generally reach their decision before that time. The award may grant any remedy or relief that is just and equitable and that is within the terms of the agreement between the parties. The arbitrators may even grant relief that has been expressly excluded by the contract if they find those provisions to be unconscionable.[15] A party may request modification of an award under the AAA rules by a letter to the AAA and a copy to the opposing party. There may be time limits involved in the request for modification. The other party is then given an opportunity to respond. The arbitrators may then agree to modify their award or, more likely, affirm it.

Enforcement

Most parties to an arbitration proceeding will comply voluntarily with the terms of an award. This will end the proceedings between the parties. However, a party will sometimes feel that the arbitration procedure was not fair or equitable and will challenge the award. The scope of judicial review is necessarily very limited because a quasi-judicial status is conferred on the proceedings.

Under the Federal Arbitration Act,[16] the parties may, by agreement, provide that a judgment by a court may be entered pursuant to the award. Then, at any time within one year after the award is made, either party may apply for an order from the court affirming the award or vacating, modifying, or correcting it. Notice of a motion to vacate or modify must be served upon the adverse party within three months after the award is entered. The award may be vacated

(a)   Where the award was procured by corruption, fraud, or undue means;

(b)   Where there was evident partiality or corruption in the arbitrators, or either of them;

---

[15]Granite Worsted Mills, Inc. v. Aaronson Cowen, Ltd., 25 N.Y.2d 451, 255 N.E.2d 168, 306 N.Y.S.2d 934 (1969).

[16]9 U.S.C. §§ 1-14 (1947).

(c) Where the arbitrators were guilty of misconduct in refusing to postpone the hearing, upon sufficient cause shown, or in refusing to hear evidence pertinent and material to the controversy; or of any other misbehavior by which the rights of any party have been prejudiced; and

(d) Where the arbitrators exceeded their powers, or so imperfectly executed them that a mutual, final, and definite award upon the subject matter submitted was not made.[17]

Where the award has been vacated, in some circumstances the court may in its discretion direct a rehearing.

The award may be modified or corrected

(a) Where there was an evident material miscalculation of figures or an evident material mistake in the description of any person, thing, or property referred to in the award;

(b) Where the arbitrators have awarded upon a matter not submitted to them, unless it is a matter not affecting the merits of the decision upon the matter submitted; and

(c) Where the award is imperfect in matter of form not affecting the merits of the controversy.[18]

Other than these grounds, courts in most states will not undertake review of an arbitration award. The courts are very careful not to reconsider any other grounds and not to review a decision on its merits.

LITIGATION

It is obvious that court action offers less flexibility than other alternatives such as negotiation or arbitration: Evidence must be presented within the formal and sometimes restrictive limits of the rules of evidence; once the suit is commenced, room for maneuvering and give-and-take on the part of the parties is restricted; and the parties are bound to the often ponderous schedule of the court. The decision to pursue court action must rest on an assessment of the advantages and disadvantages of the legal process in relation to the particular facts and problems of the individual situation. Once the choice is made to pursue litigation, a lengthy and systematic process begins.

The most important aspect of the litigation process is the substantiation of the claim through factual documentation. Successful litigation of construction cases depends primarily on the preparation and presentation of facts through documentary evidence. The documents describing the various problems that arose during the course of construction are vital for successful determination of any claim. In most construction cases settlement occurs prior to trial, and it is usually because both sides have such thorough documentation of everything that occurred that the attorneys can find a solution to the dispute.

Experts often play a vital role in construction disputes. Construction cases normally involve highly complicated issues that require detailed

[17]*Id.* § 10.
[18]*Id.* § 11.

analyses of important documents by experts. Some experts are hired during the course of the job; for example, a scheduling expert can help with the planning and set up a schedule for the work. An expert who has been on the project will have firsthand knowledge, and if a conflict does arise will understand the scope and nature of the problem. If an expert is not retained prior to the dispute, once the process has been initiated, an expert should be immediately interviewed and retained.

Written expert reports often persuade the other party to settle. A favorable expert-witness report can help an attorney sell the client's position to the other side in order to reach a favorable settlement.

Multiparty Practice

The plaintiff must decide which parties to include in its action. Construction cases necessarily involve a multiplicity of parties: the owner, design professionals, contractors, subcontractors, suppliers and the manufacturers of supplies, and surety companies. The key in construction cases involving so many parties is to initially bring in all of the parties who might be liable. In this way potential liability may be shifted to appropriate parties who have been included in the action. In addition, there are other methods available to shift potential liability. Counterclaims and cross-claims are claims that one party to an action has against someone who is already a party to the action. Third-party proceedings, on the other hand, are claims against persons who were not original parties to the action. Some claims against some parties are compulsory; that is, they must be pleaded in the original case or they are waived. Other claims are merely permissive; they may or may not be asserted in that action or may be the subject matter of a separate action. A valid counterclaim encourages both parties to settle their dispute. If the defendant counterclaims against the plaintiff, many of the advantages of a sympathetic jury can be lost. All parties should be aware of and prepared for the possibility of counterclaims.

Illustrative Example

A construction contractor brings suit against an owner to recover damages for failure to pay for repair work done on the owner's garage roof. The owner counterclaims against the contractor for damages caused by the contractor's failure to perform, resulting in leaks from the roof damaging the walls of the garage.

Persons other than parties to an original action may be made parties to an action. Joinder of parties as plaintiffs is allowed for persons who assert the right to relief based upon one transaction or a series of transactions or if there is a question of law or fact common to all the parties.[19]

[19]FED. R. CIV. P. Rule 20(a).

The practical considerations of joinder should be assessed. Although bringing in a proliferation of parties increases the chance of shifting liability onto the appropriate party, joinder may also have some disadvantages. Multiparty litigation can become very complex and confusing. The jury will be confronted with far more complex facts and issues when a number of parties are involved. Multiparty litigation also greatly increases the total cost of litigation.

Illustrative Example

The roof of a building began to leak severely and a new roof was required. The owner filed suit against the general contractor, its surety, and the design professionals. The construction parties faulted the design, and the design professionals blamed the construction. As a result of the suit, the general contractor files a third-party complaint against the roofing subcontractor and its surety and cross-claims against the design professionals for negligent design. The design professionals cross-claim against the general contractor and the roofing subcontractor to indemnify the design professionals for any liability they might incur. The roofing subcontractor files an additional third-party complaint against the supplier of the roofing felts, which it alleges are defective, cross-claims against the architect for negligent design, and counterclaims against the general contractor for monies due.

The design professionals' various errors and omissions carriers enter the picture to defend their respective insureds and also to file third-party complaints against any design consultant who had not yet been sued. The supplier has its products liability carrier defend it, and the general contractor and roofing subcontracter have their respective insurance companies defend them under their "completed operations coverage" for consequential damages alleged to have occurred. At this point in the litigation, there is a minimum of an owner, probably two or more design firms, a general contractor, a roofing subcontractor, two sureties, a manufacturer, their respective insurers, and any excess coverage insurers, all claiming against and suing one another.

Choice of Forum

The plaintiff may have the option of choosing among different forums to bring a suit. Some jurisdictions may follow different rules of law, have different statutes that govern a situation, or differ in their interpretation of the rules of evidence, appropriate defenses, and degrees of culpability. For example, when the option of choosing between federal and state jurisdictions is available, there are some general distinctions between procedure before a federal court and procedure before a state court that should be considered. One such distinction, that federal courts allow broader discovery rights than do most states, may well influence one's choice of forum. Of course, there must be jurisdiction in the forum to hear the particular case. For example, suits against the United States government brought under the Miller Act[20] must be brought "in the United States District Court for any district in which the contract was to be performed and executed and not elsewhere."[21] This section

[20]40 U.S.C. §§ 270a-270d (1935).

[21]Id. § 270b.

grants jurisdiction over such cases to the federal court irrespective of the amount in controversy. Otherwise, the federal court must have jurisdiction over a particular matter in order for it to even be considered as an option.

Judge or Jury

Another initial decision focuses on whether to present the case to a judge or to a jury. Procedural differences may favor a jury trial. For example, counsel has a greater chance of reversible error on evidentiary grounds in a trial by jury. Appeals courts often will not overturn a verdict by a judge on only the basis of improper admission of evidence. A judge is presumed to be able to give appropriate weight to questionable evidence and to be able to ignore evidence that turns out to be inadmissible. However, if a judge permits inadmissible evidence in a jury trial, counsel has a right to appeal the verdict because unfair prejudice is presumed to result from the jury being allowed to hear inadmissible evidence.

The nature of the case and parties may also have a bearing on whether the case is tried before a judge or jury. Emotional factors can be decisive in a jury trial, so counsel should carefully evaluate the evidence and the witnesses involved according to their potential impact on the jury. If the client can evoke sympathy, a jury may be more lenient in evaluating the testimony. A judge is more likely to give weight to objective factors such as the terms of the contract and less likely to be influenced by subjective factors.

Other issues to be considered are the cost and time involved. Usually it takes longer to get on the calendar for a jury trial than it does for a nonjury trial. Prospective jurors must be selected, which often is a time-consuming and expensive process. Some jurisdictions require the losing party to pay fees and mileage for jurors. If the plaintiff loses the case, the defendant's costs might be charged against the plaintiff.

The most important factor in a construction dispute is its complexity. Construction cases involve difficult issues that may require understanding of complex program analysis. For example, "critical path methods" are used by scheduling experts to evaluate the economic effect of a delay on a particular project. This is highly intricate and can easily confuse and bore a jury. Although the problem can be alleviated somewhat by simplifying the issues through the use of charts, diagrams, and expert testimony, the jury may still be confused.

The procedural choices of parties to the suit, the forum, and judge or jury are a valuable tool for winning disputes and must be assessed in light of the case and parties. All procedural requirements must be followed to avoid the embarrassment and expense that can result in having the case brought before the wrong forum.

Discovery

Discovery, the procedure that compels the disclosure of information before a trial begins, is one of the most important parts of the litigation process. The purpose of discovery is to reduce the element of surprise at trial.[22] It enables both sides to know the significant facts and theories involved in the case and brings the whole litigation process out in the open, as opposed to leaving it behind closed doors. A knowledge of the significant facts and theories involved in the case also increases the likelihood of settlement.

Before a party initiates a suit, the cost of discovery in time and money, as well as the potential results of discovery, must be considered. In some cases, the cost may outweigh the potential recovery.

A necessary strategy in a construction case is to simplify the issues and problems. Discovery in a construction case is often complex and expensive because of numerous facts and the amount of paperwork. Thorough preparation requires obtaining and organizing all of the necessary testimony and documents. After a careful review of all the documents, those that are superfluous can be set aside.

Depositions are useful devices for gaining information, preserving testimony, and committing witnesses to factual positions and can therefore aid in understanding the nature of the case and in analyzing documentary information. Witnesses and questions should be prepared in advance. Thorough preparation is critical because any statements made under oath at the deposition can later be used at trial for impeachment. Important witnesses should be deposed as early as possible while their memories are still fresh. This is especially true in construction cases because employees are highly mobile and key testimony can be lost if witnesses move on.

Oral depositions are probably the most effective discovery device. Oral depositions have all the formality of a court proceeding and all the advantages of examining a witness in person and eliciting spontaneous responses. However, the time they require and their costs for court reporters and witnesses make oral depositions extremely expensive. Counsel should balance the necessity of deposing the witness against the cost and time involved.

Interrogatories are written questions that are submitted to a party for written answers. Interrogatories are less expensive and time-consuming than oral depositions. However, they are less effective because all answers are prepared by the witness with help of opposing counsel.

Interrogatories are extremely useful in construction cases when counsel needs information involving materials and documents kept over a long period of time. The questions can be used to identify key wit-

[22]Hickman v. Taylor, 329 U.S. 495, 507 (1947).

nesses and obtain essential documents. When interrogatories are submitted directly to a corporate entity, the corporation must designate a knowledgeable person to testify on its behalf. An interrogatory directed to a corporation saves time by forcing the corporation to designate the person most qualified to be a witness, thereby avoiding the expense of deposing unnecessary witnesses. Although the witness's preparation may diminish the overall effectiveness of interrogatories, courts will take this into consideration when deciding whether to introduce any interrogatories into evidence against the party who answered them. The courts are concerned with reliability and trustworthiness of evidence. As long as the court determines that the answers are trustworthy, they will normally be allowed into evidence and the jury will be left to determine how much weight to be given to them.

Another effective discovery device is the request or notice to admit. In a majority of jurisdictions, counsel may serve on an opposing party a request that certain stated facts be admitted.[23] The notice may also be used to obtain an admission that certain documents are authentic. Counsel receiving the request then has thirty days to submit a response that

(1)   Denies the fact in the request;

(2)   States reasons for a failure to either admit or deny; or

(3)   Objects to the request.

If no response is forthcoming, the facts stated in the request are deemed admitted. Requests for admission are relatively inexpensive but can be very useful. The party who is served with a notice to admit must respond in some form or another. Silence is deemed an admission, and there are no opportunities to evade the questions or equivocate on the answers. Furthermore, if a party denies a fact that is later proved, the party served with the request may be assessed with the costs of proving the fact. The request to admit is severely restricted in some jurisdictions in that it cannot be used to try to obtain an admission from a party that it really does not have a case; that is, a request cannot seek an admission that goes to the very heart of the case.

Discovery is largely contingent on complete cooperation between the parties. However, discovery is a procedural right, and failure to respond to requests for discovery may constitute a violation of the right to a fair trial. Most jurisdictions do impose sanctions on a party who fails to respond to requests for discovery. If opposing counsel fails to cooperate, a motion compelling compliance can be made to the court. The court will issue a subpeona to the party to submit to deposition.

There are steps a party should consider when confronted with

[23]FED. R. CIV. P. 36.

requests for discovery. One of the initial decisions that the lawyer must address after the client receives a notice or motion is whether to oppose the proceeding or give the opponent what has been requested. Counsel should consider the practical effects that disclosure may have on the case and compare the harm it could do to the case with the cost of resisting discovery.

Summary Judgment

Summary judgment is a decision by the court that there is no genuine issue as to any material fact established by the pleadings and that there is no purpose in going to trial. Summary judgment can be granted on a motion by either party. If the pleadings are insufficient to establish the plaintiff's cause of action, the defendant can move that summary judgment be granted in its favor. If, however, the plaintiff's affidavits and pleadings do present genuine issues of fact, for example, if the pleadings raise a question as to whether any work was performed after the date of completion in the contract, then a summary judgment will not be granted. On the other hand, if the defendant fails to answer the complaint properly, the plaintiff's allegations will be treated as true and judgment will be entered in favor of the plaintiff.

Trial

The most important step in the litigation process is the preparation of evidence and its presentation at trial. The main purpose of the trial is to persuade the trier of fact (judge or jury) that the plaintiff is entitled to relief. The evidence is presented through the testimony of witnesses and the introduction of various documents and demonstrative (real) evidence.

The rules governing court proceedings vary from jurisdiction to jurisdiction. Some jurisdictions require pretrial conferences to review and reduce issues through stipulations. The judge, counsel, and parties all participate in an attempt to agree on facts over which there is no dispute and to authenticate documents. In federal courts and in some states, courts can assign a special master to review complex cases and recommend a decision or fact to the court. The pretrial conference and assignment of a special master can be of great benefit in complicated construction cases involving numerous issues, parties, and facts.

The principal function of direct examination of a witness is to place all pertinent facts into evidence so that the trier of fact will reach the desired conclusions. To effectuate this purpose, counsel should be able to bring out all relevant information from the witness during direct examination. An effective strategy in direct examination of a witness is to confront those issues that may be raised by opposing counsel on cross-examination. Two types of witnesses effectively used in construction cases are record witnesses and expert witnesses.

Record Witnesses

Record witnesses, the custodians of exhibits and business records introduced into evidence, are usually essential in construction cases to establish the necessary facts. Records, memos, and data in any form, made at or near the time of the incident at issue, by or from information given by a person with knowledge, are admissible. However, in order for a record to be admissible, the testimony of the custodian or another qualified witness must establish that the record was made in the regular course of business.

While often less effective than live testimony, the introduction of business records plays an important role in construction cases. Very often the records are essential evidence needed to establish liability. Moreover, the records are critical to demonstrate financial damages.

The impact on the case of these documents depends upon the accuracy of their preparation and method of storage. The record witness must be qualified by establishing his familiarity with the records and with how these records were made, used, and stored.

Illustrative Example

In an action by a contractor against a subcontractor for failure to perform additional work, the contractor must establish that a written change order for the extra work was given to the subcontractor. In order to introduce a copy of the order, the contractor must call a witness who can testify that the order was made in the regular course of business and that copies were kept in a file for safekeeping. The witness should testify that the common practice for submitting written change orders was followed. After the witness has laid a sufficient foundation establishing the reliability and accuracy of the change order, the courts normally allow the copy of the record to be introduced into evidence.

Expert Testimony

The use of expert testimony by both parties occurs frequently in construction litigation. It is standard practice to use expert testimony in complex cases to establish delay claims, trade practices, and so forth. The Federal Rules of Evidence prescribe two requirements that must be met before an expert witness may testify in court. First, the questions must be beyond the ordinary knowledge of the jury and, second, the expert must be qualified.[24]

Illustrative Example

In an action to recover damages from an architect for undue delay in responding to questions articulated by the building authority supervising the project, the alleged negligence of the architect was found to be a proper area in which to admit expert testimony. The issue to be determined was whether the special delay was unnecessarily prolonged.

[10]FED. R. EVID. Rule 702, 28 U.S.C.A.

However, expert testimony is not necessary in commonplace factual situations where the jury is capable of basing its decision on its own knowledge.

Illustrative Case

In an action by a surety on a performance bond for the alleged negligence of the architect in failing to supervise construction, the court of appeals held that the surety could recover for losses resulting from the architect's negligence. The court also held that certain duties required of the architect are within the common knowledge and experience of laypeople serving on the jury and that expert testimony is not necessary in passing on ordinary factual situations that the jury can easily grasp and understand.[25]

Demonstrative Evidence

Demonstrative evidence in the broadest sense can be anything, other than testimony, that can be perceived by the senses and presented in the courtroom. In a construction trial, models, graphs, and charts are typical forms of demonstrative evidence. The experienced trial lawyer knows that such evidence can have a significant effect on a jury. Demonstrative evidence has indicia of reliability associated with its use and can become the center of attention. Exhibits are especially effective and leave a lasting impression on the jury since they are perceived by the senses and can help a witness simplify complicated issues. Counsel should follow the litany required by the jurisdiction to establish the necessary foundation for admitting such exhibits into evidence.

Documentary evidence in construction cases is frequently used to establish a prima facie case. Authenticity of these documents is usually stipulated to by both parties to save time.

Argument

One aspect of litigation that must not be overlooked is the oral argument. The attorney must persuade the trier of fact to resolve the case in favor of his or her client. The opening statement is the attorney's first opportunity to tell the judge or jury what the case is all about. It should thus be used to initiate and develop the theory of the case by stating the facts that counsel intends to prove during the trial. The opening statement should also set the mood for the case by setting the scene, telling what occurred, and describing the charges.

The closing argument is the chronological and dramatic culmination of the trial. Some trial-advocacy experts say that the closing argument should be outlined first and that all of the elements of the trial should

---

[25]Aetna Ins. Co. v Hellmuth, Obata Kassabaum, Inc., 392 F.2d 472 (8th Cir. 1968).

lead up to the closing argument. It is clearly the most critical part of the trial. This is the attorney's last opportunity to communicate with the judge or jury. Both the strengths and weaknesses of the case should be addressed. The issues should be defined, and the outcome of the case should be clear and logical. After the closing argument, the jury should be left with only one decision to make, resolution of the case in your favor.

16 BOND RIGHTS

Bonds represent the underwriter's (surety's) guarantee that the contractor it represents is financially able to do the job. Bonds are legally required on most public-works contracts; and although some jurisdictions have statutes extending bond protection to private construction, most private work is not bonded. Bonds provide a relatively quick and easy way to protect the various interests of the owner, contractor, subcontractor, and suppliers of labor and materials on a construction project.

Three parties are involved in the issuance of a bond. First, there is the surety company, which issues the bond guaranteeing the contractor or subcontractor will perform under the plans and specifications required by the contract and that the labor and materials supplied during performance of the contract will be paid. Second, there is the contractor or subcontractor, known as the "principal," who is obligated to perform in accordance with the terms of the contract. If the contractor or subcontractor performs in accordance with the contract, then both it and the surety are discharged from any liability. However, if the contractor or subcontractor fails to perform properly or otherwise defaults on the contract, the surety is required to pay the persons benefited by the bond all damages up to a certain sum, which is usually the amount of the original contract price. The third party is the person to whom the benefit of the bond ultimately runs, the owner, or where a subcontractor is acting as the principal, the general contractor. This party, called "obligee," will recover from the surety in the event of default by the contractor or subcontractor. While a bond does not insure the owner against all problems that may occur during construction, it does provide a necessary stopgap against incurring expenses due to inadequate performance or nonpayment for labor and materials by the contractor or subcontractor.

Three kinds of bonds are normally utilized in construction: bid, performance, and payment bonds. A bid bond runs to the benefit of the owner to protect against loss in case a low bidder fails to execute a contract in accordance with its bids. The performance bond also benefits the owner. Under the terms of a performance bond, the surety guarantees that the general contractor will complete the project on time and perform the work in a satisfactory manner in accordance with the contract. A payment bond is an additional remedy for suppliers, owners, and subcontractors that protects each in the event the contractor fails to pay suppliers and subcontractors that furnish labor and materials for the project. All three bonds serve various purposes and are available at different times during the construction project.

BID BONDS

A common practice in construction is to require contractors to provide some kind of a bid guarantee when bidding a project. A bid guarantee is a guarantee required by the owner giving it some recourse if the lowest bidder fails to enter into the contract. Bid bonds are generally required by statute or regulation in the public sector but are discretionary with private owners. Private owners sometimes require the deposit of a certified check or bank draft for 10 percent of the amount of the bid. If the bid is accepted and the contractor refuses to perform the contract, the owner retains the check or bank draft. Legal requirements vary as to the amount of the bond in the public sector. Some public entities merely require a bid bond for 5 percent of the bid price, but if the contractor refuses to enter into or perform the contract, the owner's only recourse is to accept that 5 percent. The minimum amount of any bid bond should be 10 percent.

A far better alternative to the certified check, bank draft, or 5 percent bid bond is a bond providing that the contractor is liable for any costs incurred by the owner because of the bidder's failure to enter into a contract. For example, the AIA bid bond form, Document A310, guarantees that if the contractor is awarded the contract and fails to enter into the contract, the owner will be paid the difference between the contractor's bid and the next larger bid.

When a contractor has made an error in preparing a bid, the contractor may be allowed to withdraw the bid and be relieved of all obligations connected to it. This generally includes the bid bond. When the courts have allowed a contractor to withdraw a bid, they have generally required the return of the bid bond to the contractor. The courts may even require the return of the bid bond when the bid form provides that bidders will not be released on account of errors.

Illustrative Case

State Construction Company and its surety, Continental Casualty Company, submitted a bid bond to the State of Oregon's highway commissioner to ensure that if State Construction was awarded the contract by the highway commission, it would enter into a formal contract with the state. After State Construction submitted its bid, the highway commission made a change in the plans and specifications relied upon by State Construction in its original bid. State Construction later realized that it had made a mistake in its bid and notified the highway commissioner. The bid had not yet been accepted or rejected by the highway commissioner.

The highway commissioner subsequently sought to recover on the bid bond for the refusal of State Construction to execute the subcontract, and State Construction asked the court to cancel its bid. The Oregon Supreme Court found that State Construction's bid was based on an unintentional omission of the cost of a substantial item. The court held that State Construction was entitled to cancellation of its bid because the highway commissioner had not suffered any damage because of the mistake and because it would be unconscionable to allow the highway commission to take advantage of State Construction's mistake.[1]

The owner will be permitted to recover on the bid bond where the bidder by its conduct or omission fails to notify the owner of the mistake in its bid. The bidder will not be entitled to have its bid cancelled on the grounds of a mistake when the owner can show that the only reason for nonexecution of the contract is the bidder's failure to properly demonstrate due care and diligence.

Illustrative Case

John J. Bowes Company, a contractor, refused to enter into a formal contract for the construction of a schoolhouse in Milton, Massachusetts. Bowes's refusal was based upon a mistake in the amount of its final bid, in which it had omitted certain items from computation. The court held that the owner was entitled to recover on its bid bond since the parties had reached a substantial agreement as to the terms of the contract and its price and since Bowes had had full opportunity to discuss the specifications before submitting its bid.[2]

PERFORMANCE BONDS

The purpose of a performance bond is to guarantee that the contractual obligation of the contractor will be met, thus protecting the owner from possible losses if the contractor breaches its contract or defaults. It should be noted that a bond is only as good as the language it contains, and that a strong bond can be a valuable tool in the owner's hand for completing the project.

Public owners are generally required to obtain a performance bond and a payment bond for labor and materials in the amount of 100 percent for all public construction projects. For private work such bonds are entirely optional and must be requested by the owner or a lending institution.

On private construction projects where a statute is not involved, the most commonly used bond form is AIA Document A311. A311 is in fact two documents, a performance bond and a labor and material payment bond.

The choices and options of the bonding company depend entirely upon

[1]State Highway Comm. v. State Constr. Co., 203 Or. 414, 280 P.2d 370 (1955).
[2]John J. Bowes Co. v. Milton, 255 Mass. 228, 151 N.E. 116 (1926).

the way the bond form is written. Under the AIA bond form, if the general contractor is clearly in default on the construction project the surety or bonding company may

(1) Pay the amount of the bond;

(2) Bring the contractor back onto the job and finance the job until the project is completed;

(3) Propose a new contractor to the owner for the completion of the work under the same contract, which will be directly between the new contractor and the owner;

(4) Complete the work with a new contractor under a contract between the new contractor and the bonding company; or

(5) Allow the owner to obtain a new contractor and pay the cost of construction exceeding the amount of the contract funds remaining.

The bonding company may raise any defenses that are available to the contractor in order to escape performance of the bond. It is generally said that damages and liability for a bonding company are measured precisely by the liability of the contractor and are limited to the penal sum of the bond.[3] The contractor may raise any defense to its performance of the bond that a contractor might raise to a claim of default by the owner. Examples of defenses available to the contractor that can be adopted by the bonding company if the AIA standard-form General Conditions (AIA Document A201) has been used, are as follows:

(1) The owner preventing or delaying the contractor's work;

(2) The owner's failure to accede to a request for an extension of time;

(3) The owner's failure to provide access to the construction site;

(4) The design professional interfering with contract performance;

(5) Changes in the plans and specifications;

(6) Defective plans and specifications;

(7) Active interference by the owner;

(8) Acceptance by the owner of nonconforming work;

(9) Correction of the work;

(10) Substantial completion;

(11) Waiver of claims by final payment;

(12) Concealed or unknown conditions;

(13) The work stopped by the owner, court order or public authority, or the contractor for failure of payment; or

(14) Wrongful termination of the contract by the owner.

---

[3]Brown v. Nat'l Sur. of N.Y., 207 S.C. 402, 36 S.E.2d 588 (1946); Greenville Airport Comm'n v. Fidelity & Guar. Co. of Baltimore, Md., 266 S.C. 553, 86 S.E.2d 249 (1945).

If an owner elects to use the broad-form AIA Performance Bond rather than a more stringently drawn owner-oriented bond requiring the surety to complete the work and then to determine fault, the owner should realize that if the surety fails to act in a reasonable manner considering the particular circumstances of the situation, the surety can become liable for an amount in excess of the penal sum.

Illustrative Case

The general contractor defaulted and the owner filed a request with the surety under the surety's performance bond. The contractor had been certified by the architect to be in default on the construction contract. The surety refused to pay the penal sum of the bond and refused to undertake construction of the project. The surety alleged that as the bonding company, it was free from any liability under the bond due to alleged material breaches of the construction contract by the owner. The court refused to consider the bonding company's allegations and held that the architect's certificate, as reasonable grounds to terminate the contract, had triggered the surety's obligations to the owner. The court additionally held that the surety's breach of the performance bond extended its liability in an amount beyond the penal sum of the bond. In effect, the court ruled that this breach of bond obligation by the bonding company extended the liability of the surety company to all the damages sustained by the owner.[4]

PAYMENT BONDS

A payment bond is a guarantee by the bonding company that it will pay the contractor's bill for labor and materials incurred in the performance of the project's construction. Under a labor and material payment bond, a bonding company is obligated to those who furnish labor and materials to the contractor for and during construction. The bond covers supplies and labor furnished to the prime contractor or to its subcontractors. Labor and materials are generally defined as whatever is necessary to construct the work and consumed in the performance of the contract. Types of labor and materials covered are equipment rental, freight and transportation charges, minor repairs to contractor's equipment and tools, forms, scaffolding and temporary structures, gasoline and oil used in the construction, and union benefits. Capital equipment, major repairs to tools and equipment not utilized or consumed in the construction, insurance premiums and worker's compensation premiums, loans to the contractor, and taxes that have been withheld are items generally not covered under the bond.

FEDERAL BOND LAWS

All federal construction projects involving fixed-price contracts in excess of $2000 are subject to the provisions of the Miller Act. The

---

[4]Continental Realty Corp. v. The Andrew Crevolin Co., 380 F. Supp. 246 (S.D. W.Va. 1974).

Miller Act[5] was enacted to protect the government from any loss it might sustain as a result of a contractor's insolvency or inability to make payments. The purpose of the Miller Act payment bond is to protect all subcontractors and suppliers supplying labor and material to federal construction projects where lien rights are not permitted by law. The Miller Act gives subcontractors and suppliers that furnish labor and material to a federal construction project the right to sue prime contractors and their respective sureties in the United States district courts for unpaid labor and materials. Since the Miller Act was enacted for the benefit of subcontractors and suppliers, the courts have ruled that the act is to be liberally construed in favor of those subcontractors and suppliers entitled to make claims on the bond.

The Miller Act states that the payment bond protects those who supply *labor* and *material* to the prime contractor for use on a public work. The Miller Act applies only to construction, alteration, or repair projects on any public building or project belonging to the United States government. However, what constitutes a "public work" can create confusion, especially in view of the pervasive federal aid to state and local governments. The courts are often called upon to determine the "owner" of a project in order to assess its public nature. When a contract is for a public building or public work of the United States, or if the person or agency making the contract on behalf of the United States has authority to so contract, it is immaterial whether the contract was made in the name of the United States or of such person or agency—the contract is one involving a "public work." Any work for which the federal government may provide funds or in which it has an interest may be considered a public work.

NON-FEDERAL PUBLIC BONDS

Virtually all states require contractors to provide performance bonds and to pay for labor and materials supplied in connection with the contract. The bonds are normally considered a necessary ingredient of the contract, and under some statutes the state is not bound unless the bonds are given and approved. Thus the posting of a performance bond and a labor and material payment bond prevents the potentially disastrous effect of a contractor's default on its obligations.

The bonds are generally considered to be made for the benefit of the state, not for the benefit of suppliers and subcontractors, and are governed by the law of the state, even in circumstances where the contract is executed outside the state. In addition, many state bond statutes are directly modeled after the Miller Act. In such states, federal decisions interpreting the act lay the groundwork by which the state courts construe similar state statutes.

[5]40 U.S.C. §§ 270a-270d (1935).

While states may differ in statutory bond requirements, all statutes contain specific notice provisions. Failure to follow the statutory notice requirements will normally result in total forfeiture of all bond rights. The notice provision is usually applied to the timeliness of notice to preserve bond rights and also to the time limitations in which to bring suit on a bond.

PRIVATE BOND RIGHTS

In those jurisdictions that have enacted statutes permitting a private property owner to obtain from the contractor a bond protecting subcontractors, suppliers, and laborers, such statutes have met with general approval by the courts as an efficient method of protecting and enforcing liens. These statutes usually provide that where the owner files with its contract a bond to the contractor, recovery against the owner by suppliers and others is limited to the amount due on the contract.

However, those statutes *requiring* the owner to obtain a bond have met with more mixed results. Some cases have held that such statutes are invalid, at least where the owner's failure to exact the bond results in personal and individual liability to the subcontractors, suppliers, laborers, and others sought to be protected by the statute.

Illustrative Case

A Texas statute required a contractor to obtain a bond for "true and faithful performance of the contract, and the payment of all subcontractors, workmen, laborers and mechanics . . . . " The law required the owner to contract with the contractor to give a bond.

Hess contracted with J. A. Knight to build a two-story house and to furnish all labor and material for the house. Denman Lumber Company sold and delivered lumber to Knight for the construction of the house, but Knight failed to pay for it. Denman Lumber Company sued Hess because Knight became insolvent.

The Texas court held that Hess was under no obligation to pay for Knight's debts, and that the Texas statute was void by reason of its interference with liberty of contract. The court reasoned that requiring the owner to pay twice for the material would be inequitable and that the supplier had mechanic's lien rights through which it could obtain recovery for its claim.[6]

However, there are cases holding such statutes valid.

Illustrative Case

A Utah statute provided that on any project exceeding $500 the owner must secure a bond equal to the contract price. The statute also provided that any person furnishing labor or material had a direct right of action against the surety for the amount due. Should the owner fail to procure the bond, it was liable for payment of such obligations. The Utah court held that the statute could not be regarded as an unreasonable regulation, much less a violation of constitutional provisions.[7]

[6]Hess v. Denman Lumber Co., 218 S.W. 162 (Tex. 1920).
[7]Rio Grande Lumber Co. v. Darke, 50 Utah 114, 167 P. 241 (1917).

Several states have statutes requiring bonds for private work that apply at least to certain housing projects. Such legislation may either supplement the supplier's right to a mechanic's lien or provide that bond rights shall substitute for lien rights. On private construction projects where a statute is not involved, the most commonly used bond form is that recommended by the American Institute of Architects (AIA Document A311), but other forms have been furnished in private agreements. The AIA form does not require claimants who have a direct contractual relationship with the prime contractor to give written notice of a claim within ninety days of the work's completion. Those claimants who do not have a direct contractual relationship with the prime contractor must give notice by registered or certified mail to the owner, general contractor, and surety (or at least two of them) of the amount of the claim within ninety days of the last furnishing of any labor, materials, or services for which claim can be made under the bond. Failure to comply with any of these requirements defeats any action on a bond.

17 THE OWNER AND INSURANCE

Whether an owner is in the public or the private sector, one of the primary considerations any owner needs to take into account is the protection of its construction project from initiation through final completion. This protection is best obtained through the owner's purchase of insurance coverage.

Every owner should keep in mind the difference between insurance coverage obtained for the construction project and construction bonds. Insurance is basically a contract between the owner and an insurance company. This contract is, in effect, an indemnity agreement. Under such an agreement an insurance company promises to reimburse or pay the owner for a project-related loss specified in that legal document called an "insurance policy." In most states the courts have not viewed construction bonds as a form of insurance even though they are written by the insurance industry. In other words, an owner should not view a construction bond as an insurance policy. A bond is nothing more than a guarantee that the owner's construction project will be completed as specified in the contract documents and that the project will be free from liens when it is completed. Insurance, on the other hand, is used by the owner to protect the proposed construction project from physical property damage and to protect itself from liability due to project loss.

The purchase of insurance is one of two mechanisms used for reducing the owner's risk of loss during construction. The other method is to transfer the risk to others engaged in the construction. This is done by drafting risk-shifting clauses in the contracts for design services and construction.

The insurance industry serving construction is made up of two categories. One category is called "the direct writer." This type of company has its own sales force and offers no other source of coverage. The second category is the "agency." The agency is made up of brokers and agents who market or sell coverage for several companies.

The owner should develop insurance specifications early in the planning of the project so that it can study the marketplace. Insurance specifications desired for the contractor should also be drafted early so that they may be included in the contract or bid documents if the project is not negotiated. The best place for an owner to obtain advice on insurance needs is from a knowledgeable insurance counsel.

The owner must have property insurance coverage. This coverage can be placed under a master property insurance program. The standard-form AIA General Conditions (Document A201, 1976 ed.) contains provisions outlining the types of insurance coverage necessary to guard against losses due to accident, fire, or other similar occurrences during construction of the project. In reviewing these provisions, the owner should keep in mind that this is a standard-form document containing basic clauses applicable to all projects and peculiar to none. The owner should always consider its own special needs and amend these provisions to suit the proposed project.

OWNER'S LIABILITY INSURANCE

The AIA General Conditions (Document A201, 1976 ed.), at paragraph 11.2, addresses the owner's obligation to acquire liability insurance for the project. Subparagraph 11.2.1 states:

The Owner shall be responsible for purchasing and maintaining his own liability insurance and, at his option, may purchase and maintain such insurance as will protect him against claims which may arise from operations under the contract.

This subparagraph basically establishes that the owner incurs the liability and the responsibility to provide whatever liability insurance coverage it may wish to carry in order to protect itself against any possible losses or problems that may occur during project construction. The owner should carefully assess the liabilities likely to occur and act accordingly. It is a foolhardy owner that ventures into a construction project without adequate liability insurance coverage.

Paragraph 11.3 of the AIA General Conditions (Document A201) addresses the requirements for property insurance. Subparagraph 11.3.1 states in part:

Unless otherwise provided, the Owner shall purchase and maintain property insurance upon the entire work at the site to the full insurable value thereof. This insurance shall include the interests of the Owner, the Contractor, Subcontractors and Sub-subcontractors in the Work and shall insure against the perils of fire and extended coverage and shall include "all risk" insurance for physical loss or damage including, without duplication of coverage, theft, vandalism and malicious mischief.

Subparagraph 11.3.2 goes on to require that

[t]he Owner shall purchase and maintain such boiler and machinery insurance as may be required by the Contract Documents or by law. This insurance shall include the interests of the Owner, the Contractor, Subcontractor and Sub-subcontractors in the Work.

Under subparagraph 11.3.4, the owner is required to file copies of all insurance policies with the contractor.

Under subparagraph 11.3.1, if the owner does not intend to purchase insurance, the owner is required to tell the contractor, in writing, prior to commencement of construction. The contractor is then allowed to purchase insurance to cover itself and its subcontractors and charge the cost, by change order, to the owner. Subparagraph 11.3.1 further states:

[I]f the Contractor is damaged by failure of the Owner to purchase or maintain such insurance and to so notify the Contractor, then the Owner shall bear all reasonable costs properly attributable thereto.

This language, coupled with the owner's obligation to purchase and maintain insurance on the entire project, establishes that the owner bears the total risks of physical loss or damage to the project absent the purchase of insurance or notification to the contractor that insurance will not be purchased for the project.

It should be kept in mind by the wary owner that if an AIA standard-form contract is utilized, under subparagraph 11.3.6 the owner and the contractor waive all rights against each other for any damages resulting from fire or any other hazards only to the extent that a loss is covered by insurance.

In general, an extended coverage policy provides protection against fire, windstorm, hail, explosion, riot, riot attending a strike, civil unrest, aircraft damage, vehicle damage, and smoke damage. Under subparagraph 11.3.2 the owner is required to purchase boiler and machinery insurance because this coverage is normally not included in traditional policies. Vandalism, malicious mischief, construction collapse, water leakage, and water damage of any type may be also included in insurance coverage under an "all physical loss" form. In areas where earthquakes pose a danger, this special coverage should be acquired together with coverage for other special hazards.

LOSS-OF-USE INSURANCE

The AIA standard form of General Conditions (Document A201) states at subparagraph 11.4.1:

The Owner, at his option, may purchase and maintain such insurance as will insure him against loss of use of his property due to fire or other hazards, however caused. The Owner waives all rights of action against the Contractor for loss of use of his property, including consequential losses due to fire or other hazards however caused, to the extent covered by insurance under this paragraph 11.4.

This coverage is an optional provision and may be of benefit to the owner where the proposed construction involves remodeling or additions to existing structures.

CONTRACTOR'S LIABILITY INSURANCE

The AIA General Conditions (Document A201, 1976 ed.) requires as follows at subparagraph 11.1.1:

The Contractor shall purchase and maintain such insurance as will protect him from claims set forth below which may arise out of or result from the Contractor's operations under the Contract, whether such operations be by himself or by any subcontractor or by anyone directly or indirectly employed by any of them, or by anyone for whose acts any of them may be liable:

.1 Claims under worker's or workmen's compensation, disability benefit and other similar employee benefit acts;

.2 Claims for damages because of bodily injury, occupational sickness or disease, or death of his employees;

.3 Claims for damages because of bodily injury, sickness or disease, or death of any person other than his employees;

.4 Claims for damages incurred by usual personal injury liability coverage which are sustained (1) by any person as a result of an offense directly or indirectly related to the employment of such person by the Contractor, or (2) by any other person;

.5 Claims for damages, other than to the work itself, because of injury to or destruction of tangible property, including loss of use resulting therefrom; and

.6 Claims for damages because of bodily injury or death of any person or property damage arising out of the ownership, maintenance or use of any motor vehicle.

Both public and private owners preparing to engage in the construction of a project should always seek the advice of experienced insurance counsel or review standard coverage provisions in order to determine the necessary statutory coverage under employer's liability acts or worker's compensation statutes.

Subparagraph 11.1.3 requires that certificates of insurance, acceptable to the owner, shall be filed with the owner prior to commencement of the work. These certificates shall contain a provision that coverage afforded under the policies will not be cancelled until at least fifteen days' prior written notice has been given to the owner. It is the responsibility of the owner to determine that these certificates are, in fact, received and that the insurance is acceptable, so the certificate of insurance should be carefully examined. The owner should require that the certificate of insurance list policy numbers, dates of origination and expiration, and the limits of liability for worker's compensation and employees' liability. Comprehensive general liability coverage, which includes property damage, personal injury, and bodily injury as well as comprehensive automobile liability coverage that includes both property damage and provisions concerning bodily injury, should also be listed. AIA Document G705, Certificate of Insurance, describes the information that owners should be sure is in their possession. A certificate for payment should not be issued or honored until all certificates of insurance have been furnished by the contractor, reviewed, and accepted.

The general contractor should always be required, by whatever form of contract documents used, to purchase adequate insurance coverage. If an owner suffers a loss and the contractor is insolvent, as happens quite often, a comprehensive "general liability policy" is most valuable. Coverage will generally be found under this policy as long as the problem giving rise to the claim occurred while or became apparent before the contractor completed construction of the project.[1] If the loss is the result of a defect or deficiencies in the building or the work and the claim is for repair and replacement, it is a general rule that these claims are not covered under the contractor's insurance.[2] However, losses due to inability to use the construction are frequently covered under the general liability policy.[3] This problem may be avoided by phrasing the claim for defective work as a warranty claim. Although many general liability policies contain exclusions for property damage, the same policy typically states that the exclusion does not apply to a warranty of fitness or quality of the named insured product or to a warranty that work performed by or on behalf of the named insured will be done in a workmanlike manner. Faced with this ambiguity, many courts have determined that coverage applies where the claim alleges a breach of warranty.[4]

OWNER-CONTROLLED PROGRAMS

A relatively recent approach to insurance has been referred to as the "owner-controlled program" or, more commonly, "wrap-up" insurance. In using a wrap-up insurance program the owner furnishes all of the insurance for the project. The general contractor or prime multiple contractors at bid time or when proposing prices are requested to reduce their bids or offers by the sum that otherwise would be expended for liability insurance. In other words, the contractor is asked to deduct from his bid or offer the amount that the contractor would have expended in procuring insurance coverage normally obtained under a typical construction contract.

The benefit to the owner under a wrap-up program is supposedly in the return of premium cost to the owner at the completion of the construction project if there has been a good project-loss record. However, if the loss rate has exceeded the estimate on which the premium was based, the owner will then be required to pay an additional sum in

[1]Boggs v. Aetna Cas. & Sur. Co., 272 S.C. 460, 272 S.E.2d 565 (1979). *See also* United States Fidelity & Gen. Co. v. American Ins. Co., 345 N.E.2d 267 (Ind. App. 1976).

[2]Vobill Homes, Inc. v. Hartford Accident & Indem. Co., 179 So. 2d 496 (La. App. 1965).

[3]Yakima Cement Prods. Co. v. Great American Ins. Co., 608 P.2d 254 (Wash. 1980); Sola Basic Ind., Inc. v. United States Fidelity & Guar. Co., 280 N.W.2d 211 (Wis. 1979).

[4]Federal Ins. Co. v. P.S.T. Homes, Inc., 113 Ariz. 136, 547 P.2d 1050 (1976).

premiums. The wary owner should realize that premiums for wrap-up insurance are only estimated premiums and may fluctuate up and down.

If an owner is considering using wrap-up insurance, it is highly recommended that the estimated project cost exceed $75,000,000. If the estimated project cost is less than this figure, a wrap-up insurance program is not practical.

Running a wrap-up insurance program and monitoring the job for safety purposes are time-consuming occupations that the owner will be required to undertake and that will require the employment of safety engineers and an additional safety force. In addition, if the owner undertakes to oversee the safety of the project in order to manage risks, it may incur far greater liability for injury or loss than was ever intended when the project was first begun.

APPENDIX A

DBC
48A
(Rev 10/76)

ARCHITECT-ENGINEER
AND RELATED SERVICES
QUESTIONNAIRE

STATE OF NEW JERSEY
DEPARTMENT OF THE TREASURY
DIVISION OF BUILDING AND CONSTRUCTION

PURPOSE:

It is the policy of the State Government, in procuring architectural and engineering services, to encourage firms lawfully engaged in the practice of those professions to submit annually a statement of qualifications and performance data.

This standard form DBC 48-A is provided for the purpose of allowing interested A/E firms to submit appropriate information on experience and firm capabilities in order that they may become qualified to be considered for professional services to be performed for the State.

DEFINITIONS:

"**Architect-engineer and related services**" are those professional services associated with research, development, design and construction, alteration, or repair of real property as well as incidental services that members of these professions and those in their employ may logically or justifiably perform, including studies, investigations, surveys, evaluations, consultations, planning, programming, conceptual designs, plans and specifications, cost estimates, inspections, shop drawing reviews, sample recommendations, preparation of operating and maintenance manuals, and other related services.

"**Parent company**" is that firm, company, corporation, association or conglomerate which is the major stockholder or highest-tier owner of the firm completing this questionnaire, i.e., Firm A is owned by Firm B which is, in turn, a subsidiary of Corporation C. The "parent company" of Firm A is Corporation C.

"**Principals**" are those individuals in a firm who possess responsibility for its management. They may be owners, partners, corporate officers, associates, administrators, etc.

"**Discipline**", as used in this questionnaire, refers to the primary technological capability of individuals in the responding firm. Possession of an academic degree, professional registration, or certification in a given field of practice frequently reflects an individual's primary technical discipline.

MINORITY DEFINITION:

An individual, partnership, professional association or corporation of architects or engineers, legally recognized by their respective professional State Boards, whose owner, partner, or principal stockholder is an individual who is a member of a minority group as defined under New Jersey Public Laws of 1975, Chapter 127.

INSTRUCTIONS FOR FILING (Numbers below correspond to numbers contained in form):

1. Give accurate and complete name of firm and address, including zip code, name of profession and statement of specialty.

2. Provide date firm was established under name given in item 1.

3. Enter type of ownership of firm (sole proprietor, partnership, corporation, joint venture, etc.). Enter Federal Identification Number and check appropriate box regarding

Minority Ownership.

4. Insert date upon which all submitted information is current and accurate.

5. Firms which are subsidiaries of larger parent companies, or conglomerates, insert name and address of highest-tier owner.

5a. If present firm is the successor to, or outgrowth of, one or more predecessor firms, show name(s) of former entity(s) and the year of their original establishment.

6. List no more than two principals who may be contacted by the agency receiving this form. Principals must be empowered to speak for firm on policy and contractual matters and should be familiar with programs and procedures of the agency to which this form is directed.

6a. List Branch Management Personnel.

7. Beginning with the main, or home A-E office (even if previously listed), show location and telephone number of all the submitting firm's principal and satellite offices (including foreign offices). Branch offices may also submit their own "A-E and Related Services Questionnaires."

8. Enter total number of employees, by discipline, in all A-E offices. While some personnel may be qualified in several disciplines, each person should be counted only once in accord with his or her primary function. Include clerical personnel as "administrative." Write in any additional disciplines, and the number of people in each, in spaces marked "other" (sociologists, ecologists, etc.).

9. Show total professional services fees received by the submitting firm each calendar year for last five years (most recent year first). Fee totals need not be exact but should be estimated on the basis of (a) work performed directly for the State Government (not including grant and loan projects), and (b) all other work, including State assisted projects.

10. Provide information requested pertaining to partners and key personnel.

11. Select and enter in numerical sequence not more than twenty project code numbers from list on page 2 which reflect firm's demonstrated technical capabilities and project experience. For each code number show total number of, and total gross fees received for, projects of that type performed by firm during past five years. Carefully review list. If firm has capability not included on list, insert same as item 100 and include in firm listing. Do not add more than one additional capability.

12. Using the project code number(s) in same sequence as entered in item 11, give details of at least one recent (within last five years) representative project for each code number, up to a maximum of thirty (30) separate projects, or that portion of such projects for which firm was responsible. Firms listing less than 20 code numbers may provide details on 2 or more (up to 30) projects to illustrate their specialization. After each code number, (a) show whether the firm was "P," the prime professional, or "C," a consultant, or "JV," part of a joint venture, on that particular project; (b) provide name and location of a typical project which exemplifies firm's performance under that category; (c) give name and address of the owner of that project; (d) show the total project cost and the estimated construction cost (where applicable) for that portion of the project for which the firm was primarily responsible; where no construction was involved, show approximate cost of your work; and (e) list year the firm's work on that particular project was completed.

12a. Complete DBC 48A should be signed by a principal of the firm, preferably the chief Executive Officer.

13. Provide appropriate additional information.

14. Sign and date the form.

PROJECT CODE NUMBERS
For use with questions 10 and 11

001 - Acoustics & Audio Systems
002 - Aerial Photogrammetry; Mapping
003 - Air Pollution Control
004 - Airports; Terminals & Hangars
005 - Arctic Engineering
006 - Auditoriums & Theatres
007 - Automation; Controls; Instrumentation
008 - Barracks; Dormitories; Hotels
009 - Bridges
010 - Cemeteries (Planning & Relocation)
011 - Chemical Processing & Storage
012 - Churches; Chapels
013 - Commercial Buildings; Shopping Centers
014 - Communications Systems; TV (Microwave)
015 - Computer Facilities; Computer Services

016 - Construction Management
017 - Corrosion Control (Cathodic Protection)
018 - Cost Estimating
019 - Dams (Concrete; Arch)
020 - Dams (Earth; Rock), Dikes, Levees
021 - Desalinization; Process & Facilities
022 - Dining Halls; Clubs; Restaurants
023 - Ecological & Archeological Studies
024 - Educational Facilities Classrooms
025 - Electronics
026 - Elevators, Escalators & Conveyors
027 - Energy Conservation
028 - Environmental Impact Studies; Assessments
029 - Fallout Shelters; Protective Construction

030 - Field Houses; Gyms, Stadiums
031 - Fire Protection
032 - Forestry & Forest Products
033 - Fuel & Petroleum Storage & Site Dist.
034 - Garages (Vehicle Maintenance; Parking)
035 - Gas Systems (Propane; Natural, Etc.)
036 - Harbors; Jetties; Docks; Marinas
037 - Heating; Ventilating; Air Conditioning
038 - Highrise, Air Space-Type Buildings
039 - Highways; Streets; Runways; Parking Areas
040 - Historical Preservation; Bldg. Alterations
041 - Hospitals & Medical Facilities
042 - Housing (Residential and Multi-Family)

Appendix A-1. (caption)

043 - Hydraulics & Pneumatics
044 - Industrial Buildings; Manufacturing Plants
045 - Industrial Processes
046 - Interior Design & Graphics
047 - Irrigation; Flood Control
048 - Judicial and Courtroom Facilities
049 - Laboratories; Medical Research Facilities
050 - Landscaping
051 - Libraries; Museums; Galleries
052 - Lighting (Interiors; Display; Etc.)
053 - Lighting (Monumental; Stadium, Etc.)
054 - Materials Handling Systems
055 - Metallurgy
056 - Military Standard Design
057 - Mining & Minerology
058 - Missile Facilities (Silos; Fuels; Transport)
059 - Naval Architecture (Offshore Platforms)
060 - Nuclear Facilities
061 - Office Buildings
062 - Oceanographic Engineering
063 - Petroleum Drilling, Refining & Storage
064 - Pipelines-Cross Country (Liquid & Gas)
065 - Planning (Regional)
066 - Planning (Site, Urban & New Community)
067 - Plumbing & Piping Design
068 - Postal Facilities
069 - Power Generation; Transmission; Dist.
070 - Pre-Fab; Modular System Design
071 - Prisons & Correctional Facilities
072 - Product, Machine, & Equipment Design
073 - Radar; Sonar; Radio Telescopes
074 - Railroads; Rapid Transit
075 - Recreation Facilities (Parks, Etc.)
076 - Resource Recovery
077 - RF Systems & Shieldings
078 - Rivers; Canals; Waterways Improvements
079 - Security Systems
080 - Seismic Designs & Studies
081 - Sewage Treatment & Sewer Systems
082 - Soils & Geologic Studies; Foundations
083 - Solar Energy Utilization
084 - Solid Wastes; Incineration; Land Fill
085 - Special Environments; Dust Free; Cold, Etc.
086 - Surveying; Grading; Platting
087 - Swimming Pools
088 - Studies, Manuals; Reports
089 - Telephone Systems (Rural; Bldg, Etc.)
090 - Testing & Inspection Services; Wind Tunnels
091 - Traffic & Transportation Studies
092 - Towers; Poles & Guyed Systems
093 - Tunnels & Subways
094 - Urban Renewal; Rehabilitation
095 - Utilities; Gas & Steam
096 - Value Analysis; Life-Cycle Costing
097 - Warehouses & Depots
098 - Water Resources; Hydrology; Ground Water
099 - Water Treatment & Supply
100 - Other

INFORMATION AND EXPERIENCE QUESTIONNAIRE (To Be Updated Annually)

STATE OF NEW JERSEY
DEPARTMENT OF THE TREASURY
DIVISION OF BUILDING AND CONSTRUCTION

DBC
STANDARD
FORM

48A

1. Firm Name/Business Address/Profession/Specialty

2. Year Present Firm Established:

4. Date Prepared:

3. Type of Ownership:
   Federal Identification Number:
   Minority Partner or Owner: ☐ Yes ☐ No

5. Name of Parent Company, if any:

5a. Former Firm Name(s) and Year(s) Established:

6. Names of Two Principals to Contact: Title/Telephone

   1)

   2)

6a. Branch Office Management Personnel: Title/Telephone

   1)

   2)

7. Present Offices: City/State/Telephone No. personnel each office

   1)
   2)
   3)
   4)
   5)
   6)
   7)
   8)
   9)
   10)

8. Personnel by Discipline: (Include Principals and All Personnel)

____ Architects	____ Civil Engineers	____ Ecologists	____ Surveyors
____ Urban/Regional Planners	____ Structural Engineers	____ Geologists	
____ Landscape Architects	____ Mechanical Engineers	____ Specification Writers	
____ Interior Designers	____ Electrical Engineers	____ Economists	
____ Estimators	____ Sanitary Engineers	____ Construction Inspectors	
____ Draftsmen	____ Soils Engineers	____ Administrative	

____ TOTAL (Personnel)

9. Summary of Total Gross Fees Received   Last 5 Years (most recent year first)

	19 ____	19 ____	19 ____	19 ____	19 ____
Direct state contract work	$	$	$	$	$
Other domestic work	$	$	$	$	$
Foreign work	$	$	$	$	$

10. Brief Resume of Partners and Key Personnel

a. Name and Title

b. Years experience: This Firm ____   Other Firm ____

c. Education: Degree(s)/Year/Specialization

d. Active Registration: Year First Registered/Discipline

e. Other Experience and Qualifications:

a. Name and Title

b. Years experience: This Firm ____   Other Firm ____

c. Education: Degree(s)/Year/Specialization

d. Active Registration: Year First Registered/Discipline

e. Other Experience and Qualifications:

11. Profile of Firm's Project Experience, Last 5 Years

Project Code	Number of Projects	Total Gross Fees	Project Code	Number of Projects	Total Gross Fees	Project Code	Number of Projects	Total Gross Fees
1)			8)			15)		
2)			9)			16)		
3)			10)			17)		
4)			11)			18)		
5)			12)			19)		
6)			13)			20)		
7)			14)					

12. Project Examples, Last 5 Years

Project Code	"P", "C" or "JV"	Project Name and Location	Owner Name and Address	Total Cost of Project	Total Cost of Work For Which Firm Was Responsible (State Specialty)	Year Work Completed
1						
2						
3						
4						
5						
6						
7						
8						
9						

12. Project Examples (Continued)

10							
11							
12							
13							
14							
15							
16							
17							
18							
19							
20							
21							
22							
23							
24							
25							
26							
27							
28							
29							

13. Within this space, firm may provide any additional information or description of resources supporting its qualifications, including architectural achievements and awards received.

14. The foregoing is a statement of facts.

Firm Name
Signature
Name (Typed)
and Title

Date

FORM DBC 48B (REV. 10-76)

PROJECT QUESTIONNAIRE

STATE OF NEW JERSEY
DEPARTMENT OF THE TREASURY
DIVISION OF BUILDING & CONSTRUCTION

DBC
STANDARD
FORM

48B

1. Project Name/DBC No./Location & Date for which Firm is applying:

DATE OF DBC ANNOUNCEMENT _____

2. Firm (or Joint-Venture) Name & Address

Federal Identification No. _____

2a. Address of office to perform work, if different from item 2 _____

2b. No. of Personnel presently at work location _____

3. Name, Title & Telephone Number of Principal to Contact

4. If submittal is by Joint-Venture only outline specific areas of responsibility (including administrative, technical and financial) for each of the participating firms: (Attach DBC 48-A for each, if not on file with DBC.) 4a. Has joint-venture previously worked together _____

4b. Firm or joint-venture total personnel by discipline (Include Principals and all Personnel):

____ Architects ____ Civil Engineers ____ Ecologists ____ Surveyors
____ Urban/Regional Planners ____ Structural Engineers ____ Geologists
____ Landscape Architects ____ Mechanical Engineers ____ Specification Writers
____ Interior Designers ____ Electrical Engineers ____ Economists
____ Estimators ____ Sanitary Engineers ____ Construction Inspectors
____ Draftsmen ____ Soils Engineers ____ Administrative

____ Total Personnel

5. Outside Key Consultants/Associates Anticipated for this Project (Attach DBC 48A for Consultants/Associates Listed, if not already on file with DBC)

Name & Address	48A on File	Specialty	Worked with Prime before (Yes or No)
1)			
2)			
3)			
4)			
5)			
6)			
7)			
8)			

6. List of Key Personnel and Specialists anticipated for this Project.

7. Work by Firm or Joint Venture Members which Best Illustrates Current Qualifications Relevant to this Project (list not more than 20 Projects)

Project Name & Location	Nature of Firm's Responsibility	Owner's Name & Address	Completion Date	Estimated Cost	
				Entire Project	Work for which Firm was/is Responsible

8. All work by firms or Joint Venture members *currently being performed for State agencies.*

Project Name & Location DATE OF CONTRACT	Nature of Firm's Responsibility	Owner's Name & Address	Percent Complete	Estimated Cost	
				Entire Project	Work for which Firm is Responsible

9. Within this space, firm may provide any additional information and description of resources supporting its qualifications for the proposed project.

10. The foregoing is a statement of facts.

Firm Name
Signature
Name (Typed)
and Title

Date

APPENDIX B

FORM SE240
7/14/83

STATE OF SOUTH CAROLINA

STANDARD FORM

OF

AGREEMENT BETWEEN OWNER

AND ARCHITECT OR ENGINEER

_____

THIS AGREEMENT, made this _____ day of _____ in
the year of Nineteen Hundred _____ between

_____

_____

_____

hereinafter called OWNER, and _____

_____

_____

_____

hereinafter called ARCHITECT.

PROJECT

Title:_____

_____

_____

SCOPE OF WORK

It is the intent of OWNER to _____

_____

_____

_____

_____

All of the above WORK shall hereinafter be referred to as the
Project.

```
                                                  FORM SE240
                                                  7/14/83

                      CONSTRUCTION FUNDS AVAILABLE

TOTAL FUNDS available by OWNER for construction only for this

Project are:   _____

_____

_____

_____

_____

_____


(List by categories items to be designed and specified by ARCHI-
TECT such as:  Site Improvements, Landscaping, Building(s), Basic
Equipment - Fixed, etc.  Show dollar amount of each.)
but not including other Project cost such as ARCHITECT'S compen-
sation, land purchase, OWNER'S insurance, Project Representative,
contingencies, etc.

                           COMPENSATION

ARCHITECT shall provide professional services for this Project in
accordance  with  the  Terms and Conditions of this Agreement and
OWNER shall compensate ARCHITECT in accordance with the Terms and
Conditions of this Agreement as follows:

BASIC SERVICES:    Basic Compensation shall be computed on the

basis of:

_____

_____

_____


ADDITIONAL SERVICES:  Compensation shall be computed as follows:

_____

_____

_____




                              -2-
```

237 APPENDIX B

```
                                              FORM SE240
                                               7/14/83

REIMBURSABLE EXPENSES: Compensation shall be computed as follows:

_____

_____

_____


                     PAYMENT SCHEDULE TO ARCHITECT

A.  BASIC SERVICES:

    Payment  for ARCHITECT'S Basic Services shall be made monthly
    upon presentation of ARCHITECT'S statement of  services  ren-
    dered  in  proportion  to  the  amount of services performed,
    provided that the compensation of each Phase  of  Basic  Ser-
    vices shall not exceed the limits set out below:

         Schematic Design Phase...................     %

         Design Development Phase.................     %

         Construction Documents Phase.............     %

         Bidding and Bid Award Phase..............   75%*


         Construction Administration Phase

         At 25% Completed Construction............     %

         At 50% Completed Construction............     %

         At 75% Completed Construction............     %

         At SUBSTANTIAL COMPLETION................     %


         At 100% Completion, Including Furnishing
            OWNER RECORD DRAWINGS and Other
            Documents Required....................   100%

         *If  this Agreement does not require Construction Admin-
         istration Phase, then Bidding and Bid Award Phase should
         be 100% and "X" out Construction Administration Phase.

No  deduction  shall  be  made  from  ARCHITECT'S compensation on
account of penalty, liquidated damages  or  other  sums  withheld
from CONTRACTOR.



                              -3-
```

B. CONSTRUCTION COST:

The Construction Cost, when used as the basis for determining
ARCHITECT'S Compensation, shall be defined as follows:

    1. For completed construction: The total applicable
        Contract cost of all such WORK;

    2. For WORK not constructed: the lowest bona fide bid
        received from a qualified bidder for WORK within
        the stated budget;

    3. For WORK for which no such bid or proposal is
        received: the latest approved Detailed Estimate of
        Construction Cost within the stated budget.

Construction Cost does not include the compensation to ARCHI-
TECT, the cost incurred for a full-time project representative, field project manager, CONSTRUCTION MANAGER or
other special consultants, the cost of the land, rights-of-
way, advertising, Basic Equipment - Moveable or other costs
which are the responsibility of OWNER.

-4-

ARTICLE 1 - GENERAL

This Agreement incorporates the State Of South Carolina Standard Form General Conditions Of The Contract For Construction (Form SE370).

ARTICLE 2 - ARCHITECT'S BASIC SERVICES AND RESPONSIBILITIES

A. GENERAL

1. ARCHITECT'S Basic Professional Services consist of the phases described as follows and include, but are not limited to, normal architectural, structural, mechanical and electrical engineering services. ARCHITECT shall obtain written approval of OWNER before proceeding with each phase. Nothing in this Agreement shall be construed as placing any obligation on OWNER to proceed with any phase beyond the latest phase approved by OWNER.

2. ARCHITECT agrees to accept OWNER'S program and budget and further agrees to accomplish said project within the intent of the program and established budget. Should ARCHITECT determine that the project cannot be accomplished within the established budget, ARCHITECT shall notify OWNER, in writing, so that the project scope can be reviewed and modified as necessary.

3. ARCHITECT agrees to supervise the construction of WORK and to require that CONTRACTOR comply with CONTRACT DOCUMENTS. Such SUPERVISION shall include, unless otherwise specified, the general administration of the Contract; the issuance of Certificates of Payment; the keeping of accounts; the approval of materials, equipment, and apparatus used in WORK; and SUPERVISION of construction. General administration of the Contract includes, but is not limited to, the performance of all acts, services, and responsibilities described, referred to, or implied in this Contract and to the performance of all acts, services, and responsibilities described, referred to, or implied in the General Conditions (Form SE370) of the State of South Carolina.

4. ARCHITECT agrees to strictly conform to and be bound by standards, criteria, budgetary considerations and memoranda of policy furnished to him by OWNER and further agrees that he shall design WORK in strict compliance with all applicable laws, codes and industry standards.

-5-

B. ARCHITECT'S RESPONSIBILITIES IN
    CONJUNCTION WITH BASIC SERVICES

    1. DESIGN PHASE

        a. SCHEMATIC DESIGN PHASE

            (1) ARCHITECT shall review the needs and require-
                 ments of OWNER to determine the requirements
                 of the project.

            (2) ARCHITECT shall then review these project
                 requirements to determine the scope of the
                 project with OWNER.

            (3) ARCHITECT shall evaluate OWNER'S budget for
                 the project.

            (4) ARCHITECT shall provide a preliminary valua-
                 tion of the scope and requirements of the
                 project for OWNER, taking into account OWNER'S
                 project budget.

            (5) ARCHITECT shall then review with OWNER alter-
                 nate methods and approaches to design and
                 construction of the project and recommend that
                 method best suited to the needs and budget of
                 OWNER.

            (6) ARCHITECT shall, relying on OWNER'S require-
                 ments, budget restrictions of the project, and
                 method of design and construction selected by
                 OWNER and approved by STATE ENGINEER, prepare
                 for OWNER'S approval the Schematic Design
                 Documents including, but not limited to, draw-
                 ings and other documents demonstrating and
                 illustrating the scope and scale of the
                 project and the relationship of project compo-
                 nents.

            (7) ARCHITECT shall at the time of submission of
                 Schematic Design Documents furnish to OWNER a
                 Statement of Probable Construction Cost,
                 together with Estimates of Construction Costs
                 for OWNER'S review.

            (8) ARCHITECT will fully cooperate with CONSTRUC-
                 TION MANAGER, if one is utilized.

-6-

b.   DESIGN DEVELOPMENT PHASE

(1)   Prior to beginning the Design Development Phase of the project, approval in writing of the Schematic Design Documents and a Statement of Probable Project Cost shall be secured from OWNER and STATE ENGINEER by ARCHITECT.

(2)   ARCHITECT shall prepare Design Development Phase Documents based on the Schematic Design Phase Documents and any approved adjustments in the program or project budget.

(3)   Design Development Documents shall include sufficient data, information and material to define the scope of the project and to demonstrate, delineate, and define the general design of the project, including size and character of the project as to architectural, structural, mechanical and electrical systems, materials, and any other project elements appropriate under the project scope and design.

(4)   Design Development Phase Documents shall include, but not be limited to drawings, outline specifications, and a Revised Statement of Probable Construction Cost as follows:

(5)   DRAWINGS:

(a)   Drawings shall show existing topographic features and improvements affecting or relating to the proposed WORK. ARCHITECT shall indicate revisions to be made to existing topographic features and improvements such as grading construction of drainage facilities, etc. Where drainage facilities are to be provided, ARCHITECT shall indicate direction of flow and point of discharge by appropriate symbol or notes.

(b)   Drawings showing developed floor plans, proposed finished floor elevations, floor and roof framing, typical wall section, exterior elevations showing proposed floor-to-floor heights and basic details of any unusual features of construction shall be prepared.

-7-

FORM SE240
7/14/83

(c) Basic information necessary to establish space requirements and functional arrangement shall be shown.

(d) The functional layout of mechanical, electrical and electronic features, special equipment, plumbing and heating shall be furnished and shown to include, where applicable:

    (i) Location of evaporative coolers and/or air conditioning units.

    (ii) General scale layout of equipment, heater and/or boiler rooms showing space requirements and auxiliary equipment proposed.

    (iii) Location and approximate size of special equipment to be installed such as compressors, generators, transformers, electronic equipment racks, consoles, panels, distributing frames, hoists, cranes, etc.

(e) Location, dimension, sections, areas and capacities as applicable to parking areas, access roads, driveways, walks, etc. shall be illustrated.

(f) Location and size of existing or proposed sanitary sewers, water mains, gas mains and electrical service in the vicinity of the proposed buildings, as well as elevations of gravity lines and the location of proposed building connections with notations showing which of the necessary utility extensions or connections beyond the 5-foot building line will be provided.

(g) Simplified schematic electrical diagrams for each electronic or instrumentation system shall be shown for any required system functions.

(h) The Design Development Phase Documents shall reflect all architectural and/or engineering skills applicable to the project.

-8-

(6) OUTLINE SPECIFICATIONS: Outline Specifica-
     tions and Probable Construction Cost shall be
     developed by ARCHITECT to a uniform level,
     reflecting the material, trades, mechanical
     and   electrical   system, and   specialties
     required to reflect the project as a whole.

(7) STATEMENT OF PROBABLE   CONSTRUCTION   COST:
     Probable Construction Cost furnished in this
     phase shall be calculated by ARCHITECT based
     on drawings and the Outline Specifications for
     the project reflecting the changes in probable
     construction cost and taking into account the
     building trades and construction components
     utilized in the project design.

(8) Upon completion of the Design Development
     Phase, ARCHITECT shall submit to OWNER and to
     STATE ENGINEER the Design Development Docu-
     ments including Outline Specifications and the
     statement of the revised Probable Construction
     Cost, together with any other material or
     documents necessary for the design of the
     project.

c. CONSTRUCTION DOCUMENTS PHASE

(1) Prior to beginning the Construction Documents
     Phase of the project, approval in writing of
     the Design Development Documents, and specifi-
     cally the Revised Statement of Probable Con-
     struction Cost, shall be secured from both
     OWNER and STATE ENGINEER by ARCHITECT.

(2) ARCHITECT shall prepare the Construction Docu-
     ments from the approved Design Development
     Documents for approval by OWNER and STATE
     ENGINEER with a final Statement of Probable
     Construction Cost setting forth in detail the
     requirements for the construction of the
     entire project, including information neces-
     sary to bid the project.

(3) Construction Documents shall include, but not
     be limited to, drawings and specifications
     setting forth in adequate, reasonable, and
     reliable detail the final requirements for the
     construction of the project.

(4) ARCHITECT shall assist OWNER in filing all
     documents and obtaining all permits necessary

-9-

and required for the approval of the project by governmental authorities having jurisdiction over the project.

(5) Approval of the Construction Documents and Statement of Probable Construction Cost by OWNER and STATE ENGINEER shall not relieve ARCHITECT of any responsibility for design deficiencies, omissions or errors.

(6) All plans and specifications shall bear the signature and seal of ARCHITECT and his Engineer. ARCHITECT, his Engineers, Consultants, agents, and employees shall be fully responsible for all design.

d.   BIDDING AND BID AWARD PHASE

(1) Prior to beginning the Bidding and Bid Award Phase of the project, approval in writing of the Construction Documents and the Final Statement of Probable Construction Cost shall be secured from OWNER and STATE ENGINEER by ARCHITECT.

(2) ARCHITECT shall prepare the Bid Documents necessary for obtaining bids for the construction of the project.

(3) ARCHITECT shall prepare the Invitation for Bids for OWNER which shall include all contractual terms and conditions applicable to the project.

(4) ARCHITECT shall prepare and submit the construction contract and the Invitation for Bids for the written approval of OWNER and STATE ENGINEER prior to the advertising and solicitation of bids.

(5) In the event a multiple contract method of construction is utilized, ARCHITECT shall prepare all Bid Documents and Bid Packages for the multiple contracts required by the project.

(6) ARCHITECT shall design and prepare a prebid construction SCHEDULE, when necessary, as determined by the size, complexity, and scope of the project.

-10-

(7) ARCHITECT shall hold a pre-bid conference, when necessary, as determined by the size, complexity, and scope of the project.

(8) ARCHITECT shall assist OWNER by receiving, recording, and evaluating the bids received for the construction of the project.

(9) ARCHITECT shall review all bids and qualifications of the lowest responsive bidders and shall recommend to OWNER those deemed responsive. ARCHITECT shall prepare and certify the bid tabulation and mail copies of the bid tabulation to all bidders within ten (10) DAYS following the bid opening.

2. CONSTRUCTION ADMINISTRATION PHASE

a. The Construction Administration Phase shall commence with the award of the Construction Contract or contracts and will terminate with final acceptance by OWNER.

b. ARCHITECT, during Construction Administration, shall fully cooperate with CONSTRUCTION MANAGER, if one is utilized.

c. ARCHITECT shall have authority to act on behalf of OWNER to the extent provided in this Contract, State of South Carolina General Conditions (Form SE370) and Supplementary General Conditions, unless otherwise modified in writing.

d. ARCHITECT shall at all times have access to WORK.

e. ARCHITECT shall conduct a pre-construction conference with CONTRACTOR and shall take and distribute to OWNER and CONTRACTOR written minutes of the pre-construction conference and of all meetings conducted by ARCHITECT.

f. ARCHITECT shall attend job progress meetings which shall be held on a bi-weekly basis and at which time CONTRACTOR, ARCHITECT and OWNER may discuss and resolve such matters as procedures, job progress, construction problems, scheduling or other matters relating to the timely and successful completion of the project in accordance with the contract requireme:s. Additional special job site meetings, when deemed necessary by ARCHITECT, shall be held as required.

-11-

g. On the basis of these on-site visits, ARCHITECT shall keep OWNER informed through a monthly written report of the progress and quality of WORK, and shall guard OWNER against defects and deficiencies in WORK of CONTRACTOR. While periodic visits by ARCHITECT may vary with the progress of WORK and other conditions, these visits shall not be less than one visit by ARCHITECT to the project per week during the course of construction, unless otherwise agreed upon by OWNER and ARCHITECT in writing.

h. Based on observations at the site and on CONTRACTOR'S written request for payment, ARCHITECT shall determine the amount owing to CONTRACTOR and shall certify requests for payment in such amounts, on the basis that WORK has progressed to the point indicated and that the quality of WORK is in accordance with CONTRACT DOCUMENTS and sound construction practices.

i. Should CONTRACTOR fall behind in his construction SCHEDULE, ARCHITECT shall proceed as set forth in ARTICLE 15 of the General Conditions.

j. ARCHITECT will be the interpreter of the requirements of CONTRACT DOCUMENTS. ARCHITECT will render written interpretations within ten (10) DAYS of receipt of any written request or within an agreed upon time limit. These interpretations as between OWNER and CONTRACTOR will be binding upon both, unless ARTICLE 32 of the General Conditions is invoked within ten (10) DAYS.

k. ARCHITECT shall reject WORK which in ARCHITECT'S opinion does not conform to CONTRACT DOCUMENTS; to confirm the requirements of CONTRACT DOCUMENTS, ARCHITECT may request approval of OWNER for special inspection and/or testing.

l. ARCHITECT shall review and approve SHOP DRAWINGS. SHOP DRAWINGS shall only be approved if they are in conformance with the design concept of the project and in compliance with CONTRACT DOCUMENTS. SHOP DRAWINGS, samples, and other submissions of CONTRACTOR for general conformance with the design concept of the project and for compliance with the information given in CONTRACT DOCUMENTS shall be returned to CONTRACTOR within fifteen (15) DAYS of receipt thereof. If review and approval are delayed beyond the time set out above, ARCHITECT shall notify CONTRACTOR and OWNER in writing stating the reason for the delay.

-12-

m. ARCHITECT shall review and analyze all requests for CHANGE ORDERS including any documents offered to substantiate such requests. ARCHITECT shall submit written recommendations and shall prepare those CHANGE ORDERS recommended for approval by OWNER.

n. ARCHITECT shall require that no changes may be made in WORK by any party without prior written consent of OWNER.

o. The responsibility of ARCHITECT for enforcing the faithful performance of the Contract is not relieved or affected in any respect by the presence of any other agents, consultants, or employees of OWNER.

p. ARCHITECT shall obtain from a competent LAND SURVEYOR or MATERIAL TESTING ENGINEER, selected by and employed by ARCHITECT, all plats, reports, tests, and engineering data, as further defined in Paragraph D of ARTICLE 4 of this Agreement, upon approval of the costs by OWNER.

q. ARCHITECT shall (a) enforce the faithful performance of the Contract and (b) assure himself that WORK has been or is being installed in accordance with CONTRACT DOCUMENTS and good construction practices before allowing it to be covered.

r. ARCHITECT is fully responsible for any WORK designed, approved, certified, or accepted by his Engineers, Consultants, agents and employees the same as if the said WORK were designed, approved, certified, or accepted by him. Additionally, ARCHITECT shall determine the amount, quality, acceptability and fitness of kind of WORK and materials which are to be paid for under this Contract.

s. ARCHITECT shall make decisions promptly and in any event shall respond within ten (10) DAYS after presentation of an issue, claim or complaint by the parties to the Construction Contract.

t. Should CONTRACTOR fail to comply with the orders of ARCHITECT relative to any particular portion of WORK, then ARCHITECT shall have the authority to stop WORK for 24 hours. Thereafter, if the suspension is to continue, ARCHITECT shall so advise OWNER, recommend the suspension stating the reasons therefor, and obtain the written authorization of OWNER for transmittal to CONTRACTOR.

-13-

u.   If CONTRACTOR shall be adjudged bankrupt, or if he should make a general assignment for the benefit of his creditors, or if a receiver should be appointed on account of his insolvency, or if he should persistently or repeatedly refuse or fail to supply enough properly skilled workman or proper materials, or if he should fail to make prompt payment to SUBCONTRACTORS or for material or labor, or persistently disregard laws, ordinances or the instructions of OWNER, or otherwise be guilty of a material violation of any provision of the contract, or if he should fall behind the progress SCHEDULE as described in CONTRACT DOCUMENTS, then ARCHITECT may serve notice to CONTRACTOR and his surety setting forth the asserted violations and demanding compliance with the contract. Unless within ten (10) consecutive calendar DAYS after serving such notice, such violations shall cease and satisfactory arrangements for correction be made, ARCHITECT may declare CONTRACTOR to be in default and shall advise OWNER in writing either to suspend CONTRACTOR'S right to proceed with WORK or to terminate the contract with CONTRACTOR.

v.   If CONTRACTOR refuses or fails to prosecute WORK, or any part thereof, with such diligence as will insure its completion within the time specified in the contract, or any extension thereof, or fails to complete said WORK within such time, or refuses to correct defective WORK, ARCHITECT may suspend WORK and may advise OWNER to terminate the contract.

w.   ARCHITECT, at the completion of the entire WORK or a designated portion thereof, shall issue a Certificate of SUBSTANTIAL COMPLETION which shall state that WORK is acceptable to ARCHITECT and that WORK is in accord with all requirements of CONTRACT DOCUMENTS except for minor items which, in the opinion of ARCHITECT, will not interfere with complete and satisfactory use of the facilities.

x.   ARCHITECT shall provide a close-out program for the project including, but not limited to, the preparation and enforcement of "punch lists". ARCHITECT shall also:

    i.   Assist and cooperate with CONTRACTOR in the completion of punch list WORK.

    ii.   Transmit from CONTRACTOR to OWNER all guarantees, warranties, equipment, and maintenance manuals and operating instructions.

-14-

iii. Require CONTRACTOR to schedule and coordinate all start-up and shake-down operations of all equipment with OWNER'S operating personnel and shall require brief periods of instruction for OWNER'S operating personnel as required in the specifications, and shall arrange for, coordinate, and monitor the balancing of all systems.

iv. Obtain from CONTRACTOR and furnish to OWNER all guarantees and required affidavits of releases from CONTRACTOR.

y. Upon completion of the Construction Phase, ARCHITECT shall modify the original drawings to RECORD DRAWINGS showing all changes made during construction. These modifications to the original drawings shall be made from "marked-up" sets of drawings prepared by CONTRACTOR in accordance with ARTICLE 36 of the GENERAL CONDITIONS. Such changes to the original drawings shall be made in a professional manner, and original drawings shall be stamped and signed by ARCHITECT as said drawings being RECORD DRAWINGS and these drawings shall be transmitted to OWNER.

z. ARCHITECT shall arrange for final inspection and shall require that all WORK performed by CONTRACTORS is in accordance with the requirements of CONTRACT DOCUMENTS.

aa. Subsequent to the final completion of construction operations and the occupancy of the project by OWNER, ARCHITECT shall review all outstanding claims which have not been settled during the construction phase of the project and shall prepare a written report outlining the background and status of such claims and making recommendations as to the ultimate disposition of such outstanding claims.

bb. One month prior to the expiration of the oneyear warranty period as called for in the Construction Documents, ARCHITECT shall inspect the project for any deficiencies that may have developed under the one-year warranty. Upon completion of inspection, a written report shall be furnished to OWNER, STATE ENGINEER and CONTRACTOR, and ARCHITECT shall take the necessary action to see that the deficiencies are corrected at no cost to OWNER.

ARTICLE 3 - ADDITIONAL SERVICES

A. GENERAL: The following additional Services shall be provided only when authorized in writing by OWNER and shall be paid for by OWNER:

1. Providing special analyses of, and programming for, OWNER'S needs and providing financial feasibility or other special studies.

2. Providing special planning surveys, special site evaluations, special environmental studies or special comparative studies of prospective sites, and preparing special surveys, special studies and special submissions required for approvals of governmental authorities or others having jurisdiction over the project.

3. Providing services relative to future facilities, systems and equipment, which are not intended to be constructed during the Construction Phase or providing services to investigate existing conditions of facilities or to make measured drawings thereof, or to verify the accuracy of drawings or other information furnished by OWNER.

4. Preparing documents for separate or sequential bids if not contemplated under the initial contract.

5. Providing coordination of WORK performed by separate CONTRACTORS or by OWNER'S own forces if not contemplated under the initial contract.

6. Providing interior design and all other similar services required for or in connection with the selection, procurement or installation of moveable furniture, furnishing and related equipment.

7. Making revisions in drawings, specifications or other documents when such revisions are inconsistent with written approvals or instructions previously given, or required by enactment or revision of codes, laws or regulations subsequent to the preparation of such documents

8. Preparing drawings, specifications and supporting data, providing other services in connection with CHANGE ORDERS to the extent that the adjustment in the Basic Compensation resulting from the adjusted Construction Cost is not commensurate with the services required of ARCHITECT, provided such CHANGE ORDERS are required by causes not solely within the control of ARCHITECT, including those requested by OWNER.

-16-

9. Making investigations, surveys, valuations, inventories or detailed appraisals of existing facilities, and services required in connection with construction performed by OWNER.

10. Providing consultation concerning replacement of any WORK damaged by fire or other causes during construction.

11. Providing services made necessary by the default of CONTRACTOR or by failure of performance of either OWNER or CONTRACTOR under the Contract for Construction.

12. Providing special services after issuance to OWNER of the final Certificate for Payment, or in the absence of a final Certificate for Payment, more than sixty (60) DAYS after the Date of SUBSTANTIAL COMPLETION of WORK.

13. Preparing to serve or serving as OWNER'S expert witness in connection with any public hearing or legal proceeding.

14. Providing consultation or design services for other than the normal architectural, structural, mechanical and electrical engineering services for the project.

15. If OWNER and ARCHITECT agree that more extensive representation at the site than is described in ARTICLE 2 shall be provided, ARCHITECT shall provide one or more Full-Time Project Representatives to assist ARCHITECT in carrying out such responsibilities at the site. Such Full-Time Project Representatives shall be selected, employed and directed by ARCHITECT, and ARCHITECT shall be compensated, therefore, as mutually agreed between OWNER and ARCHITECT as set forth in ARTICLE 14 of this Agreement which shall describe the duties, responsibilities and limitations of authority of such Full-Time Project Representative.

ARTICLE 4 - OWNER'S RESPONSIBILITIES

A. OWNER shall provide full information regarding his requirements for the project including related budgetary information and shall cooperate fully with ARCHITECT at all times.

B. If OWNER observes or otherwise becomes aware of any fault or defect in the project or non-conformance with CONTRACT DOCUMENTS, he shall give prompt WRITTEN NOTICE thereof to ARCHITECT.

C. OWNER shall furnish information required of him as expeditiously as necessary for the orderly progress of WORK so as not to unreasonably delay ARCHITECT in the performance of the duties.

-17-

D. OWNER shall reimburse ARCHITECT for the cost of obtaining the following information by ARCHITECT from LAND SURVEYOR or MATERIAL TESTING ENGINEER, selected by and employed by ARCHITECT, provided the cost is approved by OWNER before it is incurred:

 1. Survey of Building Site Conditions. A complete and accurate survey of the building site giving the grades and lines of streets, pavements, and adjoining properties, contours of the building site, and full information as to sewer, water, gas, electrical service, telephone lines, or other utilities, and

 2. Report on Subsurface Investigations. Test borings or test pits and chemical, mechanical, laboratory or other tests.

 3. All other tests deemed necessary by ARCHITECT.

 4. The surveys, tests, engineering data, and any other information described under this ARTICLE shall be obtained by ARCHITECT only, not OWNER.

ARTICLE 5 - ALTERNATES

A. Upon approval by OWNER, ARCHITECT may include in the project additfve and/or deductive alternates. The alternates when bid must be accepted in numerical order.

B. When OWNER requires ARCHITECT, subsequent to the execution of this Agreement, to include alternates to the project, the cost of the preparation of those alternates shall be used to negotiate ARCHITECT'S additional compensation whether the alternates are accepted or not accepted.

C. When ARCHITECT elects to include alternates for the purpose of determining cost, or to protect the budget established for the Base Bid(s), or for any other reason, no compensation will be allowed ARCHITECT for alternates not accepted.

D. Alternates shall not render the project unusable. Therefore, ARCHITECT, in determining his final estimate, must include Base Bid and necessary alternate costs within the funds available for construction, unless otherwise approved by OWNER.

ARTICLE 6 - REIMBURSABLE EXPENSES

A. Reimbursable Expenses are defined as direct costs which may be in addition to the compensation for Basic and/or Additional Services and may include, but are not necessarily limited to, the following:

-18-

1. Mileage, meals and lodging. The latest rules and regulations promulgated by the State of South Carolina for lodging and travel expenses shall apply to travel by ARCHITECT, his Engineers, and his employees.

2. Reproduction, postage and telephone at actual cost.

B. Cost of surveys and tests furnished in ARTICLE 4 which shall be provided by ARCHITECT at direct cost times 1.25.

C. Reimbursable expenses shall be submitted by ARCHITECT for approval of OWNER on a monthly basis. Approved reimbursable expenses shall be paid promptly.

ARTICLE 7 - ARCHITECT'S ACCOUNTING RECORDS

A. Daily records of ARCHITECT'S Direct Personnel, Consultants and Reimbursable Expenses pertaining to the project shall be kept on a generally recognized accounting basis and shall be available to OWNER or his authorized representatives upon request.

ARTICLE 8 - ARCHITECT'S COOPERATION

A. ARCHITECT agrees to perform his services under this Contract in such manner and at such times so that OWNER and/or any CONTRACTOR who has WORK to perform, or contracts to execute, can do so without unreasonable delay.

ARTICLE 9 - OWNERSHIP OF DOCUMENTS

A. OWNER shall have unlimited rights in the ownership of all drawings, designs, specifications, notes and other WORK developed in the performance of the Agreement, including the right to use same on any other OWNER'S projects without additional cost to OWNER, and with respect thereto ARCHITECT agrees to and does hereby grant to OWNER a royalty-free license to all such data which he may cover by copyright and to all designs as to which he may assert any rights or establish any claim under the design patent or copyright laws.

B. In the case of future reuse of the documents, OWNER reserves the right to negotiate with ARCHITECT for compensation for the acceptance of any professional liability.

C. In the event OWNER does not exercise the option to negotiate with ARCHITECT for ARCHITECT'S acceptance of any professional liability, it is understood that ARCHITECT'S name and seal shall be removed from the documents and ARCHITECT shall no longer be liable in the reuse of those documents and OWNER shall hold ARCHITECT harmless with regard to the reuse of these documents.

-19-

ARTICLE 10 - SUCCESSORS AND ASSIGNS

A. OWNER and ARCHITECT each binds himself, his partners, successors, assigns and legal representatives to the other party to
this Agreement and to the partners, successors, assigns and legal
representatives of such other party with respect to all covenants
of this Agreement. Neither OWNER nor ARCHITECT shall assign,
sublet or transfer his interest in this Agreement without the
written consent of the other.

ARTICLE 11 - TERMINATION

A. THIS AGREEMENT, for any reason including the convenience of
OWNER or for cause, may be terminated by OWNER by WRITTEN NOTICE
to ARCHITECT specifying the termination date which shall be
effective within seven (7) DAYS from the date to be stated by
OWNER in the notice to ARCHITECT.

B. In the event of termination which is not the fault of ARCHI-
TECT, OWNER shall pay to ARCHITECT the compensation properly due
for services properly performed prior to the effective date of
the termination and for any reasonable reimbursable expenses
properly incurred.

C. In the event ARCHITECT through any cause fails to perform any
of the terms, covenants, or provisions of this Contract on his
part to be performed, or if he for any cause fails to make progress in WORK hereunder in a reasonable manner, or if the conduct
of ARCHITECT impairs or prejudices the interests of OWNER, or if
ARCHITECT violates any of the terms, covenants, or provisions of
this Contract, OWNER shall have the right to terminate this Contract by giving notice in writing of the fact and date of such
termination to ARCHITECT, and all drawings, specifications, and
other documents relating to the design or SUPERVISION of WORK
shall be surrendered forthwith by ARCHITECT to OWNER, PROVIDED
HOWEVER: That in such case ARCHITECT shall receive equitable
compensation for such services as shall in the opinion of STATE
ENGINEER have been satisfactorily performed by ARCHITECT up to
the date of termination of this Contract, such compensation to be
fixed by STATE ENGINEER, and PROVIDED FURTHER: That OWNER may
take over WORK to be done hereunder and may prosecute the same to
completion by contract or otherwise, and ARCHITECT shall be liable to OWNER for all reasonable cost occasioned OWNER thereby.

ARTICLE 12 - INSURANCE

A. Within ten (10) DAYS after execution of the Agreement and
during the entire period of ARCHITECT'S responsibility under this
Agreement, ARCHITECT shall obtain and maintain professional liability insurance coverage. ARCHITECT shall file with OWNER the
certificate from an insurance company authorized to do business

-20-

in the State of South Carolina showing issuance of professional liability insurance (errors and omissions insurance) in the amount of $ _____ coverage with a maximum of $ _____ deductible pertaining to <u>this project only.</u> The certificate shall bear an endorsement in words exactly as follows:

> The insurance company certifies that the insurance covered by this certificate has been endorsed as follows: "The insurance company agrees that the coverage is on a project basis only and shall not be cancelled, changed, allowed to lapse, or allowed to expire until ten DAYS after notice to: _____
> _____ ".

ARTICLE 13 - DISPUTES AND REMEDIES

A. ARCHITECT hereby agrees that all claims made by OWNER against ARCHITECT and by ARCHITECT against OWNER including controversies based on breach of contract, mistake, misrepresentation, contract modification or recession or any other claims which arise under or by virtue of the contract between them, shall be settled by the State CHIEF PROCUREMENT OFFICER for Construction under the Consolidated Procurement Code Procedures as outlined in South Carolina Code of Laws 1976 (as amended) §§11-35-4230(3),(4) and (5), with all appeal rights as defined in §11-35-4410 to PROCUREMENT REVIEW PANEL being applicable.

B. ARCHITECT hereby further agrees that should any CONTRACTOR file a claim concerning any dispute or controversy with CHIEF PROCUREMENT OFFICER for Construction which involves allegations of architectural or engineering errors and omissions including but not limited to defects in the plans or specifications, errors or omissions in the administration of the contract by ARCHITECT, and inadequate construction phase services as defined and required by the contract between ARCHITECT and OWNER, then ARCHITECT shall consent to participate and to be joined in the Protest Procedures as outlined in Article 17 of the South Carolina Consolidated Procurement Code, entitled Legal and Contractual Remedies, and to be bound by any decisions rendered thereunder.

C. ARCHITECT further agrees that should he be found liable for any errors and omissions under this contract, then OWNER shall recover its attorney's fees, expert witness costs, cost of consultants necessary for evaluation of the project, and any other costs incurred.

-21-

FORM SE240
7/14/83

ARTICLE 14 - OTHER CONDITIONS

-22-

FORM SE240
7/14/83

EXTENT OF AGREEMENT

THIS AGREEMENT represents the entire and integrated Agreement between OWNER and ARCHITECT and supersedes all prior negotiations, representations or agreements, either written or oral. This Agreement may be amended only by written instrument signed by both OWNER and ARCHITECT.

THIS AGREEMENT entered into as of the day and year first written above.

OWNER   ARCHITECT

_____   _____

_____   _____

_____   _____

BY_____   BY_____

-23-

APPENDIX
C

STATE OF SOUTH CAROLINA

STANDARD BOND FORM

FOR BIDS

_____

KNOW ALL MEN BY THESE PRESENTS:

That _____ ,
             (Legal Title and address of CONTRACTOR)

_____ ,

as Principal (hereinafter referred to as "Principal"), and

_____
          (Legal Title and address of Surety)

_____

as Surety (hereinafter referred to as "Surety") are held and

firmly bound unto _____

_____

as Obligee (hereinafter referred to as "OWNER"), in the amount

of twenty percent (20%) of the Principal's Bid to which payment

Principal and Surety bind themselves, their heirs, executors,

administrators, successors and assigns, jointly and severally,

firmly by these presents.

    The conditions of the above obligation is such that whereas

the Principal has submitted to OWNER a certain Bid, attached

hereto and hereby made a part hereof, to enter into a contract in

writing, for the _____
              (Set forth the Name of Project)

_____ .

NOW THEREFORE,

    (a)   If said Bid shall be rejected, or, in the alternate,

    (b)   If said Bid shall be accepted and the Principal shall execute and deliver a contract in the Form of Agreement attached hereto and shall execute and deliver Performance and Payments Bonds in the Forms attached hereto (all properly completed in accordance with said Bid), and shall in all other respects perform the agreement created by the acceptance of said Bid,

Then, this obligation shall be void, otherwise the same shall remain in force and effect; it being expressly understood and agreed that the liability of the Surety for any and all default of the Principal hereunder shall be the difference between the bid of the Principal and the next bona fide low bid but shall not exceed the amount of the obligation as stated herein.

The Surety, for value received, hereby stipulates and agrees that the obligations of said Surety and its bond shall be in no way impaired or affected by any extension of the time within which OWNER(S) may accept such Bid; and said Surety does hereby waive notice of any such extension.

The parties hereto agree that ARTICLE 32 of GENERAL CONDITIONS apply to all disputes arising out of the performance of the parties hereto described under this agreement and agree to be bound thereby and shall constitute the sole disputes remedy of the parties.

-2-

IN WITNESS WHEREOF, the above-bounded parties have executed this instrument under their several seals this _____ day of _____, 19____, the name and corporate seal of each corporate party being hereto affixed and these presents duly signed by its undersigned representative, pursuant to authority of its governing body.

In presence of

_____ _____(SEAL)
(INDIVIDUAL PRINCIPAL)

_____ _____
(ADDRESS) (BUSINESS ADDRESS)

_____ _____(SEAL)
(INDIVIDUAL PRINCIPAL)

_____ _____
(ADDRESS) (BUSINESS ADDRESS)

Attest: _____
(CORPORATE PRINCIPAL)

_____
(BUSINESS ADDRESS)

_____ BY_____

_____

AFFIX CORPORATE SEAL

Attest: _____
(CORPORATE SURETY)

_____
(BUSINESS ADDRESS)

_____ BY_____

_____

-3-

APPENDIX
D

STATE OF SOUTH CAROLINA
BUDGET AND CONTROL BOARD
DIVISION OF GENERAL SERVICES
STATE ENGINEER

QUESTIONNAIRE FOR GENERAL CONTRACTORS

PURSUANT TO SECTION 11-35-1810 OF THE
SOUTH CAROLINA CODE, 1976 AS AMENDED

INSTRUCTIONS:

Each General Contractor submitting a bid must complete this form as a description of Bidder's Qualifications. This questionnaire and all other information requested herein shall be placed in a separate sealed envelope and submitted as part of the Contractor's Bid. The outside of the envelope shall show:

TITLE: BIDDER'S QUALIFICATIONS
NAME AND LOCATION OF PROJECT
NAME AND ADDRESS OF BIDDER

This description of qualifications will be considered part of the Contractor's Bid. Any Bid submitted without this information will be incomplete. The Architect/Engineer and/or Owner will examine only the qualifications of the apparent low Bidder. The envelopes submitted by unsuccessful Bidders will be returned unopened.

PLEASE COMPLETE THE FOLLOWING:

1. Name of Bidder:

    _____

    _____

2. Address of Bidder:

    _____

    _____

3. Name of Project:

    _____

    _____

4. Location of Project:

    _____

    _____

5. Bidder's Contractors License Number:

_____

_____

6. Who will be the superintendent on this job? If you are not certain, name the possible superintendents.

_____

_____

7. Give the name and address of your certified public accountant.

_____

_____

8. Give the name and address of your insurance agent and surety company.

_____

_____

9. If you are the apparent low bidder, will you furnish your most recent certified financial statements. (If you do not have certified financial statements, a statement of condition from your CPA showing verifiable payables and receivables will be sufficient.)
Yes __ No __

10. What is or will be your bonding capacity on the date of your bid?

_____

11. What amount of your bonding capacity will have been used on the date of your bid?

_____

12. How many applications for bonds have you made in the last five (5) years? How many of these applications have been to the same surety company?

_____

_____

13. Have any claims been paid by your surety bond company in the last five (5) years? If so, describe the nature of the claim and give the name of the surety company, date of claim, amount of claim, and identifying number of the claim.

_____

_____

_____

14. List the following for *all* projects done for the State of South Carolina in the past three (3) years. (Use additional sheets if necessary.)

PROJECT #1

a. Name and Location of Project:

_____

_____

_____

b. Name and Address of Owner:

_____

_____

_____

c. Name and Address of Architect:

_____

_____

_____

d. Name of your Superintendent on the Job:

_____

e. Date of Signed Construction Contract:

_____

f. Date of Final Completion:

_____

g. Amount of Bid:

_____

h. Final Cost:

_____

i. Explain Difference:

_____

_____

_____

15. List selected projects done for private owners or the Federal Government which exemplify your expertise in this particular building type and/or projects done by the proposed superintendent. (Use additional sheets if necessary.)

PROJECT #1

a. Name and Location of Project:

_____

_____

_____

b. Name and Address of Owner:

_____

_____

_____

c. Name and Address of Architect:

_____

_____

_____

d. Name of your Superintendent on the Job:

_____

e. Date of Signed Construction Contract:

_____

f. Date of Final Completion:

_____

g. Amount of Bid:

_____

h. Final Cost:

_____

i. Explain Difference:

_____

_____

_____

I, the undersigned, do hereby declare that the foregoing statements are true and correct, all as of the date hereinafter set forth, and that those examining this document may, with my permission, contact any or all of those parties listed in this questionnaire.

COMPANY: _____

NAME (typed): _____

SIGNATURE: _____

TITLE: _____

DATE: _____

APPENDIX
E

STANDARD FORM
APPLICATION FOR PAYMENT
FOR CONSTRUCTION CONTRACT

Form SE470
7-14-83

TO: Agency/Institution _____ _____
                        Code   Name

PROJECT: _____ _____
           Number   Name

A P P L I C A T I O N   F O R   P A Y M E N T   Application No. :

                                                       Application Date:
FROM: Contractor _____   For the Period
                                                                       From:
         Contract for _____   To:

         Contract Date _____

In accordance with the provisions of this Contract, application is made for Payment as
indicated herein. Schedules supporting the amounts claimed for Work in Place and for
Materials Stored are attached, and are a part of this Application.

1. ORIGINAL CONTRACT SUM. . . . . $ _____
2. NET CHANGE BY CHANGE ORDERS. $ _____
3. CONTRACT SUM TO DATE . . . . $ _____
----
4. VALUE OF WORK IN PLACE (Schedule attached) . . . . $ _____
5. VALUE OF MATERIALS STORED (Schedule attached). . . . . $ _____
6. TOTAL EARNED TO DATE . . . . $ _____
7. RETAINAGE:
         From Schedule of Work in Place $ _____
         From Schedule of Materials Stored $ _____
                    TOTAL RETAINAGE . . . . $ _____
8. TOTAL EARNED LESS RETAINAGE. $ _____
9. LESS PREVIOUS CERTIFICATES FOR PAYMENT . . . . $ _____
10. CURRENT PAYMENT DUE. . . . . $ _____

The undersigned Contractor certifies under Section 29-7-20 of Code of Laws of South
Carolina (1976), as amended, that the Work covered by this Application for Payment has
been completed in accordance with the Contract Documents, that all amounts have been
paid by him for Work for which previous Certificates for Payment were issued and payments
received from the Owner, and that the current payment shown herein is now due.

Subscribed and sworn to before me this _____   _____
day of_____, 19_____   Contractor

Notary Public:_____   By: _____

My Commission Expires: _____   Date: _____

A R C H I T E C T / E N G I N E E R   P A Y M E N T   C E R T I F I C A T E

In accordance with the Contract Documents, based on observation at the site and the data
comprising the above Application, the A/E certifies to the Owner that the Work has progressed to the point indicated; that the quality of the Work is in accordance with the
Contract Documents and sound construction practices; and that the Contractor is entitled
to payment of the AMOUNT CERTIFIED. This Certificate is not negotiable. The AMOUNT CER-
TIFIED is payable only to the Contractor named herein. Issuance, payment, and acceptance
of payment are without prejudice to any rights of the Owner or Contractor under this Contract.

A/E FIRM: _____   AMOUNT CERTIFIED $ _____

By: _____   Date: _____

SCHEDULE OF VALUES, MATERIALS STORED
(Amounts are stated to the nearest dollar)

Item	Description	Value of Material Stored Previous Periods, Less Materials Used	Value of Materials Stored This Period	Total Value of Materials Presently Stored	RETAINAGE
TOTALS:					

SUMMARY OF CHANGE ORDERS

Prior to the period of this Application, Change
Order(s) Number(s) _____ was/were approved
and included in previous Applications for Payment,
with a resulting NET CHANGE PRIOR TO THIS PERIOD of. . . $

Subsequent to submission of preceding Applications,
additional Change Order(s) numbers(s) _____
have been approved, with a resulting net change of . . . $

TOTAL CHANGE AS OF THIS APPLICATION . . . $

	ADDITION	DEDUCTION
	$ _____	$ _____
	$ _____	$ _____
	$ _____	$ _____

SCHEDULE OF VALUES, WORK IN PLACE
(Amounts are stated to the nearest dollar)

| Item | Description | Total Cost** | WORK COMPLETED | | | RETAINAGE |
			A Previous Applications	B This Application	C (A+B) Total To Date	
TOTALS:						

**Values listed include approved Change Orders.

APPENDIX
F

```
                         STANDARD FORM
                       CHANGE ORDER TO
                     CONSTRUCTION CONTRACT              Form SE 480
                                                          7-14-83
FROM:     Agency/Institution _____ _____
                             Code              Name

PROJECT: _____ _____
            Number                 Name

CHANGE ORDER                           Change Order No.: 
                                       Initiation Date :

TO:     Contractor _____
        Contract for _____
        Contract Date _____
```

In accordance with the provisions of this Contract, you are directed to make the following changes in this Contract:

```
----------------------------------------------------------------------
Not valid until signed by Owner, Architect/Engineer, and approved by State Engineer.
Signature of Contractor indicates his agreement herewith, including any adjustment in
the Contract Sum or Contract Time.
----------------------------------------------------------------------
The Original Contract Sum was. . . . . . . . . . . . . . . . . . .$_____
Net Change by previously approved Change Orders. . . . . . . . . . . .$_____
The Contract Sum prior to this Change Order was. . . . . . . . . . . .$_____
The Contract Sum will be (increased)(decreased)(unchanged) by this
   Change Order . . . . . . . . . . . . . . . . . . . . . . . . . . .$_____
The new Contract Sum including this Change Order will be . . . . . . . . .$_____
The Contract Time will be (increased)(decreased)(unchanged) by . . . . . .(      ) Days
The Date for Substantial Completion as of the date of this Change Order is:_____
----------------------------------------------------------------------

Architect/Engineer          Contractor              Owner
By:_____        By:_____     By:_____

Date: ___ _____        Date: _____     Date: _____
----------------------------------------------------------------------
Budget & Control Board By: _____ State Engineer   Date: _____
```

APPENDIX
G

FORM SE410
7/14/83

STATE OF SOUTH CAROLINA

STANDARD FORM

OF

AGREEMENT BETWEEN OWNER AND CONTRACTOR

_____

THIS AGREEMENT, made the _____ day of _____

in the year of Nineteen Hundred and _____

by and between _____

_____

_____ hereinafter

called CONTRACTOR and _____

_____

_____ hereinafter

called OWNER.

    WITNESSETH, that CONTRACTOR and OWNER, for the consideration stated herein agree as follows:

    ARTICLE 1. STATEMENT OF WORK. CONTRACTOR shall furnish all labor and materials and perform all WORK required for furnishing and installing all labor, materials, equipment and transportation and everything necessarily inferred from the general nature and tendency of the plans and specifications for the proper execution of WORK in strict accordance with the Specifications and the Drawings, all of which are made a part hereof and designated as follows: "Plans and Specifications for

_____

(Project Title)

_____

_____ "

and shall do everything required by this agreement, GENERAL CONDITIONS of the contract, specifications and drawings and all other CONTRACT DOCUMENTS.

ARTICLE 2.   TIME OF COMPLETION.   Time is of the essence of
this contract. WORK to be performed under this contract shall be
commenced within ten (10) DAYS after WRITTEN NOTICE TO PROCEED is
received from OWNER, and WORK covered by this contract shall be
completed within _____ consecutive DAYS from, and
including the date specified in the written order from OWNER,
instructing CONTRACTOR to commence said WORK.

ARTICLE 3. CONTRACT SUM. OWNER shall pay CONTRACTOR for the
prompt, faithful and efficient performance of the conditions and
undertakings   of   this   contract,   subject   to additions and
deductions as provided herein, in current funds the sum of
_____
Dollars.

OWNER hereby accepts and reserves and CONTRACTOR is hereby
bound   thereby,   Alternate Bids of the Proposal submitted as
follows:

Payments may not be started until thirty (30) DAYS after
CONTRACTOR has commenced WORK, and thereafter, partial payments
shall be made in accordance with the provisions of the contract.

ARTICLE 4.   CONTRACT DOCUMENTS.   CONTRACT DOCUMENTS shall
consist of the following component parts:

        1.   Advertisement for Bids
        2.   Instructions to Bidders
        3.   Affidavit of Non-Collusion
        4.   CONTRACTOR'S Proposal Form
        5.   Questionnaire for General CONTRACTORS
        6.   The Contract
        7.   CONTRACTOR'S Progress SCHEDULE (CPM)
        8.   GENERAL CONDITIONS

-2-

```
 9.   Supplementary Conditions
10.   The Drawings
11.   The Technical Specifications
12.   CONTRACTOR'S Proposal as accepted by OWNER
13.   A. Required Certificate of Insurance
      B. Performance Bond (SE430)
      C. Labor and Material Bond (SE440)
14.   NOTICE TO PROCEED
```

ARTICLE 5.   OTHER CONDITIONS.

IN WITNESS WHEREOF, THIS AGREEMENT entered into as of day, month
and year first written above.

OWNER: CONTRACTOR:

_____   _____

_____   _____

_____   _____

BY_____   BY_____

-3-

APPENDIX
H

FORM SE370
7/14/83

STATE OF SOUTH CAROLINA

STANDARD FORM

GENERAL CONDITIONS OF THE CONTRACT

FOR CONSTRUCTION

INDEX

GENERAL CONDITIONS

STATE OF SOUTH CAROLINA

STANDARD FORM

GENERAL CONDITIONS OF THE CONTRACT

FOR CONSTRUCTION

GENERAL

A. These General Conditions apply to each section of these specifications and must be carefully read by all CONTRACTORS and
SUBCONTRACTORS who are all subject to the provisions contained
herein.

B. The General Conditions are intended to establish certain
rules and provisions governing the operation and performance of
WORK so that WORK may be continued and completed in a safe,
orderly, expeditious and workmanlike manner.

ARTICLE 1 - DEFINITIONS:

A. As used in these CONTRACTS DOCUMENTS, the following terms
shall have the meanings and refer to the parties designated in
these definitions.

1. "ARCHITECT": When the term "ARCHITECT" is used herein,
it shall refer to ARCHITECT or Engineer specified and
defined in the Supplementary Conditions, or his duly
authorized representative.

2. "CHANGE ORDER": A contract modification which is a
written alteration in specifications, delivery point,
rate of delivery, period of performance, price, quantity
or other provisions of the contract accomplished by
mutual agreement of the parties to the contract.

3. "CHIEF PROCUREMENT OFFICER": STATE ENGINEER for areas
of construction, architectural and engineering, construction management, and land surveying services.

4. "CONSTRUCTION MANAGER": A professional manager secured
under contract by OWNER for the purpose of providing
that group of management activities required to plan,
SCHEDULE, coordinate, and manage the design and construction of a State project in a manner that contributes to the control of time, cost, and quality of construction as specified in the construction management
contract.

5. "CONTRACT DOCUMENTS": "CONTRACT DOCUMENTS" shall consist of the executed Contract, the Special Conditions,
Instructions to Bidders, the Proposals, the Specifications and Drawings, including all modifications as
set forth in Addenda or CHANGE ORDERS to any of the
above, the required Certificates of Insurance, Labor and
Material Payment Bond, Performance Bond, Notices to
Proceed, and CPM, together with updates thereof containing authorized time changes.

6. "CONTRACTOR": Party or parties who have entered into a
contract with OWNER for a fixed price, commission, fee
or wage to undertake the construction or superintending
of construction of any building, sewer, grading,
improvement, reimprovement, structure or part thereof
and to furnish any other WORK required under the specifications and drawings of that contract.

7. "DATE OF CONTRACT AWARD": "DATE OF CONTRACT AWARD"
shall be the date when CONTRACTOR receives notification
in writing that his Bid has been accepted.

8. "DAYS": Means calendar DAYS.

9. "LAND SURVEYOR": A person engaging in the practice of
land surveying which is defined as including the surveying of areas for their correct determination and
description and for conveyancing or for the establishment or reestablishment of land boundaries and the platting of land and subdivisions thereof.

10. "MATERIAL TESTING ENGINEER": An engineer that special-
izes in the element of inspection that generally denotes
the determination by technical means of the properties
or elements of supplies, material, equipment, or compo-
nents thereof, and involves the application of established scientific and engineering principles and procedures.

11. "NOTICE TO PROCEED": "NOTICE TO PROCEED" shall be the
written communication issued by OWNER to CONTRACTOR
authorizing him to proceed with WORK and establishing
the date of commencement of WORK.

12. "OWNER": Whenever the term "OWNER" is used, it shall
mean the State of South Carolina or one of its agencies,
departments, or institutions.

13. "PROCUREMENT REVIEW PANEL": South Carolina PROCUREMENT
REVIEW PANEL is the body charged with the responsibility

-2-

of providing an administrative review of formal protests of decisions arising from the solicitation and award of contracts, and as further defined under Section 11-35-4410 of the South Carolina Consolidated Procurement Code.

14. "RECORD DRAWINGS": Construction drawings revised to show changes made during the construction process. The drawings are to be based on marked-up prints, drawings, and other data furnished by CONTRACTOR to ARCHITECT.

15. "SCHEDULE": "SCHEDULE" shall be either CPM or BAR CHART showing a logical method of sequences and interdependent nature of WORK activities in detail for the construction of the project as called for by ARCHITECT in the Supplementary General Conditions of the Contract. SCHEDULE shall indicate the dates for starting and the dates for completion of the various stages of construction and shall be revised and up-dated at four (4) week intervals.

   (a) "CRITICAL PATH METHOD" (CPM): That method which depicts parallel activities that can be worked on concurrently and the length, in calendar DAYS, of their duration. The critical path of the project is the longest collective chain of consecutive activity necessary to be performed before the project is complete. The parallel activities not on the critical path are characterized by slack time or float (i.e., within certain limits, their delay causes no delay in the project; whereas a delay of an activity on the critical path will delay the entire project).

   (b) "BAR CHART": A form of chart for time SCHEDULES whereby items or events in the construction progress of the project are represented by "bars", the length of which indicate quantity or time.

16. "SHOP DRAWINGS": Drawings, diagrams, illustrations, SCHEDULES, performance charts, brochures, catalog data, and other data which are prepared by CONTRACTOR or any SUBCONTRACTOR, manufacturer, supplier or distributor, and which illustrate some portion of WORK.

17. "STATE ENGINEER": The person holding the position as head of STATE ENGINEER'S Office, and as further defined under Section 11-35-830 of the South Carolina Consolidated Procurement Code.

-3-

18. "SUBCONTRACTOR": Party or parties who contract under, or for the performance of part or all of the contract between OWNER and CONTRACTOR. The subcontract may or may not be direct with CONTRACTOR.

19. "SUBSTANTIAL COMPLETION": The completion of the entire WORK or a designated portion thereof acceptable to ARCHITECT in strict accord with all requirements of the drawings and specifications except minor items which in the opinion of ARCHITECT will not interfere with complete and satisfactory use of the facilities.

20. "SUPERVISION": Observation of WORK for the purpose of guarding OWNER against defects and deficiencies in WORK and from variations by CONTRACTOR from CONTRACT DOCUMENTS.

21. "WORK": Labor, material, supplies, plant and equipment required to perform and complete the service agreed to be performed or provided by CONTRACTOR in safe, expeditious, orderly and workmanlike manner so that the project upon which WORK is performed shall be complete and finished in the best manner known to each respective trade.

22. "WRITTEN NOTICE": Any Notice from one party to the other relative to any part of this contract shall be in writing and considered delivered and service thereof complete when receipt is acknowledged by the addressee or said notice is posted by registered or certified mail to OWNER or CONTRACTOR at his last given address, or delivered in person to OWNER or CONTRACTOR or his authorized representative.

ARTICLE 2 - DRAWINGS AND SPECIFICATIONS:

A. Drawings are intended to show general arrangements, design and extent of WORK and are partly diagrammatic. As such, they are not intended to be scaled for roughing-in measurements or to serve as SHOP DRAWINGS.

B. Specifications are separated into titled divisions for convenience of reference only and to facilitate letting of contracts and subcontracts. Such separations shall not, however, operate to make ARCHITECT or OWNER an arbiter to establish limits of subcontracts or to establish responsibility as between CONTRACTORS or SUBCONTRACTORS.

C. In case of discrepancy between drawings and specifications, specifications shall govern.

-4-

D. Anything shown on drawings and not mentioned in the specifications or vice versa, as well as any WORK which is obviously
necessary to complete the project within the limits established
by the drawings and specifications, although not shown on or
described therein, shall be performed by CONTRACTOR as a part of
his contract.

E. Data concerning lot size, ground elevations, present obstruc-
tions on or near the site, locations and depth of sewers, conduits, pipes, wires, etc., position of sidewalks, curbs, pavements, etc., and nature of ground and subsurface conditions have
been or will be obtained from sources ARCHITECT and/or OWNER
believe reliable, although accuracy of such data is not guaranteed.

F. Upon encountering conditions differing materially from those
indicated in CONTRACT DOCUMENTS, or any discrepancy in the documents, CONTRACTOR shall, within fourteen (14) calendar DAYS,
notify in writing ARCHITECT, OWNER, and CONSTRUCTION MANAGER, if
one is utilized, with recommendations in writing within fourteen
(14) calendar DAYS.

ARTICLE 3 - ARCHITECT'S RIGHTS AND RESPONSIBILITIES:

A. ARCHITECT shall determine the amount, quality, acceptability
and fitness of WORK and materials which are to be paid for under
this contract. In the event any question shall arise between the
parties hereto relative to the contract or specifications, a
determination or decision of ARCHITECT shall be a condition
precedent to the right of CONTRACTOR to receive any money or
payment for WORK under the contract affected in any manner or to
any extent by such question.

B. ARCHITECT may file WRITTEN NOTICE to CONTRACTOR and OWNER
advising CONTRACTOR when any of his SUBCONTRACTORS, superintendents, foremen, workmen, watchmen or other employees shall be
deemed by ARCHITECT to be incompetent, careless or a hindrance to
proper or timely execution of WORK. CONTRACTOR shall remedy such
condition as promptly as practicable without detriment to WORK or
its progress and if CONTRACTOR should fail to do so within a
reasonable time, ARCHITECT may proceed as per ARTICLE 33 of the
General Conditions..

C. ARCHITECT shall have the rights, responsibilities, and
authority to carry out the specific duties required of ARCHITECT,
as described in other articles of the General Conditions, the
Supplementary Conditions and ARCHITECT'S Contract with OWNER
(SE240).

-5-

D. ARCHITECT will not be responsible for and will not have control, direction, or charge of any CONTRACTOR'S construction
means, methods, techniques, sequences or procedures, or for safety precautions and programs in connection with WORK.

E. Should any CONTRACTOR fall behind in his construction SCHED-
ULE, ARCHITECT shall proceed as outlined in ARTICLE 15-C.

F. ARCHITECT will be the interpreter of the requirements of
CONTRACT DOCUMENTS. ARCHITECT will render interpretations in
writing of these documents within ten (10) DAYS of receipt of any
request in writing or within an agreed upon time limit. These
interpretations as between OWNER and CONTRACTOR will be binding
upon both OWNER and CONTRACTOR unless ARTICLE 32 is invoked within ten (10) DAYS.

ARTICLE 4 - INSPECTION OF WORK:

A. ARCHITECT, OWNER, and CONSTRUCTION MANAGER, if one is utilized, and their representative shall at all times have access to
WORK whenever it is in preparation or progress, and CONTRACTOR
shall provide proper facilities for such access and for inspection and SUPERVISION.

B. During progress of WORK, OWNER will be represented at the
project by ARCHITECT and CONSTRUCTION MANAGER, if one is utilized, whose duties it will be to see that the contract is properly fulfilled.

C. Inspection by ARCHITECT or CONSTRUCTION MANAGER is for the
purpose of assuring OWNER that the drawings and specifications
are being properly executed. Although ARCHITECT is instructed to
confer with CONTRACTOR regarding interpretation of plans and
specifications, such assistance shall not relieve CONTRACTOR of
any responsibility for WORK.

D. The fact that ARCHITECT, OWNER, or CONSTRUCTION MANAGER, if
one is utilized, has failed to observe faulty WORK, or WORK done
which is not in accordance with the drawings and specifications,
or has failed to provide WRITTEN NOTICE to CONTRACTOR of such
errors or omissions, shall not relieve CONTRACTOR from responsibility for correcting such WORK without additional compensation.

E. If any WORK is covered up without approval or consent of
ARCHITECT or CONSTRUCTION MANAGER, if one is utilized, it must,
if requested, be uncovered by CONTRACTOR as provided for in
ARTICLE 21.

F. No inspection shall be construed as constituting or implying
acceptance and any such inspection is for the benefit of OWNER

-6-

and shall not relieve CONTRACTOR of the responsibility for providing quality control measures to assure that WORK strictly
complies with the contract requirements.

ARTICLE 5 - PERMITS AND TAXES:

A. CONTRACTOR shall, without additional expense to OWNER, be
responsible for obtaining all necessary licenses and permits
other than building permits, and for complying with all applicable Federal, State, and municipal laws, codes, and regulations,
in connection with the prosecution of WORK. He shall be similarly responsible for all damages to persons or property that occur
as a result of his fault or negligence. He shall take proper
safety and health precautions to protect WORK, the workers, the
public, and the property of others. He shall also be responsible
for all materials delivered and WORK performed until completion
and acceptance of the entire construction WORK, except for any
completed unit of construction thereof which theretofore may have
been accepted.

B. General building permits are not required by Title 6, Chapter
9, Subsection 6-9-11, Code of Laws of South Carolina 1976, as
amended, except in order that inspection services of municipal or
county building departments might be available for plumbing,
heating, air conditioning and electrical WORK. CONTRACTOR or
SUBCONTRACTOR shall obtain and pay the cost of a permit and
inspection fees for that specialty for which he is CONTRACTOR or
SUBCONTRACTOR, provided that this WORK is to be constructed within a municipality or county offering such services. Should
municipality or county refuse to issue a permit, CONTRACTOR shall
so notify ARCHITECT and CONSTRUCTION MANAGER, if one is utilized,
and STATE ENGINEER in writing.

C. CONTRACTOR shall pay all taxes for WORK or his portion thereof which are legally enacted at the time bids are received
whether or not yet effective.

D. CONTRACTOR'S attention is directed to Title 12, Chapter 9,
Code of Laws of South Carolina (1976), as amended, concerning
withholding tax for non-residents, employees, CONTRACTORS and
SUBCONTRACTORS.

ARTICLE 6 - NONDISCRIMINATION IN EMPLOYMENT:

A. CONTRACTOR and his SUBCONTRACTORS will not discriminate
against any employee or applicant for employment because of sex,
race, creed, color, religion, age, veteran or handicap status, or
national origin, unless with respect to sex, age or the handi-
capped it can be determined that such employment restrictions
relate to a bona fide acceptance qualification. CONTRACTOR and

-7-

SUBCONTRACTORS will take affirmative action to insure applicants are employed and employees are treated during employment without regard to the above considerations. Such action shall include, but not be limited to, the following: employment, upgrading, demotion and transfer; recruitment or recruitment advertising; layoff or termination; rates of pay or other forms of compensation; and selection for training, including apprenticeship.

B. CONTRACTOR and SUBCONTRACTORS will, in all solicitations or advertisements for employees, state that all qualified applicants will receive consideration for employment without regard to the above considerations.

C. In the event of CONTRACTOR'S or SUBCONTRACTOR'S noncompliance with the nondiscrimination clause of this contract, OWNER may cancel this contract in whole or in part or require CONTRACTOR to terminate his contract with SUBCONTRACTOR under the procedures outlined in ARTICLE 34, with no additional cost to OWNER.

ARTICLE 7 - CONDITIONS AFFECTING WORK:

A. CONTRACTOR shall be responsible for having taken steps reasonably necessary to ascertain the nature and location of WORK, and the general and local conditions which can affect WORK or the cost thereof. Any failure by CONTRACTOR to do so will not relieve him from responsibility for successfully performing WORK without additional expense to OWNER. OWNER assumes no responsibility for any understanding or representations concerning conditions made by any of its agents prior to the execution of this contract, unless such understanding or representations by OWNER are expressly stated in the contract.

ARTICLE 8 - SITE INVESTIGATIONS:

A. CONTRACTOR acknowledges that he has investigated and satisfied himself as to the conditions affecting WORK, including but not restricted to those bearing upon transportation, disposal, handling and storage of materials, availability of labor, water, electric power, roads and uncertainties of weather, river stages, tides or similar physical conditions at the site, the conformation and conditions of the ground, the character of equipment and facilities needed preliminary to and during prosecution of WORK. CONTRACTOR further acknowledges that he has satisfied himself as to the character, quality and quantity of surface and subsurface materials or obstacles to be encountered insofar as this information is reasonably ascertainable from an inspection of the site, including all exploratory WORK done by ARCHITECT, or CONSTRUCTION MANAGER, if one is utilized, or OWNER and results thereof reported to CONTRACTOR, as well as from information presented by the drawings and specifications made a part of this contract. Any

-8-

failure by CONTRACTOR to acquaint himself with the available information will not relieve him from responsibility for estimating properly the difficulty or cost of successfully performing WORK. OWNER assumes no responsibility for any conclusions or interpretations made by CONTRACTOR on the basis of the information made available by OWNER.

ARTICLE 9 - DELAYS AND EXTENSIONS OF TIME:

A. If CONTRACTOR is delayed at any time in the progress of its WORK by:

    1. any act or negligence of OWNER;

    2. unusually severe weather, not reasonably anticipated, as referenced to the nearest U. S. Weather Bureau 40 year statistical climatical data; a rain gauge shall be used on the job site by CONTRACTOR for measuring rainfall and a daily record shall be maintained to substantiate any claims for time made under this item;

    3. changes ordered by OWNER in WORK;

    4. labor disputes;

    5. delays authorized by OWNER; or

    6. delays caused by casualties or causes beyond CONTRACTOR'S control;

Then, in such event, the Time of Completion shall, at CONTRACTOR'S request, be extended by CHANGE ORDER to such reasonable time as OWNER may determine. CONTRACTOR shall make such request for a time extension in writing to ARCHITECT, complete with all supporting data, within fourteen (14) DAYS after the commencement of the delay or such delay will be waived by CONTRACTOR.

B. No payment or monetary compensation of any kind shall be made to CONTRACTOR for damages because of hindrance or delay from any cause in the progress of WORK, whether such delays be avoidable or unavoidable, and extension of time shall be CONTRACTOR'S sole remedy.

ARTICLE 10 - COMMUNICATIONS:

A. All notices, requests, instructions, approvals and claims must be in writing. All such communications shall be delivered to ARCHITECT, unless other specified by OWNER in writing to the contrary.

-9-

ARTICLE 11 - DUTIES OF CONTRACTOR:

A. CONTRACTOR shall supply all labor, material, plant and equipment required for the proper execution and completion of WORK;
and shall pay, when due, any laborer, SUBCONTRACTOR or supplier
for WORK or supplies furnished, and shall otherwise prosecute
WORK with diligence to prevent WORK stoppage and insure completion thereof within the time specified.

B. CONTRACTOR and each of his SUBCONTRACTORS shall submit to
ARCHITECT or CONSTRUCTION MANAGER, if one is utilized, such
SCHEDULES of quantities and costs, Progress SCHEDULES, CPM, payrolls, reports, estimates, records and other data concerning WORK
performed or to be performed under the contract and concerning
materials supplied or to be supplied.

C. CONTRACTOR shall give access to, upon written request from
OWNER, all time cards, material invoices, payrolls, and evidence
of all other direct or indirect costs related to this WORK.

D. Each CONTRACTOR shall be responsible for laying out his own
WORK and for any damage which may occur to WORK of any other
CONTRACTOR or SUBCONTRACTOR because of his own errors or inaccu-
racies, as well as be responsible for unloading, uncrating and
handling of all materials and equipment to be erected or placed
by him, whether furnished by CONTRACTOR or others. Layout of
mechanical and electrical WORK shall be coordinated with layouts
of CONTRACTOR for general construction WORK. Unless otherwise
directed by ARCHITECT or CONSTRUCTION MANAGER, if one is utilized, salvage materials, waste and scrap resulting from such
WORK shall be promptly removed from the site by the responsible
CONTRACTOR.

E. CONTRACTOR, SUBCONTRACTORS and material suppliers shall be
responsible for inspecting all job conditions affecting the
installation of any item and taking all field measurements
required prior to fabrication of any item to insure that the item
concerned will integrate properly with all adjacent materials and
fit all other conditions as they exist or will exist in the finished building. WORK in connection with the installation of any
item will be coordinated with all other affected WORK and trades.
Sleeves, anchors and other items that must be embodied in or that
otherwise affect other portions of WORK will be located and set
while such portions of WORK are in progress.

F. Unless otherwise specifically mentioned, all anchors, bolts,
screws, fittings, fillers, hardware, accessories, trim and other
parts required for or in connection with any item of material to
make a complete, serviceable, finished and first quality installation shall be furnished and installed as part of the item
whether or not called for by the specifications.

-10-

G. All materials shall be shipped and stored and handled in a
manner that will afford protection and insure their being in
first-class condition at the time they are incorporated in WORK.
After installation, they shall be properly protected against
damage to insure their being in first-class condition when the
building as a whole is completed and accepted by OWNER.

H. When standard specifications such as The American Society for
Testing and Materials, Federal Specifications, Department of
Commerce (Commercial Standards), American Institute of Steel
Construction, or other well known public or trade associations
are cited as a standard to govern materials and/or workmanship,
such specifications or portions thereof as referred to shall be
equally as binding and have the full force and effect as though
copied into these specifications. Such standards as are mentioned are generally recognized by and available to the trades
concerned. ARCHITECT will, however, upon request of a bidder or
CONTRACTOR, either furnish for inspection a copy of any standard
specifications mentioned or direct the bidder or CONTRACTOR to
any easily available copy. Unless otherwise specifically stated,
the standard specifications referred to shall be considered as
the latest edition and/or revision of such specifications that is
in effect on the date of the Invitation for Bids. In case of any
conflicts between standard specifications and the written portion
of the specifications, the specifications as actually written
herein will govern.

I. Any part of finish damaged during installation or prior to
final acceptance of WORK shall be repaired so as to be unno-
ticeable and to be equal in quality, appearance, serviceability
and other respects to an undamaged item. Where this cannot be
fully accomplished, the damaged item or part will be replaced.
After installation, all exposed surfaces and parts of an item
shall be cleaned in a manner that will not damage the finish or
any of the parts of the item and the finish job left in first-
class condition, free of all visible defects. All damaged or
defaced WORK shall be repaired or replaced to OWNER'S satisfaction at the expense of CONTRACTOR.

J. CONTRACTOR shall procure and furnish to OWNER all guarantees
and warranties that are called for by the specifications or that
are promised by a manufacturer or any item in the manufacturer's
published catalog or literature. Guarantees and warranties shall
commence as of the date of SUBSTANTIAL COMPLETION of the project.

K. CONTRACTOR shall pay all royalties and license fees. He
shall defend all suits or claims for infringement of any patent
rights and shall save OWNER harmless from loss on account thereof, except that OWNER shall be responsible for all such loss when
a particular design, process or the product of a particular manu-

-11-

facturer or manufacturers is specified, but if CONTRACTOR has
reason to believe that the design, process or product specified
is an infringement of a patent, he shall be responsible for such
loss unless he promptly gives such information to ARCHITECT.

L. Unless otherwise specifically stated, all manufacturer's
catalogs, specifications, instructions or other information or
literature that are referred to in the specifications shall be
considered as the latest edition and/or revision of such publication that is in effect on the date of the Invitation or Advertisement for Bids.

M. CONTRACTORS shall limit operations to the area within the
project, except as necessary to connect to existing utilities,
and shall not, without permission, encroach on neighboring property.

N. CONTRACTORS shall prearrange time with ARCHITECT or CONSTRUC-
TION MANAGER, if one is utilized, whenever it becomes necessary
to interrupt any service to make connections, alterations or
relocations and shall fully cooperate with OWNER in doing WORK so
as to cause the least annoyance and interference with the continuous operation of OWNER'S business or official duties. Unless
otherwise specified in these documents, all connections, alterations or relocations will be performed during normal working
hours.

O. CONTRACTOR shall coordinate all WORK so there shall be no
prolonged interruption of the use of existing equipment. Any
existing plumbing, heating, ventilating, air conditioning or
electrical disconnections necessary which affect portions of this
construction or building or any other building must be coordinated with ARCHITECT or CONSTRUCTION MANAGER, if one is utilized,
to avoid any disruption of operation within the building or construction or other building or utilities. In no case, unless
previously approved in writing by ARCHITECT or by CONSTRUCTION
MANAGER, if one is utilized, shall utilities be left disconnected
at the end of a work day or over a weekend. Any interruption of
utilities either negligently, intentionally, or accidentally
shall not relieve CONTRACTOR responsible for the interruption
from liability for loss or damage caused by such interruption, or
from his responsibility for repairing and restoring the utility
to normal service. Repairs and restoration shall be made before
the workmen responsible for the repair and restoration leave the
job.

P. CONTRACTOR shall be responsible for repair of damage to property on or off the project caused by his omission or negligence
occurring during construction of project, and all such repairs
shall be made to the satisfaction of OWNER of said property.

-12-

Q. CONTRACTOR shall not overload, or permit others to overload, any part of any structure during performance of WORK.

R. CONTRACTOR shall be responsible for shoring required to protect WORK or adjacent property and improvements of OWNER, and shall be responsible for shoring or for giving any required notice to adjacent property owners and shall pay for any damage caused by failure to shore or by improper shoring or by failure to give proper notice. Shoring shall be removed only after completion of permanent supports.

S. During the performance of WORK, CONTRACTOR shall be responsible for providing and maintaining warning signs, lights, signal devices, barricades, guard rails, fences and other devices appropriately located on site which will give proper and understandable warning to all persons of danger of entry onto land, structure or equipment.

T. CONTRACTOR shall be responsible for protection, including weather protection, and proper maintenance of all equipment and materials installed or to be installed by him.

U. CONTRACTOR shall designate a responsible member of his organization available at the job site whose duty shall be the preservation of safety and health and the prevention of accidents and injury to all persons coming on WORK site.

V. CONTRACTOR is responsible for replacing or making good any theft or damage.

W. If CONTRACTOR receives WRITTEN NOTICE from ARCHITECT or CONSTRUCTION MANAGER, if one is utilized, to dismiss any of his SUBCONTRACTORS or employees, as described in ARTICLE 3, Paragraph B, CONTRACTOR agrees to replace those dismissed without delay to the project and at no additional cost to OWNER.

X. CONTRACTOR shall superintend and direct WORK. He shall be solely responsible for all construction means, methods, techniques, sequences and procedures, and safety precautions, and for coordinating all portions of WORK under the contract.

Y. ARCHITECT shall furnish CONTRACTOR with a set of drawings to maintain during the progress of WORK. CONTRACTOR shall keep these drawings up to date as changes are made and these drawings shall be available for inspection and use by ARCHITECT as required in ARTICLE 36.

Z. CONTRACTOR shall maintain a daily log of all events occurring on the job site with particular notice being given to the weather conditions, persons visiting the site, number of workmen by trades, date of major events, deliveries, etc.

-13-

ARTICLE 12 - BOND:

A.   CONTRACTOR shall provide and pay the cost of the Performance
and Payment Bonds on The State Bond Forms, "PERFORMANCE BOND" and
"LABOR AND MATERIAL BOND".   Each shall be in the full amount of
the contract sum, issued by a surety company licensed in South
Carolina with an "A" minimum rating of performance as, stated in
the most current publication of "Best's Key Rating Guide, Property Liability" which shall show a financial strength rating of
at least five (5) times the contract price. Each Bond shall be
accompanied by a "Power of Attorney" authorizing the attorney-
in-fact to bind the surety and certified to include the date of
the Bond.

ARTICLE 13 - COMMENCEMENT AND COMPLETION OF WORK:

A.   The items listed below must be received by OWNER within fourteen (14) consecutive DAYS after DATE OF CONTRACT AWARD.   If not,
ARCHITECT may, at his option, treat the failure to timely submit
them as a refusal by CONTRACTOR to accept a contract for WORK.

   1.   Contract.

   2.   Performance/Payment Bond as described in ARTICLE 12.

   3.   Certificates of Insurance, or the actual policies them-
        selves, showing that CONTRACTOR has obtained the insur-
        ance coverage required by ARTICLE 23.

   4.   A Progress and a Payment SCHEDULE as described in
        ARTICLE 15.

   5.   A complete list of all SUBCONTRACTORS, major suppliers
        and other suppliers, as requested by ARCHITECT, not
        previously named who will be used for this project.

B.   Within ten (10) DAYS following receipt of "NOTICE TO PRO-
CEED", CONTRACTOR shall submit to ARCHITECT for approval a complete breakdown of CONTRACTOR'S proposal into line item costs.
No payments to CONTRACTOR will be made until CONTRACTOR has submitted these items and they have been approved by ARCHITECT and
OWNER; provided, however, that should CONTRACTOR not receive
written notification from either ARCHITECT or OWNER of the disap-
proval of any of these items within twenty-one (21) DAYS of their
receipt by ARCHITECT, CONTRACTOR may consider them approved.

ARTICLE 14 - SUBSTANTIAL COMPLETION:

A.   Only certification by ARCHITECT as to SUBSTANTIAL COMPLETION
of WORK within the time specified shall be conclusive and binding
on OWNER and CONTRACTOR.

-14-

B. If WORK embraced by the terms of this contract is not SUB-STANTIALLY COMPLETED on or before the time specified in this contract because of any act or omission of CONTRACTOR, then, without prejudice to any other rights, claims, or remedies of OWNER, the architectural, engineering, and inspection costs and expenses incurred by ARCHITECT upon WORK, from the originally agreed upon completion date to SUBSTANTIAL COMPLETION date of all WORK, shall be borne by CONTRACTOR and will be deducted by OWNER from any amount owing and due CONTRACTOR.

C. SUBSTANTIAL COMPLETION does not relieve CONTRACTOR of the requirements concerning final completion and of ARTICLE 37 - General Conditions.

ARTICLE 15 - PROGRESS AND SCHEDULING:

A. When separate contracts are awarded for different portions of the project, CONTRACTOR in CONTRACT DOCUMENTS in each case shall be CONTRACTOR who signs each separate contract.

B. The Progress SCHEDULE shall show the rate of progress that CONTRACTOR agrees to maintain and the order in which CONTRACTOR proposes to carry on various phases of WORK. The Payment SCHED-ULE shall show the percentage of WORK to be completed on a bi-weekly basis and the anticipated monthly payments by OWNER.

C. Bi-weekly job progress meetings shall be held by the general CONTRACTOR shall be attended by ARCHITECT who shall monitor CON-TRACTOR'S progress and performance. The general CONTRACTOR shall take and distribute written minutes of these meetings to OWNER, ARCHITECT and all attendees.

D. If ARCHITECT'S bi-weekly review of CONTRACTOR'S performance, on the basis of this SCHEDULE, shows that any part of WORK is behind CONTRACTOR'S projected SCHEDULE, ARCHITECT shall promptly notify CONTRACTOR and OWNER in writing. Upon receipt of this WRITTEN NOTICE, CONTRACTOR shall submit a revised SCHEDULE for the next two week period and enact appropriate measures to put WORK back on SCHEDULE by the next bi-weekly meeting. This will be done at no additional cost to OWNER. If WORK is not back on SCHEDULE by that next bi-weekly meeting, ARCHITECT, at his option, shall proceed in accordance with ARTICLE 29, ARTICLE 33 and/or ARTICLE 34. Adoption of one remedy will not waive the right to invoke another.

E. Values employed in preparation of any SCHEDULES will be used only for determining the basis for partial payments and will not be considered as a basis for additions to or deductions from the contract price.

-15-

F. There will be no payments of any periodic estimates until the
Progress SCHEDULE has been approved by ARCHITECT and CONSTRUCTION
MANAGER, if one is utilized.

G. CONTRACTOR shall employ and supply a sufficient force of
workmen, material, and equipment and will pay when due, any workman, SUBCONTRACTOR or supplier and other prosecute WORK with such
diligence so as to maintain the rate of progress indicated on the
Progress SCHEDULE, prevent WORK stoppage, and insure completion
of the project within the time specified.

H. Time is of the essence of this agreement. CONTRACTOR shall
be responsible for maintaining such SCHEDULE and the failure to
do so may be a material breach of this agreement. Any additional
or unanticipated cost or expense required to maintain SCHEDULE
shall be solely CONTRACTOR'S obligation and shall not be charged
to OWNER.

ARTICLE 16 - SUBSTITUTIONS AND "OR EQUALS":

A. Specific reference in the specifications to any article,
device, product, materials, fixture, form or type of construction, etc., by name, make, or catalog number, with or without the
words "or equal" shall be interpreted as establishing a standard
of quality and shall not be construed as limiting competition and
CONTRACTOR in such cases may, at his option, use any article,
device, product, material, fixture, form or type of construction
which, in the judgment of ARCHITECT expressed in writing, is
equal to that named and approval by ARCHITECT shall not be unreasonably withheld.

ARTICLE 17 - SUPERINTENDENCE:

A. CONTRACTOR shall keep on his WORK during its progress, a
competent superintendent satisfactory to OWNER.   The superintendent shall represent CONTRACTOR in his absence and all directions given to him shall be as binding as if given to CONTRACTOR.
He shall carefully study and compare all drawings, specifications
and other instructions and shall, at once, report to ARCHITECT
and CONSTRUCTION MANAGER, if one is utilized, any error, inconsistency or omission which he may discover.

ARTICLE 18 - SHOP DRAWINGS AND DOCUMENTS:

A. CONTRACTOR shall maintain at the site for OWNER and the use
of ARCHITECT and/or CONSTRUCTION MANAGER one copy of all drawings, specifications, bulletins, addenda, approved SHOP DRAWINGS,
catalog data, manufacturers' operating and maintenance instructions, certificates, warranties, guarantees and other modifications, in good order and marked daily by CONTRACTOR to record all

-16-

approved changes made during construction. These shall be turned
over to ARCHITECT by CONTRACTOR at the time of SUBSTANTIAL COM-
PLETION of the contract for the purpose of assembling and corre-
lating said material for use by OWNER.

B. CONTRACTOR shall submit to ARCHITECT or CONSTRUCTION MANAGER,
if one is utilized, with such promptness as to cause no delay in
his WORK or in that of any other CONTRACTOR, all SHOP DRAWINGS as
required by the construction documents.

C. Each drawing and/or series of drawings submitted must be
accompanied by a letter of transmittal giving a list of the
titles and number of the drawings. Each series shall be numbered
consecutively for ready reference and each drawing shall be
marked with the following information:

    1.   Date of Submission

    2.   Name of Project

    3.   Location

    4.   Branch of WORK

    5.   State Project Number

    6.   Name of Submitting CONTRACTOR

    7.   Name of SUBCONTRACTORS

D. All SUBCONTRACTORS' SHOP DRAWINGS and SCHEDULES shall be
submitted by CONTRACTOR and shall bear written approval by CON-
TRACTOR as evidence that he has checked them. Any SHOP DRAWINGS
and SCHEDULES submitted without this approval, or without having
been checked, will be returned for resubmission and the drawings
and SCHEDULES will be considered as not having been submitted.

E. CONTRACTOR shall include with SHOP DRAWINGS, a letter indicating all deviations from ARCHITECT'S drawings and/or specifications. Failure to so notify of such deviations will be ground
for subsequent rejection of the related WORK or materials. If,
in the opinion of ARCHITECT, the deviations are not acceptable,
CONTRACTOR will be required to furnish the item as specified and
indicated on ARCHITECT'S drawings.

F. It is CONTRACTOR'S obligation and responsibility to check all
of his SHOP DRAWINGS and SCHEDULES and to be fully responsible
for them and for their coordination with connecting WORK. SHOP
DRAWINGS and SCHEDULES shall indicate in detail all parts of an

-17-

item of WORK, including erection and setting instructions and engagements with WORK of other trades.

G. By approving and submitting SHOP DRAWINGS and samples, CONTRACTOR thereby represents that he has determined and verified all field measurements, field construction criteria, materials, catalog numbers and similar data, or will do so, and that he has checked and coordinated each SHOP DRAWING and sample with the requirements of WORK and of CONTRACT DOCUMENTS.

H. ARCHITECT shall check SHOP DRAWINGS and within fifteen (15) DAYS of receipt thereof return them to CONTRACTOR or CONSTRUCTION MANAGER, if one is utilized. If review and approval are delayed beyond the time set out above, ARCHITECT shall notify CONTRACTOR and OWNER in writing stating the reason for the delay. Approval shall not relieve CONTRACTOR from the responsibility for deviations from the drawings and specifications, unless he has called ARCHITECT'S attention to same, in writing, at the time of submission. An approval of any such modification will be given only if it is in the intent of OWNER, to affect an improvement in WORK, does not increase the contract sum and/or completion time, is subject generally to all contract stipulations and covenants, and is without prejudice to any and all rights under the surety bond.

I. No extension of time will be granted CONTRACTOR because of his failure to submit SHOP DRAWINGS in ample time to allow for review, possible resubmittals and approval. Fabrication of WORK shall not commence until CONTRACTOR has received approval. He shall furnish prints of his approved SHOP DRAWINGS to all CONTRACTORS whose WORK is in any way related to the WORK under the contract. Only prints bearing this approval will be allowed on the site of construction.

J. On completion of WORK, and as a condition precedent to receiving final payment, all SHOP DRAWINGS of all WORK or all trades shall be corrected to a true and actual representation of WORK actually performed, erected and installed. Drawings showing the actual installation of all underground services, utilities and structures of every description shall be furnished OWNER upon completion of WORK. See ARTICLE 35.

ARTICLE 19 - SAMPLES, TESTS AND CERTIFICATES:

A. CONTRACTOR shall prepare samples of all items requested or required by the specifications. Samples shall be properly identified and submitted with such promptness as to cause no delay in WORK or in that of any other CONTRACTOR and to allow time for consideration by ARCHITECT and OWNER.

-18-

B.   Each set of samples submitted must be accompanied by a letter
of transmittal containing the following information:

    1.   Date of Submission

    2.   Location

    3.   Branch of WORK

    4.   State Project Number

    5.   Name of Submitting CONTRACTOR

    6.   Name of SUBCONTRACTOR

C.   ARCHITECT shall require CONTRACTOR to furnish a certificate
guaranteeing that material or equipment as submitted hereunder
complies with contract requirements. Certificates shall be in
notarized affidavit form. If statement originates with manufacturer, CONTRACTOR shall endorse all claims and submit a statement
of compliance in his own name.

D.   Approval of material is general and shall not constitute
waiver. of OWNER'S right to demand full compliance with contract
requirements.

E.   Unless ARCHITECT is authorized at the time of submittal to
return samples at CONTRACTOR'S expense, rejected samples will be
destroyed.

F.   After delivery of materials, ARCHITECT may make such tests as
he deems necessary, with samples required for such tests being
furnished by and at the cost of the appropriate CONTRACTOR. Any
test is for the benefit of OWNER and shall not relieve CONTRAC-
TOR of the responsibility for providing quality control measures
to assure that WORK strictly complies with the contract requirements. No test shall be construed as implying acceptance.

G.   On the basis of the tests results, materials, workmanship,
equipment or accessories may be rejected even though general
approval has been given. If items have been incorporated in
WORK, ARCHITECT shall have the right to cause their removal and
replacement by items meeting contract requirements or to demand
and secure such reparation to OWNER from CONTRACTOR.

H.   All tests required by the specifications shall be paid for by
CONTRACTOR.

-19-

ARTICLE 20 - MATERIALS AND WORKMANSHIP:

A.   Unless otherwise specified, all materials shall   be   new   and suitable   for the purpose intended and both workmanship and mate- rials shall be of the best quality.   If   required   by   ARCHITECT, satisfactory evidence shall be furnished as to the kind and qual- ity of the materials and workmanship.

B.   Unless otherwise provided and stipulated within these   speci- fications,   CONTRACTOR   shall   furnish, construct, and/or install and pay for materials, devices, mechanisms, equipment, all neces- sary   personnel,   utilities including, but not limited to, water, heat, light and electric power, transportation services, applica- ble   taxes   and licenses of every nature and all other facilities necessary for the proper execution and completion of WORK.

C.   CONTRACTOR shall, at all times, enforce strict discipline and good   order among his employees, and shall not employ on WORK any unfit person or anyone not skilled in WORK assigned to him.

D.   CONTRACTOR shall carefully examine the plans and drawings and shall   be   responsible   for   the   proper fitting of his material, equipment and apparatus into the building.

E.   CONTRACTOR shall base his proposal only on materials, methods of construction and equipment as indicated by CONTRACT DOCUMENTS.

F.   CONTRACTOR   shall   promptly   remove   at   his   own expense all rejected materials from site of WORK.

ARTICLE 21 - UNCOVERING OF WORK:

A.   If any portion of WORK should   be   covered   contrary   to   the request of ARCHITECT or CONSTRUCTION MANAGER, if one is utilized, or to requirements specifically expressed in CONTRACT   DOCUMENTS, it   must,   if   required in writing by ARCHITECT, be uncovered for his observation and shall be replaced at CONTRACTOR'S expense.

B.   If any other portion of WORK has been covered which ARCHITECT or CONSTRUCTION MANAGER, if one is utilized, has not specifically requested to observe prior to being covered,   ARCHITECT   or   CON- STRUCTION   MANAGER,   if   one is utilized, may request to see such WORK and it shall be uncovered by CONTRACTOR.   If   such   WORK   be found in accordance with CONTRACT DOCUMENTS, the cost of uncover- ing and replacement shall, by appropriate CHANGE ORDER be charged to   OWNER.   If such WORK be found not in accordance with CONTRACT DOCUMENTS, CONTRACTOR shall pay such costs   unless   it   be   found that   this condition was caused by OWNER or a separate CONTRACTOR as provided in ARTICLE 6, in which event OWNER shall be responsi- ble for the payment of such costs.

-20-

ARTICLE 22 - CORRECTION OF WORK:

A. CONTRACTOR shall promptly correct all WORK rejected by ARCHI-
TECT or CONSTRUCTION MANAGER, if one is utilized, as defective or
non-conforming or as failing to conform to CONTRACT DOCUMENTS
whether observed before or after SUBSTANTIAL COMPLETION and
whether or not fabricated, installed or completed. CONTRACTOR
shall bear all costs of correcting such rejected WORK, including
the cost of ARCHITECT'S additional services thereby made necessary. Failure to correct rejected WORK shall be a material
breach of this contract.

B. If within one (1) year after the date of SUBSTANTIAL COMPLE-
TION any of WORK is found to be defective or not in accordance
with CONTRACT DOCUMENTS, CONTRACTOR shall correct it promptly
after receipt of WRITTEN NOTICE from OWNER to do so, unless OWNER
has previously given CONTRACTOR a written acceptance of such
specific condition.

C. Nothing contained in Paragraph B shall be construed to establish a period of limitation with respect to any other obligation
of CONTRACTOR under CONTRACT DOCUMENTS. The establishment of the
time period of one (1) year after the date of SUBSTANTIAL COMPLE-
TION relates only to the specific obligation of CONTRACTOR to
correct WORK, and has no relationship to the time within which
his obligation to comply with CONTRACT DOCUMENTS may be enforced
or to the time within which proceedings may be commenced to
establish CONTRACTOR'S liability with respect to his obligations
other than the obligation to correct WORK. Proceedings may be
commenced at any time within the applicable statute of limitations following discovery of any defect in workmanship or materials, discovery of any failure to follow the plans and specifications of ARCHITECT, or discovery of any failure on the part of
CONTRACTOR to furnish OWNER with a project sufficient and fit for
its intended purpose.

D. All such defective or non-conforming WORK under Paragraphs A
and B of this section shall be removed from the site where necessary, and WORK shall be corrected to comply with CONTRACT DOCU-
MENTS without cost to OWNER.

E. CONTRACTOR shall bear the cost of making good all WORK of
separate CONTRACTORS destroyed or damaged by such removal or
correction.

F. If CONTRACTOR does not remove such defective or nonconforming
WORK within a reasonable time fixed by WRITTEN NOTICE from ARCHI-
TECT, OWNER may remove it and may store the materials or equipment at the expense of CONTRACTOR. If CONTRACTOR does not pay
the cost of such removal and storage within ten (10) DAYS there-

-21-

after, OWNER may upon ten (10) additional DAYS WRITTEN NOTICE
sell such WORK at auction or at private sale and shall account
for the net proceeds thereof, after deducting all the costs that
should have been borne by CONTRACTOR, including compensation for
additional professional services. If such proceeds of sale do
not cover all costs which CONTRACTOR should have borne, the difference shall be charged to CONTRACTOR and an appropriate CHANGE
ORDER shall be issued. If the payments then or thereafter due
CONTRACTOR are not sufficient to cover such amount, CONTRACTOR
shall pay the difference to OWNER.

G. If CONTRACTOR fails to correct such defective or non-conforming WORK, OWNER may correct it at CONTRACTOR'S expense.

H. The obligations of CONTRACTOR under this Section shall be in
addition to and not in limitation of any obligations imposed upon
him by special guarantees required by CONTRACT DOCUMENTS or otherwise prescribed by law.

ARTICLE 23 - INSURANCE:

A. CONTRACTOR shall purchase and maintain in a company or companies acceptable to OWNER such insurance as will protect him
from claims set forth below which may arise out of or result from
CONTRACTOR'S operations under the contract, whether such operations be by himself and by any of his SUBCONTRACTORS or by anyone
directly or indirectly employed by them or by anyone for whose
acts they may be liable:

    1.   Claims under workers' or workmen's compensation, dis-
          ability benefit and other similar employee benefits
          acts;

    2.   Claims for Employers' Liability;

    3.   Claims for damages because of bodily injury. Bodily
          injury means bodily injury, sickness or disease sus-
          tained by any person, including death at any time
          resulting therefrom.

    4.   Claims for damages insured by personal injury liability
          coverage which are sustained (1) by any person as a
          result of an offense directly or indirectly related to
          the employment of such person by CONTRACTOR, or (2) by
          any other person. Personal injury includes false
          arrest, libel and slander and wrongful entry or evic-
          tion.

    5.   Claims for damages other than to WORK itself because of
          injury to or destruction of tangible property, including

-22-

loss of use resulting therefrom; and loss of use of tangible property which has not been physically injured or destroyed provided such loss is caused by an occurrence.

6. Claims for damages because of bodily injury or death of any person or property damage arising out of the ownership, maintenance or use of any motor vehicle.

B. The insurance required by Subparagraph A shall be written for not less than any limits of liability specified in CONTRACT DOCUMENTS, or required by law, whichever is greater.

C. The minimum limit for the following types of insurance is $_____. The limit may be insured by excess or umbrella policies providing total limits of $_____ per occurrence. (B.I. = Bodily Injury; P.D. = Property Damage)

1. Workmen's Compensation, including:

    (a) Workmen's Compensation insurance statutory coverage.

    (b) Employers' Liability - $_____

2. Comprehensive General Liability, $_____ B.I./P.D., including:

    (a) Premises and Operations - including xcu hazards

    (b) CONTRACTOR'S Protective Liability

    (c) Products Liability, including Completed Operations Coverage - including coverage for one (1) year beyond completion of project.

    (d) Broad Form Contractual Liability, providing coverage for all written and oral contracts. This coverage should specifically cover indemnity included under this contract.

    (e) Broad Form Property Damage

    (f) Personal Injury Liability

3. Comprehensive Automobile Liability, $_____ B.I./P.D., including:

    (a) All OWNER Automobiles

-23-

(b) Non-OWNER Automobiles

(c) Hired Car Coverage

D. Coverage under both Comprehensive General and Comprehensive Automobile forms shall include "occurrence" basis wording, which means an event, or continuous or repeated exposure to conditions which unexpectedly causes injury or damage during policy period.

E. CONTRACTOR shall either (a) require each of his SUBCONTRACTORS to procure and maintain during the life of the subcontract, SUBCONTRACTOR'S Comprehensive General Liability, Automobile Liability, and Property Damage Liability Insurance of the type and in the same amounts as specified in this Subparagraph, or (b) insure the activities of his SUBCONTRACTORS in his own policy.

F. The insurance required by Subparagraph A shall include contractual liability insurance applicable to CONTRACTOR'S obligations under ARTICLE 27.

G. Certificate of Insurance must be filed through ARCHITECT on form approved by ARCHITECT, by an insurer authorized to do business in South Carolina by South Carolina State Insurance Commission. All blanks and questions on Certificate must be filled out completely. Incomplete or inadequate Certificate will be returned to CONTRACTOR as unsatisfactory and commencement of his WORK will be delayed until satisfactory Certificate is submitted. Such delay will not warrant extension of contract time.

H. Certificates of Insurance acceptable to OWNER shall be filed with OWNER prior to commencement of WORK. These Certificates shall contain a provision that the company certifies the policy will not be amended to reduce coverage, cancelled or non-renewed without at least sixty (60) DAYS advance WRITTEN NOTICE given to OWNER.

I. OWNER'S LIABILITY INSURANCE:

1. GENERAL:

CONTRACTOR shall be responsible for purchasing and maintaining complete OWNER'S Protective Liability Insurance covering claims which may arise from operations under the contract. CONTRACTOR shall file a copy of all OWNER'S Protective Liability Insurance policies with OWNER before any exposure to loss may occur. Limits shall be the same as specified for General Liability and Property Damage Insurance.

-24-

PROPERTY DAMAGE:

(a) Unless otherwise provided, OWNER shall purchase and
maintain Property Insurance upon the entire WORK at
the site to the full insurable value thereof. This
insurance shall include the interest of OWNER,
CONTRACTOR, SUBCONTRACTORS and Sub-subcontractors
in WORK and shall insure against the perils of
fire, extended coverage, vandalism, glass breakage
and malicious mischief. A deductible of $1,000
shall apply to each loss on a per occurrence basis.
THE DEDUCTIBLE SHALL BE BORNE BY CONTRACTOR. In
the event of a loss involving more than one party,
such as CONTRACTOR and SUBCONTRACTOR and/or
Sub-subcontractor, the deductible will be borne by
all parties involved on a prorata basis. This
insurance shall NOT cover any tools owned by
mechanics, any tools, equipment, scaffolding, stag-
ing towers, and forms owned or rented by CONTRACTOR
which are NOT intended to become part of the project. This insurance shall NOT cover any loss by
theft or burglary, or damage to the building or
contents as a result of said theft or burglary.
The interest of OWNER, CONTRACTOR, SUBCONTRACTORS
and Sub-subcontractors in this insurance shall only
be effective during the construction of the project
and all rights and interest of CONTRACTOR, SUBCON-
TRACTORS and Sub-subcontractors in this insurance
shall end upon the acceptance of the project by
OWNER as evidenced by the certificate of SUBSTAN-
TIAL COMPLETION.

(b) OWNER shall purchase and maintain such boiler and
machinery insurance as may be required by CONTRACT
DOCUMENTS or by law. This insurance shall include
the interest of OWNER, CONTRACTOR, SUBCONTRACTORS
and Sub-subcontractors in WORK. The interest of
CONTRACTOR, SUBCONTRACTORS and Sub-subcontractors
in this insurance shall only be during the time of
the construction of the project and all rights and
interest in this insurance shall end upon acceptance of the project by OWNER.

(c) If applicable, any insured loss is to be adjusted
with OWNER and made payable to OWNER as trustee for
the insured, as their interests may appear, subject
to the requirements of any applicable mortgage
claims.

-25-

(d) OWNER shall file a certificate of all policies with CONTRACTOR before an exposure to loss may occur. If OWNER does not intend to purchase such insurance, he shall inform CONTRACTOR in writing prior to commencement of WORK. CONTRACTOR then shall effect insurance which shall protect the interest of himself, his SUBCONTRACTORS and the Sub-subcontractors in WORK, and by appropriate CHANGE ORDER the cost thereof shall be charged to OWNER. If CONTRACTOR is damaged by the failure of OWNER to purchase or maintain such insurance and so notifies OWNER, then OWNER shall bear all reasonable costs appropriately attributable thereto.

(e) If CONTRACTOR requests in writing that insurance for special hazards be included in the Property Insurance Clause, OWNER shall, if possible, include such insurance, and the cost thereof shall be charged to CONTRACTOR by an appropriate CHANGE ORDER.

(f) OWNER and CONTRACTOR waive all rights against each other for damages caused by fire and other perils to the extent covered by insurance provided under Paragraph I-2, except such rights as they may have to the proceeds of such insurance held by OWNER as trustee. CONTRACTOR shall require similar waivers by SUBCONTRACTORS and Sub-subcontractors in accordance with ARTICLE 25. This waiver does not apply to any defects due to faulty materials or workmanship by CONTRACTOR. SUBCONTRACTORS, Sub-subcontractors, and CONTRACTOR shall remedy any defects due to such faulty materials or workmanship and pay for any damage to other WORK resulting therefrom, which shall appear within a period of one year from the date of acceptance as defined in the General Conditions, and in accordance with the terms of any special guarantees provided in the contract. OWNER shall give notice of observed defect within ninety (90) DAYS of the time that the defect was observed by OWNER.

(g) If required in writing by any party in interest, OWNER as trustee shall, upon the occurrence of an insured loss, deposit in a separate account any money received for such loss, and he shall distribute it in accordance with such agreement as the parties in interest may reach. If after such loss no other special agreement is made, replacement of damaged WORK shall be covered by appropriate CHANGE ORDER.

-26-

(h)   OWNER as trustee shall have the power to adjust and settle with the insurers.

(i)   If OWNER finds it necessary to occupy or use a portion or portions of WORK prior to substantial completion thereof, such occupancy shall not commence prior to a time mutually agreed to by OWNER and CONTRACTOR and to which the insurance company or companies providing the property insurance have consented by endorsement to the policy or policies. This insurance shall not be cancelled or lapsed on account of such partial occupancy. Consent of CONTRACTOR and of the insurance company or companies to such occupancy or use shall not be unreasonably withheld.

(j)   OWNER, at his option, may purchase and maintain such insurance as will insure him against loss of use of his property due to fire and other hazards, however caused.

ARTICLE 24 - SEPARATE CONTRACTS AND COOPERATION:

A.   OWNER reserves the right to let other contracts in connection with this WORK, or perform WORK himself. CONTRACTOR shall afford other CONTRACTORS reasonable opportunity for the introduction and storage of their materials and the execution of their WORK and shall properly connect and coordinate his WORK with theirs.

B.   CONTRACTORS shall consult the documents of and for all other CONTRACTORS in connection with WORK. Any WORK conflicting with WORK to be performed by CONTRACTOR shall be brought to the attention of ARCHITECT and CONSTRUCTION MANAGER, if one is utilized, before WORK is performed. If CONTRACTOR fails to notify ARCHITECT of such conflicting WORK, he shall remove any part so conflicting and rebuild same, as directed by ARCHITECT and CONSTRUCTION MANAGER, if one is utilized, at no additional cost to OWNER.

C.   No CONTRACTOR shall delay any other CONTRACTOR by neglecting to perform his WORK at the proper time. Each CONTRACTOR shall be required to coordinate his WORK with other CONTRACTORS so as to afford others reasonable opportunity for execution of their WORK.

D.   Each CONTRACTOR shall be responsible for damage to OWNER'S or other CONTRACTOR'S property done by him or persons in his employ through his or their fault or negligence.

E.   Should a CONTRACTOR sustain any damage through any act or omission of any other CONTRACTOR having a contract with OWNER, CONTRACTOR so damaged shall have no claim or cause of action

-27-

against OWNER for such damage and hereby waives such a claim, but shall have a claim or cause of action against the other CONTRAC-TOR to recover any and all damages sustained by reason of the acts or omissions of such CONTRACTOR. The phrase "acts or omissions" as used in this section shall be defined to include, but not be limited to, any unreasonable delay on the part of any such CONTRACTORS.

ARTICLE 25 - SUBCONTRACTS:

A. SUBCONTRACTOR assignments, as identified in the bid proposal, shall not be changed without written approval of OWNER. No prime CONTRACTOR shall substitute any person as SUBCONTRACTOR in place of SUBCONTRACTOR listed in the original bid, except with the written consent of OWNER.

B. CONTRACTOR agrees that he is as fully responsible to OWNER for the acts and omissions of his SUBCONTRACTORS and of persons either directly or indirectly employed by them, as he is for the acts and omissions of persons directly employed by him.

C. Every SUBCONTRACTOR shall be bound by the applicable terms and provisions of CONTRACT DOCUMENTS, but no contractual relationship shall exist between any SUBCONTRACTOR and OWNER, unless the right of CONTRACTOR to proceed with WORK is suspended or the contract is terminated as herein provided, and OWNER in writing elects to assume the subcontract.

ARTICLE 26 - ASSIGNMENT OF CONTRACT:

A. No assignment by CONTRACTOR of any amount or any part of the contract or of the funds to be received thereunder will be recognized unless such assignment has had the prior written approval of OWNER and the surety on CONTRACTOR'S bond has been given due notice of such assignment and has given written consent thereto. In addition to the usual recitals in assignments of contracts, the following language must be set forth: "It is agreed that the funds to be paid to the assignee under this assignment are subject to performance by CONTRACTOR of the contract and to claims or liens for services rendered or materials supplied for the performance of WORK called for in said contract in favor of any persons, firms or corporations rendering such services or supplying such materials."

ARTICLE 27 - INDEMNIFICATION:

A. CONTRACTOR agrees to indemnify and save harmless OWNER, ARCHITECT, and CONSTRUCTION MANAGER, if one is utilized, their agents and employees, from and against any and all liability for damage arising from injuries to persons or damage to property

-28-

resulting from the negligence in whole or in part by any acts or omissions of CONTRACTOR, any SUBCONTRACTORS, their agents, or employees, including any and all expense, legal or otherwise, which may be incurred by OWNER or ARCHITECT, their agents or employees. In no case, however, shall CONTRACTOR be liable for claims, expenses, loss or damage caused by the sole negligence of OWNER, its independent CONTRACTORS, ARCHITECT, their agents, or employees.

ARTICLE 28 - CHANGES IN WORK:

A. OWNER, and no other, may order extra WORK or make changes by altering, adding to or deducting from WORK, the contract sum being adjusted accordingly. The contract sum and the contract time may be changed only by CHANGE ORDER. All such WORK shall be executed under the conditions of the original contract except that any claim for extension of time caused thereby shall be adjusted at the time of ordering such change. No such CHANGE ORDER shall have the effect of invalidating the contract or relieving CONTRACTOR or surety of their liability on the Performance Bond. Any notice of CHANGE ORDERS required by the surety shall be the responsibility of CONTRACTOR, and the cost of any additional bond premiums shall be the obligation of CONTRACTOR.

B. The amount of any adjustment in the contract price for authorized changes shall be agreed upon before such change becomes effective and shall approximate the actual cost to CONTRACTOR and all costs incurred by CONTRACTOR shall be justifiably compared with prevailing industry standards, including reasonable profit. Costs shall be properly itemized and supported by substantiating data sufficient to permit evaluation before commencement of the pertinent performance or as soon thereafter as practicable, and shall be arrived at through whichever one of the following ways is the most valid approximation of the actual cost to CONTRACTOR:

1. by unit prices specified in the contract or subsequently agreed upon;

2. by the costs attributable to the events or situations under such clauses with adjustment of profits or fee, all as specified in the contract or subsequently agreed upon;

3. by agreement on a fixed price adjustment;

4. in such other manner as the contracting parties may mutually agree; or

-29-

5. in the absence of agreement by the parties, through
    unilateral determination by STATE ENGINEER of the costs
    attributable to the events or situations under such
    clauses, with adjustment of profit or fee, all as com-
    puted by STATE ENGINEER in accordance with Section
    11-35-3040 of the South Carolina Consolidated Pro-
    curement Code and subject to the provisions of ARTICLE
    32 of the General Conditions.

C. In determining the cost or credit to OWNER resulting from a
change in WORK, the allowances for all extended overhead and
profit combined, included in the total cost to OWNER, shall not
exceed the percentages herein scheduled, as follows:

1. For the Prime CONTRACTOR, for any WORK performed by his
    own forces, 15% of the cost;

2. For each SUBCONTRACTOR involved, WORK performed by his
    own forces, 15% of the cost;

3. For the Prime CONTRACTOR, for WORK performed by his
    SUBCONTRACTOR, 7% of the amount due SUBCONTRACTOR.

D. The "cost" as used herein may include all items of labor or
materials, the use of power tools and power equipment and all
such items of cost as public liability, workmen's compensation
insurance, pro rata charges for additional time of foremen,
social security, and old age and unemployment insurance and bond
premiums. Among the items to be considered as overhead are
insurance other than that mentioned above, SUPERVISION, travel,
superintendence, timekeepers, clerks, watchmen, small tools,
incidental job burdens and general office expense, and all other
items not included in the cost as defined above.

E. If CONTRACTOR claims that any instructions involve extra cost
under this contract, he shall give OWNER WRITTEN NOTICE thereof
within fourteen (14) DAYS after the receipt of such instructions,
and in any event before proceeding to execute WORK. No such
claim shall be valid unless so made and authorized by OWNER in
writing.

F. In an emergency affecting the safety of life or of the structure or of adjoining property, CONTRACTOR, without special
instruction or authorization from OWNER, is hereby permitted to
act at his discretion to prevent such threatened loss or injury.
Any compensation claimed by CONTRACTOR on account of such emergency WORK shall be determined by agreement with OWNER.

-30-

ARTICLE 29 - PAYMENT TO CONTRACTORS:

A. PAYMENTS:

1. Payments on account of this contract will be made month-ly as WORK progresses. CONTRACTOR shall submit to OWNER, in the manner and form prescribed, an application for each payment, and, if required, receipts or other vouchers showing his payments for materials and labor, including payments to SUBCONTRACTORS. OWNER will make partial payments as specified in the Supplemental Condi-tions, for WORK done during the preceding calendar month on estimates certified by ARCHITECT and CONSTRUCTION MANAGER, if one is utilized, to OWNER. All bills, claims and demands for labor performed, WORK done or materials furnished, shall be submitted in six (6) cop-ies by CONTRACTOR. OWNER shall retain one (1) percent of the adjusted contract sum from the payment due at SUBSTANTIAL COMPLETION until final payment is due. The general CONTRACTOR shall not hold any retainage from his SUBCONTRACTORS

2. For contracts, the cost of which is $5,000.00 or less, Paragraph A of this article shall not apply. CONTRAC-TORS falling within this category shall require but a single payment which shall become due and payable on completion and acceptance of all WORK specified there-under.

3. Each payment made to CONTRACTOR shall be on account of the total amount payable to CONTRACTOR and all material and WORK covered by paid partial payment shall thereupon become the sole property of OWNER. Nothing in this Article shall be construed as relieving CONTRACTOR from the sole responsibility for care and protection of mate-rials and WORK upon which payments have been made or restoration of any damaged WORK or as a waiver of the right of OWNER to require fulfillment of all terms of CONTRACT DOCUMENTS.

4. CONTRACTOR'S Application for Payment shall be on a form as follows:

   (a) The form of Application for Payment shall be on the Standard State Form, Application and Certification for Payment (SE470), which shall include the fol-lowing statement:

-31-

State of:

County of:

The undersigned CONTRACTOR certifies under Section 29-7-20 of Code of Laws of South Carolina (1976), as amended, that the WORK covered by this Application for Payment has been completed in accordance with the CONTRACT DOCUMENTS, that all amounts have been paid by him for WORK for which previous Certificates for Payment were issued and payments received from the OWNER, and that the current payment shown herein is now due.

CONTRACTOR:

By:

Date:

Subscribed and sworn to before me this ___ day of _____, 19___.

Notary Public:

My Commission Expires:

5. Rental equipment such as, but not limited to, mobile equipment, pans, patented forms, scaffolding, compressors, etc., shall not be considered material stored on the site.

6. CONTRACTOR'S attention is directed to the Code of Laws of South Carolina, (1976), and all amendments thereto, and specifically to Title 29, Chapter 7, Code of Laws of South Carolina, (1976), as amended, concerning laborers' liens and to Title 9, Chapter 12, concerning the withholding of income tax.

7. Interest on late payments shall be paid in accordance with Section 11-35-45 of Code of Laws of South Carolina, (1976), as amended.

B. PAYMENTS WITHHELD:

1. OWNER may withhold or nullify in whole or in part any certificate for payment to such extent as may be necessary to protect OWNER from loss on account of:

    (a) Defective WORK not remedied.

-32-

(b) Failure of CONTRACTOR to make payment properly to SUBCONTRACTORS for material or labor.

(c) Claims filed or reasonable evidence indicating probable filing of claims.

(d) A reasonable doubt that the contract can be completed for the balance then unpaid.

(e) CONTRACTOR'S failure to perform any of his contractual obligations, or in default under CONTRACT DOCUMENTS, or has failed to maintain the agreed upon time SCHEDULE (as described in ARTICLE 15).

When OWNER is satisfied CONTRACTOR has remedied any such deficiency, payment shall be made of amount withheld.

C. FINAL PAYMENT:

1. Upon receipt of WRITTEN NOTICE from CONTRACTOR to ARCHITECT that WORK is ready for final inspection and acceptance, OWNER, ARCHITECT, and CONSTRUCTION MANAGER, if one is utilized, shall promptly make such inspection. If WORK is acceptable and the contract fully performed, CONTRACTOR will be directed to submit a final estimate for certification and the entire balance shall be due and payable upon a certification of completion by ARCHITECT that WORK is in accordance with plans and specifications.

D. RELEASES:

1. The final payment shall not become due until CONTRACTOR delivers to ARCHITECT or to CONSTRUCTION MANAGER, if one is utilized, a complete file of releases from SUBCONTRACTORS.

2. If any lien or claim remains unsatisfied after all payments are made, CONTRACTOR shall refund to OWNER all monies that the latter may be compelled to pay in discharging such a lien or claim including all costs and a reasonable attorney's fee.

ARTICLE 30 - CLEAN-UP:

A. CONTRACTOR shall at all times keep the construction area, including storage areas used by him, free from accumulations of waste material or rubbish and prior to completion of WORK remove any rubbish from the premises and all tools, scaffolding, equip-

-33-

ment, and materials not the property of OWNER. Upon completion of the construction, CONTRACTOR shall leave WORK and premises in a clean, neat and workmanlike condition satisfactory to OWNER.

B. If CONTRACTOR fails to clean up and keep the premises and all adjoining areas as required above, then OWNER may do so and charge the cost to CONTRACTOR.

ARTICLE 31 - OCCUPANCY:

A. OWNER may, with the written approval of ARCHITECT and CON-TRACTOR, fully occupy the facility upon SUBSTANTIAL COMPLETION. No provisions in this document shall be construed to prevent partial occupancy by OWNER so long as the partial occupancy does not materially affect the construction process.

B. CONTRACTOR agrees that OWNER, upon advance notification to CONTRACTOR in writing and with the written approval of CONTRAC-TOR, will be permitted to occupy and use any completed or par-tially completed portions of the project when such occupancy and use is to OWNER'S best interest.

ARTICLE 32 - DISPUTES AND DISAGREEMENTS:

A. In order to prevent all disputes or disagreements between the parties in relation to the performance required by CONTRACT DOCU-MENTS, it is hereby expressly agreed and understood that, in case of any controversy or difference of opinion which should arise as to the quantity or value of WORK, or material, the interpretation of plans, specifications, and provisions of CONTRACT DOCUMENTS, or any other matter connected with WORK, or the performance of the covenants and agreements contained herein, or any controversy arising under or by virtue of CONTRACT DOCUMENTS, including, without limitation, controversies based upon breach of contract, mistake, misrepresentation or other cause for modification or recision, all disputes or disagreements shall first be submitted to ARCHITECT. ARCHITECT shall render a written decision within fifteen (15) DAYS following the receipt of a written demand for resolution of a dispute or controversy by either OWNER or CON-TRACTOR and this decision shall be final and binding, unless that decision is appealed to CHIEF PROCUREMENT OFFICER within ten (10) DAYS following its receipt.

B. All appeals arising under or out of this contract shall be submitted to CHIEF PROCUREMENT OFFICER who in accordance with Section 11-35-4230(3) shall issue a written decision within ten (10) DAYS of receipt of notice of appeal, unless the time is extended by agreement of the parties. This decision shall be final and conclusive unless CONTRACTOR submits a written appeal within ten (10) DAYS from the date of receipt of the decision to

-34-

SOUTH CAROLINA PROCUREMENT REVIEW PANEL stating the grounds for the appeal.

C. PROCUREMENT REVIEW PANEL shall hear the appeal under procedures set forth in the South Carolina Consolidated Procurement Code and any pertinent regulations thereo and shall render its decision within thirty (30) DAYS.

D. The Determination of the REVIEW PANEL shall be conclusive and final unless the decision is set aside by a court of competent jurisdiction subsequent to judicial review under the South Carolina Administrative Procedures Act.

E. The provisions under this Article shall be the sole remedy of the parties and the parties shall be bound thereby.

F. CHIEF PROCUREMENT OFFICER and PROCUREMENT REVIEW PANEL shall each have the right to consolidate all claims, protests, and controversies arising under or out of this contract.

G. The surety for the general CONTRACTOR shall be bound by the provisions of this Article and the provisions herein shall be the sole remedy of the surety.

ARTICLE 33 - SUSPENSION OF WORK AND FAULT OF CONTRACTOR:

A. Should CONTRACTOR fail to comply with the orders of ARCHITECT or CONSTRUCTION MANAGER, if one is utilized, relative to any particular parts of WORK, ARCHITECT or CONSTRUCTION MANAGER, if one is utilized, can stop WORK for 24 hours. Thereafter, for the suspension to continue, it must be with the written authorization of OWNER. In case of such suspension, which shall be considered due to the fault of CONTRACTOR, no extension of time shall be given and no allowance will be made for the expense of CONTRACTOR on account of idle equipment or labor during the terms of such suspension.

B. Ten (10) DAYS Notice of Suspension shall be given if WORK is suspended pursuant to ARTICLE 34-A.

ARTICLE 34 - TERMINATION:

A. If CONTRACTOR shall be adjudged bankrupt, or if he should make a general assignment for the benefit of his creditors, or if a receiver should be appointed on account of his insolvency, or if he should persistently or repeatedly refuse or fail to supply enough properly skilled workmen or proper materials, or if he should fail to make prompt payment to SUBCONTRACTORS or for material or labor, or persistently disregard laws, ordinances or the instructions of OWNER, or otherwise be guilty of a material vio-

-35-

lation of any provision of the contract, or if he should fall behind the progress SCHEDULE as described in CONTRACT DOCUMENTS, then ARCHITECT may serve notice to CONTRACTOR and his surety setting forth the asserted violations and demanding compliance with the contract. Unless within ten (10) consecutive calendar DAYS after serving such notice, such violations shall cease and satisfactory arrangements for correction be made, ARCHITECT or CONSTRUCTION MANAGER, if one is utilized, may declare CONTRACTOR to be in default and OWNER may suspend CONTRACTOR'S right to proceed with WORK or OWNER may terminate the contract.

B. If CONTRACTOR refuses or fails to prosecute WORK, or any separable part thereof, with such diligence as will insure its completion within the time specified in the contract, or any extension thereof, or fails to complete said WORK within such time or refuses to correct defective WORK, ARCHITECT may suspend WORK as set forth in ARTICLE 33 and may advise OWNER to terminate the contract.

C. In the event that ARCHITECT, CONSTRUCTION MANAGER, if one is utilized, or OWNER suspends CONTRACTOR'S right to proceed with WORK or OWNER terminates the contract OWNER may demand that CON-TRACTOR'S surety take over and complete WORK on the contract, and upon its failure or refusal to do so within ten (10) consecutive DAYS after demand therefor OWNER may take over WORK and prosecute the same to completion by bid or negotiated contract, or OWNER may elect to take possession of and utilize in completing WORK such materials, supplies, appliances and plant as may be on the site of WORK, and all SUBCONTRACTORS, if OWNER elects, shall be bound to perform their contracts.

D. CONTRACTOR and his surety shall be liable for all costs nec-essary for repair and completion of the project over and beyond the amount of CONTRACTOR'S original bid. CONTRACTOR and his surety shall be liable for all legal fees and costs rendered necessary by any litigation required to enforce the provisions of this contract.

E. CONTRACTOR, in the event of such suspension or termination, shall not be entitled to receive any further payments under the contract until WORK is wholly finished. Then if the unpaid bal-ance under the contract shall exceed all expenses of OWNER as certified by ARCHITECT, such excess shall be paid to CONTRACTOR; but, if such expenses shall exceed the unpaid balance as certi-fied by ARCHITECT, CONTRACTOR and his surety shall be liable for and shall pay the difference and any damages to OWNER.

F. In exercising OWNER'S right to secure completion of WORK under any of the provisions hereof, OWNER shall have the right to exercise OWNER'S sole discretion as to the manner, methods and reasonableness of costs of completing WORK.

-36-

G. The rights of OWNER to suspend or terminate as herein provided shall be cumulative and not exclusive and shall be in addition to any other remedy provided by law.

ARTICLE 35 - TERMINATION FOR CONVENIENCE:

A. The performance of WORK under this contract may be terminated by OWNER in accordance with this clause in whole, or from time to time in part, whenever CHIEF PROCUREMENT OFFICER FOR CONSTRUCTION shall determine that such termination is in the best interest of OWNER. Any such termination shall be effected by delivery to CONTRACTOR of a Notice of Termination specifying the extent to which performance of WORK under the contract is terminated, and the date upon which such termination becomes effective.

B. After receipt of Notice of Termination, and except as otherwise directed by CHIEF PROCUREMENT OFFICER FOR CONSTRUCTION, CONTRACTOR shall:

    1. Stop WORK under the contract on the date and to the extent specified in the Notice of Termination;

C. After receipt of a Notice of Termination, CONTRACTOR shall submit to CHIEF PROCUREMENT OFFICER FOR CONSTRUCTION his termination cost, in the form and with the certification prescribed by CHIEF PROCUREMENT OFFICER FOR CONSTRUCTION. Such claim shall be submitted promptly but in no event later than one year from the effective date of termination, unless one or more extensions in writing are granted by CHIEF PROCUREMENT OFFICER FOR CONSTRUCTION upon request of CONTRACTOR made in writing within such one-year period or authorized extension thereof.

D. Subject to the provisions of paragraph C, and subject to any review required by PROCUREMENT REVIEW PANEL'S procedures in effect as of the date of execution of this contract, CONTRACTOR and CHIEF PROCUREMENT OFFICER FOR CONSTRUCTION may agree upon the whole or any part of the amount or amounts to be paid to CONTRACTOR by reason of the total or partial termination of WORK pursuant to this clause, which amount or amounts may include a reasonable allowance of profit on WORK done. Provided; That such agreed amount or amounts exclusive of settlement costs, shall not exceed the total contract price as reduced by the amount of payments otherwise made and as further reduced by the contract price of WORK not terminated. The contract shall be amended accordingly, and CONTRACTOR shall be paid the agreed amount. Nothing in paragraph E of this clause, prescribing the amount to be paid to CONTRACTOR by reason of termination of WORK pursuant to this clause, shall be deemed to limit, restrict, or otherwise determine or affect the amount or amounts which may be agreed upon to be paid to CONTRACTOR pursuant to this paragraph.

-37-

E. In the event of the failure of CONTRACTOR and CHIEF PROCURE-MENT OFFICER FOR CONSTRUCTION to agree as provided in paragraph D upon the whole amount to be paid to CONTRACTOR by reason of the termination of WORK pursuant to this clause, CHIEF PROCUREMENT OFFICER FOR CONSTRUCTION shall, subject to any review required by PROCUREMENT REVIEW PANEL'S procedures in effect as of the date of execution of this contract, determine, on the basis of information available to him, the amount, if any due to CONTRACTOR by reason of the termination and shall pay to CONTRACTOR the amounts determined as follows:

1. With respect to all contract WORK performed prior to the effective date of the Notice of Termination, the total (without duplication of any items) of:

   i. The cost of such WORK;

   ii. The cost of settling and paying claims arising out of the termination of WORK under subcontracts or orders, said claims being limited to the same types of cost that the general CONTRACTOR is limited to hereunder, exclusive of the amounts paid or payable on account of supplies or materials delivered or services furnished by SUBCONTRACTOR prior to the effective date of the Notice of Termination of WORK under this contract, which amounts shall be included in the cost on account of which payment is made under i above; and

   iii. A sum, as profit on i, above, determined by CHIEF PROCUREMENT OFFICER FOR CONSTRUCTION pursuant to South Carolina Consolidated Procurement Code Regulations, in effect as of the date of execution of this contract, to be fair and reasonable: Provided, however, That if it appears that CONTRACTOR would have sustained a loss on the entire contract had it been completed, no profit shall be included or allowed under this subdivision and an appropriate adjustment shall be made reducing the amount of the settlement to reflect the indicated rate of loss; and

2. The reasonable cost of the preservation and protection of property incurred; and any other reasonable cost incidental to termination of WORK under this contract, including expense incidental to the determination of the amount due to CONTRACTOR as the result of the termination of WORK under this contract.

-38-

The total sum to be paid to CONTRACTOR under 1 above shall not exceed the total contract price as reduced by the amount of payments otherwise made and as further reduced by the contract price of WORK not terminated. Except for normal spoilage, and except to the extent that OWNER shall have otherwise expressly assumed the risk of loss, there shall be excluded from the amounts payable to CONTRACTOR under 1 above, the fair value, as determined by CHIEF PROCUREMENT OFFICER FOR CONSTRUCTION, of property which is destroyed, lost, stolen, or damaged so as to become undeliverable to OWNER.

F. Costs claimed, agreed to, or determined pursuant to paragraphs C, D, and E of this clause shall be in accordance with the contract cost principles and procedures of the South Carolina Consolidated Procurement Code Regulations in effect on the date of this contract.

ARTICLE 36 - RECORD DRAWINGS:

A. CONTRACTORS shall at the completion of their WORK, complete and turn over to ARCHITECT or CONSTRUCTION MANAGER, if one is utilized, a marked-up set of the drawings provided for construction. The corrections shall show all field changes that were made to adapt to field conditions, changes resulting from contract CHANGE ORDERS and all buried installations of piping, conduit, and utility services. All buried and concealed items both inside and outside the building shall be accurately located as to depth and referenced to two permanent features such as interior or exterior wall faces and finished floors. The drawings shall be clean and all corrections/dimensions shall be noted as changes are made and shall be given in a neat and legible manner in a contrasting colored pencil or ink and shall become the property of OWNER.

ARTICLE 37 - WARRANTIES AND OPERATING INSTRUCTIONS:

A. CONTRACTOR warrants to OWNER and ARCHITECT that all materials and equipment furnished under this contract shall be new, unless otherwise specified, and that all WORK shall be of good quality, free from faults and defects and in conformance with CONTRACT DOCUMENTS. All WORK not so conforming to these standards may be considered defective or non-conforming. If required by ARCHITECT or OWNER, CONTRACTOR shall furnish satisfactory evidence as to the kind and quality of materials and equipment. Where there is an approved substitution of material or equipment, CONTRACTOR warrants that such installation, construction, material, or equipment will perform the function for which the original material or equipment was specified. CONTRACTOR explicitly warrants the merchantability and the fitness for use and quality of all

-39-

substituted items provided for by him in addition to any warranty given by the manufacturer or supplier. CONTRACTOR shall deliver to ARCHITECT all warranties required under the contract or to which CONTRACTOR is entitled from manufacturers, suppliers, materialmen and/or SUBCONTRACTORS.

B. Warranties and operating instructions of various equipment items, according to the manufacturer's policy covering their products, shall be delivered to ARCHITECT prior to submission of the final pay estimate.

C. The warranty provided in this Section shall be in addition to and not in limitation of any other warranty or remedy provided by law or by CONTRACT DOCUMENTS.

ARTICLE 38 - GENERAL GUARANTEE:

A. Neither the final certificate of payment nor any provision in CONTRACT DOCUMENTS nor partial use of occupancy of the premises by OWNER shall constitute an acceptance of WORK not done in accordance with CONTRACT DOCUMENTS or relieve CONTRACTOR or his sureties of liability respect to any express warranties or responsibility for faulty materials and workmanship.

B. CONTRACTOR or his sureties shall remedy any defects in WORK and pay for any damage to other WORK resulting therefrom. OWNER will give notice of observed defects with reasonable promptness.

C. In case of default on the part of CONTRACTOR in fulfilling this part of the contract, OWNER may correct WORK or repair the damage and the cost and expense incurred in such event shall be paid by or recoverable from CONTRACTOR.

D. Should CONTRACTOR be required to perform tests that, due to climatic conditions must be delayed, it is understood that such tests will be accomplished by CONTRACTOR at the earliest possible date with the provisions of the General Guarantee beginning upon satisfactory completion of said test. The responsibility of CONTRACTOR under this Section will not be abrogated if OWNER should elect to initiate final payment.

E. CONTRACTOR shall guarantee that the entire project will conform to CONTRACT DOCUMENTS or in CONTRACTOR'S respective section of the specifications if multiple contracts are awarded by OWNER.

ARTICLE 39 - TIME:

A. Time is of the essence of this agreement. CONTRACTOR shall be responsible for maintaining such SCHEDULE and the failure to do so may be a material breach of this agreement. Any additional

-40-

or unanticipated cost or expense required to maintain SCHEDULE
shall be CONTRACTOR'S obligation.

End of Section

-41-

APPENDIX I

STATE OF SOUTH CAROLINA

STANDARD BOND FORM

FOR PERFORMANCE OF THE WORK

_____

KNOW ALL MEN BY THESE PRESENTS:

That_____,
      (Legal Title and address of CONTRACTOR)

_____,

as Principal (hereinafter referred to as "Principal"), and

_____
      (Legal Title and address of Surety)

_____

as Surety (hereinafter referred to as "Surety") are held and

firmly bound unto _____

_____

as Obligee (hereinafter referred to as "OWNER"), in the amount of

_____Dollars ($_____), to which
  (Insert Contract Price)

payment Principal and Surety bind themselves, their heirs, executors, administrators, successors and assigns, jointly and severally, firmly by these presents.

    IN WITNESS WHEREOF, we have hereunto set our hands and
affixed our seals this _____ day of _____,
19___.

    PROVIDED, HOWEVER, that the condition of this obligation
is such that whereas the above bound Principal entered into a
certain Contract with the said

_____
                 (OWNER)
for the _____
      (Set forth the Name of the Project)

_____.

NOW, THEREFORE, THE CONDITION OF THIS OBLIGATION is such
that, if CONTRACTOR shall promptly and faithfully perform and
comply with the terms and conditions of CONTRACT DOCUMENTS which
are incorporated herein, then this obligation shall be null and
void; otherwise it shall remain in full force and effect.

PROVIDED, further, that upon either the default of the Principal or a declaration of default by OWNER in accordance with
ARTICLE 34 of the GENERAL CONDITIONS, the above bound
_____, as
Surety, shall either remedy the default of the Principal or shall
take charge of said WORK and complete the contract at his own
expense, pursuant to its terms, receiving, however, any balance
of the funds in the hands of said
_____
(OWNER)
due under said contract.

It shall be the duty of the Surety to give an unequivocal
notice in writing to OWNER within ten (10) DAYS after receipt of
a declaration of default of the Surety's election either to
remedy the default or defaults promptly or to perform the contract promptly or to pay to OWNER the penal sum of the bond, time
being of the essence. In said notice of election, the Surety
shall indicate the date on which the remedy or performance will
commence, and it shall then be the duty of the Surety to give
prompt notice in writing to OWNER immediately upon completion of
(a) the remedy and/or correction of each default, (b) the remedy
and/or correction of each item of condemned WORK, (c) the furnishing of each omitted item of WORK, and (d) the performance of
the contract. The Surety shall not assert solvency of its Principal or its Principal's denial of default as justification for
its failure to give notice of election or for its failure to
promptly remedy the default or defaults or perform the contract.

In the event the said Surety shall fail to act promptly as
hereinbefore provided, then STATE ENGINEER shall cause ten (10)
DAYS' notice of such failure to be given, both to said Principal
and Surety, and at the expiration of said ten (10) DAYS, the
Obligee shall have the authority to cause said WORK to be done,
and when the same is completed and the cost thereof estimated,
the said Principal and Surety shall and hereby agree to pay any
excess in the cost of said WORK above the agreed price to be paid
under said contract, and not limited to the penal sum of the
bond.

Upon the completion of said contract pursuant to its terms,
if any funds remain due on said contract, the same shall be paid
to said Surety.

-2-

The said Principal and Surety further agree as part of this obligation to pay all such damages of any kind to person or property that may result from a failure in any respect to perform and complete said contract including, but not limited to, all repair and replacement costs necessary to rectify construction error, architectural and engineering costs and fees, all (but not limited to) consultant fees, all testing and laboratory fees, and all legal fees and litigation costs incurred by OWNER.

The parties hereto agree that ARTICLE 32 of the GENERAL CONDITIONS apply to all disputes arising out of the performance of the parties hereto described under this agreement and agree to be bound thereby and shall constitute the sole disputes remedy of the parties.

The Surety agrees that other than as is provided in this Bond it may not demand of OWNER that OWNER shall (a) perform any thing or act, (b) give any notice, (c) furnish any clerical assistance, (d) render any service, (e) furnish any papers or documents, or (f) take any other action of any nature or description which is not required of OWNER to be done under CONTRACT DOCUMENTS.

The Advertisement for Bids, Instructions to Bidders, Proposal, General Conditions of the Contract, any special condition of the Contract, Detailed Specification Requirements and Drawings, and the Contract Agreement hereinbefore referred to, and the Payment Bond are made a part of this obligation, and this instrument is to be construed in connection therewith.

IN WITNESS WHEREOF, the above parties have executed this instrument under their several seals this _____ day of _____, 19___, the name and corporate seal of each corporate party being hereto affixed and these presents duly signed by its undersigned representative, pursuant to authority of its governing body.

In the Presence of: PRINCIPAL:

_____   _____
WITNESS
                                       BY_____
                                              (TITLE)

_____   SURETY:
WITNESS

                                       _____

                                       BY_____
                                              (TITLE)

-3-

APPENDIX
J

STATE OF SOUTH CAROLINA

STANDARD BOND FORM

FOR LABOR AND MATERIAL PAYMENT

_____

KNOW ALL MEN BY THESE PRESENTS:

That_____ ,
                    (Legal Title and address of CONTRACTOR)

_____ ,

as Principal (hereinafter referred to as "Principal"), and

_____
                    (Legal Title and address of Surety)

_____

as Surety (hereinafter referred to as "Surety") are held and

firmly bound unto_____

_____

as Obligee (hereinafter referred to as "OWNER"), in the amount of

_____Dollars ($_____), to which
    (Insert Contract Price)

payment Principal and Surety bind themselves, their heirs, executors, administrators, successors and assigns, jointly and severally, firmly by these presents.

   WHEREAS, the above bounden Principal has entered into a contract with OWNER dated _____ for

_____ in accordance with
           (Insert Name of WORK)

drawings and specifications, prepared by _____

_____
           (Here insert full name and title)

which contract is incorporated herein by reference and made a
part hereof, and is hereinafter referred to as the Contract.

NOW, THEREFORE, THE CONDITION OF THIS OBLIGATION is such that if the Principal shall promptly make payment to all claimants as hereinafter defined, for all labor and materials supplied in the prosecution of WORK provided for in said Contract, then this obligation shall be void; otherwise, it shall remain 'in full force and effect, subject, however, to the following conditions.

1. The said Surety to this bond, for value received, hereby stipulates and agrees that no change or changes, extension of time or extensions of time, alteration or alterations or addition or additions to the terms of the Contract or to WORK to be performed thereunder, or the specifications or drawings accompanying same shall in any wise affect its obligation on this bond, and it does hereby waive notice of any such change or changes, extension of time or extensions of time, alteration or alterations or addition or additions to the terms of the Contract or to WORK or to the specifications or drawings.

2. Pursuant to South Carolina Code of Laws (1976) as amended, Section 11-35-3030:

    a. Suits on Payment Bonds - Right to Institute. Every person who has furnished labor or material to CONTRACTOR or SUB-CONTRACTORS for WORK specified in the contract, in respect of which a payment bond is furnished under this section, and who has not been paid in full therefor before the expiration of a period of ninety DAYS after the day on which the last of the labor was done or performed by such person or material was furnished or supplied by such person for which such claim is made, shall have the right to sue on the payment bond for the amount, or the balance thereof, unpaid at the time of institution of such suit and to prosecute such action for the sum or sums justly due such person. Any person having a direct contractual relationship with SUBCONTRACTOR of CONTRACTOR, but no contractual relationship express or implied with CONTRACTOR furnishing such payment bond, shall have a right of action on the payment bond upon giving WRITTEN NOTICE to CONTRACTOR within ninety DAYS from the date on which such person did or performed the last of the labor or furnished or supplied the last of the material upon which such claim is made, stating with substantial accuracy the amount claimed and the name of the party to whom the material was furnished or supplied or for whom the labor was done or performed. Such WRITTEN NOTICE to CONTRACTOR shall be personally served or served by mailing the same by registered or certified mail, postage prepaid, in an envelope addressed to CONTRACTOR at any place CONTRACTOR maintains an office or conducts its business.

    b. Suits on Payment Bonds - Where and When Brought. Every suit instituted upon a payment bond shall be brought in a court of competent jurisdiction for the county or circuit in which the construction contract was to be performed, but no such

-2-

suit shall be commenced after the expiration of one year after the day on which the last of the labor was performed or material was supplied by the person bringing suit. The obligee named in the bond need not be joined as a party in any such suit.

Signed and sealed this _____ day of _____ A.D. 19___ .

IN THE PRESENCE OF:

_____(SEAL)
(PRINCIPAL)

_____   _____
                                           (TITLE)

                                     _____(SEAL)
                                           (SURETY)

_____   _____
                                           (TITLE)

-3-

APPENDIX
K

FORM SE250
7/14/83

STATE OF SOUTH CAROLINA

STANDARD FORM

OF

AGREEMENT BETWEEN OWNER AND CONSTRUCTION MANAGER

THIS AGREEMENT, made this _____ day of _____

in the year of Nineteen Hundred and _____

between _____

_____

_____

hereinafter called CONSTRUCTION MANAGER.

PROJECT

TITLE:_____

_____

_____

SCOPE OF WORK

It is the intent of OWNER to _____

_____

_____

_____

_____

All of the above WORK shall hereinafter be referred to as the
Project.

FORM SE250
7/14/83

CONSTRUCTION FUNDS AVAILABLE

TOTAL FUNDS available by OWNER for construction only for this

Project are: _____

_____

_____

_____

_____

_____

COMPENSATION

CONSTRUCTION MANAGER shall provide professional services for this Project in accordance with the Terms and Conditions of this Agreement and OWNER shall compensate CONSTRUCTION MANAGER in accordance with the Terms and Conditions of this Agreement as follows:

BASIC SERVICES: Basic Compensation shall be computed on the

basis of:_____

_____

_____

_____

ADDITIONAL SERVICES: Compensation shall be computed as follows:

-2-

REIMBURSABLE SERVICES: Compensation shall be computed as follows:

_____

_____

_____

_____

PAYMENT SCHEDULE TO CONSTRUCTION MANAGER

A. **BASIC SERVICES:**

Payment for CONSTRUCTION MANAGER'S Basic Services shall be made monthly upon presentation of CONSTRUCTION MANAGER'S statement of services rendered in proportion to the amount of services performed, provided that the compensation of each Phase of Basic Services shall not exceed the limits set out below:

Schematic Design Phase................ %

Design Development Phase.............. %

Construction Documents Phase.......... %

Bidding and Bid Award Phase........... % (Max. 40%)

Construction Administration Phase

At 25% Completed Construction......... %

At 50% Completed Construction......... %

At 75% Completed Construction......... %

At SUBSTANTIAL COMPLETION............. % (Max. 90%)

At 100% Completion, Including
Furnishing OWNER RECORD DRAWINGS
and Other Documents Required...... 100%

-3-

B. CONSTRUCTION COST:

The Construction Cost, when used as the basis for determining
CONSTRUCTION MANAGER'S Compensation, shall be defined as
follows:

     1.   For completed construction: The total applicable
        Contract cost of all such WORK;

     2.   For WORK not constructed: The lowest bona fide bid
        received from a qualified bidder for WORK within
        the stated budget;

     3.   For WORK for which no such bid or proposal is
        received: The latest approved Detailed Estimate of
        Construction Cost within the stated budget.

The Construction Cost does not include the compensation to
ARCHITECT, the cost incurred for a full-time project representative, field project manager, CONSTRUCTION MANAGER or
other special consultants, the cost of the land, cost of
insurance, rights-of-way, advertising or other costs which
are the responsibility of OWNER.

-4-

ARTICLE 1 - GENERAL

This Agreement incorporates the State of South Carolina Standard Form General Conditions of the Contract for Construction (Form SE370).

ARTICLE 2 - CONSTRUCTION MANAGER'S
BASIC SERVICES AND RESPONSIBILITIES

A. GENERAL

1. CONSTRUCTION MANAGER'S Basic Professional Services shall consist of the furnishing of management activities required to plan, schedule, coordinate, and manage the design and construction of a state project in a manner that insures the control of time, cost, and quality of construction of that project.

2. CONSTRUCTION MANAGER will fully cooperate with ARCHITECT in the design and development of the project and shall guard the interests of OWNER in order to ensure a project most advantageous and cost effective to OWNER within the construction funds available.

3. CONSTRUCTION MANAGER shall work with ARCHITECT in the development of the design and shall review all plans and specifications during the design of the project so as to provide direction on foundations, systems and materials, construction feasibility, availability of labor and materials, time requirements for procurement, installation and construction costs, relative costs, and provide any other recommendations for the project as appropriate and necessary so as to guard OWNER against errors and omissions in the performance of ARCHITECT.

4. CONSTRUCTION MANAGER agrees that the Prime CONTRACTORS are third party beneficiaries of this Contract and are entitled to relief against CONSTRUCTION MANAGER for damages resultant from CONSTRUCTION MANAGER'S breach of obligations under this Contract.

5. CONSTRUCTION MANAGER agrees to supervise the construction of WORK and to require that CONTRACTOR comply with CONTRACT DOCUMENTS. Such SUPERVISION shall include, unless otherwise specified, the general administration of the Contract; the issuance of Certificates of Payment; the keeping of accounts; the approval of materials, equipment, and apparatus used in WORK; and SUPERVISION of construction. General Administration of the Contract includes, but is not limited to, the performance of all acts, services, and responsibilities

-5-

described, referred to, or implied in this Contract and to the performance of all acts, services, and responsibilities described, referred to, or implied in the General Conditions (Form SE370) of the State of South Carolina, which are incorporated by reference herein.

6. CONSTRUCTION MANAGER agrees to strictly conform to and be bound by industry standards, criteria, budgetary considerations, and the requirements of the project and further agrees that he shall supervise WORK to ensure strict compliance with all applicable laws, codes, and industry standards.

B. CONSTRUCTION MANAGER'S RESPONSIBILITIES
IN CONJUNCTION WITH BASIC SERVICES

1. DESIGN PHASE

    a. SCHEMATIC DESIGN PHASE

        (1) CONSTRUCTION MANAGER shall review with OWNER, and with ARCHITECT, the needs and requirements of the project.

        (2) CONSTRUCTION MANAGER shall assist ARCHITECT in reviewing the project requirements so as to assist in determining the scope of the project.

        (3) CONSTRUCTION MANAGER shall participate in and advise OWNER on site selection and improvement.

        (4) CONSTRUCTION MANAGER shall evaluate the requirements for the project and the scope of the project taking into account the construction funds available for the project.

        (5) CONSTRUCTION MANAGER shall prepare a project budget for OWNER'S written approval as soon as the major project requirements have been identified and determined.

        (6) CONSTRUCTION MANAGER shall review the Schematic Design Phase Documents so as to ensure that the design is proceeding in a manner most cost effective to OWNER and within the construction budget.

        (7) CONSTRUCTION MANAGER shall immediately advise OWNER and ARCHITECT if it shall appear that

-6-

the project budget will be exceeded and shall make recommendations for corrective measures to OWNER and to ARCHITECT.

(8) CONSTRUCTION MANAGER shall recommend to OWNER the feasibility of the construction contemplated, and shall advise OWNER and ARCHITECT as to the availability of materials, labor, installation of selected construction materials and systems, and all other factors, including alternative design or alternative construction materials or systems available.

(9) Prior to beginning the Design Documents Phase of the project, CONSTRUCTION MANAGER shall provide OWNER and ARCHITECT a written statement as to recommendations for alternative designs or construction materials or shall state approval of the Schematic Design Phase Documents, together with a Statement of Probable Construction Cost.

b. DESIGN DEVELOPMENT PHASE

(1) The Design Development Phase shall commence upon receipt of the written authorization of OWNER and STATE ENGINEER to proceed with the preparation of the Design Development Phase Documents.

(2) Following receipt of written authorization to proceed, CONSTRUCTION MANAGER shall advise and assist ARCHITECT in preparation of the Design Development Phase Documents which shall be based on the Schematic Design Phase Documents and any adjustments in the program or project budget.

(3) CONSTRUCTION MANAGER shall assist ARCHITECT and require that the Design Development Phase Documents meet the requirements of ARTICLE 2, Section B, 1.b of Standard Form of Agreement Between Owner and Architect or Engineer (SE240), and shall include sufficient data, information and material to define the scope of the project and to demonstrate, delineate, and define the general design of the project, including size and character of the project as to architectural, structural, mechanical and electrical systems, materials, and any other project elements appropriate under the project scope and design.

-7-

(4) Prior to beginning the Construction Documents Phase of the project, CONSTRUCTION MANAGER will provide OWNER and ARCHITECT a written statement as to recommendations for alternative designs or construction materials or acknowledge approval of the Design Development Phase Documents together with a Revised Statement of Probable Construction Cost.

c. CONSTRUCTION DOCUMENTS PHASE

(1) CONSTRUCTION MANAGER shall assist ARCHITECT and require that the Construction Phase Documents meet the requirements of ARTICLE 2, Section B, 1.c of Standard Form of Agreement Between Owner and Architect or Engineer (SE240), and shall include sufficient data, information and material to define the scope of the project and to demonstrate, delineate, and define the general design of the project, including size and character of the project as to architectural, structural, mechanical and electrical systems, materials, and any other project elements appropriate under the project scope and design.

(2) CONSTRUCTION MANAGER shall create and prepare a preliminary construction SCHEDULE for OWNER which shall reflect the sequence of WORK and the construction time.

(3) CONSTRUCTION MANAGER shall create and update each thirty (30) DAYS a project time SCHEDULE which shall coordinate and integrate ARCHITECT'S services with the preliminary construction SCHEDULE.

(4) CONSTRUCTION MANAGER shall provide ARCHITECT with a continuous cost consultation service for the duration of the project and shall prepare detailed cost estimates relative to all early procurement of materials and equipment.

(5) CONSTRUCTION MANAGER shall review the plans and specifications and shall recommend in writing as they are prepared, alternative solutions when the design affects construction feasibility, the construction SCHEDULE, or may cause construction cost to exceed OWNER'S construction funds.

-8-

(6)   STATEMENT OF PROBABLE CONSTRUCTION COST:
The Probable Construction Cost furnished in
this phase shall be calculated by CONSTRUCTION
MANAGER based on drawings and Outline Specifications for the project reflecting the changes
in construction cost and taking into account
the building trades and construction compo-
nents utilized in the project design. This
Revised Statement shall be submitted to OWNER
for OWNER'S written approval and CONSTRUCTION
MANAGER shall advise OWNER and ARCHITECT if it
appears that the construction funds available
for the project will be exceeded and shall
make written recommendations for corrective
action.

d.   BIDDING AND BID AWARD PHASE

(1)   Prior to beginning the Bidding and Bid Award
Phase of the project, approval in writing of
the Construction Documents and the Final
Statement of Probable Construction Cost shall
be secured from OWNER and STATE ENGINEER by
ARCHITECT.

(2)   CONSTRUCTION MANAGER shall advise OWNER as to
the best method for the award of contracts and
for selecting CONTRACTORS.

(3)   CONSTRUCTION MANAGER shall review the design,
drawings and specifications to verify that:

(a)   Areas of jurisdiction do not overlap;

(b)   All WORK necessary for the project has
been included;

(c)   All codes, regulations, and industry
standards have been complied with; and

(d)   That phased construction or separate
contracts is the method of construction
most advantageous to OWNER.

(4)   CONSTRUCTION MANAGER shall identify, recommend
in writing any purchase, and expedite the
procurement of, receipt, and storage of all
equipment, materials, and systems or supplies
requiring a long lead time so as to obtain
delivery when required for the construction of
the project.

-9-

(5) CONSTRUCTION MANAGER shall furnish to OWNER and ARCHITECT in writing an analysis of the types and quantity of labor required for the project and the appropriate categories of labor required for the phases.

(6) CONSTRUCTION MANAGER shall assemble the Bid Documents necessary for obtaining bids for the construction of the project.

(7) CONSTRUCTION MANAGER shall prepare the Invitation for Bids for OWNER which shall include all contractual terms and conditions applicable to the project.

(8) CONSTRUCTION MANAGER shall prepare and submit the construction contract and the Invitation for Bids for the written approval of OWNER and STATE ENGINEER prior to the advertising and solicitation of bids.

(9) In the event a multiple contract method of construction is utilized, CONSTRUCTION MANAGER shall assemble all Bid Documents and Bid Packages for the multiple contracts required by the project.

(10) CONSTRUCTION MANAGER shall design and prepare a pre-bid construction SCHEDULE, when necessary, as determined by the size, complexity, and scope of the project.

(11) CONSTRUCTION MANAGER shall prepare prequalification criteria for CONTRACTORS where prequalification is determined by ARCHITECT and CONSTRUCTION MANAGER to be in the best interest of OWNER.

(12) CONSTRUCTION MANAGER shall hold a pre-bid conference and shall take and distribute the minutes thereof to ARCHITECT, OWNER and all attendees.

(13) CONSTRUCTION MANAGER shall assist OWNER by receiving, recording and evaluating the bids received for the construction of the project.

(14) CONSTRUCTION MANAGER shall review the bids with OWNER and ARCHITECT and shall recommend to OWNER and ARCHITECT those bids deemed responsive and responsible.

-10-

2. CONSTRUCTION ADMINISTRATION PHASE

    a. The Construction Administration Phase shall commence with the award of the Construction Contract or contracts and will terminate with final acceptance by OWNER.

    b. CONSTRUCTION MANAGER, during Construction Administration, shall fully cooperate with ARCHITECT.

    c. CONSTRUCTION MANAGER shall have authority to act on behalf of OWNER to the extent provided in this Contract, State of South Carolina General Conditions (Form SE370) and Supplementary General Conditions, unless otherwise modified in writing.

    d. CONSTRUCTION MANAGER shall at all times have access to WORK.

    e. CONSTRUCTION MANAGER, together with ARCHITECT, shall conduct a pre-construction conference. Written minutes will be taken and distributed to all attendees by CONSTRUCTION MANAGER.

    f. CONSTRUCTION MANAGER shall assist CONTRACTOR in obtaining all necessary building permits, inspection permits, and permits for temporary facilities.

    g. CONSTRUCTION MANAGER shall assist OWNER in obtaining all permits and approvals from all authorities having jurisdiction.

    h. CONSTRUCTION MANAGER shall conduct job progress meetings which shall be held on a bi-weekly basis and at which time CONSTRUCTION MANAGER, ARCHITECT and OWNER may discuss and resolve such matters as procedures, job progress, construction problems, scheduling or other matters relating to the timely and successful completion of the project in accordance with the contract requirements. Additional special job site meetings, when deemed necessary by CONSTRUCTION MANAGER, shall be held as required. CONSTRUCTION MANAGER shall take and distribute written minutes of all meetings conducted to OWNER, ARCHITECT, CONTRACTOR and STATE ENGINEER.

    i. CONSTRUCTION MANAGER shall review the construction SCHEDULE on a bi-weekly basis, and shall submit to OWNER a monthly written report of his findings and of the progress of WORK.

-11-

j.   CONSTRUCTION MANAGER shall keep OWNER informed of the progress and quality of WORK, and shall guard OWNER against defects and deficiencies in WORK of CONTRACTOR.

k.   CONSTRUCTION MANAGER shall immediately advise OWNER and ARCHITECT in writing should any CONTRACTOR fall behind in the construction SCHEDULE.

l.   CONSTRUCTION MANAGER shall advise CONTRACTOR in writing that additional WORK force is needed whenever appropriate and shall notify OWNER and ARCHITECT in writing.

m.   CONSTRUCTION MANAGER shall advise OWNER and ARCHITECT in writing whenever CONTRACTOR fails to comply with CONTRACT DOCUMENTS or fails to carry out WORK in accordance with CONTRACT DOCUMENTS and shall recommend that payment be withheld, that WORK be decertified, that CONTRACTOR be terminated, or any other remedy appropriate under the contract.

n.   CONSTRUCTION MANAGER shall provide to OWNER detailed estimates of construction cost, cash flow forecasts, detailed quantity surveys, and inventories of material stored on job site, equipment and labor.

o.   CONSTRUCTION MANAGER shall review in collaboration with ARCHITECT, all SHOP DRAWINGS promptly and shall approve them only if they are in conformance with the design concept of the project and in compliance with CONTRACT DOCUMENTS.

p.   CONSTRUCTION MANAGER shall plan, direct, coordinate, manage, schedule, supervise, and monitor the progress and WORK of the CONTRACTORS so as to meet the project SCHEDULE and to ensure the completion of WORK in accordance with CONTRACT DOCUMENTS.

q.   CONSTRUCTION MANAGER, in order to expedite equipment and materials delivery and utilization, shall assist CONTRACTORS in the planning and coordinating of the ordering, receipt, storage, and delivery to the job site of construction materials and equipment.

r.   CONSTRUCTION MANAGER shall review and approve the various SCHEDULES of CONTRACTORS, including activity sequences and durations, allocation of labor and construction materials, processing of SHOP

-12-

DRAWINGS and samples, and delivery of materials requiring long lead time procurement.

s. CONSTRUCTION MANGER, based on an approval of the progress SCHEDULE of each CONTRACTOR and based on CONSTRUCTION MANAGER'S observations at the site and the determination that all WORK performed by CONTRACTOR is in conformity with CONTRACT DOCUMENTS and sound construction practices, shall assist ARCHITECT in determining the amount owing to CONTRACTOR under CONTRACTOR'S written request for payment.

t. CONSTRUCTION MANAGER shall monitor the construction SCHEDULE as construction progresses and shall advise OWNER and ARCHITECT in writing immediately if it appears likely that a delay in completion of the project may occur stating the reason for that prospective delay.

u. CONSTRUCTION MANAGER shall review SHOP DRAWINGS. It is CONSTRUCTION MANAGER'S responsibility to see that SHOP DRAWINGS are processed according to ARTICLE 18 of the General Conditions (SE370).

v. CONSTRUCTION MANAGER shall inspect WORK of CONTRACTORS to ensure that WORK is in compliance with CONTRACT DOCUMENTS and to protect OWNER against defects and deficiencies in WORK.

w. CONSTRUCTION MANAGER has the authority to stop WORK pursuant to ARTICLE 33 of the General Conditions (SE370).

x. CONSTRUCTION MANAGER shall reject WORK which, in CONSTRUCTION MANAGER'S opinion, does not conform to CONTRACT DOCUMENTS and good construction practices, and shall immediately give WRITTEN NOTICE to OWNER and ARCHITECT of the rejection of WORK.

y. CONSTRUCTION MANAGER shall, after consultation with ARCHITECT, make recommendations to OWNER for such changes in WORK as CONSTRUCTION MANAGER may consider necessary or desirable.

z. CONSTRUCTION MANAGER shall review all requests for changes and coordinate alternate solutions with ARCHITECT and OWNER, review design changes and solicit proposals from CONTRACTORS, conduct cost negotiations and prepare CHANGE ORDER requests.

-13-

aa. CONSTRUCTION MANAGER shall review and process all applications by the separate CONTRACTORS for final payments and make recommendations to ARCHITECT for certification thereof.

bb. CONSTRUCTION MANAGER shall allow no changes in WORK without the written authorization of OWNER.

cc. CONSTRUCTION MANAGER shall review and analyze all requests for CHANGE ORDERS, including any documents offered to substantiate such requests.

dd. CONSTRUCTION MANAGER shall submit written recommendations on all requested CHANGE ORDERS to ARCHITECT and OWNER and shall prepare recommended CHANGE ORDERS for approval by OWNER.

ee. The responsibility of CONSTRUCTION MANAGER for enforcing the faithful performance of the contract is not relieved or affected in any respect by the presence of any other agents, consultants, or employees of OWNER.

ff. In the event an interpretation of the meaning and intent of the plans and specifications becomes necessary during construction, CONSTRUCTION MANAGER shall consult with OWNER and ARCHITECT, obtain the interpretation in writing and shall transmit this interpretation to the appropriate separate CONTRACTORS.

gg. CONSTRUCTION MANAGER shall make decisions promptly and in any event shall respond within ten (10) DAYS after presentation of written claim or complaint by any party to the Construction Contract.

hh. CONSTRUCTION MANAGER shall maintain at the job site on a current basis, records of all contracts, OWNER-furnished, CONTRACTOR-installed materials and equipment, SHOP DRAWINGS, samples and any other related documents and revisions thereto which arise out of this Agreement or the construction WORK.

ii. CONSTRUCTION MANAGER shall maintain cost accounting records with respect to portions of WORK to be performed by CHANGE ORDER.

jj. CONSTRUCTION MANAGER shall maintain a daily detailed diary of all events occurring on the job site or connected with progress of the project. The diary shall be open to OWNER, ARCHITECT, CONTRACTOR and SUBCONTRACTOR at all times.

-14-

kk. CONSTRUCTION MANAGER shall insure that RECORD DRAW-INGS are maintained in accordance with ARTICLE 36 of the General Conditions (SE370) and shall upon completion of construction, turn over the marked set to ARCHITECT for correction of the original drawings.

ll. CONSTRUCTION MANAGER shall accompany ARCHITECT in making all inspections and shall coordinate the preparation of the punch lists indicating the items of WORK remaining to be accomplished and shall expedite and supervise completion of the punch list items.

mm. CONSTRUCTION MANAGER shall assist ARCHITECT in implementing a close-out program for the project in accordance with ARTICLE 2, paragraph (x) of Standard Form of Agreement Between Owner and Architect or Engineer (SE240).

nn. CONSTRUCTION MANAGER shall assist ARCHITECT in arranging for all inspections and shall require that all WORK performed by CONTRACTOR is in accordance with the requirements of CONTRACT DOCUMENTS.

oo. Subsequent to the final completion of construction operations and the occupancy of the project by OWNER, CONSTRUCTION MANAGER shall assist in reviewing all outstanding claims which have not been settled during the construction phase of the project and shall prepare a separate written report outlining the background and status of such claims and making recommendations as to the ultimate disposition of such outstanding claims.

pp. SUBSTANTIAL COMPLETION: CONSTRUCTION MANAGER shall, upon CONTRACTORS' determination of SUBSTANTIAL COMPLETION of WORK or designated portions thereof, prepare for ARCHITECT a list of incomplete or unsatisfactory items and a schedule for their completion. After ARCHITECT certifies the date of SUBSTANTIAL COMPLETION, CONSTRUCTION MANAGER shall supervise the correction and completion of WORK in accordance with CONTRACT DOCUMENTS and the instructions to ARCHITECT.

qq. FINAL COMPLETION: CONSTRUCTION MANAGER shall assist ARCHITECT in determining final completion and shall provide WRITTEN NOTICE to OWNER and ARCHITECT that WORK is ready for final inspection. CONSTRUCTION MANAGER shall secure and transmit to

-15-

ARCHITECT required guarantees, affidavits, releases, bonds and waivers. CONSTRUCTION MANAGER
shall turn over to ARCHITECT all keys, manuals,
RECORD DRAWINGS and maintenance stocks.

rr. One month prior to the expiration of the one-year
warranty period as called for in the construction
documents, CONSTRUCTION MANAGER shall assist ARCHI-
TECT in inspecting the project for any deficiencies
that may have developed under the one-year warranty. Upon completion of inspection, a written
report shall be furnished to OWNER, ARCHITECT,
STATE ENGINEER, and CONTRACTOR, and CONSTRUCTION
MANAGER shall assist OWNER in taking necessary
action to see that the deficiencies are corrected
at no cost to OWNER.

ARTICLE 3 - STAFF

A. GENERAL

1. CONSTRUCTION MANAGER shall establish organization and
line of authority, naming individuals assigned to the
project to carry out requirements of this Agreement. No
substitution of any key personnel shall be made by CON-
STRUCTION MANAGER without the prior consent of OWNER.
Before any such substitution, CONSTRUCTION MANAGER shall
submit to ARCHITECT a detailed justification supported
by the qualifications of any proposed replacement.

2. CONSTRUCTION MANAGER shall maintain a competent full-
time SUPERVISION staff at the job site under the direction of a licensed general CONTRACTOR or a registered
ARCHITECT by the State of South Carolina for the coordination and direction of WORK of separate CONTRACTORS and
determine the adequacy of separate CONTRACTORS' personnel and equipment and the availability of necessary
materials and supplies to maintain the job SCHEDULE.

ARTICLE 4 - CONSTRUCTION SCHEDULE

A. GENERAL

1. CONSTRUCTION MANAGER shall, in collaboration with ARCHI-
TECT and the separate CONTRACTORS, produce a construction SCHEDULE that integrates the various separate CON-
TRACTORS' and their SUBCONTRACTORS' plans into one complete SCHEDULE. CONSTRUCTION MANAGER shall include in
this SCHEDULE the preparation, processing and approval
of SHOP DRAWINGS.

-16-

2. CONSTRUCTION MANAGER shall maintain copies of the con-
    struction SCHEDULE at the job site to reflect current
    conditions and provide copies to OWNER and ARCHITECT
    with bi-weekly reports as to deviations from SCHEDULE,
    the causes of the deviations, and the corrective action
    taken.

3. CONSTRUCTION MANAGER shall provide for an occupancy
    schedule prepared in coordination with ARCHITECT.

4. CONSTRUCTION MANAGER shall provide a monthly progress
    report to OWNER and ARCHITECT.

5. CONSTRUCTION MANAGER shall inform OWNER and ARCHITECT in
    writing of variances between estimated completion dates
    and scheduled completion dates and the effect which
    these SCHEDULE variances will have on the scheduled
    completion date of the total project on a monthly basis.

ARTICLE 5 - PROGRESS MEETINGS

A. GENERAL:

CONSTRUCTION MANAGER shall conduct meetings with ARCHITECT
and CONTRACTORS to discuss progress, problems and scheduling.
Meetings will be conducted as required, but no less often
than on a bi-weekly basis. CONSTRUCTION MANAGER shall take,
transcribe and distribute complete and accurate minutes of
such meetings to those in attendance and distribute information copies to OWNER and to ARCHITECT. The minutes, as a
minimum, will establish responsibility and a deadline for
items under consideration.

ARTICLE 6 - OWNER'S RESPONSIBILITIES

A. GENERAL

1. OWNER shall provide full information regarding his
    requirements for the project.

2. OWNER shall have ARCHITECT furnish sufficient copies of
    the construction documents to CONSTRUCTION MANAGER to
    permit bidding of the various construction contracts.

3. OWNER shall furnish for CONSTRUCTION MANAGER'S review
    copies of ARCHITECT'S and/or other consultants' con-
    tracts with OWNER for coordination with this Agreement.

-17-

4. OWNER shall not be responsible for any costs or damages resulting from errors and omissions or any delays caused by CONSTRUCTION MANAGER, ARCHITECT, Engineer or CONTRACTOR.

5. CONSTRUCTION MANAGER'S sole remedy for any delay caused by OWNER shall be an extension of time.

6. If OWNER observes or otherwise becomes aware of any fault or defect in the project or non-conformance with CONTRACT DOCUMENTS, he shall give prompt WRITTEN NOTICE thereof to CONSTRUCTION MANAGER and ARCHITECT.

7. OWNER shall see that ARCHITECT furnishes to CONSTRUCTION MANAGER all necessary surveys, borings, and tests obtained as necessary to the project.

ARTICLE 7 - REIMBURSABLE EXPENSES

A. Reimbursable Expenses are defined as direct costs which may be in addition to the compensation for Basic and/or Additional Services and may include, but are not necessarily limited to, the following:

1. Mileage, meals and lodging. The latest rules and regulations promulgated by the State of South Carolina for lodging and travel expenses shall apply to travel by CONSTRUCTION MANAGER and his employees.

2. Reproduction, postage and telephone at actual cost.

B. Reimbursable Expenses shall be submitted by CONSTRUCTION MANAGER for approval of OWNER on a monthly basis. Approved reimbursable expenses shall be paid promptly.

ARTICLE 8 - CONSTRUCTION MANAGER'S ACCOUNTING RECORDS

Daily records of CONSTRUCTION MANAGER'S direct personnel, consultants and reimbursable expenses pertaining to the project shall be kept on a generally recognized accounting basis and shall be available to OWNER or his authorized representatives upon request.

ARTICLE 9 - CONSTRUCTION MANAGER'S COOPERATION

CONSTRUCTION MANAGER agrees to perform his services under this contract in such manner and at such times so that OWNER, ARCHITECT and/or any CONTRACTOR who has WORK to perform, or contracts to execute, can do so without unreasonable delay.

-18-

ARTICLE 10 - SUCCESSORS AND ASSIGNS

OWNER and CONSTRUCTION MANAGER each binds himself, his partners, successors, assigns and legal representatives to the other party to this Agreement and to the partners, successors, assigns and legal representatives of such other party with respect to all covenants of this Agreement. Neither OWNER nor ARCHITECT shall assign, sublet or transfer his interest in this Agreement without the written consent of the other.

ARTICLE 11 - INDEMNIFICATION

A. CONSTRUCTION MANAGER shall defend, indemnify and hold OWNER free and harmless from all claims, demands, liabilities and losses, including injury or death of any person and damage to or destruction of property provided such claims, demands, liabilities or losses arise out of performance of this contract by CONSTRUCTION MANAGER, his agents or consultants.

B. In no case shall CONSTRUCTION MANAGER be liable for any claims, demands, liabilities or losses caused by the sole negligence of OWNER.

ARTICLE 12 - TERMINATION

A. THIS AGREEMENT, for any reason, including the convenience of OWNER or for cause, may be terminated by OWNER by WRITTEN NOTICE to CONSTRUCTION MANAGER specifying the termination date which shall be effective within seven (7) DAYS from the date to be stated by OWNER in the notice to CONSTRUCTION MANAGER.

B. In the event of termination which is not the fault of CONSTRUCTION MANAGER, OWNER shall pay to CONSTRUCTION MANAGER the compensation properly due for services properly performed prior to the effective date of the termination and for any reasonable reimbursable expenses properly incurred.

C. In the event CONSTRUCTION MANAGER through any cause fails to perform any of the terms, covenants, or provisions of this contract on his part to be performed, or if he for any cause fails to make progress in WORK hereunder in a reasonable manner, or if the conduct of CONSTRUCTION MANAGER impairs or prejudices the interests of OWNER, or if CONSTRUCTION MANAGER violates any of the terms, covenants, or provisions of this contract, OWNER shall have the right to terminate this contract by giving notice in writing of the fact and date of such termination to CONSTRUCTION MANAGER, and all drawings, specifications, and other documents relating to the design or

-19-

SUPERVISION of WORK shall be surrendered forthwith by CON-
STRUCTION MANAGER to OWNER, PROVIDED HOWEVER: That in such
case CONSTRUCTION MANAGER shall receive equitable compensation for such services as shall in the opinion of STATE ENGI-
NEER have been satisfactorily performed by CONSTRUCTION MAN-
AGER up to the date of termination of this contract, such
compensation to be fixed by STATE ENGINEER, and PROVIDED
FURTHER: That OWNER may take over WORK to be done hereunder
and may prosecute the same to completion by contract or otherwise, and CONSTRUCTION MANAGER shall be liable to OWNER for
all reasonable cost occasioned OWNER thereby. The parties
agree that the decision of STATE ENGINEER in regard to the
matter set forth in this ARTICLE shall be final.

ARTICLE 13 - INSURANCE

A. Within ten (10) DAYS after execution of this Agreement and
during the entire period of CONSTRUCTION MANAGER'S responsibility under this Agreement, CONSTRUCTION MANAGER shall
obtain and maintain professional liability insurance coverage. CONSTRUCTION MANAGER shall file with OWNER the certificate from an insurance company authorized to do business in
the State of South Carolina showing issuance of professional
liability insurance (errors and omissions insurance) in the
amount of $_____ coverage with a maximum of
$_____ deductible pertaining to this project
only. The certificate shall bear an endorsement in words
exactly as follows:

The insurance company certifies that the
insurance covered by this certificate has
been endorsed as follows: "The insurance
company agrees that the coverage is on a
project basis only and shall not be cancelled, changed, allowed to lapse, or
allowed to expire until ten days after
notice to_____
_____".

ARTICLE 14 - DISPUTES AND REMEDIES

A. CONSTRUCTION MANAGER hereby agrees that all claims made by
OWNER against CONSTRUCTION MANAGER and by CONSTRUCTION MAN-
AGER against OWNER, including controversies based on breach
of contract, mistake, misrepresentation, contract modifica-
tion or recession or any other claims which arise under or by
virtue of the contract between them, shall be settled by
STATE CHIEF PROCUREMENT OFFICER FOR CONSTRUCTION under the
Consolidated Procurement Code Procedures as outlined in South

-20-

Carolina Code of Laws (1976), as amended, Sections 11-35-4230(3), (4) and (5), with all appeal rights as defined in Section 11-35-4410 to PROCUREMENT REVIEW PANEL being applicable.

B. CONSTRUCTION MANAGER hereby further agrees that should any CONTRACTOR file a claim concerning any dispute or controversy with CHIEF PROCUREMENT OFFICER FOR CONSTRUCTION which involves allegations of any acts, errors and omissions of CONSTRUCTION MANAGER, including, but not limited to, defects, errors or omissions in the administration of the contract by CONSTRUCTION MANAGER, and inadequate construction phase services as defined and required by the contract between CONSTRUCTION MANAGER and OWNER, then CONSTRUCTION MANAGER shall consent to participate and to be joined in the Protest Procedures as outlined in Article 17 of the South Carolina Consolidated Procurement Code, entitled Legal and Contractual Remedies, and to be bound by any decisions rendered thereunder.

C. CONSTRUCTION MANAGER further agrees that should he be found liable for any errors and omissions under this contract, then OWNER shall recover its attorney's fees, expert witness costs, cost of consultants necessary for evaluation of the project, and any other costs incurred.

D. The remedy defined in this ARTICLE shall be the sole remedy of the parties.

ARTICLE 15 - OTHER CONDITIONS

-21-

EXTENT OF AGREEMENT

THIS AGREEMENT represents the entire and integrated Agreement between OWNER and CONSTRUCTION MANAGER and supersedes all prior negotiations, representations or agreements, either written or oral. This Agreement may be amended only by written instrument signed by both OWNER and CONSTRUCTION MANAGER.

Under this Agreement CONSTRUCTION MANAGER shall provide to OWNER the services set forth in this Agreement in connection with the project described and under the conditions enumerated under this Agreement. It is expressly understood that the relationship between OWNER and CONSTRUCTION MANAGER is that of an independent CONTRACTOR and CONSTRUCTION MANAGER is not and shall not be deemed as an agent of OWNER.

THIS AGREEMENT entered into as of the day and year first written above.

OWNER   CONSTRUCTION MANAGER

_____   _____

_____   _____

_____   _____

BY_____   BY_____

-22-

TABLE OF CASES

INDEX

ABOUT THE AUTHORS

MCNEILL STOKES is a partner in the law firm of Stokes, Shapiro, Fussell & Genberg of Atlanta, Georgia. Acknowledged as one of the nation's leading experts on construction law, Mr. Stokes is a frequent speaker at conventions and seminars and has on many occasions testified before congressional committees and at White House conferences. A graduate of Vanderbilt University with degrees in chemical engineering and law, Mr. Stokes is also the author of *Construction Law in Contractors' Language; Labor Law in Contractors' Language; International Construction Contracts, Second Edition;* and *Conquering Government Regulations,* all published by McGraw-Hill.

JUDITH L. FINUF is General Counsel for the Medical University of South Carolina. A former Assistant Attorney General for the State of South Carolina, Ms. Finuf has represented the state and numerous public agencies in construction law disputes, negotiated construction contracts for public owners and design professionals, and monitored construction contract problems in both prime contractor and multiple prime contract situations. Widely renowned in her field, Ms. Finuf has conducted construction law seminars for the public and private sectors and the state bar association, and has moderated panels and spoken before the National Association of Attorney Generals on construction law. Ms. Finuf was instrumental in developing the South Carolina construction form contracts and serves as a member of the National Association of Attorneys General Model Construction Document Committee.